EMMA LAZARUS IN HER WORLD

Life and Letters

Emma Lazarus

EMMA LAZARUS IN HER WORLD

Life and Letters

Bette Roth Young

With a Foreword by Francine Klagsbrun

THE JEWISH PUBLICATION SOCIETY

Philadelphia   Jerusalem

5755   1995

Copyright © 1995 by Bette Roth Young

Foreword © 1995 by Francine Klagsbrun

First Edition   All rights reserved

Manufactured in the United States of America

Library of Congress Cataloging-in-Publication Data

Young, Bette Roth, 1937–
Emma Lazarus in her world : life and letters / Bette Roth Young ;
with a foreword by Francine Klagsbrun. — 1st ed.
p.   cm.
Includes bibliographical references and index.
ISBN 0–8276–0516–1 (cloth)
ISBN 0–8276–0618–4 (paper)
1. Lazarus, Emma, 1849–1887—Biography.   2. Lazarus, Emma,
1849–1887—Correspondence.   3. Women poets, American—19th century—
Correspondence.   4. Women poets, American—19th century—Biography.
5. Jews—New York (N.Y.)—Biography   6. New York (N.Y.)—Biography.
I. Title.
PS2234.Y68   1995
811'.4—dc20   95-3005
[B]   CIP

TYPESET IN MINION BY COGHILL COMPOSITION
DESIGNED BY KRISTIE LEE

For my children

For my sisters

And for my husband, Mike,
with whom all is possible

Contents

Foreword   FRANCINE KLAGSBRUN   ix

Preface   FINDING EMMA   xvii

Acknowledgments   xix

PART I   The Life

1. *The Statue*   3

2. *The Chronology*   6

3. *The Myth*   12

4. *The Experience*   22

5. *The Work*   28

6. *Jewish Themes*   36

7. *A Jewish Identity*   43

8. *A Jewish Polemic*   52

PART II   The Letters

9. *Helena deKay Gilder*   67

10. *Thomas Wren Ward*   170

CONTENTS

11. *Rose Hawthorne Lathrop*   186

12. *Edwin Robert Anderson Seligman*   201

13. *Henry James*   210

Notes   221

Glossary of Proper Names   263

Bibliography   275

Index   291

Photographs follow page 63

Foreword

FRANCINE KLAGSBRUN

In a letter of comfort and advice to the first group of exiles who left Jerusalem for Babylon in 586 B.C.E., the prophet Jeremiah wrote, "Build houses and live in them, plant gardens and eat their fruit. . . . Multiply there, do not decrease. And seek the welfare of the city to which I have exiled you and pray to the Lord on its behalf; for in its prosperity you shall prosper" (Jeremiah 29: 4–7).

It was a message the Babylonian exiles took to heart, for when, some fifty years later, they were allowed to return to Judah, many remained in Babylon, settled comfortably in the houses they had built, with the gardens they had planted. And it was a message that has continued to guide Jews living outside the land of Israel to this day. Wherever they put down roots, they sang of Zion and prayed for the welfare of the lands in which they lived, never completely forgetting the former but always accommodating themselves to the latter. To one degree or another, that mixture of trying to remember while trying to accommodate, of multiplying as Jews while eating the fruits of other cultures, has been the source of some of the most basic tensions in Jewish life in the Diaspora for more than two thousand years.

In the American Diaspora, Emma Lazarus personifies those tensions more than any writer before her, both in her work and her personal life. She may be remembered today chiefly for her sonnet "The New Colossus," whose words "Give me your tired, your poor,/ Your huddled masses yearning to breathe free . . ." are inscribed on the pedestal of the Statue of Liberty. But in her prime, during the 1870s and 1880s, she received much recognition as a "poetess, a magaziness, and a Jewess," in the words of Henry James. Her poems and essays appeared in *The Century, Lippincott's, The Critic,* and other leading magazines. At the same time she wrote assertively on Jewish themes in such journals as the *American Hebrew* and sought to help the masses of Jewish immigrants who had fled to America from the pogroms of Czarist Russia. In every way she seemed to have achieved a fine balance between her Jewish heritage and the Gentile society in which she made her name.

Yet closer examination reveals some holes in that seemingly seamless surface. During the period when she was publishing impassioned defenses of Jews and Judaism in the magazines, she barely mentioned issues of Jewish concern in the dozens of letters she wrote to her non-Jewish friends. Although her work for the immigrants was fervent, almost frenetic, it lasted less than two years and then faded into the background of her life. Lauded by some Jewish mourners as a prophet in the tradition of the biblical Deborah, she was described by Joseph Gilder, editor of *The Critic,* as being "as much a Christian as a Jewess—perhaps it would be better to say, neither one nor the other." In other words, like the exiles to Babylon and generations of Jews after them, she strove to straddle two worlds—the Gentile and the Jewish—but was not completely comfortable in either.

Born in 1849, she came to maturity during the industrial boom of the post-Civil War years. Businesses burgeoned, railroads began to criss-cross the country, and men amassed great fortunes as bankers, investors, and manufacturers. The Lazarus family, of Sephardic origins, had acquired wealth generations earlier, and like others in their aristocratic circles, they looked down on the new-monied folk. Theirs was the genteel Victorian society of New York's exclusive Union and Knickerbocker clubs, and their children grew up tutored in music, languages, literature, and arts, far removed from the excesses of the Gilded Age.

In her cultivated environment, Lazarus could be accepted as both a writer and a Jew. In fact, writing was one of the few vocations in which women had already gained considerable recognition. Emily Dickinson, Harriet Beecher Stowe, Julia Ward Howe, and other New England authors stand out, but many other women wrote novels and published stories, poems, and articles in popular magazines—so many that Nathaniel Hawthorne, in an outburst of envy at their commercial success, labeled them a "damned mob of scribbling women." Writing was seen as a suitable occupation for women because it did not necessarily interfere with domestic activities. Even the unmarried like Lazarus could fulfill the accepted ideal of "true womanhood," pursuing their writing while still devoting themselves to parents and home.

Lazarus's Jewishness was another matter. It set her apart from others in her world, but it also drew them to her. Ralph Waldo Emerson's daughter Ellen put her finger on part of Lazarus's appeal when she described her family's excitement at actually meeting "a real unconverted Jew (who had no objections to calling herself one. . . .)." There was something mysterious and alluring about this distinguished Jewish woman who did not deny her tradition even if she did not practice it. Even the word "Jewess," in popular usage then, had romantic overtones. It conjured up visions of dark-eyed biblical women—Sarah, Rebecca, Rachel—and the biblical creeds that had formed the foundation of American life from the days of the early Puritans.

Christian America had ambivalent attitudes toward Jews. In the abstract they revered these descendants of the great prophets and heroes of the Bible whom they spoke of as God's chosen people. In real life, however, cartoons, plays, and novels often portrayed Jews in the age-old stereotypes of Shylocks, business sharks, and killers of Christ. In "The Jewish Cemetery at Newport" (a poem Lazarus would later imitate), written in 1867, Henry Wadsworth Longfellow could lament the end of a once-thriving Jewish population in Newport, Rhode Island, convinced that they were members of one of the world's "dead nations" that would "never rise again." In his monumental *Education,* on the other hand, Henry Adams would vent hatred on the very-much-alive Jewish immigrants he had seen in New York, "still reeking of the Ghetto."

It was not hard for Gentile society to welcome Lazarus into its midst. With her cultured manners and refined intelligence, she fit the best ideals of the ancient "Hebrew" nation as they imagined it, a world apart from the growing numbers of Jews appearing on the scene.

Those numbers increased greatly as the nineteenth century wore on. The population consisted of only about 6,000 Jews in 1830, most of them, like the Lazarus family, descendants of Sephardim or of early German Jewish settlers who had married into Sephardic families and assumed their traditions. Several new waves of German Jewish immigrants raised the ranks to about 50,000 in 1850 and 250,000 in 1870. The huge influx of East European immigrants in the 1880s and 1890s brought the total to close to two million by the turn of the century.

By the 1870s, even before the arrival of the East Europeans, American Jews of both Sephardic and German descent had begun to feel themselves more vulnerable than ever before. Anti-Semitism (a word coined in Germany at the end of the 1870s) had risen in Europe, particularly Germany, and German American Jews, who had pointed with pride to the culture and spirit of enlightenment in their homeland, felt shocked and betrayed. More important, vibrations of anti-Jewish sentiment could be felt in the United States—Judge Henry Wilton's exclusion of the highly respected banker Joseph Seligman from his Grand Union Hotel in Saratoga in 1877 was only the most publicized example of a prejudice against Jews that was cropping up in many parts of the country. In this climate, the advent of thousands of new immigrants compounded the anxiety of American Jews. Poor, Orthodox in their religious practice, highly visible because of their numbers, the newcomers seemed to threaten the very security of the more established and assimilated Jews.

The growing sense of vulnerability coupled with the overwhelming presence of poor immigrants catapulted Lazarus into the Jewish scene.

As Bette Roth Young shows, Lazarus had dealt with some Jewish themes even before they became the focus of her energies in 1882. Most of her early work, however, centered on heroic subjects taken from ancient mythology and were little different from the poetry and prose appearing in many popular magazines. Even in the one poem—"Echoes"—in which she examines her place as a writer, she maintains her conventional stance. As if to reassure the reader that she is not overstepping the role society allotted her, she refers to her poems as "echoes" of the more forceful subjects of male writers, her art as "veiled and screened by womanhood."

Only when she threw herself wholeheartedly into her Jewish subject matter did those veils and screens begin to come down. By the time Lazarus took up the cause, European anti-Semitism and the Russian pogroms had sparked much debate among both Jews and Gentiles about the "Jewish Problem" (a term with unforgettable resonance in the twentieth century). For Christians, the "problem" referred to a view of the Jews as aliens wherever they lived because of their stubborn refusal to relinquish either their religious beliefs or their group solidarity. For Jews, the "problem" was the fact that others defined them as a problem; that they did not know how to combat the anti-Jewish sentiments that seemed to well up all around them.

Lazarus tackled the issue head on. Her poems and essays in *The Century* and other publications appealed to the non-Jewish public to recognize the part Christian prejudice and persecutions had played in creating the "problem." Her writings in the Jewish magazines appealed to her own people to reform and renew themselves. With determination, she called on Jews to establish a national homeland in Palestine as a haven from anti-Semitism, and to that end she organized the Society for the Improvement of East European Jews to help resettle victims of Russian oppression in Palestine.

No Jewish writer before her had displayed such energy and verve. A few male journalists of the early nineteenth century, among them Isaac Harby and the diplomat Mordecai M. Noah, had written plays and articles that occasionally dealt with a Jewish topic. Several female writers—Rebecca Gratz and Penina Moise among the best—had written letters, hymns, or poems that appeared in Jewish magazines. But none of these people equalled Lazarus in talent or the ability to reach both the general and the Jewish publics.

And with all that, when we look at Lazarus and her work today what we see is a person writing from the outside, a person set apart from the people she seeks to guide and aid. We see a defender of the Jews who is hardly of them.

Assimilated, with no religious affiliations of her own, she had little appreciation for the traditions and rituals that had governed Jewish life in Eastern

Europe for centuries. She viewed the immigrants as backward, their religion as "superstition." Her image of Jewish renewal was of a return to an idealized past, to that heroic biblical age that Christians so accepted and admired. Wealthy and well bred, she had little understanding of the skills and culture the new arrivals brought with them. She urged that they work as domestics and manual laborers or form agricultural colonies in rural areas—occupations that had been pressed on and rejected by waves of earlier Jewish immigrants. Concerned lest American Jews be seen as disloyal, she envisaged a Jewish homeland in Palestine only as a haven for the oppressed of other nations and not as a national center for all Jews. In making that distinction she also recognized—at least on some level—that sending the impoverished immigrants off to Palestine would ease the insecurity their presence caused American Jews. As sympathetic as she was to their plight, she needed to maintain the separateness of Jews like herself from them.

Lazarus's own sense of separateness from her people, and the need for it, comes across particularly in the letters she wrote to her non-Jewish friends from the 1870s until close to her death in 1887.

The bulk of the letters in this collection are to her good friend Helena deKay Gilder, who, with her husband Richard Gilder, editor of *The Century Magazine*, formed the nucleus of New York intellectual society. There are gaps in the correspondence: no letters exist from the end of September, 1882, until Lazarus began her first trip abroad in May, 1883—months when she was deeply involved in her Jewish ventures—and none for the year 1884. Were these letters lost or destroyed, or were they simply never written? We may never know. But it seems fairly safe to conjecture that had Lazarus written to Helena during those times, her letters would have provided little more insight into her Jewish involvement than did the rest of her correspondence.

Certainly her lively, newsy letters from Europe barely touched on the Jewish issues with which she had become so caught up before leaving and whose pursuit was one of the purposes of her trip. She alludes on May 31, 1883 to a forthcoming meeting with Claude Montefiore, leader of Liberal Judaism in England, but reports nothing more about it. She jokes a short time later about her disappointment at not "seeing the slightest prospect of marrying Sir Moses Montefiore. . . . He is approaching his 99th birthday," but gives no other information about him. Yet it seems likely that she discussed her plans for Jewish resettlement in Palestine with both Montefiores, who were great Jewish philanthropists (Sir Moses was Claude's grand-uncle) and other Jewish leaders she met, for on her return home she wrote to E.R.A. Seligman, a member of her Society on East European Jews, that she was eager to hold a meeting to present a report on her findings abroad.

Moreover, compared to the effusiveness with which she describes many of her activities, in the few references she does make to Jewish matters she seems to be detached, standing away from the event she recounts. On July 4, 1883, for example, she writes almost indifferently of having met "the original of George Eliot's *Mirah*—a very handsome Jewess." Yet it was Eliot's book *Daniel Deronda,* of which Mirah is the heroine, that inspired Lazarus's dream of Jewish nationalism. We might have expected more enthusiasm and a more detailed description than this cool reference to the "handsome Jewess."

Why the reticence on Lazarus's part? Perhaps because she believed Helena would have little interest in the details of her Jewish mission. Or perhaps because she believed that she could enjoy a greater intimacy with her friend by keeping that aspect of her life muted in their personal relationship.

The one Jewishly connected event that she does elaborate on is her depiction in the July fourth letter of a day she and her sister Annie spent with Robert Browning. The elderly poet, she writes, "is a great enthusiast of the Jews, & I think this may be the secret of his immense kindness to Annie & myself." That enthusiasm led him to invite the sisters to his home, where, with "pathetic" sadness, he showed them Hebrew and Greek books that had belonged to his wife, who had died some twenty years earlier. Before they left, Browning gave them a photograph of himself, which he inscribed in Hebrew. The visit offered a rare insight into the private Browning. Of this encounter Lazarus could write comfortably, knowing that Helena would appreciate the special attentions she enjoyed from such a world-revered figure.

Lazarus's letters to her friend Rose Hawthorne Lathrop, daughter of Nathaniel Hawthorne, are less intimate than those to Helena, and do mention some Jewish undertakings. On August 23, 1882, she writes of her "imperative duties" in regard to the Russian Jews and her absorption with the "Jewish Question," which, she hastens to say, was now a topic of major interest in the general press. A few weeks later, on September 30th, she sends Rose a copy of her new book of Jewish poetry, *Songs of a Semite.*

Rose Lathrop was an odd choice to receive that book, for her brother, the author Julian Hawthorne, wrote anti-Semitic novels that portrayed Jews in the crudest stereotypes. Sister and brother had been estranged over family matters, but Lazarus's letters seem to indicate a warm reconciliation. Lazarus would have been too polite to criticize Hawthorne to his sister—in fact she refers to him sympathetically a number of times. Could she have sent Rose her poems as an indirect response to Julian? Possibly. It seems more likely, however, that the book was a gift of friendship and that she separated her friendship with Rose, and perhaps Julian as well—as she did her other close Gentile friendships—from her work on behalf of the Jews Julian mocked.

By the time Lazarus returned from her first trip to Europe, in the fall of 1883, some of her passion for that work had abated. The trip had been a personal triumph. With letters of introduction from the Gilders and others, she had met some of the luminaries of the continent: the great pianist Anton Rubinstein; the pre-Raphaelite painter Edward Burne-Jones, the reformer-artist William Morris; and the writer Matthew Arnold among others. Her descriptions of them in her letters are a treasure-trove of social history. (Of Henry James, whom she saw in England several times, she wrote, "He is overworked, & over-dined and over-bored & over-everything.") On her return, she tried to keep her Society for resettling the immigrants alive, but it expired by the end of 1884. Though she wrote some poems and essays on Jewish themes for the rest of her life, she was never again as actively committed to Jewish causes as she had been in 1882 and early 1883.

How, then, do we assess Emma Lazarus today, more than a hundred years after her death? In her own time many saw her as a beacon of light, much like the Statue of Liberty itself, reaching out to downtrodden immigrants, the "wretched refuse" of other lands, in the words of her famous sonnet. Jews took pride in her spirited criticisms of Christian anti-Semitism. Gentiles praised her as a leader of her people. Her call for a national homeland, limited though it was, anticipated the Zionist idea that would soon capture Jewish thought.

Yet her work has not held up well over time. Except for her sonnet it is mostly unknown and unread. It has not held up in part because her talent was not a major one—many of her poems are too high-flown; her essays too polemical. But it has not held up also because much of it no longer rings true. Like her letters, it reflects the discomfort of a woman who was not totally at home in the Christian world she inhabited but had not quite found her footing in the Jewish one either. It has the feel of outsideness, of a writer who held herself too much apart, too much above the people she sought to defend and counsel. The outsideness has stood in the way of its survival.

One of Lazarus's last published works, the prose poem "By the Waters of Babylon," traces Jewish exiles through history, flashing back to the earliest exiles to Babylon. It ends with an appeal for acceptance of the new exile, the East European Jew, who, "ignorant" because of decades of oppression, now "crawls blinking forth from the loathsome recesses of the Jewry." She could not have known then that from those "loathsome recesses" would emerge a new literature, one in which writers—Anzia Yezierska or Henry Roth in the early generations, Saul Bellow or Philip Roth later—would not hide the tensions they felt living in two worlds but would consciously grapple with them. She could not foresee then that from the "huddled masses" of immigrants that worried her and other Jews of the nineteenth century would come a true and vibrant American Jewish culture in the twentieth.

Preface

FINDING EMMA

My odyssey with Emma Lazarus began as an extra credit project in a graduate course in Jewish History at the University of Michigan. In the course of my research, I received a roll of microfilm from the New York Public Library from the Richard Watson Gilder collection. Among the many letters written to Gilder by a variety of Lazarus sisters were two letters from Emma to Helena Gilder. They were astonishing. Here was not a reclusive spinster but the Emma now found in these pages.

About four years later, I called the NYPL to see if there were more letters from Emma to Helena Gilder. By then I had obtained copies of the letters to Thomas Wren Ward, housed in the Houghton Library at Harvard and those to E.R.A. Seligman and from Henry James, in the Butler Library at Columbia. The librarian informed me that two of the Gilder daughters, both octogenarians, still lived in Manhattan and gave me their phone number. I called only to be told that Rosamond Gilder, who was in charge of her mother's correspondence, was in the hospital. And that, I thought, was that.

About two years later, however, I felt compelled to write to Rosamond Gilder, telling her of my interest in her mother's letters. She replied that she had no letters in her home in Gramercy Park but would be spending the summer at the family summer home in Tyringham, near Lenox, Massachusetts, and would look there. In July of that year, she wrote that she had some one hundred letters from Emma and her sisters to Helena Gilder. Three days later, I arrived at Four Brooks Farm, the Gilder summer residence, built in 1896.

Rosamond Gilder led me through her home, an American historical treasure to be sure, to the attic where I confronted wood cupboards on all sides of a rather large room. These cabinets contain the correspondence of Helena deKay Gilder. What a collection it is. Ms. Gilder gave me several files of letters from Emma, Annie, Sarah, and Josephine Lazarus. I asked her if I might copy them. With generosity and trust, she told me to go to the Lenox post office where I would find the only Xerox machine available on that Saturday afternoon. I spent the rest of the day copying some three hundred pieces of paper.

That evening, in my attic room at a bed and breakfast in Lenox, I began to read the letters. I found them more extraordinary than I could have imagined. For the next two years I transcribed Emma's experiences. For the next ten years I lived her life: I read her books, heard the music she loved, walked 14th Street and 57th Street and 10th Street in Manhattan, and became acquainted with the remarkable men and women she knew.

I found the Lathrop letters at last by following a footnote that mentioned Rose Hawthorne Lathrop and Rosary Hill Home, the hospice she founded, in a biography of Augustus St. Gaudens. I wrote to the hospice, since I had read of the strong friendship between Emma and Rose. Not only was I sent Emma's letters but Helena Gilder's letters to Rose Lathrop as well.

Let me say, finally, that the letters transcribed in this book could be only a beginning. While I think I have looked into all possible resources, there just might be another trove of letters, hidden in another attic cupboard just waiting to be discovered.

Editor's Note on Orthography and Punctuation in the Letters

The letters in this collection have been transcribed word for word from photocopies of the originals; sometimes the spelling was inconsistent or incorrect. The use of dashes and of ampersands (&) for the word "and" are transcribed faithfully from Emma Lazarus' letters as are her idiosyncratic spellings.

As can be seen from the photo of one of her letters, Emma's handwriting was often illegible; the author struggled for years to decipher some of the words. The use of the ellipsis or multiple periods (. . . . . .) indicates the illegibility of a word or words. In some cases the paper of the original letter had been torn or the quality of the reproduction was so poor that a complete transcription of the text was not possible.

Acknowledgments

I n my eighteen-year journey with Emma Lazarus, I have been given the
support of many people. Special thanks to Dr. Jehuda Reinharz, with
whom I first met Emma; Lazarus scholar Morris U. Schappes, who has been a
generous and conscientious adviser and friend; Sara Bell, who helped me in
my search; Dr. Patricia Pilling, whose always sage advice and warm support
fortified me; and Carol Rich, who was the first to read the manuscript.

I want to thank Dr. Jacob R. Marcus at the American Jewish Archives and
Bernard Wax at the American Jewish Historical Society for their advice and
support and for furnishing me with primary materials, indispensable to my
work.

For the ceaseless encouragement of my friends in Detroit and Columbus, I
say thank you.

My children, my sisters, and my husband know how indispensable their love
and support have been to this book. "Thank you" would never be enough.

Working with The Jewish Publication Society has been a joy: Dr. Ellen Fran-
kel, Editor-in-Chief; Diane Zuckerman, Managing Editor; Barbara O'Neil
Phillips, copy editor; I thank them for their enthusiasm and advice.

This volume would not have happened without the hospitality and generosity of the late Rosamond Gilder, who opened her wonderful historic home to
me for two summers in 1980 and 1981. She entrusted me with more than one
hundred precious letters, which I photocopied at the local post office, and she
invited me to lunch and to tea, to see her priceless photographs and to hear her
wonderful memories. I am grateful for her permission to publish the letters of
Emma Lazarus to her mother and father, Helena deKay and Richard Watson
Gilder.

Thanks to Helena Pappenheimer for the wonderful photos of her grandparents and for permission to use them.

Rosary Hill Home, a hospice founded by Rose Hawthorne Lathrop (Mother Alphonsa), sent me the original letters written by Emma Lazarus to Rose Lathrop and the photograph of their foundress and gave me permission to publish them. I thank them for their generosity and trust.

Special Collections at the Brown University Library has given permission to publish an excerpt from a letter of Emma Lazarus to James Russell Lowell, housed there.

The Rare Book and Manuscript Library of the Butler Library, Columbia University, has given permission to publish letters from Emma Lazarus to Edwin Robert Anderson Seligman in the Edwin Robert Anderson Seligman Papers and to Robert Underwood Johnson in the Robert Underwood Johnson Papers; and the letters from Henry James to Emma Lazarus in the Emma Lazarus Papers, which reside there.

Thank you to the Columbia University Library, Stephen Crane Papers, Rare Book and Manuscript Library, for permission to publish the photograph of Henry James.

The Houghton Library at Harvard University has given permission to publish the letters from Emma Lazarus to Thomas Wren Ward, in the Ward Papers, housed there in the Autograph File.

The Rare Books and Manuscript Division of the New York Public Library, Astor, Lenox, and Tilden Foundations, has given permission to publish the letters of Emma Lazarus to Richard Watson and Helena deKay Gilder, in the Richard Watson Gilder Papers, housed there.

The Stanford University Library has given me permission to publish an excerpt from a letter from Mary Hallock Foote to Helena deKay Gilder in the Mary Hallock Foote Papers, housed there. I thank them for sending me the whole cycle of that correspondence on film. It was most illuminating.

Thank you to Evelyn Foote Gardiner for permission to quote her grandmother, for the photograph of Emma's friends, and for so generously answering my questions.

The American Jewish Historical Society has given permission to quote the poem titled "Assurance" from Emma Lazarus' Notebook and to publish a photograph of Emma Lazarus.

Morris U. Schappes has given permission to quote excerpts from the following three poems written by Emma Lazarus, published in 1978 in a volume edited by him, *Emma Lazarus: Selections from Her Poetry and Prose*: "The Banner of the Jews," "The Crowing of the Red Cock," and "Echoes."

This volume would not have been published without the consent of Emma's family to share her hidden life. I am most appreciative of their permission to publish her letters. A special thank you to Henry Geyelin for his hospitality, his generosity and his friendship.

ACKNOWLEDGMENTS

Alexander James has graciously given consent to publish letters from his great-uncle Henry James to Emma Lazarus.

The University of Virginia Library has given permission to publish a photograph of Emma Lazarus.

A special thank you to Ormonde deKay for making available to me the photograph of his grandfather and for his help through the years.

Thanks to the Redwood Library and Athenaeum Publishers for providing the photo of the Lazarus summer home in Newport, Rhode Island. The photo was taken from a book by George Champlin Mason titled, *Newport and Its Cottages*, published by the James R. Osgood Company in 1874.

PART I

The Life

1

The Statue

THE NEW COLOSSUS

Not like the brazen giant of Greek fame,
With conquering limbs astride from land to land;
Here at our sea-washed sunset gates shall stand
A mighty woman with a torch, whose flame
Is the imprisoned lightning, and her name
Mother of Exiles. From her beacon-hand
Glows world-wide welcome; her mild eyes command
The air-bridged harbor that twin cities frame.

"Keep ancient lands, your storied pomp!" cries she
With silent lips. "Give me your tired, your poor,
Your huddled masses yearning to breathe free,
The wretched refuse of your teeming shore.
Send these, the homeless, tempest-tost to me,
I lift my lamp beside the golden door."

Emma Lazarus, nineteenth century American poet, is best remembered for her sonnet, "The New Colossus." History needn't apologize; the poem has become an American anthem. It was written in 1883 to be auctioned at the Art Loan Fund Exhibition in Aid of the Bartholdi Pedestal Fund for the Statue of Liberty, and was the only entry read at the gala opening of that exhibit on 3 December of that year. James Russell Lowell wrote Emma that her poem had given the Statue a "raison d'être." Except for an appearance in one daily after that, however, it fell into obscurity. At the unveiling of the Statue in 1886, both Emma and her sonnet were absent. Nevertheless, she thought the piece important enough to give it first place in her notebook of poems, transcribed a year before her death.[1]

The sonnet was rescued from oblivion in 1901, when Georgina Schuyler set in motion a successful attempt to memorialize her friend by placing the poem, inscribed on a bronze tablet, inside the pedestal of the Statue. On 6 May 1903, after two years of red tape, Schuyler was able to report to her friends that "dear Emma's poem" was in place.[2]

The relationship between the Statue of Liberty and "The New Colossus" is taken for granted. In 1986, in honor of the tandem renovations of the Statue of Liberty and Ellis Island, liberty coins were struck on which the Statue, the immigrant, and the lines of the sonnet were inscribed. To quote Oscar Handlin, the Statue, the immigrant, and the sonnet are "connected."[3]

"Liberty Enlightening the World" was given to the United States by the French people in honor of each country's revolution. At the unveiling ceremonies on 28 October 1886, President Grover Cleveland viewed the Statue as a goddess who had "made her home here." He said that the fires from her "chosen altar" would be kept alive by "willing votaries" and would shine "upon the shores of our sister republic in the east." Liberty's light would "pierce the darkness of man's ignorance and oppression," until Liberty enlightened the world.[4]

Emma Lazarus gave the Statue a very different name and purpose. Calling her "Mother of Exiles," she brought America's most illustrious immigrant down to earth to welcome exiles from around the world. Her Statue could not wait for the concept of liberty to triumph in distant lands; she offered liberty now, to the globe's great unwashed. Lazarus' poem reinforced the concept of America as a haven for the homeless. It came, appropriately, at a time when this country was overwhelmed by an unending torrent of immigrants. To this day, hyphenate Americans continue to claim the Statue as their own.[5]

Furthermore, various segments of American society, pleading for social justice, continue to use the Statue as a kind of intercessor. With an absence of awe, some have climbed her stairways and chained themselves to the railing around her crown. Many have used Emma's words as proof-text for their cause.[6] In addition, the sonnet has become a part of America's musical repertoire. Put to music by Irving Berlin, it is sung by schoolchildren at vocal music concerts as a replacement for "America the Beautiful."[7]

Emma Lazarus gave a goddess to a world full of strangers and called her Mother. She breathed life into that icy majesty, rescuing her from the "stuff of Fourth of July oratory."[8] The Statue of Liberty is an American icon. So, in a sense, is Emma Lazarus. But while the Statue "lives" in a New York harbor, "battered and assaulted by wind and weather," Emma Lazarus has been put on a pedestal of sorts. She is viewed as brilliant, morbid, reclusive, and pure, an unapproachable American aristocrat. Nevertheless, she is a "patron saint" for American Jews. Seen in her time as the leading spokesperson for an East European Jewry forced to leave the barbarity of Czarist Russia, she is still honored today by such diverse groups as the Emma Lazarus Federation of Jewish Women's Clubs and the American Jewish Historical Society, for example.

The federation, founded in 1951, is an offshoot of the Jewish People's Fraternal Order. The JPFO, which grew out of the Jewish-American section of the International Workers Order, was liquidated during the McCarthy era. The Federation continues to exist. Its members are octogenarian Jewish women, for the most part, whose commitment to the principles of Karl Marx informs their group. The publication of Lazarus' poetry and prose has been an ongoing project of this national organization that sees Emma Lazarus as a "progressive," i.e., socialistic, Jew. Her one essay on William Morris as well as her "secular" humanistic Judaism inspires this view.[9]

The American Jewish Historical Society, housed on the campus of Brandeis University, is one of two archives for American Jewish artifacts. The Emma Lazarus Foundation is one of three endowments created by the Society for the purpose of raising funds. In addition, in 1986, in honor of the Centennial of the Statue of Liberty, the Society inaugurated the Emma Lazarus Statue of Liberty Award Dinner, "the only national event during the centennial celebration of the Statue of Liberty to focus on the role American Jewish immigrants have played in the development of our nation."[10]

Emma Lazarus was never "radical," nor was she comfortably Jewish. She was more at home in the cultured milieu of New York, Newport, Concord, and London than in the Jewish world she so ardently embraced in the last years of her life. Said to have had a "conversion" experience upon meeting East European Jewish refugees at Ward's Island, she became their spokesperson in poetry and prose. Nevertheless, her world remained as it had been, one of gentility and high culture.

2

The Chronology

Emma Lazarus was born on 22 July 1849 in New York City and died there on 19 November 1887. She was thirty-eight years old. The fourth of six daughters and one son born to Moses and Esther Nathan Lazarus, she belonged to "one of the best known and oldest Hebrew families" in New York.[1] In fact, at the time of her birth, both the Lazarus and Nathan families had been well established in Manhattan for four generations.

The first twenty-three Jews to settle in this country, exiles from Recife in Brazil, landed on the shores of New Amsterdam in 1654. It is from this nucleus that the American Jewish community evolved. By the Revolutionary Era, all of Emma's ancestors were members of this close-knit, interrelated community. The Nathan branch of the family was particularly prolific. Emma's grandparents, Sarah Seixas and Isaac Mendes Seixas Nathan, had fifteen children. From these roots would spring Emma's first cousins, some seventy in number, many of whom would distinguish themselves in social, political, and literary life.[2]

Emma's father was a prosperous sugar refiner who is said to have retired in 1865, having amassed a fortune. He was a member of the exclusive Union Club and was one of the founders of the Knickerbocker Club. Other founders included John Jacob and William Astor, August Belmont, John Hay, and William Vanderbilt. Her maternal uncle, Benjamin Nathan, a vice-president of the New York Stock Exchange, was also a member of the city's most prestigious clubs. Emma's paternal uncle, Jacob Hart Lazarus, was one of the city's most proficient portrait artists.[3]

Although we know nothing about the education of the Lazarus children, Emma's poems and translations, first published in 1866 by her father for private distribution, show evidence of a strong classical education with expertise in German and French. In 1868, she sent a copy of her book to Ralph Waldo

Emerson, whom she had met at the home of Samuel Gray Ward some time before. He liked the book and became her mentor and friend. Emma visited him in 1876 and again in 1879 and maintained a relationship with his family until her death.[4]

In 1870, Moses Lazarus built a summer cottage on fashionable Bellevue Avenue in Newport and called it The Beeches.[5] His daughters belonged to the exclusive Town and Country Club there. Headed by Julia Ward Howe, its membership was confined to fifty families, meeting once a week "in some of the most agreeable houses in Newport" for "some scientific and literary entertainment." The eminent participants included Richard H. Hunt, John LaFarge, Dr. Silas Weir Mitchell, Thomas W. Higginson, and Vincenzio Botta.[6]

By 1874, at the age of twenty-five, Emma was recognized as an author of note. Her second volume of poetry, *Admetus and Other Poems,* published in 1871, met with critical praise. The *Westminster Review* compared the title poem with Browning's *Balaustion's Adventure.* The *Athenaeum* said, "There is . . . something—and not much—wanting to complete her success, and place her alongside the masters."[7] The publication of her *Alide: An Episode of Goethe's Life* (1874) won warm praise from Ivan Turgenev, who wrote her, "An author who writes as you do is not 'a pupil in art' anymore; he [*sic*] is not far from being himself a master." *Lippincott's* reviewed this adaptation of Goethe's autobiography, a sketch of his brief interlude with Friederike Brion, stating that "in the character of the heroine, Miss Lazarus had a legitimate field and fair scope of the exercise of her imaginative powers." Her treatment of the story "justified strong expectations in regard to any venture she may hereafter make on the broad sea of fiction under her own flag."[8]

Probably Lazarus' strongest early talent was her ability to translate the works of German, French, and Spanish Jewish poets. As early as 1867, her translations of Dumas, Hugo, Heine, and Schiller were described in the *New York Times* as "quite passable."[9] Her publication of Heine's poems in 1881 met with wide acclaim. The *Critic* said, "To say that Miss Lazarus' rendering into English of several hundreds of Heine's beautiful poems is the best, would be paying her a small compliment. Little can be said of the three most widely known previous translators of Heine." The *Century* confirmed her "right to be heard," by reason of her "strong enthusiasm in the man and his work" and "a delicate appreciation of the quality of Heine's verse."[10]

By 1882, Emma Lazarus had published more than fifty poems and translations, the majority of which appeared in *Lippincott's Magazine.*[11] She counted as her friends many artists and thinkers, among them Edmund Clarence Stedman, E. L. Godkin, Charles Dana, Constance Cary Harrison, Georgina Schuyler, E. R. A. Seligman, and Felix Adler, key figures in the cultural history of New York City. Lazarus corresponded with such luminaries as Thomas W.

Higginson, Ivan Turgenev, Henry George, Henry James, John Burroughs, and the Italian Shakespearean actor, Tommaso Salvini.[12]

Rose Lathrop, Nathaniel Hawthorne's daughter, was Emma's intimate friend. They probably met at the home of Richard and Helena deKay Gilder. Gilder was both her editor at the *Century* magazine and her friend; Helena was one of her closest confidantes. Many of Emma's friends were friends of the Gilders. She was a member of the group of artists and thinkers who orbited around that remarkable couple. Richard Watson Gilder was an editor at *Scribner's Monthly* when Emma met him; Helena deKay Gilder was an artist of some note. Their home, The Studio, a stable remodeled by Stanford White, became the gathering place for the best and brightest actors, artists, musicians and public figures in America at century's end.[13]

Not only was Emma a friend of the Gilders', she was close to members of their families. At least two sources have suggested that Emma's relationship with Helena's brother, Charles deKay, was more than platonic. DeKay, literary and art editor of the *New York Times*, was a poet. Emma loved his work; others found it morbid and strange.[14]

New York in the 1880s had come of age. Although all roads might once have led to Concord, artists, musicians, and authors were congregating in Manhattan. The Society of American Artists and the Authors' Club held organizing meetings at the Gilder home as young writers and artists established themselves.[15] By 1885, a permanent home for the Metropolitan Museum of Art, the Metropolitan Opera, and three symphony orchestras were in existence as well.[16] Emma Lazarus was a vital presence in that city of flowering culture. Her poems and essays on music, literature and art were given voice in both the *Century* and the *Critic*, a magazine edited by Richard Gilder's brother and sister, Joseph and Jeannette. It was Lazarus who was chosen by Gilder to write the memorial essay on Emerson for the June number of the *Century* in 1882.[17] Edmund Stedman called her the "natural companion to scholars and thinkers."[18]

Not only had New York become the meeting place for artists and thinkers, it became the destination for Jewish immigrants fleeing the Czar's Russia. In 1881, Alexander II was assassinated. His son, Alexander III, instituted severe discriminatory laws against the Jews, who had never enjoyed a satisfactory status in Russian society. Pogroms ordered by government officials decimated Jewish communities, causing great injury and loss of life. The pogroms were decried in London and New York; Christian spokespersons deplored the destruction caused by a Christian Russian populace.[19]

Emma's friends participated in the protests; soon, she too noticed the plight of her co-religionists. She met Jewish immigrants face to face and seems to have been transformed. Now she wrote strident poetry and prose, calling upon her fellow Jews to rise up as in biblical times. She became the American spokesperson for the resettlement of Jews in a re-nationalized Palestine. Thus, she advocated Zionism thirteen years before Theodor Herzl coined the term. She worked with unskilled immigrants, setting up classes for them, settling them in suitable housing. In addition, she met with Jewish leaders in the city to put forth her ideas for the Hebrew Technical Institute she felt was so needed.[20]

Emma was able to publish her "Jewish" essays in the *Century*, probably because of her relationship with Richard Gilder. She became the mediator of Jewish history and culture to thousands of readers, Christian and Jewish. She used the pages of the Jewish weekly, the *American Hebrew*, to introduce Jewish history, Jewish patriotism, and the need for the education of East European Jews in the manual arts to an affluent, acculturated "uptown" Jewish population.[21]

Emma's vision of Jewish rebirth was two-pronged. She saw two centers of revival, Palestine and the United States. Unpublished correspondence tells us that when she composed "The New Colossus" in 1883, she was trying to keep alive her fledgling organization, the Society for the Improvement and Colonization of East European Jews. The major purpose of this group was the resettlement of Jewish exiles in Palestine.[22]

During this time, Emma tried to embrace both the uptown world of the arts and the downtown world of an immigrant population trying to survive. She went to England in May 1883, ostensibly to gain support for her resettlement scheme from leading British Jews. But her purpose seems to have been eclipsed by the sights and sounds of England and France. She met and dined with no less than forty prominent Britons, visited the studios of George du Maurier and George Frederic Watts, and spent some unforgettable days with Robert Browning and William Morris.[23] As Henry James wrote her, "You appear to have done more in three weeks than any lightfooted woman before; when you ate or slept I have not yet made definite."[24] From Paris she wrote that she had "hardly seen my people [the Jews] . . . as I have had too many other things to do even to deliver my letters of introduction."[25]

The year 1884 saw the collapse of the Society for the Improvement and Colonization of East European Jews. Emma's concerns seem to have become more universalized. She wrote her lengthy essay on William Morris, which was published two years later in the *Century*, as well as an essay on Heine as a poet.[26] An early member of the Nineteenth Century Club, she resumed participation in its events. This nonsectarian club met fortnightly in private residences for discussion of current social problems and other subjects of interest.

Gustav Gottheil, rabbi at Temple Emanu-El, and Emma's good friend, was one of the founding members.[27]

Lazarus helped organize the so-called Workingmen's Concerts, free concerts for workers and their families, under the direction of Maestro Theodore Thomas, conductor of the New York Philharmonic Orchestra.[28] During this time, her Jewish activity seems to have consisted of contributions of essays and poetry to Jewish and general journals.

An illness in the summer of 1884 forced curtailment of Emma's activities. Shortly thereafter, her father became mortally ill; he died in March 1885. Two months later, she set off with her sisters for what was to be an eighteen-month tour of Europe. Some time before January 1887, however, Emma Lazarus became critically ill. She could not be moved from her bed in Paris until the end of July, when she was brought home to die. Four months later, she succumbed.[29]

When Emma Lazarus died she was memorialized as the "bravest singer of the Semitic race" since "Miriam sang of deliverance and triumph by the Red Sea."[30] It hardly mattered that she had chosen to spend eighteen months in Europe rather than in active assistance to the East European Jews she had championed in 1882 and 1883. Furthermore, during her "Jewish" years she had become a subject of controversy in the Jewish community, because of her secular Jewishness and her call for a Jewish nation. At the same time, however, many saw her as the greatest Jewish poet of the nineteenth century. At her death all quarrels were set aside as Jewish weeklies across the country mourned her.[31]

The *American Hebrew* devoted a special issue to Emma Lazarus and called upon Jewish communal leaders and international literary figures to memorialize her.[32] John Greenleaf Whittier compared her works to those of Robert Browning. He noted that she had his "rugged strength" and "verbal audacity." Browning admired her "genius." *New York Sun* editor Charles Dana said she had "the courage and logic of a man." John Hay saw her as one of "our best writers, those whose extraordinary gifts have added an ardent and self-sacrificing devotion to justice, to purity, and to humanity." Naturalist John Burroughs said, "She was one of my best friends."

Jacob Schiff, the most prominent American Jewish philanthropist of that day, placed her in the "pantheon of our own race," her name would "stand with that of Deborah and Miriam." Anna Laurens Dawes summed up the reason for the esteem and awe in which Emma was held. "More than any other woman," she said, "she represented her people to the world at large, and by token of her own force and power she seemed to lift the whole race of Israel in the public mind, to its due and rightful position."

Mary M. Cohen, intellectual member of a prominent Philadelphia Jewish family, described her first visit to Emma, showing us how widespread her popularity was.

> I was so familiar with the thoroughness, power and lofty beauty of her literary works as to feel great timidity in approaching her. . . . After hesitation, the steps of her house were mounted, the bell rung, a faltering question asked. . . . Presently a young woman came into the parlor, and entered into the conversation. Was this the far-reaching mind, the subtle soul, the glorious imagination—an embodiment of womanly grace, graceful calm, the very essence of modesty, the type of noble genius. . . . She moved easily and spoke with a gentleness very engaging, but I was more struck by the entire absence of self-consciousness in her manner than by any other of her traits.

Her soul, said Cohen, was dedicated to the aid of the oppressed.

Emma Lazarus was a Jewish celebrity when she died, as the *London Jewish Chronicle* had noted.[33] Her absence of two years from New York seemed to have added to her mystique. Her untimely death, however, poses questions for biographers and scholars. Would she have continued her involvement with Jews after her tour of the Continent? While she was there, she seems to have made no effort to contact "her people." Would she have gained increasing prestige as a poet and a critic? Would her interest in such activists as Henry George and William Morris have developed into political activism? What would have been her involvement in the Women's movement? These issues and more can be addressed only hypothetically. In the meantime, Emma's public has created her to their own specifications. They seem to own her as they do the Statue, to whom she gave an identity.

3

The Myth

Since the day of her death in 1887, Emma Lazarus' life has been increasingly covered with "fictionalized crystals."[1] A paucity of primary materials has inhibited serious research. This has not stopped the publication of numerous biographical entries in encyclopedias and dictionaries, popular journals and newspapers, and treatment in monographs and juvenile texts. Precisely because Lazarus is a folk hero, her life could not be ignored until suitable data were discovered; authors have used what they could and called it truth. Two cycles of letters have been the only available primary sources for those who write Emma's life. However, a questionable essay written by her sister Josephine one year after Emma's death has been used as additional primary material. All three resources are severely limited.

In 1939, Emerson scholar Ralph L. Rusk edited a Columbia University edition of seventy-five letters to Emma Lazarus, *Letters to Emma Lazarus in the Columbia University Library,* twenty-three of which were written by Ralph Waldo Emerson. Additional contributors included: John Burroughs, Henry George, Thomas W. Higginson, William James, John LaFarge, William Morris, Ivan Turgenev, and others. The edition's sparse annotations are incorrect in some instances. Nevertheless, the letters are clear evidence that Emma Lazarus was a respected artist and thinker.

In 1949, the New York Public Library issued seventy-eight letters from Emma Lazarus, *The Letters of Emma Lazarus, 1868–1885,* forty-one of which were written to Philip Cowen, editor of the *American Hebrew.*[2] Edited and annotated by Lazarus scholar Morris U. Schappes, these letters are significant because they portray Lazarus as both professional and Jew. The letters to Cowen are formal and aloof, in contrast to the somewhat ingratiating letters to Emerson and his family, also included in the collection.

Although both cycles are informative, they present an incomplete view.

They do not show us adequately the social life or the "personality" of the writer. Emma Lazarus was vitally interested in and emotionally involved with her family, her friends, her city, and her people. Her thought was a curious mixture of intellect and strong passion. These aspects of her life have been ignored, eclipsed by a myth that sees her as her sister Josephine had seen her. That portrait drawn by Josephine Lazarus has remained remarkably unchanged in the one hundred years since it was written.

"One hesitates to lift the veil and throw light upon a life so hidden and a personality so withdrawn as that of Emma Lazarus." This, the opening statement of an unsigned essay in the *Century* magazine, written by Josephine Lazarus in 1888, informs the contents of that essay and virtually every subsequent biographical treatment of her sister in the years since her death.[3] In most instances, Josephine's sibling authority is accepted without question. Because Emma Lazarus' portrayal has remained so constant through the years, we must first examine the persona her sister created and then look at some representative samplings of her biographies. These studies have a life of their own, perpetuating the memory of their subject in hyperbolic distortion. They are as much a "fact" of Emma's life as the sonnet that gave her immortality.

Josephine Lazarus saw her sister Emma as a one-dimensional, tragic Jewish priestess, whose "somber streak" was rooted in her membership in a "race born to suffer." Josephine portrayed her as a shy, sensitive child, a "born singer," for whom poetry was the natural language. "To write was less effort than to speak." Her winters in New York and summers "by the sea" were essentially "quiet and retired." There was no "dramatic episode or climax" in Emma's life.[4]

Even her mentor Ralph Waldo Emerson, the foremost American thinker of that day, failed to "elate the young poetess, or even to give her a due sense of the importance and value of her work or the dignity of her vocation." Josephine tells us that this was because "Emma Lazarus was a true woman, too distinctly feminine to wish to be exceptional or to stand alone and apart, even by virtue of superiority."[5]

Josephine contended that Emma reclaimed her Jewishness quite suddenly in 1882. Public protest in London and New York to Russian excesses against Jews was "a trumpet call that awoke slumbering and unguessed echoes" in the tragic poet. Furthermore, she asserted that the "almost fatal juxtaposition" of an enigmatic and seemingly equivocal essay Emma wrote on Benjamin Disraeli, "Was the Earl of Beaconsfield a Representative Jew?," to an anti-Jewish piece by Russian expatriate Mme. Zénaide Ragozin, "Russian Jews and Gentiles, from a Russian Point of View," in the April 1882 number of the *Century*, served as the catalyst for Lazarus' pro-Jewish response in the next number.

From that time "dated the crusade which she undertook in behalf of her race."[6]

According to Josephine, Emma experienced a personality change on her trip to Europe in the summer of 1883. "We have difficulty in recognizing the tragic priestess we have been portraying," she wrote, "in the enthusiastic child of travel who seems new-born in a new world." We are told that after her trip, however, she gave herself up, once again, "to quiet retrospect and enjoyment with her friends of the life she had had a glimpse of and the experiences she had stored—a restful, happy period."[7]

In 1885, Emma's father was "stricken," as we know. The winter months were a "long strain of acute anxiety, which culminated in his death" in March 1885. "The blow was a crushing one," Josephine wrote. "Truly the silver cord was loosed, the golden bowl was broken. Life had lost its meaning and its charm. Her father's sympathy and pride in her work had been her chief incentive and ambition, had spurred her on when her own confidence and spirit failed. Never afterwards did she find complete and spontaneous expression."[8]

Josephine ended her essay as she began it. Having described Emma's final illness and death, she reinforced her sister's Jewish identity. "To be born a Jewess was a distinction for Emma Lazarus," she wrote, "and she conferred distinction upon her race."[9]

Josephine Lazarus did not do her sister justice. She imprisoned her in an identity Emma would not have recognized. Emma's favorite youngest sister, Annie, had problems with that persona also, some forty years after the essay was published. On 25 February 1926, in a letter addressed to Bernard G. Richards, she denied his request for the rights to publish Emma's so-called Jewish poems for which she had the copyright. "There has been a tendency on the part of her public," Annie wrote, "to overemphasize the Hebraic strain of her work, giving it this quality of sectarian propaganda, which I greatly deplore, for I understand this to have been merely a phase in my sister's development, called forth by righteous indignation at the tragic happenings of those days. Then, unfortunately, owing to her untimely death, this was destined to be her final word."[10]

Annie, who had lived with Emma in Europe the last two years of her life, converted some years later to Anglican Catholicism. Her statement has been questioned by some who write of Emma's life, with no definitive resolution. Most Lazarus biographers have been unaware of or have ignored Annie's opinion, however. They have done little more than mimic or exaggerate Josephine's essay.

Almost immediately after the essay was published, it was noticed and enlarged upon. In the decade following her death, Emma Lazarus was thought important enough to be included in three biographical encyclopedias. The first entry appeared in 1888, in *Appleton's Cyclopedia of American Biography.* Published simultaneously with Josephine's essay, it asserted that Emma was educated privately at home. This "shard" has been incorporated in subsequent biographies, reinforcing the image of her privileged and secluded existence.[11]

The *National Cyclopedia of Biography,* published in 1893, used and embroidered upon Josephine's essay. Here we see Emma as a "shy and impressible child" whose melancholy was "the unconscious expression of the inherited sorrow of her race." The third volume, *Women of the Century,* published in 1897, stated that Emma Lazarus was "noted in her childhood for her quickness and intelligence," that she received a liberal education under private tutors," and that she was a "profound thinker."[12]

When on 6 May 1903, twenty years after it was written, Emma's sonnet "The New Colossus," engraved on a bronze tablet, was placed on a wall within the pedestal of the Statue of Liberty, both the *New York Times and the New York Tribune* covered the event. Sixteen years after her death, Emma Lazarus was characterized by the *Tribune* as "the most talented woman the Jewish race has produced in this country." Because of her devotion to the "persecuted and exiled Jews," the piece continued, she had "come to be regarded as almost a saint by the Jews of this country and England." Using Josephine's words, the daily told its readers that Judaism was a "dead letter" for Emma until she had been made aware of her East European co-religionists. After that, the *Tribune* asserted, it was "largely through her efforts that Jewish refugees met with help in New York." Both stanzas of the poem were printed, reacquainting the readers with the sonnet.[13]

Henrietta Szold, who would become one of America's foremost Zionists, wrote an essay that appeared in the *Jewish Encyclopedia* in 1904. Szold called Lazarus doubtless the "most distinguished literary figure produced by American Jewry and possibly the most eminent poet among Jews since Heine and Judah Loeb Gordon." She mentioned the placement of the bronze tablet "commemorative of" Lazarus, but not the sonnet.[14]

Through the years, biographies of Emma Lazarus have continued to be informed by Josephine's essay. Consider, for example, Allen Lesser's article published in 1938 in the *Menorah Journal,* the organ of the Menorah Society, a national Zionist youth organization on college campuses. Without the slightest hesitation, he asserted that Emma found religious services "dull and uninspiring at the Spanish and Portuguese Synagogue which she attended perfunctorily with her parents." He said that she was a "strange, shy child, precocious in her studies and sensitive to nature and to people." Lesser knew that Emerson "carefully" supervised the "reading and development of his youthful protégée." Again, of her visit to Ward's Island, he knew, of course, that she "had gone there rather timidly with a group of women." Actually, she went with a group of men, leaders in the Jewish community, the day of the infamous riot there.[15]

Lesser enlarged upon Josephine's description of Emma's relationship with her father. She had been "fonder of him than of any other member of her family." At the time of his death, he continued, "the bond between them had grown stronger than ever since her mother's death ten years before." Lesser ended the essay by stating the mythic "fact" that "save for her father, she had been in love with no man."

The essay is replete with exaggeration and misinformation. The most glaring error is Lesser's assertion that on her journey from Paris to New York during her final illness, she was "too weak to take notice of the shining bronze plaque on the pedestal of the Statue of Liberty upon which her famous sonnet had been inscribed."[16]

The first book-length biography of Emma Lazarus was written in 1949, the centenary of her birth, by Heinrich E. Jacob. A refugee from Germany, he had been in this country only a decade when his questionable volume, *The World of Emma Lazarus*, was published. The *New York Times* review of the book said that although "many unprinted diaries, manuscripts, and letters seem to have been lost, making the biographer's task most difficult, . . . Mr. Jacob, through indefatigable research, has managed to give us a fascinating picture, not only of the gifted, if frustrated woman, but also of her world—New York from the Mexican War to the late Eighties."[17]

Morris Schappes challenged that claim, saying bluntly that whatever "his merits as a German novelist and dramatist, Mr. H. E. Jacob demonstrates his inability to write a biography in which original research was required." Schappes' judgment of the author is correct. "[N]ot only does this first biography of Emma Lazarus (1849–1887) not add anything verifiable to the already accessible record, this book by misstating simple facts, creates confusion and distortion." Jacob's lack of documentation "compounds the mess," and the bibliography is inaccurate. Schappes ended by saying that in view of "Mr. Jacob's less than responsible handling of verifiable data, these materials must be approached with great caution."[18]

The World of Emma Lazarus is so faulty that it is really not worthy of discussion. Unfortunately, it is seen as the only "scholarly" biography of the subject, and authors of popular literature and scholarly monographs have made use of it. Furthermore, such reputable research tools as the *Encyclopaedia Judaica* and *Notable American Women* cite Jacob's work as a source.

Jacob used Josephine's essay to create a grotesque caricature in support of his central thesis that Emma was fixated on her father. He wrote that at the age of eighteen, when normally she would have fallen in love with some young man, she was so emotionally tied to her father that she became more and more a "father's girl." He went on to say that this "mild intelligent, cultivated man cast his shadow upon her verses. . . . He gave her far more at this stage of life than she could have received from any other man. For he studied with her and she studied with him." In addition, Jacob found that her works and her relationships were informed by her fixation. *Alide*, Emma's novel on an episode in Goethe's life, is said to have been written after her "complete breakdown," the result of her exclusion from Emerson's monumental poetry collection, *Parnassus*. In fact, she wrote *Alide* before she was excluded from the volume. Jacob seems to have needed this erroneous time sequence to develop his thought that Emma's "dread of love—dread of what the French call 'l'abandon"—informed this work. "Fear of the faithlessness of men. . . . It was to this virgin soul, infected by a lifelong fear of being jilted, that so terrible a thing as the *Parnassus* incident had happened!"[19]

In Jacob's fantasy, Josephine's shy and precocious poet became "so delicate, so fragile a person that too great an exposure to the raw realities of the world would have smothered, not fostered, her abilities." He characterized her as one who was "not even completely a woman; she was a daughter only." According to Jacob, one of the strongest facets of Emma's personality was the absence of a sense of humor, a trait he must have derived from Josephine's descriptions of her melancholy, morose sister.[20]

Jacob's book is full of chronological and factual mistakes. But the importance of the volume is its use as a source for further characterizations and for alleged motivations in analyses of her works.

Both a dissertation and a scholarly monograph focus on Emma Lazarus as an author. Arthur Zeiger's dissertation, "Emma Lazarus: A Critical Study," was the first scholarly attempt to understand the author and her work. Zeiger argued that her subjects were borrowed from other sources and were in many cases only slight adaptations. Zeiger was thorough in his documentation of his assertion that she "never managed to invent a living fable, or to plot an original story, or to exorcise the ghosts of her genteel exemplar. Where she found anything which interested her, she borrowed it."[21] When he dealt with motivation, however, he used the same erroneous biographical sources as did his predecessors.

From the beginning, Zeiger imitated Josephine. For example, in discussing the "funereal atmosphere which shrouds" Emma's youthful poems, he quoted her suggestion that a third reason for her "mournfulness" was hereditary, namely, that Emma's birth and temperament had the "stamp and heritage of a race born to suffer." On the other hand, in attempting to understand Emma's so-called sudden pro-Semitism in the 1880s, Zeiger suggested that "displaced sexuality" may have been a dynamic in her conversion. "If ever Emma Lazarus had a love affair, all traces have vanished utterly," he asserted.

"Did her passionate energy sublimate, flow into different channels? There are any number of analogies to be found in textbooks of psychology; but the end of the enquiry, like the beginning, is bounded by a guess."[22]

Similarly, Zeiger reinforced the idea that "Emma Lazarus never married, apparently never formed a deep attachment to any man, and had an abnormally strong attachment to her father." This "insight" was used to try to explain her unpublished poem "Assurance." "It would be difficult to interpret it as anything but a lesbian fantasy," he said, "a variety of autism unique in her work":

> Last night I slept, and when I woke her kiss
> Still floated on my lips. For we had strayed
> Together in my dream, through some dim glade,
> Where the shy moonbeams scarce dared light our bliss.
> The air was dank with dew, between the trees,
> The hidden glow-worms kindled and were spent.
> Cheek pressed to cheek, the cool, the hot night-breeze
> Mingled our hair, our breath, and went,
> As sporting with our passion. Low and deep
> Spake in mine ear her voice: "And didst thou dream,
> This could be buried? This could be sleep?
> And love be thralled to death! Nay whatso seem,
> Have faith, dear heart; THIS IS THE THING THAT IS!"
> Thereon I woke, and on my lips her kiss.[23]

To date, no evidence has been revealed to support the contention that Emma Lazarus was a lesbian.

Dan Vogel's monograph, *Emma Lazarus*, published in 1980, is an incisive analysis of Lazarus' poetry and prose. His treatment of her personality, however, is an example of the durability of both Josephine's essay and Jacob's book. In the introductory chapter, Vogel compared his subject to that other literary recluse, Emily Dickinson. He said that her mother's death in 1874 "thrust Emma into herself and into a deep emotional dependence on her father." Like Dickinson, though, Emma "once loved and lost. He was Washington Nathan, a cousin on Emma's mother's side."[24]

Washington Nathan was the son of Benjamin Nathan, her mother's brother. Although she dedicated her poem "Lohengrin" to him, we have no evidence that Emma thought of him as anything other than her cousin.

Vogel wrote that Emma "tried to shake off, but never really could, early melancholy tendencies." He knew, somehow, that "on the sly she surely read Edgar Allan Poe, who offered vicarious, delicious death, not uplift, to the impressionable teenager." Happiness was not often an "inspirational emotion for Emma Lazarus," he stated. "Poems describing joy are so infrequent and even then so rarely realized as experience, that when they do come they dazzle by contrast." He compared Lazarus to Elizabeth Barrett Browning: "[T]wo artistic women, two poets dependent upon dreams, both untouched by human passion, until one meets her man and the other is fated to imagine that condition."[25]

Vogel's analysis of Emma's relationship to Emerson was less pathological than Jacob's, but his word usage trivialized it. "Thus began a master-disciple relationship that lasted for ten years," he said. "He was, first of all, a source of inspiration and pride to her. A Brahmin from the New England pantheon took an abiding interest in a little Jewish girl from New York!" He said that "shyness and modesty did not prevent Lazarus from a long correspondence with another popular American author of that time, the naturalist, John Burroughs." However, in listing her "admirers," Charles Dudley Warner, John Greenleaf Whittier, Charles Dana, Henry James, William James, and James Russell Lowell, he found them a rather "illustrious group for a presumably young woman who cared little for her public posture," thus challenging Josephine's pronouncements.[26]

Virtually all histories of American Jews include Emma Lazarus. Several popular histories are good examples of the caricature developed from Josephine's essay. Solomon Liptzin, a reputable Jewish scholar, wrote at least two histories in which Emma Lazarus was included. In *Generation of Decision*, he wrote that in the 1880s "only a single Jewish writer, the Sephardic poetess Emma Lazarus, succeeded in groping her way during solitary and tragic years from early ignorance and indifference to profound insight and prophetic vision. Phoenix-like, the tired heiress of Colonial Jewry arose resplendent in fresh vigor and heralded a heroic resurgence of her ancient people." In *The Jew in American Literature*, Liptzin wrote that with "missionary zeal, the frail poetess undertook to defend her people against all detractors and defamers. . . . At first, the timid poetess could merely grope her way step by step."[27]

Harry Simonhoff's treatment of Lazarus in his history, *Saga of American Jewry, 1865–1914*, is almost identical to Liptzin's. He tells us how the shy Emma was "overawed when she met the Olympian god of American literature, Ralph Waldo Emerson. The shrinking Emma, in a rash moment," had mailed him her book. His portrayal of her spinsterhood is reminiscent of Jacob's:

> Emma was nearing spinsterhood without getting anywhere in poetry or in life. Reared in a wealthy home, without men, she lived in her ivory tower secluded and protected from the world and its strife. Personally not unattractive and gifted, yet she neither sought nor attracted prospective wooers, and her poetry reflected the inner frustration of an existence that remained uneventful and unfulfilled. In her *Admetus* she unconsciously identifies herself with Alcestis who welcomes death.[28]

An almost accurate portrayal of Emma Lazarus was written in 1987, on the occasion of the centenary of the poet's death, by Carole S. Kessner for the *Jewish Book Annual.* We forgive her use of literary license when she described the young poet as "beautiful." Kessner challenges Josephine's portrayal of her sister's reluctance to "assert herself or claim any prerogative," citing, as did Vogel, her "tutelary relationships" with "important literary figures." However, she seems to use the *Century*'s perception of Lazarus' first essay on Heine, stating that Emma "plays down Heine's Jewishness and attributes his Jewish consciousness to his general sentiments regarding egalitarianism and liberal causes."[29]

Kessner's hypotheses become questionable when she speculates on Emma's "latent" Jewishness. Although she challenges Josephine's statement that Judaism had been a "dead letter" to Emma, she credits Emerson's not including Lazarus in *Parnassus* for her slight shift to Jewish subjects in the 1870s. She feels that he "may have wounded her ego considerably by omitting her" from that work. Kessner does not tell us why that wound may have led to an interest in Jewishness. She does speculate, however, that it may have manifested itself in the poet's subsequent work. She cites the "penniless alienated Eastern European artist, Sergius Azoff," the central character in Emma's short story "The Eleventh Hour" (1878), as "undoubtedly" a Jew.[30] We have no evidence to suggest that Emma implicitly gave her immigrant that label.

The most recent monograph to mention Emma Lazarus is a biography of her friend Rose Hawthorne Lathrop, *To Myself a Stranger*, published in 1991. The author uses Jacob as a reference for a "conversation" between Lathrop and Lazarus. In addition, she places Emma's sonnet on "a bronze plaque on the statue's pedestal" in 1886, the year of the placement of the Statue of Liberty in New York Harbor.[31]

The discovery of more than one hundred letters sheds astonishing new light on Emma Lazarus. They provide the social life and the personality of a vital young woman who, contrary to the persona her biographers created, went a great many places with a great many people, and met life with an unfailing sense of humor. Letters to Helena and Richard Gilder, Thomas Wren Ward, Rose Hawthorne Lathrop, and Edwin R. A. Seligman are most instructive.

From 1876 until her death, Emma Lazarus wrote at least sixty letters to the Gilders, the majority of which are addressed to Helena. They cannot be overestimated. They are intimate, gossipy, thoughtful, and highly emotional. Furthermore, the majority of the people she mentions are significant to the era. Although many of the names are now unfamiliar, they are important to an understanding of American social history at century's end. Her letters from

Europe are visual masterpieces and talk of the many people she met. For a "reclusive spinster" she got around.

Letters to Thomas Wren Ward from 1876 to 1881 reveal yet another facet of Emma Lazarus. Ward, the son of Samuel Grey Ward, was the boyhood friend of Emerson's and James' children. "Tom" was an introspective and sensitive young man, deaf since childhood. Emma shared with him her love of literature. Her letters are more than intellectual, however; they are flirtatious. In reading them, we find it difficult to remember that Tom Ward was a married man.[32]

Emma's correspondence with Rose Lathrop began in January 1882. These two unique women became intimate friends, according to Lathrop's biographer, Theodore Maynard. Although the fourteen letters are too few to see the friendship in depth, they provide us with Emma's views on Oscar Wilde's outrageous visit to this country in 1882, Matthew Arnold's controversial lecture on Emerson during his celebrated visit in 1884, and what Emma called her plunging "wrecklessly" into the Jewish Question.

Eleven letters to Edwin Seligman from April, 1883 to April 1884 are probably the most historically significant. Lazarus wrote to Seligman, then a graduate student in political science and law at Columbia, asking him to join a group she had founded, including, among others, Daniel De Leon, then lecturing at Columbia. The primary purpose of the Society for the Improvement and Colonization of Eastern European Jews (S.I.C.E.E.J) was, as mentioned earlier, the resettlement, in Palestine, of Jews from Romania and Russia.

Although Emma Lazarus has long been recognized as a precursor of Zionism, she was seen only as a zealous literary champion of her people and as a genteel Lady Bountiful to the immigrants at New York Harbor. With the discovery of these letters, we not only learn what Seligman and De Leon were doing in these years, information unknown until now, we see the assertive activism of their author. The letters are also an important footnote in the history of American Zionism, as they are the only available record of the existence of the S.I.C.E.E.J.

One additional cycle of letters is included in this volume. Henry James wrote at least seven letters to Emma Lazarus from 1883 to 1885. Wonderfully Jamesian, they are strong evidence of a friendship only halted by Emma's early death.

4

The Experience

Who, then, was Emma Lazarus and how did she live? From both the letters included in this volume, and from what we know about New York City in the second half of the nineteenth century, we can question some of Josephine's assumptions about her sister's life there. From a review of Emma's works, we can challenge Josephine's statements about her interests and ideas. And finally, from astonishing and hitherto unrevealed data about her father's business connections, we may gain a new perspective on Emma's point of view.

New York City was the fastest-growing, most interesting metropolis in the United States in the second half of the nineteenth century. By 1849, the year of Emma's birth, New York had a polyglot population of more than 500,000 persons. By the time she was twenty, the population of the city had almost doubled.[1] When she was eight years old, Emma's family moved to 36 West Fourteenth Street, one block west of Union Square.

Fourteenth Street was the hub of activity for a fast-growing Manhattan in the third quarter of the century. The Academy of Music, Steinway Hall, the Metropolitan Museum of Art, Pursell's Ladies Restaurant, R. H. Macy's, F. A. O. Schwarz, and Tammany Hall were located there, between Third and Seventh avenues.[2]

Union Square between Fourteenth and Seventeenth streets and Broadway and Fourth Avenue was the locus for "political protests, triumphant marches, and popular celebrations" in the years before and during the Civil War. When Emma was ten years old, for example, the Square was the site for a great meeting in support of the Union cause. In addition, the grand Metropolitan Fair for the United States Sanitary Commission was held there in 1864.[3]

It is difficult to believe that any child growing up on that street at that time in the city's history could have lived in an "ivory tower," so to speak. It is especially difficult to believe that Emma Lazarus would have been unaffected by that dynamic environment. In fact, we see evidence to the contrary in both her correspondence and her poems and essays. Interestingly, she wrote to Helena Gilder in 1881 that "[l]ong imprisonment in the house" would be "almost unbearable" to her.[4]

Emma's letters to the Gilders exhibit her active participation in the cultural life of New York City before 1882, the year that Josephine contended she came down from that ivory tower. The 1870s and 1880s witnessed a cultural explosion in this country as artists and artifacts from Europe made their American debut. Not only was Emma present at these events, she met and became friends with many of the artists who performed. In 1872, she met virtuoso pianist Anton Rubinstein after his greatly acclaimed first concert in this country. She "lost [her] head musically" when she heard Hungarian pianist Rafael Joseffy in February 1880. During that month, she attended the American production of Berlioz's *Damnation of Faust* six times in ten days.[5]

In February 1881, Emma saw, met, and wrote about Tommaso Salvini in his first American performance as Macbeth. Her "blunted sensibilities" were restored when she heard a Schubert song sung by George Henschel, who had made his American debut some two months earlier. Also on the program with Henschel was the "wonderful Brazilian boy-violinist," Maurice Dengremont.[6]

Emma shopped at Sypher's and Abraham & Straus, dined at Pursell's Restaurant, supped at Martinelli's and was a frequent presence at the Gilders' famous Friday Evenings and the Samuel Gray Wards' Sunday suppers. She visited the Emersons twice, alone, in 1876 and 1879, where she enlarged her growing circle of friends. In addition, she went with her sisters to Ocean City and Nantucket and visited the Josiah G. Hollands' Bonnie Castle in the Thousand Islands.[7]

Both Charles deKay and Thomas Wren Ward seem to have been not infrequent visitors to the Lazarus home. DeKay escorted Emma to cultural events; Ward gave her gifts of poetry. Edwin R. A. Seligman, twelve years her junior, was a member of her short-lived "Zionist" organization, and he was a social friend as well.[8]

By the late 1870s, Emma had joined the Gilder circle of friends. Her friendships with artists Maria Oakey and Olivia Ward are documented in the Gilder letters. She visited Olivia in Morristown, New Jersey, Helena in Staten Island and Milton, Massachusetts, and spent a great deal of time with Maria in her studio. Later, she joined her friend Margaret Crosby's Review Club, a group of some thirty to forty women who discussed current literature and art.[9]

On a stormy February evening in 1881, Emma attended the dedication of Cleopatra's Needle at the so-called Obelisk Entertainment, where a hymn by

Richard Gilder was performed. In June of that year, she and her friend Olivia Ward sat "like two tramps" in Madison Square, viewing the newly dedicated Farragut Statue.[10]

Emma Lazarus was not a recluse. In the context of late nineteenth-century society in New York City, however, she would not have been considered "social." Although her father was a member of both the Union and Knickerbocker clubs, with the Astors, Vanderbilts, and other members of the so-called Champagne Aristocracy, Emma and her sisters seem to have escaped the intricate banalities of that world, described so well by Emma's friend Henry James and his friend Edith Wharton.

Emma seems to have been groomed to be noticed from an early age. Of her five sisters and one brother, it was only she whom her father singled out for her precocious talent. Contrary to Emma's having led a life "so hidden," as Josephine asserted, her talent was first made known when she was seventeen years of age—her father published her first volume of poetry and translations for his friends. The next year the volume was amended and offered to the public.

When she was nineteen years old, Emma was presented to Ralph Waldo Emerson, the most famous thinker of the age. Her relationship with him has been misunderstood. Lazarus biographers have asserted that her exclusion from *Parnassus*, Emerson's encyclopedic volume of poetry, marked the end of their relationship. But Emma's response to that slight is indicative of both the strength of their friendship and of her assertive, not reclusive personality. She wrote him a lengthy and spirited letter when she found that she had been excluded, reviewing for him all of his laudatory comments on her work, in an angry attempt to understand the injury.[11]

Emma remained friendly with Emerson and his family, as correspondence suggests. She visited him in Concord in 1876, two years after her disappointment. The Gilder letters describe a second visit to them in 1879, a visit unrevealed until now. Emma described Emerson as having treated her with an "almost fatherly affection."[12]

Perhaps the most enigmatic aspect of Lazarus' life is her relationship with her own father. Although Josephine would have us believe it territorial and exclusionary, Emma did correspond with more than a few talented and powerful men and had close friendships with at least two admirers, Charles deKay and Thomas Wren Ward. For all of her supposed timidity, Emma sent her work to be critiqued by such luminaries as Ivan Turgenev, Thomas Wentworth Higginson, Richard Gilder, and, of course, Ralph Waldo Emerson. Moses Lazarus shared his daughter with some challenging competitors. Nevertheless, we know that Emma and her sisters were attentive daughters, worried terribly when their father was ill, and lived with him until his death in 1885.

Emma addressed the relationship of fathers and daughters in two plays and an essay. The first, *The Spagnoletto*, a grotesque tragedy, was written some time before October 1876. Although it was never performed, Turgenev and Emerson both read it, as did Emma's friend Helena Gilder, who sent it to her friend Mary Hallock Foote.[13]

The play takes place in Naples and Palermo. It is a fictional incident in the life of Spanish painter José Ribera (1591–1652), who was also known as Lo Spagnoletto, the Little Spaniard. Ribera has an obsessive attachment to his beautiful flaxen-haired daughter, Maria. Unfortunately, Maria falls in love with a handsome young prince, Don John of Austria. Amid promises of marriage, she leaves with him, in the night, without a word to her father. Ribera, who has had a strong hatred for the nobility, never trusted John and, discovering his daughter's elopement, is wild with anger. He disowns his daughter, renounces his life as a painter, in shame, and becomes a monk.

Meanwhile, Maria's lover has jilted her and returned to Austria to marry a princess chosen by his father, the king. She is devastated and retires to a monastery. Believing she has caused her father's death, she dreams of him for three nights, his dead face "Bleached, ghastly, dripping as of one that's drowned." Her father, hidden in monk's cowl, visits Maria. Believing he is a monk, she humbles herself before him, calling herself a "cast-away, a trait'ress, a murderess, a parricide!" She begs for "grace," for hope "beyond a million years of purgatory!" The monk, her father, tells her that even if perchance her father is not dead, she has "murdered him in spirit." She must not cheat herself with "empty dreams—thy God hath judged thee guilty!" Maria tries to justify her actions, saying that she had been seduced by a betrayer with the face of an angel.

> His were all gifts,
> All grace, all seeming virtue. I was plunged,
> Deaf, dumb and blind, and hand-bound in the deep.

"If a poor drowning creature craved thy aid," she pleads, "Thou wouldst not spurn it." And she cries,

> Help! Help!
> Let me not perish! Wrest me from my doom!
> Say not that I am lost!

Ribera tells her that her punishment "is huge as thy offense":

> Death shall not help,
> Neither shall the pious life wash out the stain.
> Living thou art doomed, and dead, thou shalt be lost,
> Beyond salvation.

Maria cries that her father would have mercy could he but see her in her agony. Her father throws back his cowl and tells her that her "parricidal hands" have murdered him and that he is "the spirit of blind revenge." His sole motivation has been to track down his daughter, to see her tortured body "writhe" beneath his feet, and to curse her stricken spirit.

When Maria begs him not to kill her, her father tells her not to worry, he would not "do thee that much grace to ease thee of the gross burden of the flesh." She must suffer for her sin; for the murder of her father she would find no prayer. Telling her that to all "dreams that haunt thee of past anguish, shall be added the vision of this horror," he stabs himself in the heart. Maria prostrates herself upon his body.[14]

The second play, *The Dance to the Death*, written in 1880, was published in 1882.[15] The play takes place in Nordhausen in Germany at the time of the Black Death. It is a platform for Lazarus' polemic on Christian anti-Semitism. It is also a tragic story of fathers and daughters. Liebhaid von Orb is, unknown to herself, the adopted daughter of Susskind von Orb, a Jew. Her birth father is the protagonist, Henry Schnetzen, whose castle von Orb had destroyed. He wants the Jewish community eradicated. Even though Liebhaid is in love with Prince William, Landgrave Frederick's son, and even when she finds out the truth about her lineage, she stays with her adoptive father and her people, all of whom are immolated by Schnetzen in their synagogue. In grotesque irony, Lazarus tells us that Schnetzen realizes that Liebhaid is his daughter as the flames envelop her.

The third piece to focus on the father-daughter relationship is an essay Lazarus wrote for the *Century* in May 1883, "Salvini's King Lear." She uses her evaluation of Italian Shakespearean actor Tommaso Salvini to put forth a unique interpretation of Lear's paternal behavior. She sees as normal his wild rage when he hears Cordelia's "discourteous and irreverent" rebuff, "The first stranger who appears and claims me as his wife will obtain from me a greater need of affection than you can possibly expect." "Whoever transports himself mentally into the period, place and circumstances of that scene," Emma asserts, "will not consider the wrath of 'Lear' exaggerated." His "insanity" is "occasioned" not by "dotage and decrepitude" but by the "stunning blows of unparalleled misfortunes." His daughters Regan and Goneril were, according to Lazarus, "unnatural monsters such as no human foresight, much less the loving heart of a parent, could divine."[16]

For Emma, Salvini's Lear is majestic, generous, tender, and self-abnegating, "broken, helpless and defeated—not with the helplessness of a violent, doting old man, but with the despair of a Titan at war with demons." He recognizes the true loyalty of Cordelia too late, of course. She is dead. "Nothing can be more beautiful, more piercingly pathetic than the dissolution of all fever and frenzy in a flood of refreshing tears, and the heart-broken, passionate tenderness with which he clasps her to his breast and bows his head above her own."[17]

Common to all three pieces is Emma's endorsement of the supremacy of filial piety. Even Ribera is portrayed sympathetically. When he tells his daughter, Maria, that he will renounce his life as an artist and will live as a recluse, he rejects her pleadings, telling her that his heart is "dead as stone." But he tells us he said this so that the "last link" would be "snapt":

> Had I not steeled my heart,
> I fain had kissed her in farewell.
> 'Tis better so. I leave my work unfinished.
> Could I arise each day to face this spectre,
> Or sleep with it at night?—to yearn for her
> Even while I curse her? No! the dead remain
> Sacred and sweet in our remembrance still;
> They seem not to have left us; they abide
> And linger nigh us in the viewless air.
> The fallen, the guilty, must be rooted out
> From heart and thought and memory. With them
> No hope of blest reunion; they must be
> As though they had not been; their spoken name
> Cuts like a knife.[18]

Lazarus' punishments are more devastating than those of Shakespeare. Maria must watch her father kill himself and must live with the horror. Lear, however, will find his daughter hanged. But he is more fortunate than Maria, for the shock will kill him. Emma's analysis of Lear provides a peculiar perspective through which to analyze her own play.

The father-daughter relationship in *The Dance to the Death* is one in which filial piety is raised to its most exalted form in Lazarus' eyes, heroic sacrifice. When Liebhaid forsakes her true love, Prince William, she acts correctly in Lazarus' scheme of things. Although she must die with her father, she dies a heroine.

Emma Lazarus' treatment of fathers and daughters in her writings leaves little room for doubt that, for her, love and obedience are expected. She seems to suggest that a daughter's disobedience can cause in a father a blind and insane rage.

None of the Lazarus sisters married until after the death of their father. It has been suggested that Emma and Charles deKay did not marry because Emma's father would have disapproved of deKay, who was a Christian. It is questionable, however, whether Moses Lazarus, who would join all of the right clubs and summer in the right places, would then object to his daughter marrying out of the faith. Nevertheless, Emma's filial expectations seemed to demand absolute devotion.[19]

5

The Work

When we look at additional subjects for Emma's poetry and prose, we find a significant number of artists, heroes, and great men who transcended geography and time: medieval French King Robert Capet; mythic heroes Admetus, Orpheus, Lohengrin, and Tannhauser; the Talmudist, Rashi; Spanish artist José Ribera; German authors Goethe and Heine; Shakespearean actor Tommaso Salvini; virtuoso pianist Rafael Joseffy, composer Ludwig van Beethoven; French authors Eugène Fromentin and Henri Regnault; British author and artist William Morris; American authors Ralph Waldo Emerson and Henry Wadsworth Longfellow; political leaders President James Garfield, Czar Alexander, and Prime Minister Benjamin Disraeli. Furthermore, Lazarus used her heroes to discuss her concerns about life and art. We find recurrent themes in her works that deal with destiny and greatness, odd subjects for a reclusive dreamer.

Could it be that Emma Lazarus identified with her characters, the heroes about whom she wrote? Could she have been living vicariously through them? She seems to suggest this as the only role appropriate for women in "Echoes," a short poem she wrote in 1880:

> Late-born and woman-souled I dare not hope,
> The freshness of the elder lays, the might
> Of manly, modern passion shall alight
> Upon the Muse's lips, nor may I cope
> (Who veiled and screened by womanhood must grope)
> With the world's strong-armed warriors and recite
> The dangers, wounds, and triumphs of the flight;
> Twanging the full-stringed lyre through all its scope.
> But if thou ever in some lake-floored cave
> O'erbrowed by rocks, a wild voice wooed and heard,

> Answering at once from heaven and earth and wave,
> Lending elf-music to thy harshest word,
> Misprize thou not these echoes that belong
> To one in love with solitude and song.[1]

Less than two years after this poem was written, Emma began her aggressive campaign in behalf of beleaguered East European Jews. We will see that her public reclamation of her Jewishness was not a sudden response to the excesses of the hour, but an evolutionary journey. From the first, we witness her need for a faith, a belief system that she could adopt, a teleology with which to handle the age. Her involvement with concepts like Destiny would ride in tandem with her problem with the Church, a problem that would come down to earth with an immediacy she could not ignore, in the anti-Jewish excesses in Europe. Her attention to current events would help her deal with the cosmic problems she addressed as a young woman.

Emma lived in a particularly anomic period in the nation's history. The Civil War, which she experienced as an adolescent, was followed by an industrialization out of control. Secular messianism competed with religious doctrine in an attempt to provide answers to social problems and teleological questions.

The country's anomic sense of self extended to the cultural arena, even though a genteel aristocracy of arts and letters, Gilder, Stedman, and other friends of Lazarus, tried to preserve old values. The sense of a historical void permeated the essays of thinkers like George Woodberry and Edmund Stedman, who lamented the fact that this country had no noble history, no inspiration for a uniquely American culture.[2]

Emma addressed herself to that issue with great passion in an essay in the 18 June 1881 number of the *Critic* and in a letter to Stedman. She told him that she had "never believed in the want of a theme, wherever there is humanity," she said, "there is the theme of a great poem." But she protested too loudly, perhaps, and in the end she found another people, another history for her grand theme.[3]

Implicit in Emma's work is her infatuation with heroism. She articulated this in an early letter to Helena Gilder in reference to Turgenev's *Virgin Soil*:

> I am sure Mr. Gilder has the same idea about it that I have. Why do you find it so sad & depressing? To me it is hopeful, *not* because it ends with a marriage & the chief characters in whom our sympathy is enlisted, turn out ardently happy, but because the whole book is so permeated with an atmosphere of aspiration & heroism. Whenever I look into it or think of it I am reminded of a verse in the Koran that promises to the faithful—"one of the two most excellent things, martyrdom or victory." Viewed in this light, even Nedzhdanoff ceases to be a failure, & his suicide becomes a noble necessary

act. In that little band of enthusiasts of which he is leader, there is nothing mean.[4]

Emma would find in Jewish Nationalism a noble and heroic cause, a focus for her passion. But we are ahead of our story.

"Bertha," Emma Lazarus' first long poem, covers fifty-five pages and was written before she was seventeen years old. Historical figures carry her message. Robert Capet, son of tenth-century French King Hugh Capet, and his wife Bertha are her central characters. The Pope discovers these two star-crossed lovers are cousins and orders the marriage annulled. They refuse to obey his decree and are excommunicated. Bertha, however, gives birth to a son, who is kidnapped by the abbot of the nearby monastery and is drowned. The child is replaced with a grossly deformed infant in the care of the abbot. Bertha, believing the child to be her own, retires, in penance, to a convent. There, in a bridal gown, she prostrates herself on the altar and dies. From the first, the Church was a grotesque villain for the young Emma.[5]

"Tannhauser" is included in Emma's second published volume of verse, *Admetus and Other Poems.* Her hero's conflict is explicitly with the Church; his descent into Venusberg is an attempt to find spiritual peace. He wishes he could "kneel and hail the Virgin and believe." His description of Christianity leaves little room for doubt about his displeasure or about Emma's:

> The world is run by one cruel God,
> Who brings a sword, not peace. A pallid Christ,
> Unnatural, perfect, and a Virgin cold,
> That gives us for a heaven of living gods,
> A creed of suffering and despair, walled in
> On every side by brazen boundaries,
> That limit the soul's vision and her hope
> To a red Hell or an unpeopled heaven.
> Yet I am lost already,—even now
> Am doomed to flaming torture by my thought
> O Gods! O Gods! Where shall my soul find peace?[6]

When Tannhauser rejects Venus and her bacchanal, he becomes a penitent ascetic whose pilgrimage to Rome is informed by an obsessive need for expiation of the sin of his orgy with Venus. But he finds a brutal and unforgiving Pontifical College, as excessive in their hatred as is Venus in her love, a stark contrast to Tannhauser's self-enforced penury. Rather than forgiveness, they offer self-righteous rebuke. Having been rejected, he comes then, alone, to the "broad of the Campagna" and suddenly snaps the "Cord that held the cross about his neck," flinging it far from him. The "leaden burden" flung, he kneels and cries,

> O God! I thank Thee, that my faith in Thee
> Subsists at last, through all discouragements.

> Between us must no type or symbol stand,
> No mediator, were he more divine
> Than the incarnate Christ. All forms, all priests,
> I part aside, and hold communion free
> Beneath the empty sky of noon, with naught
> Between my nothingness, and thy high heavens—
> Spirit with spirit.[7]

Tannhauser dies, "His fleshly weeds of sin forever doffed." At the end of the poem, "Tannhauser lay and smiled, for in the night / The angel came who brings eternal peace." And he is forgiven. "The pastoral rods had borne green shoots of spring, / and leaf and bloom. God is merciful." Tannhauser is the first of Emma's exiles who find peace outside the Church.[8]

In fact, "Outside the Church" is the title of Lazarus' fifteen-stanza poem published in the *Index*, the journal of the Free Religious Association, in 1872. She appealed to "Mother Church" for the "utter peace" the liturgical chants inspired, asking for "refuge from distress and sin, / the grace that on thine own elect falls," and longing with one great wish to "hear the mastering word, to yield, to adore, / conquered and happy, crying 'I am thine!'" And she waited, "but the message did not come; . . . the lifeless rites no comfort could impart." It was only "outside the Church," beneath the open sky, that Lazarus found her "religion," a part "of all the moving, teeming, sun-lit earth." "O simple souls," she cried, "who yearn with no reply, / too reverent for religion, ye may find / All patience, all assurance life can bring / In this free prospect, 'neath the open sky!"[9]

Many who study Emma Lazarus have seen this poem as evidence of Lazarus' whole-hearted acceptance of transcendentalism. But as Dan Vogel says, "Lazarus came to Nature by a process of elimination."[10]

But Lazarus would extend her dialogue with the Church in an unequivocal attack. When we examine her poetry, we see a preoccupation with Christian anti-Semitism, strange business for a woman whose best friends were Christian. Her argument with the Church finds its way into her long poems and into her plays. In defending the East European Jews in later work, she takes an apologetic position, blaming their "faults" on centuries of Christian anti-Semitism.

We have no biographical data to tell us why anti-Semitism was such an issue in Lazarus' work, but we have the literary record to support this contention. Although she seems to have been comfortable as a Jew in a Christian milieu, her writing suggests a conflict in her thought. She is almost brazen in her exposure of a corrupted clergy, a primitive dogma, and a barbaric Christian populace. We could say, perhaps, that her early works were only fantasies, typical of the time. But in her Jewish polemic, she transferred these issues from what appeared to be medieval fantasy to "current events," making it mandatory to take her early work seriously. Although she used fantasy and myth before 1880, her message remained the same when she brought the subject into her own era.

Perhaps the most explicit example of Lazarus' rejection of Christian doctrine is seen in one of her Jewish poems, "An Epistle," published in the *American Hebrew* in June 1882. It is subtitled "From Joshua ibn Vives of Allorqui to His Former Master, Solomon Levi-Paul de Santa-Maria, Bishop of Cartagena, Chancellor of Castile, and Privy Councillor to King Henry III of Spain." The author tells us that in the poem she has done "little more than elaborate and versify the account given in Graetz's History of the Jews . . . of an Epistle actually written in the beginning of the 15th century by Joshua ben Joseph ibn Vives to Paulus de Santa Maria."[11]

In the epistle, Joshua ibn Vives, a Jew, asks his former Jewish mentor and now Jew-baiter, Paulus de Santa Maria, why he chose to convert to Christianity. With sarcasm and irony, ibn Vives rejects three motives—ambition, doubt, and fear. In questioning the fourth motive, conviction, Lazarus leaves no doubt as to her own opinion of Christianity. Through ibn Vives, she says that she will not argue about the "Virgin's motherhood" or the resurrection, she who knows "not how mine own soul came to earth, / Nor what should follow death." And man can never know "even in thought the height and girth / Of God's omnipotence; . . . but that He should dwarf Himself to us—it cannot be!"[12]

Lazarus looks at the works of nature and sees in them the wonder of God:

> The God who balances the clouds, who spread
> The sky above us like a molten glass,
> The God who shut the sea with doors, who laid
> The corner-stone of earth, who caused the grass
> Spring forth upon the wilderness, and made
> The darkness scatter and the night to pass.

"That he should clothe Himself with flesh, and move," she challenges, "Midst worms a worm—this sun, moon, stars disprove." The epistle ends with ibn Vives bending his "exile-weary feet" to his former "boyhood guide," whom he implores to teach him the "invisible to divide, / Show me how three are one and One is three!" He cries, "How Christ to save all men was crucified, / Yet I and mine are damned eternally."[13]

We do not know when this poem was actually written, but it is evidence of the enduring enmity Lazarus felt for Christianity. On 3 October 1882, she wrote to her friend Rabbi Gustav Gottheil after reading an excerpt in the *New York Times* of a talk he had given. She asked him if he had really said "as was reported in yesterday's *Times* that 'the Christian Church is a noble and vital institution.' I hope not!" she exclaimed.[14]

Emma's problem with both Christian doctrine and Christian anti-Semitism served as a negative motivation for much of her poetry. But a more positive impetus for her creativity came with her need to explicate her ideas about the interrelationship of her concepts of Destiny, Nature, and Talent.

In her only novel, *Alide* (1874), Lazarus' central character, Goethe, is a great man called by Destiny to develop his talent. He is the author's voice. He expounds upon Shakespeare to articulate a concept of Destiny. "Shakespeare's plots," he says, are "no plots. All his plays turn upon the hidden point which no philosopher has yet seen and defined, in which the peculiarity of our EGO, the pretended freedom of our will, clashes with the necessary course of the whole."[15]

Lazarus had more interest in the concept of free will than its use as a literary construct. In a letter to her friend Tom Ward, she wrote that she had "never seen the 'free will' problem stated in a more satisfactory way than in a translation I lately read of an Indian poem." Her transcription echoes Goethe's words:

> Man follows the bent of his will, subdues or is led by his passions, respects life or ruthlessly snaps it, bows to the law of his conscience or willfully lives in rebellion. He says to himself, "I am free!" He says true; he is free to grow noble, he is free too to work his undoing. But let him act as he will he is a tool in the hands of Destiny, used to perfect the fabric of life. There are sons of the night & their portion is blackness; there are sons of the Dawn & the daylight is theirs; both are workers for Destiny—from the labors of both issues harmony. But of evil comes good, but not for the doer of evil; he has earned for himself sorrow, that he did freely; he has worked for the good of the universe,—that he did *blindly* in obedience to the hidden pleasure of Destiny![16]

In this passage, Lazarus seems to see man as a puppet whose strings are pulled by an invisible Destiny. But her construct has another facet: Destiny is a controlling force calling individuals with talent to greatness.

Goethe is an artist who must follow his calling whatever the moral consequences. He is a necessary cog in Destiny's wheel. In Goethe's analysis of Hamlet's renunciation of Ophelia, the author uses Shakespeare to elucidate her concept of the overriding duty of talent. He feels that Hamlet sincerely loved Ophelia "before the beginning of the play":

> She was the sweetheart of his boyhood, the companion of his hours of recreation. But from the moment that his capacities are disclosed to him by the revelation from another world, he is bound by the highest duty of man—that which he owes to himself—to discard everything that can cramp or impede

the development of his own nature, and the fulfillment of the sacred office to which he is called. The beauty and sweetness of Ophelia's character cannot be exaggerated, yet she is no mate for Hamlet. He simply outgrows her; or rather, in binding himself to her, he has underestimated his own powers, and after these have been supernaturally revealed to him, it is impossible for him to return to his earlier position.[17]

In hearing this pronouncement, Alide (Friederike Brion) realizes that, like Hamlet, Goethe has a higher duty to his art. She renounces him for the sake of his talent. Critics view Alide's renunciation of Goethe the poet as an expression of Lazarus' own feeling of martyrdom as a woman. But clearly, her issue is with Goethe, not with Alide, who simply acts as she must in Lazarus' thought system. As Dan Vogel wrote, Goethe is "an Artist and an Artist has a duty beyond the ken of simple innocent country girls."[18]

Alide is an example of Lazarus' infatuation with charisma. Her description of Goethe as a "great man" is implicit in her drawings of the other men she chose to spotlight. "It is this faculty of great men which makes their simplest action fresh and original," she says. "They are generous of their soul. They meet with abundant vitality the demands of every hour, and thus shed a peculiar glory upon whatever claims their regard." And in describing Goethe, she says, "It needed no keen observer to perceive that 'nothing he did but smacked of something greater than himself,' for the magnetism of his personality bore as emphatically the impress of his genius as anything he has left behind."[19]

Lazarus believed that talent in designated individuals was crucial for Destiny's grand design and that Destiny demanded obedience. But informing this command was an optimistic worldview. Destiny was Progress, an idea she articulated in her short story "The Eleventh Hour," published in *Scribner's* in 1878. Her only other work of fiction, it is a panegyric to that "colossal experiment," the United States, where one could witness the "execution of divinely simple laws."[20]

Sergius Azoff, a disillusioned Romanian artist, is the foil for Richard Bayard, an upper-class New Yorker who in the end saves the artist from suicide. Azoff finds no inspiration as an artist in America and becomes a day laborer. He fails in this pursuit and becomes an "opium eater." Bayard, quite by accident, reaches him as he is about to end his life. In his gentle rebuke to Azoff, he is Lazarus' voice. Through him, she introduces her somewhat fatalistic concept of "art" as a talent guided by Nature, or Destiny.

Bayard tells Azoff that the world seems to him "an immense working-place, a factory, if you will, where each of us has his special task assigned, which he cannot honorably shirk. A certain amount of labor has to be accomplished for some universal end which we cannot conceive, the law is Progress; in generations we scarcely see a step of advance."[21]

For Lazarus, Nature gives each person an unnegotiable place in the universe. Bayard tells Azoff that he is right in saying that Nature has refused him a place "among the diggers and delvers of soil. Nature," he says, "makes no mistake; she does not create a sensitive, receptive brain, an accurate eye, an uncommon touch, a poet's imagination, an ardent heart of universal sympathies, for the purpose of securing one more beast of burden."[22]

Emma Lazarus believed that there were "natural inequalities" in man and in "races," as we shall see in her Jewish polemic. Ironically, "progressive" Jews have lauded her so-called commitment to the principles of Karl Marx. Although she may have admired the heroism in a Turgenev novel, she disliked social systems that tried to equalize human beings. She stated this in a letter to Thomas Wren Ward, in 1877, telling him that her mind had been "very much exercised by the Railroad Strikes and Communism in general." She asked him if he agreed that "there is something essentially unjust about the whole theory of Communism[.] I shall never believe in it," she said, "as long as there are such natural inequalities in the minds & capacities of men."[23]

Although Lazarus was concerned with only one fallen individual, one artist, in "The Eleventh Hour," she generalized her idea to an entire population, her people, the East European Jews, four years later. By then, she ordered the people of the planet into races, in a social construct modeled after those of Charles Darwin and Herbert Spencer. For Emma, Nature or Destiny had been thwarted by a Christian anti-Semitism causing grotesque permutations in the Jewish "race." In the grand scheme, Jews had been intended for greatness; detoured, they were physically and psychically destroyed.

"The Eleventh Hour" is an ode to the grand possibilities in the American experience. Although Emma Lazarus is known for her devotion to Jewish Nationalism, her belief in the heroism in American history and the viability of an American "culture" was expressed in her poetry, essays, and correspondence. Her celebration of America in "The Eleventh Hour" exhibits an intuitive understanding of and endorsement of the young nation's capabilities.

Bayard tells a disillusioned Azoff that America is midway between "the Utopian fancies you brought here and the gloomy conclusions to which you have arrived now." He tells Sergius that he has made the "common mistake of most Europeans in bringing the miniature standard of Europe with which to measure and judge a colossal experiment." Here, he believes, "art and beauty must and will survive," although it was impossible in that time of transition to determine what forms they would assume. Lazarus through Bayard observed "immense forces at work" building cities of "gigantic scale." The "prosperity" of the continent would be assured in the "execution of divinely simple laws."[24]

6

Jewish Themes

Although Lazarites have hardly noticed Emma Lazarus' attention to Jewish themes before 1882, it was in evidence as early as 1867, when she wrote "In the Jewish Synagogue at Newport."[1] Modeled after Longfellow's poem "In the Jewish Cemetery at Newport,"[2] it is relevant to her later work, because the focus of the piece is on the tragedy of "lone exiles of a thousand years, from the fair sunrise land that gave them birth!" She wrote a number of significant works dealing with the excesses of anti-Semitism before 1882, when she began her overt campaign against anti-Jewish persecution.

In 1876, Lazarus added two "imitations" to the translation of Heine's "Donna Clara." All three poems were published in the *Jewish Messenger*. In this work Emma addressed medieval anti-Semitism, using a cleric as villain. "Donna Clara" is the story of the anti-Semitic daughter of the Alcalde, the mayor of the town, who meets and falls in love with "a handsome unguilty stranger." He tells her, after hearing her anti-Semitic excesses, that he, her beloved, is the son of the "respected, worthy, erudite Grand Rabbi, Israel of Saragossa." Here the ballad ends. Lazarus wrote the two additional "imitations" to fulfill the poet's intention to write a trilogy "in which the son, conceived in this illicit moment, grows up hating Jews and then, becoming a Dominican monk, cruelly persecutes them." Pedro, the lovers' offspring, is the central character of Emma's "Don Pedrillo" and "Fra Pedro."[3]

In "Don Pedrillo," Donna Clara has become a penitent, living like a nun, "first at matins, first at vespers." Her son is zealous in his hatred of Jews, and coaxes his pet parrot to "speak thy lesson, thief and traitor, / Thief and traitor" croaked the parrot / "Is the yellow skirted Rabbi." A rabbi whom his mother has befriended confronts the child, chiding him for his "evil words." Pedrillo replies that it is "no slander to speak evil of the murderers of our Savior." He is only biding his time till manhood, when he may "wreak all my lawful hatred on thyself." He tells the rabbi, "[A]ll your tribe offends my senses,/ They're an eyesore to my vision, / And a stench upon my nostrils." He hates these "disbelievers" with their "thick lips and eagle noses."[4]

In "Fra Pedro," Lazarus' ironic treatment of the brutality of the cleric is gentle yet instructive. Pedro has been asked to save Saragossa's "finest physician" from the intended destruction of the Jewish community. He refuses to do so, asserting that should he find a single drop of Jewish blood in his "vein's pure current," he would not shrink from ending his life to "purge it." "Shall I gentler prove to others?" he asks. "Mercy would be sacrilegious." After his statement that he would "exterminate" these Jewish "abominations" and more, the poem ends with the sun dropping "down behind the purple hillside" while "above the garden / Rang the Angelus' clear cadence / Summoning the monks to vespers."[5]

Lazarus' imitations are faithful to Heine's verse in both meter and word usage. His poem was written, she said, "not to excite laughter, still less to denote a mocking spirit." It was written to "render with epic impartiality in this poem an individual circumstance, and at the same time something general and universal, . . . conceived . . . in a spirit which was anything rather than smiling, but serious and painful, so much so that it was to form the first part of a tragic trilogy."[6]

Heine, we know, confronted anti-Jewish persecution in Germany and, because of that, became an embittered expatriate. But why did the acculturated Emma Lazarus, at that time just twenty-seven years of age, choose to finish Heine's task? This was her first work published in a Jewish journal.

In March and April 1880, Henry Ward Beecher's journal, the *Independent*, published two long poems by Lazarus. "Rashi in Prague" and "The Death of Rashi" confront anti-Semitism in twelfth-century Prague.[7] Rashi is another of Lazarus' great men. He was a legend during his life and is still considered one of the most erudite Talmudists in Jewish history. The poems are fables; her history is out of sequence. Nevertheless, in these works she clarifies her position, painting a landscape of sharp contrast between the brutality of the Christian mob and the serenity of the Jews it destroys.

Rashi enters Prague, in his "wide wanderings," and is hosted by Rabbi Jochanan and his beautiful daughter, Rebekah. His triumphant welcome on the Jewish streets raises the ire of the duke, Wladislaw, and his bishop. Ruffian soldiers storm the rabbi's house and carry both Rashi and the rabbi to the duke. The bishop recognizes Rashi as the "physician" who miraculously healed him in Palestine, and so both are freed. In "The Death of Rashi," a Christian stabs him during a Passover seder. Rebekah, who is his wife by this time, feeds him the herb potion that brings him back from the dead. He lives on to continue his good works.

Lazarus' descriptions in the first poem are excessive, as in her account of the destruction of the rabbi's house, for example:

> The strong doors split asunder, pouring in
> A stream of soldiers, ruffians, armed with pikes,
> Lances and clubs—the unchained beast, the mob.
> Then, while some stuffed their pockets with baubles snatched,
> From board and shelf, or with malignant sword
> Slashed the rich orient rugs, the pictured woof
>   That clothed the wall.

She polarizes her characters in caricature. Rebekah, the rabbi's daughter, represents the ideal Jewish woman, the "radiant girl" who dared not "lift / Shy, heavy lids from pupils black as grapes / That dart the imprisoned sunshine from their core." Rashi is the consummate hero:

> From his clear eyes youth flamed magnificent;
> Force, masked by grace, moved in his balanced frame,
> An intellectual, virile beauty reigned
> Dominant on domed brow, on fine, firm lips,
> An eagle profile cut in gilded bronze,
> Strong, delicate as a head upon a coin,
> While as an aureole crowns a burning lamp,
> Above all beauty of the body and brain
> Shone beauty of a soul benign with love.

Duke Wladislaw is a stereotypical anti-Semite who "heard / With righteous wrath his injured subjects' charge / Against presumptuous aliens." He remembers how Prague

> Harbored first,
> Out of contemptuous ruth, a wretched band
> Of outcast paupers, gave them leave to ply their
> Moneylending trade and lease them land
> On all too facile terms. Behold! today
> They batten on Bohemia's poverty;
> They breed and growl like adders, spit back hate
> And venomed perfidy for Christian love.

Rashi is Emma Lazarus' first Jewish "exile." In addition, in this work she returns to Jews as a community in exile. Rashi brings "glad tidings" of his brethren in the Diaspora. He tells of the papal treasurer who is a Jew; the flourishing academies at Babylon, Bagdad, and Damascus; and ben Maimuni, the "pearl, the crown of Israel," in Cairo, the "second Moses, gathering at his feet the Sages from all over the world." But he forgets or ignores, according to Lazarus, the "chief shrine, the Exile's Home, whereunto yearned all hearts":

> All ears strained for tidings, someone asked,
> "What of Jerusalem? Speak to us of Zion."

The light died from his eyes. From depths profound
Issued his grave, great voice: "Alas for Zion!"
Verily she is fallen! . . .
One, only one, one solitary Jew
The Rabbi Abraham Haceba, flits
Ghostlike amid the ruins; every year
Beggars himself to pay the idolaters
The costly tax for lease to hold agape
This heart's live wound; to weep, a mendicant,
Amidst the crumbled stones of palaces
Where reigned his ancestors, upon the graves
Where slept the priests, the prophets, and the kings
Who were his forefathers. Ask me no more![8]

This poem is complete fable. Rashi died some thirty years before ben Maimuni (Maimonides) was born. From all accounts, he never traveled to Prague. And Lazarus' conception of Zion as bereft of all save one Jew is excessive. From the fall of the Second Temple in 68 A.D., small and often impoverished communities of Jews had lived in Palestine.

The poem is significant for a number of reasons. First, it shows clearly Emma's knowledge of and concern with the problem of Exile for the Jew. Second, she is aware of the longing of her people for a return to their homeland as early as 1880, two years before her active advocacy in their behalf. As a matter of fact, she had been attracted to the Spanish Jewish poets some years earlier. She chose to translate a number of their poems, some of which addressed with eloquent poignancy that longing. The *Jewish Messenger* in 1879, for example, published her translation of a poem by Judah HaLevi:

Oh, City of the world, with sacred splendor blest,
My spirit yearns to thee from out the far-off West,
A stream of love wells forth when I recall thy day,
Now is the Temple waste, thy glory passed away.

. . . .

Oh! how I long for thee! Albeit thy King has gone.
Albeit where balm once flowed, the serpent dwells
Could I but kiss thy dust, so would I fain expire,
As sweet as honey then, my passion, my desire![9]

Probably Emma Lazarus' most acclaimed work of fiction is *The Dance to the Death*, a dramatization of the German prose narrative "Der Tanz zum Tode."[10] In this tragedy, Lazarus magnifies her treatment of Christian anti-Semites. In the terror of the Black Death, the Jews in France have been tortured and burned. Blind Rabbi Jacob Cresselin comes to tell the Jewish community at Nordhausen that they must exile themselves or suffer the same fate.

At the same time, Henry Schnetzen is advising Landgrave Frederick to destroy the community, as we know, not because of the plague but because it has been discovered that Prince William is in love with Liebhaid von Orb, the adopted daughter of Susskind von Orb. Schnetzen has no idea that Liebhaid is his own daughter, whom he assumes is dead. This constellation of facts provides the personal tragedy set within the larger tragedy of the immolation of the entire Jewish population in the synagogue. When Schnetzen learns of Liebhaid's true identity, he thinks it a trick and realizes the tragic truth only as the flames engulf her.

Lazarus' characterization of the cleric Prior Peppercorn is a logical extension of that of Fra Pedro. He is terrifying. In the play form, she is able to develop his rage more fully. The prior's speeches are filled with lethal language and show Lazarus' acute perception of a European anti-Semitism rooted in Christian theology. Peppercorn tells the princess, William's mother, that it is better for her son, who has been locked in a palace apartment, "to perish in time than in eternity."

> No question here of individual life; our sight
> Must broaden to embrace the scope sublime
> Of this trans-earthly theme. The Jew survives
> Sword, plague, fire, cataclysm—and must since Christ
> Cursed him to live till doomsday, still to be
> A scarecrow to the nations. None the less
> Are we beholden in Christ's name at whiles
> When maggot-wise Jews breed, infest, infect
> Communities of Christians, to wash clean
> The Church's vesture, shaking off the filth
> That gathers round her skirts—A perilous germ!
> Know you not, all the wells, the very air
> The Jews have poisoned?—Through their arts alone
> The Black Death scourges Christendom.[11]

The princess urges Peppercorn to permit Liebhaid to convert and marry her son. Although the prior acquiesces, Liebhaid refuses, even after she has learned of her lineage. Saying that she loves the prince "as my soul," she proclaims "no more of that" and announces that she is "all Israel's nor—till this cloud passes, / I have no more thought, no passion, no desire. / Save for my people."[12] Lazarites view this speech as autobiographical. Because it was published in *Songs of a Semite,* at the height of her Jewish campaign, they view Lazarus as a martyr who gave her personal life for her cause. Josephine's essay validates this contention. But the play was written at least two years earlier, when some of the same sources insist her Jewishness was as yet unborn.

Probably one of Lazarus' favorite exiles was Harry [sic] Heine. In addition to her translations of his works, she composed and published two lengthy essays about him. The first, written in 1878, became the introduction to a volume of her translations of his poetry, published in 1881.[13] A review in the *Century* chastised her for failing to consider Heine "from the standpoint of an Israelite, and something authoritative as to the position in Germany, both as a student and exile. . . . Now that the JUDENHETZE is once more in Prussia and Russia," the critic noted, "it is time for a well-informed co-religionist to be heard. . . . Here is a chance for one so well-fitted by birth, education, and a poetical nature as Emma Lazarus. The main objective would be the consideration of Heine as a Hebrew poet, who used German as his native, and French as his adopted tongue."[14]

This criticism is significant, first of all, because it is incorrect. Emma's essay is based on the tragedy of Heine's Jewish birth in a virulently anti-Semitic Germany. Second, Josephine seems to have accepted the *Century*'s criticism. According to her, Emma was "as yet unaware or only vaguely conscious of the real bond between them—the sympathy in the blood, the deep, tragic, Judaic passion of eighteen hundred years that was smoldering in her own heart, soon to break out and change the whole current of her thought and feeling."[15] Biographers address Emma's treatment of Heine from the points of view of the critic in the *Century* and Josephine Lazarus.

Lazarus' second essay on Heine, published in the *Century* in 1884, seems purposefully defiant of her earlier critic.[16] In "The Poet Heine," she stated that Heine could be seen as Hellene or Hebrew, but he was above all and only a poet, and she would treat him as an artist in discussing his work. Nevertheless, because the essay was published in 1884, during her "Jewish" phase, Lazarus' biographers have lauded her attention to Heine as a Jew.

Heinrich Heine is known as a renegade from his Jewish heritage. In the first essay, Lazarus tried to correct this assumption, saying that his baptism occurred only after he had exhausted ways to alleviate the restrictions against Jews who wished to become attorneys, a profession for which he was trained. She explained that he then dedicated himself "more entirely to upholding the rights of [his] unhappy brethren." Eventually, he found it beneath his dignity to live in Germany as a baptized Jew and settled in Paris, a more benign climate for Jews, according to Lazarus.[17]

Lazarus compares Goethe's Germany to that of Heine. His "cheerful-burgher life" is contrasted to the "gloomy JUDENGASSE" where "squalid, painful Hebrews were banished to scour old clothes." In this "wretched by-way," which was "relegated" to Heine, he must be "locked in like a wild beast, with his miserable brethren every Sunday." And she asks, "How shall we characterize a national policy which closed to such a man as Heine every career that could give free play to his genius and offer him the choice between money changing and medicine?"[18]

Lazarus deals with Heine's Jewishness when she discusses the "Rabbi of Bacharach," which, like her works, illustrates the persecutions of their people during the Middle Ages. Heine, "one of the most subjective of poets," treated his theme "in a purely objective manner," allowing himself "not a word of comment or condemnation." And although he painted "the scene as an artist, not as the passionate fellow-sufferer and avenger that he is, . . . what subtle eloquence lurks in that restrained cry of horror and indignation which never breaks forth." Lazarus tells us that Heine never signed his Christian name Heinrich, but he never surrendered his love for the country that loathed his people.[19]

In spite of the *Century*'s criticism in 1882, or perhaps because of it, Lazarus' second essay was informed, not by her need to exonerate Heine as a Jew, but by her purpose to defend his right to be judged as a poet. Lazarus, like Heine, would try to remain objective; her emotion, like his, would bleed through the words. She admitted in 1884 that there was a duality about Heine, whose Greek traits of "laughter and sunshine," the "intellectual clearness of his vision," and his "pure and healthy love of art for art's sake," were in "perpetual" conflict with his "somber Hebrew" side. "A mocking voice, Hebrew, Christian, tragedy, comedy, an adorer of despotism incarnate in Napoleon, an admirer of Communism embodied in Proudhon—a Latin, a Teuton, a beast, a devil, a god!" For Lazarus, Heine was "all and none of these; he is a poet." And that was how she would "consider him in these pages." Her discussion of his Jewishness consisted of two sentences explaining that his "home-life and surroundings were strictly Jewish" and that he was baptized "not from conviction, but in order to secure freedom in the choice of a profession, as the German code of that day obliged every Jew to become either a physician or a money-lender."[20]

Emma Lazarus felt a kinship with Harry Heine. Although she never experienced the paralysis of Heine's Germany, her sensitivity to Christian anti-Semitism became outrage in 1882. She began dealing with anti-Semitism in 1876, six years before the start of her aggressive campaign in behalf of her co-religionists in the East, and dressed the topic in medieval disguise. By 1882, she lifted the mask, presenting contemporary Christian anti-Semitism to Christian and Jew, with a terrible honesty.

7

A Jewish Identity

Amajor concern in dealing with Emma Lazarus is, precisely, her Jewishness. First, the so-called Jewish Problem or Jewish Question was a
matter of concern to both Gentile and Jew in the 1880s. It became a conceptu-
alization with the advent of political anti-Semitism, and anti-Jewish sentiment
became ominously racist as the years went on. Jews, either too cosmopolitan
or too exclusive, as was true of those who were observant, were seen to under-
mine the nation-state. They were perceived as Socialists and Capitalists, unable
to integrate into and become loyal citizens of the countries in which they
resided. In both cases, their detractors endowed them with a superhuman or
demonic ability to gain control of or overthrow any system of government.
Solutions to the problem ranged from reinstitution of restrictive laws to pogroms to expulsion—and eventually to Hitler's "Final Solution."

Emma came to be recognized as an authority on the subject by her non-
Jewish friends and colleagues. As we have seen, after her death she was remem-
bered not for her sonnet but for her strident poetry and prose in behalf of East
European Jews. Probably more important, she is regarded even today not as a
New York intellectual, which she certainly was, but as a Jew who "rechose"
her Jewishness in the thirty-third year of her life.

Emma Lazarus was an improbable champion of a people she scarcely knew.
As Joseph Gilder, her editor at the *Critic*, said at the time of her death, the
children of Moses Lazarus "had Christians for playmates and schoolmates and
most of Emma's friends were Christian. . . . She died, as she lived, as much a
Christian as a Jewess—perhaps it would be better to say neither one nor the
other."[1] Emma had told Ellen Emerson on her visit to Concord in 1876 that
her family was "outlawed now" because they "no longer keep the Law," but
Christian institutions, she told her hostess, did not interest her either.[2]

Moses and Esther Nathan Lazarus were descendants of the early members of the Spanish-Portuguese Synagogue, Shearith Israel, the oldest Jewish congregation still in existence in this country. Following Sephardic ritual, members of the congregation observe the laws of kashrut and the ages-old ritual prescribed in the Torah. They would be considered Orthodox today. Both Emma's paternal and maternal ancestors were active members of this, their family synagogue. Her great-grandfather, Samuel Lazarus, had been clerk of the synagogue from 1788 to 1795. Jacob Hart, her father's maternal grandfather, was a major benefactor. Emma's grandfather, Eleazer Lazarus, was proficient enough in Hebrew to officiate at High Holiday services and to co-author the first revised Hebrew-English prayerbook in the Sephardic ritual in this country, *The Form of Daily Prayer*, in 1826. He was president of the synagogue in 1842 and from 1846 to 1849.[3]

On her mother's side, Emma's great-great-grandfather, Isaac Seixas, and great-grandfather Simon Nathan, served as president of Shearith Israel. Her uncle, Benjamin Nathan, served as president from 1851 to 1854. Another uncle, the Rev. J. J. Lyons, was cantor at the synagogue for thirty-eight years.[4]

Moses Lazarus seems to have made a deliberate break with the religious tradition of the Lazarus and Nathan families. In fact, he made a successful effort to integrate his family into the greater life of the city. As one of the few Jewish members of both the Union and the Knickerbocker clubs, he seems to have "passed." Furthermore, his friendship with Samuel Gray Ward was an entrée into Concord society. When we review Emma's life, we notice that with the exception of E. R. A. Seligman, none of her many friends was Jewish. Her life was little different from that of her friends. Or was it? Just how was Emma Lazarus seen by her friends?

At least ten years before her public announcement of her Jewishness, Thomas Wentworth Higginson clearly saw her as a Jew. In 1872 he wrote his sisters from Newport, asking if they had ever heard of "any poems by Emma Lazarus? She is rather an interesting person," he said, "and her volume of poems are better received in England than here." He went on to say that she was a "Jewess; they are very rich and in fashionable society in New York."[5]

In 1876, Ellen Emerson wrote her niece of her meeting with Emma. "Then think of what nuts it was to me, old S.S. [*sic*] teacher that I am, to get at a real unconverted Jew (who had no objection to calling herself one, and talked freely about 'Our Church' and 'we Jews') and hear how the Old Testament sounds to her."[6] In that same year, author and illustrator Mary Hallock Foote wrote to her dearest friend, Helena deKay Gilder, about Emma's interest in Helena's brother, Charles deKay. "You cannot really be worried about Charley's interest in Miss L!" she said.

> It seems to me to be so very inappropriate as to be quite absurd—not that he should be interested in her but that he should be entangled, so to speak.

After such women as Miss Stickney, Olivia Ward—but this is very absurd of me, whose ideas of what would suit Charley are necessarily colored by what would suit me.—and who have never seen the young lady. Must I confess that the facts of her being of Jewish blood and an aspiring young poetess are my great stumbling blocks in her case. Was there ever anything so unreasonable in one who is herself of a "peculiar people" and one of the pitiful aspirers! It seems a pity that she should be so gushing about Charley. That sort of thing is always very dreadful to other women—a lowering of the pride of us all, and it is very bad for men.[7]

"Charley" deKay had some interesting things to say about Emma, one year after her death. The *Christian Union* published his essay entitled "Sibyl Judaica," which was reprinted in 1889 in the *American Hebrew* with the caveat that the "value of his essay is impaired by his failure to properly appreciate the character and temperament of the Jews." The editor took issue with deKay's error in "thinking that because Jews are successful in commercial pursuits, they are therefore insensible to literature and art." In addition, he erred in "describing the Hebrew religion as monarchical, when it is essentially democratic." His final error was in characterizing the Hebrew nature as "material, pleasure-loving practical." These were, said the *American Hebrew*, "but the surface phenomena of a small number of shallow youth."[8]

DeKay drew upon Josephine's essay to canonize Emma Lazarus, a woman some say he loved. In the process, he revealed his own antipathy to American Jews. DeKay saw them as interlopers: America was not the land of their ancestry, only the land of their birth. Emma's ancestors came to this continent, of course, before the United States was a nation, as did only a relatively small number of non-Jews. Nevertheless, deKay seems to have singled out the Jews when he said that they "readily assimilate the traits of a nation" and that these are "often the worst traits." But Emma was "different," she was different from those "young Hebrew women" one saw in public, "forward, pert and bad mannered." DeKay agreed with Josephine that everything in her "birth, training, and social position" deterred Emma from "thrusting herself forward." Her Oriental Jewish "training" taught her to curb the "instinct to be bold." And so it required more than ordinary strength for her to take a public position with regard to her people. Emma's value, said deKay, lay in her power to "reach the ears of that great world of finance in Europe which is Hebrew, which is so powerful through money-bags and acquired titles, and which seems to use its wealth to so little purpose."[9]

In Europe, through the centuries, there had always been a handful of court Jews, or "exception Jews." They often took the role of intercessors, seeking favors for their routinely oppressed people. It is clear that deKay saw Emma Lazarus as an exception Jew, an advocate for her people. It is also certain that his stereotype of Jews in the late nineteenth century differed little from the representations of those anti-Semites against whom Emma railed. We shall see, however, that her own equivocal description of the East European Jews is almost identical to deKay's.

We may assume that Emma never read her friends' letters, although she might have known of her friend Charles deKay's sentiments. It is safe to say that she would have read of the so-called Hebrew Controversy or Seligman-Hilton affair in the pages of the *New York Times*, a newspaper to which she was a contributor. In June 1877, New York banker Joseph Seligman was denied admittance to the Grand Union Hotel in Saratoga, New York, because he was a Jew. The hotel's department store magnate, A. T. Stewart, had recently died, and management of the hotel was turned over to Judge Henry Hilton. Although Seligman had frequented the hotel in years past, Hilton blatantly refused entry to him and to his co-religionists. The judge had come to the conclusion that "Christians did not like their [Jews'] company and for that reason shunned the hotel."[10]

In a front-page interview in the *New York Times* of 20 June 1877, Hilton differentiated between Hebrews and Jews, calling his unwanted guests Seligman Jews. Hebrews were Jews like the Nathans and the Hendrickses, Emma's relatives. In noting that difference, he also said "shysters" were different from lawyers. Calling him a "Sheeney," Hilton said that the Seligman Jew "has made money; he must advertise it in his person":

> He is of low origin, and his instincts are all of the gutter—his principles small—they smell of decayed goods, or of decayed principles. But he has extracted cash out of his gutter, his rags, his principles, and he shoves his person upon respectability. He is too obtuse or too mean to see his vulgarity, or to go where it may not be on public exhibition. He is shoddy, false, squeezing—unmanly; but financially he is successful. And that is the only token he has to push himself upon the polite. He is as audacious as he is vulgar; he is as fussy as he is worthless; he is as vain as he is devoid of merit; and he is puffed out with as much importance as he is poor of any value. He comes to the Grand Union big with himself and little with everybody else in the decent world. . . .

Furthermore, Seligman Jews "deserved the common contempt they get," Hilton continued, "and they have brought the injurious reflection of their vulgarity upon the true Hebrews. It is no wonder that Americans are down on the Seligman Jew," he asserted.

> The richness of this new country has tended to propagate the breed, and the breed has cursed the Hebrew race socially in this country. People won't go to hotels where the Seligman Jew is admitted. And the very fact that the Seligman "Jew" makes such a fuss because people don't want his society, and

makes such a noise to force himself where he is unwelcome, instead of going elsewhere, proves him to be just what I have described him.[11]

With the exception of Rothschild banker August Belmont, Joseph Seligman was probably the most prominent Jewish financier in the United States in 1877. He had emigrated from Germany some forty years earlier and had subsequently established an international banking empire in which branches were run by his various brothers and brothers-in-law. J. and W. Seligman and Company represented the United States in Europe, selling bonds during the Civil War. Joseph Seligman was so patriotic that he named his five sons after Civil War heroes. He saw himself as so assimilated that he helped found the New York Society for Ethical Culture, which was regarded as an Americanized, ecumenical secularization of Reform Judaism. It is still in existence.[12]

The blatantly racist action of Judge Henry Hilton was the first publicized act of discrimination against Jews since the Civil War. The fact that such a prestigious Jew as Joseph Seligman could be so openly discriminated against outraged the Jewish community. According to Judge Hilton's obituary in the *New York Times* in August 1899, a "nine days' sensation followed." Two non-Jewish notables, the Reverend Henry Ward Beecher and William Cullen Bryant, protested publicly, Beecher preaching a sermon that was a "panegyric on the Jews." One hundred "Hebrew" merchants were said to have withdrawn their business from Hilton's establishments. Henry Hilton did not revoke his ban, however. For several years, no Jews were admitted to his hotel or to others in Saratoga and other favored summer resorts.[13]

The significance of this incident for our story is that Emma Lazarus would become friendly with Joseph Seligman's son, Edwin Robert Anderson, known as E. R. A. Seligman, named for Civil War hero Robert Anderson. In 1883, Seligman would join Emma in her Society for the Improvement and Colonization of East European Jews. We can infer, perhaps, that she thought he would be sympathetic because of his father's treatment at the Grand Union Hotel.

On 23 July 1879, the front page of the *New York Times* carried an item titled "Mr. Corbin and the Jews." Austin Corbin, president of the Manhattan Beach Railway Company, announced that "Jews, as a class" were not welcome at his hotel at Manhattan Beach on Coney Island. He found them "vulgar and unclean" and said that he would "leave nothing undone to get rid of them, in order to save his business from ruin."[14] Although Saratoga catered to the wealthy, Manhattan Beach was a favorite resort for New Yorkers who wanted to escape the oppressive sidewalks on their tenement-lined streets. It is interesting to note that Emma's polemic would exhibit much of the negative stereotyping found in both Hilton's and Corbin's diatribes. She would temper it with a Darwinian apology.

But why would Emma Lazarus, an acculturated, privileged young Jewess, even notice anti-Jewish behavior? Why would she react to it? Why would she be so outraged about anti-Jewish persecution that she would become her people's most militant advocate? An "outlaw" in her extended family, she certainly was not an observant Jew. Did she feel her "difference," after all, with friends like her beloved Helena Gilder? What about her own nuclear family? Was there anything in her own family life that would have sensitized her to anti-Semitic stereotyping?

We know little about Emma's parents' personal or social lives; her father's business associations are another matter, however. It has been a long-standing assumption that Moses Lazarus was a respectable businessman whose wealth had earned him an envied position in the community. But while we know little about his business life, we have found enough information about his business partner to know that he was a man of questionable character who, like Lazarus, nevertheless achieved a prominent place in New York society.

Moses Lazarus and one Bradish Johnson became partners in 1845 and remained so until at least 1865. Their business was listed as Rectifier of Spirits, Sugar Refiners, and Distillers in various city directories.[15] They were in the sugar business.

Bradish Johnson was born on Magnolia Plantation in Plaquemines Parish, Louisiana, forty-six miles below New Orleans. His father, George Johnson, and William Martin Bradish, both riverboat pilots, had settled there in 1795 to establish a sugar plantation and live there with their families. Even though Bradish Johnson was named for his father's partner, the two men soon parted company. Johnson sold his shares of the Magnolia Plantation to Bradish and established Woodland Plantation, just down the road. There he planted and milled sugarcane.[16]

Bradish Johnson inherited the plantation and became an absentee slave owner, spending at least six months of the year at his residence on Fifth Avenue in Manhattan. In that city, he established a distillery and an adjacent dairy on Sixteenth Street. The dairy was the object of notoriety in January 1853, when it was exposed in a pamphlet by John Mullaly. The findings were summarized in a *New York Times* article entitled "Death in the Jug."[17]

Attached to large distilleries in New York were "vast cow-stables" where the animals' feed was the swill produced in the distilling process. Johnson, who was reported to have owned one of the largest such businesses in the city, boarded two thousand cows at $0.06 a day each or some $40,000 a year. The stench from the stables was noticeable even a mile away, and the "disgusting" exterior conveyed "no adequate conception of the interior." After a few weeks of feeding on the swill, the cows developed a "leaden expression." The effect of this feed "upon the constitution and health of the animal [was] something similar to alcoholic drinks upon the human system." The process of milking the cows was so careless and unclean that the milk was dangerously contaminated. The result for the children of New York was tragic: Some 8,000 children died each year, at least half of whom were less than one year of age. For the *Times*, the identity of one of the culprits was perfectly clear, such were the "effects of the villainous compound" distilled and fed to cattle "on the premises and under the sanction of the man Johnson."[18] We have found nothing to suggest that Johnson was ever prosecuted for his dairy, but at that time Johnson and Lazarus had been in business for at least eight years.

Although he was an absentee slaveholder during the Civil War, Bradish Johnson played a significant role in Louisiana's reentry into the Union in 1863. He was a member of a group of conservative Unionist slaveholders who were ready to repudiate Louisiana's secession but "earnestly hoped" to preserve slavery. For that purpose, he was one of three men who traveled to Washington to petition Abraham Lincoln, asking that the "General Government" fully recognize the "rights of the State as they existed previous to the passage of an act of secession upon the principle of the existence of the State Constitution unimpaired." Their request was denied.[19]

Johnson's plantation in Louisiana was as disreputable as his dairy in New York. In April 1863, Major General Nathaniel Banks received a report from the Office of Negro Labor about plantations "on the right bank of the river downward from New Orleans." On the plantation owned by Bradish Johnson, "who does not live on the Estate," and run by the overseer Decker, "great illfeeling and discontent" existed. Decker was the "object" of this discontent. The "laborers" said that they would "accept even the Devil for an Overseer, if you will only remove this man!" They begged to be given permission to enlist in the army. They complained that their rations were "unfairly curtailed" by Decker and that he was "lecherous toward their women." After the inspectors had left, Decker is said to have "harangued the Negroes, boasted of his unlimited power over them," and "used seditious and insulting language towards the Government of this Department."[20]

It seems obvious that Moses Lazarus was untouched by his partner's attitudes and actions. Although the *New York Times* stated in Moses Lazarus' obituary that he retired from the sugar business in 1865, the New York Business Directory lists Johnson and Lazarus as sugar refiners until 1885. Lazarus is listed in the New York City Directory as a refiner in 1884–85. His son Frank is listed in 1885–86 as a member of the firm, as is Bradish Johnson, Jr.[21]

What was the effect of Moses Lazarus' business relationship on his daughter? As we know, Emma Lazarus was associated professionally and socially with a group of artists and writers defined by their gentility and refinement.

In an age when commerce was seen as a necessary but contaminating vocation for those who must engage in it, art was given an almost religious ability to uplift the human soul. Moreover, Emma's very close friends, Helena and Richard Gilder, saw themselves and were seen as arbiters of taste. They helped give rise to the "Aesthetic Movement," which offered art as a "counterbalance to materialism."[22]

Known as the "Age of Ideality," the post–Civil War era was an age when upper-class intellectuals believed in the idealism they preached. Emma and her circle took seriously what they saw as their responsibility to teach the middle and lower classes how to live and what to think, through magazines like the *Century*. For them, life went further than imitating art; life was art. Art was emphasized in the production of everything, from household articles to textiles, wallpaper, and books.

The Aesthetic Movement was, in a real way, an extension of the values of Emerson and his group, redefined in a metropolitan milieu. In a sense, art became a substitute for nature in that setting. It is significant to note that Emerson, Higginson, Gilder, and others had been or had supported abolitionists. Did this present problems for Emma Lazarus? Did she have an attitude toward slavery? Just how did she integrate her father's questionable business relationships into her genteel thought system?

If we review Emma's early poetry, we find several poems about the Civil War, but none about slavery. Surely she had heard of *Uncle Tom's Cabin*; perhaps she had even read it. But if she wrote about the subject, it was never published, nor was it included in her own handwritten notebook. Except for a poem about Henry George's *Progress and Poverty*, she seems to have ignored the misery practically under her feet in a Manhattan that had never been able to house, feed, clothe, and employ the poor.[23] Could it be that her loyalty to and love for her father prevented her either consciously or subconsciously from noticing or addressing these issues?

One poem, "The South," appears in *The Poems of Emma Lazarus*, published posthumously by Mary and Annie in 1889. Interestingly, the central character of the poem is a beautiful Creole with "still-burning, languid eyes, / Voluptuous limbs and incense-breathing mouth." The woman is haunted by "dark visions." She is aware of the ruin about her and "Ever midst those verdant solitudes, / The soldier's wooden cross, / O'ergrown by creeping tendrils and rank moss."[24]

Lazarus idealizes the southern experience—"broad plantations . . . swart freemen bend / Bronzed backs in willing labor." But the maid lies in her hammock listlessly, with "pathetic, passive, broken mien, / Of one who, sorely proved, / Great-souled, hath suffered much and much hath loved!" The poem ends with the optimistic expectation that the South will rise again. Having awakened, through "clear air she sees the pledge, the brightening ray, / And leaps from dreams to hail the coming day."[25]

We do not know if Emma ever visited Louisiana, the southern home of her father's partner, but the poem exhibits a knowledge of its terrain, its "tangled everglades" and "majestic streams" winding through "lush savanna or dense forest shades" to "broad bayous." She visualizes the "savage splendor of the swamp" where strange insects "whir" and "oft looms the great-jawed alligator's head." The postbellum South was apparently a safe subject for her muse.[26]

There seems to have been only one safe social problem into which Emma could direct her imprisoned passion. In a unique historical coincidence, Emma Lazarus lived in that moment when Jewish persecution was being noticed by "well-bred" people in America and England. Emma noticed it too, and the role she would come to play was the logical consequence of matching her own personal feeling and needs with a respectable cause that would not conflict with her loyalty to her father. In her crusade against the persecution of her people, she could validate her own Jewish self without risking the censure of her Gentile friends.

In Jewish Nationalism, Lazarus found a focus for her passion. As one of her friends described her, "She was always on fire about something." And as she wrote her friend Rose Lathrop, she had "plunged . . . wrecklessly & impulsively" into the Jewish Question, which had opened "such enormous vistas in the Past & Future." It came to absorb more and more of her mind and heart. Significantly, the Jewish Question was so "palpitatingly alive at the moment— being treated with more or less ability & eloquence in almost every newspaper and periodical you pick up—that it has about driven out of [her] thought all other subjects." The excesses perpetrated against Jews in Romania and Russia were decried by Christian spokespersons, Emma's friends, in journals and in public meetings, reinforcing her interest in the problem.[27]

8

A Jewish Polemic

In 1882, Emma Lazarus published a book of poetry that she titled, audaciously, *Songs of a Semite*. "Anti-Semitism," a word coined by German anti-Jewish agitator Wilhelm Marr in 1879, came to be a general label for all forms of hostility to Jews throughout history. Marr used it proudly to proclaim his intense antipathy toward Jews.[1] Emma took the Semitic label every bit as proudly in public identification with a despised people. From 1882 until her death, she published powerful poetry with Jewish themes. Strident, passionate polemic, the works were written to two audiences, Jewish and Christian. She urged her people to renew themselves, to recapture their past glory, to reclaim their ancestral homeland, and she reminded her Christian readers of their historic and recurring anti-Semitism, as in "The Crowing of the Red Cock":

> Where is the Hebrew's fatherland?
> The folk of Christ is sore bestead;
> The Son of Man is bruised and banned,
> Nor finds whereon to lay his head,
> His cup is gall, his meat is tears,
> His passion lasts a thousand years.
>
> . . . .
>
> When the long role of Christian guilt
> Against his sires and kin is known
> The flood of tears, the life blood spilt,
> The agony of ages shown,
> What oceans can the stain remove
> From Christian law and Christian love?[2]

In "The Banner of the Jew" she called on Jews to reclaim their nation:

> "Oh for Jerusalem's trumpet,
> To blow a blast of shattering power,

To wake the sleepers high and low,
And to rouse them to the urgent hour!
No hand for vengeance—but to save,
A million naked swords would wave.

O deem not dead that martial fire,
Say not the mystic flame is spent!
With Moses' law and David's lyre,
Your ancient strength remains unbent,
Let but an Ezra rise anew,
To lift the BANNER OF THE JEW.[3]

Although Emma's poems and essays seem to have been addressed to the same audiences, the essays were both patronizing and apologetic. In her poetry she stood with her people; in her prose she stood above them. She wrote three essays on Jewish themes for the *Century* and fifteen for the *American Hebrew*.[4] Many assert that her first *Century* essay, "Was the Earl of Beaconsfield a Representative Jew?," was an aberration for which she atoned in later essays. They are incorrect. In that piece we find characteristics of the Jew that would remain consistent in her later polemic in defense of her people.

When the Disraeli essay was published in April 1882, the Jewish community was outraged. At first glance, Lazarus seems to have presented "hardly a cliché which the anti-Semite would seriously oppose."[5] The problem with this less-than-flattering essay was that it appeared in the same issue of the *Century* as that questionable essay by Mme. Ragozin, and Emma would respond to her scathing presentation of Russian Jews exploiting Russian peasants. Emma's portrayal of Disraeli seemed to echo some of Ragozin's ideas.

Lazarus wrote the Disraeli article in response to a monograph by Georg Brandes in which he asserted that Disraeli was not a representative Jew, that he lacked the "many-sidedness" of the Jew. He lacked the noble qualities of a Spinoza.[6] On the contrary, Lazarus asserted that Disraeli had the qualities of both a Spinoza and a Shylock, that as prime minister of England, "poet, novelist, orator, satirist, wit and dandy," he could lay claim to "many-sidedness of sympathy and mind." However, Disraeli was not a "first class man," she asserted.

[H]is qualities were not those of the world's heroes; he possessed talent, rather than genius; he was a sagacious politician aiming at self-aggrandizement; not a wise statesman building his monument in enduring acts of public service, and the study of his career is calculated to dazzle, to entertain, even to amuse, rather than to elevate, to stimulate, or to ennoble.

"But," she continued, "do all these derogatory facts preclude him from being considered a representative Jew? On the contrary, we think they tend to confirm his title." Calling Disraeli a "brilliant Semite," she wrote that his "typical national character" developed from "centuries of persecution."[7]

Lazarus contended that "centuries of persecution and the enforced narrowness of their sphere of action" had caused the Jewish "race" to be second rate. For example, much might have been heard of their achievement in the arts, but "among no modern people has the loftiest embodiment of any single branch of creative art been a Jew." And the "great modern revolution in science" had gone on without their participation or aid. In her opinion, the next hundred years would "be the test of their vitality as a people." The "phase of toleration upon which they are only now entering" would "prove whether or not they are capable of growth."[8]

For Lazarus, Disraeli's Jewishness informed his activities and actions. She noted that he had

> in an eminent degree the capacity which seems to us the most characteristic feature of the Jew, whether considered as a race or an individual, . . . the faculty which enables this people, not only to perceive and make the most of every advantage of their situation and temperament, but also, with marvelous adroitness, to transform their very disabilities into instruments of power.

And he had that "patient humility which accepted blows and contumely in silence." This was not "the inertia of a broken will, but the calculating self-control of a nation imbued with persistent and unconquerable energy." Emma said that no other Jewish trait was "more conspicuously exemplified than this in the career of Benjamin Disraeli. It was this which supported him through his repeated defeats before securing a seat in Parliament and again through the disgraceful exhibition of Parlimentary brutality which attended his maiden speech." On that day, his "peculiar manner and outlandish costume" was, according to Emma, "something deeper than the so-called Oriental love of show. . . . [I]t is probable that the wily diplomat adopted it deliberately as a conspicuous mark for the shafts of scorn— . . . to divert attention from the natural race peculiarities of his apppearance. The ridicule he foresaw as inevitable; rather let it be poured on the masquerade dress, which could be doffed at will, than upon the inalienable characteristics of his personality."[9]

Emma continued her adulation, telling the reader that no Englishman could ever forget that Disraeli was a Jew; therefore "he himself would be the first to proclaim it, instead of apologizing for it." Rather than "knock servilely at the doors of the English aristocracy," he "conquered them with their own weapons, he met arrogance with arrogance, the pride of descent based upon a few centuries of distinction, with the pride of descent supported by hundreds of centuries of intellectual supremacy and even of divine anointment."[10]

As these passages make quite clear, Emma Lazarus had a chauvinistic attitude about her own Jewishness. Her admiration of Disraeli is equally explicit. "In the attitude which he assumed, politically, socially and aesthetically, toward his race," she said, "we do not know which to admire more—the daring originality of his position, or the pluck and consistency with which he maintained it." Emma probably identified with Disraeli, whom she saw as a Jew in Christian society. More significant, however, he was a Sephardic Jew, as was she, and he "knew himself to be the descendant, not of pariahs and pawnbrokers, but of princes, prophets, statesmen, poets, and philosophers, and in his veins was kindled that enthusiasm of faith in the genius and high vocation of his own people, which strikes outsiders as an anomaly in a member of an habitually despised race." Moreover, the "narrowness, the arrogance, the aristocratic pride, the passion for revenge, the restless ambition, the vanity and love of pomp of Benjamin Disraeli, no less than his suppleness of intellect, his moral courage, his dazzling talents, and his triumphant energy, proclaim him, to our thinking, a representative Jew."[11]

Emma Lazarus presented Disraeli, blemishes and all. Instead of criticizing him, she celebrated his traits as representative of his Jewishness. It was her contention that Disraeli and all modern Jews were products of centuries of oppression. She saw the Jewish "race" as a mutation, a distortion from its pure and heroic state in biblical times. Its survival as a group was a miracle.

At the risk of tarnishing her halo, we must point out that today Emma Lazarus would be known as a racist. Her stereotypical concept of the Jewish "race" is almost as offensive as that of those European anti-Semites she held in such great disdain. As we shall see, the words she used and the ideas she put forth to describe Disraeli do not disappear. On the contrary, her paradigm is well thought out in her subsequent Jewish essays, and was borrowed, in fact, from a woman for whom she had a great deal of admiration and respect, George Eliot.

In her last novel, *Daniel Deronda*, and in "The Modern Hep! Hep!," a late essay, Eliot, a philo-Semite, designed a Jewish thought system. Her work would become the basis for future Zionist thought. For Eliot, the potentially "noble" character of the Jews had become corrupted in their effort to survive. It was true, for example, that Jews were ambitious and avaricious. This was the result of de-nationalization. "It is certainly worth considering," she said, "whether an expatriated, denationalized race, used for ages to living among antipathetic populations, must not inevitably lack some of the conditions of nobleness."[12]

Jews as a race had lost their nation, a geographical space in which to reside or to love from afar. Herein lay the problem. "[E]ndowed with uncommon tenacity, physical and mental, feeling peculiarly ties of inheritance both in blood and faith, remembering national glories, trusting in their recovery, abhorring apostasy, . . . they would cherish all differences that mark them off from their hated oppressors. . . . Doubtless such a people would get confirmed in vices." Re-nationalization, on the other hand, had the mystical ability to change the negative character traits of the people who accepted it. "The nobleness of a nation" depended on the "presence of a national consciousness," as did the nobleness of each individual citizen.[13]

We do not know when Lazarus first read George Eliot's Jewish works, but she quoted the novel and the essay throughout her own Jewish essays. In Eliot she apparently found a focus for her emotion and her thought. Interestingly, although Eliot has been seen as a philo-Semite, "The Modern Hep! Hep!" displays a chilling racism. Perhaps Emma's knowledge of Eliot's bias strengthened her own concept of the enforced separateness of her Jewish "race" and of herself as a member of that people.

Eliot believed that "[t]he pride which one identifies with a great historic body is a humanizing, elevating habit of mind, inspiring sacrifices of individual comfort, gain, or other selfish ambition, for the sake of the ideal whole; and no man swayed by that sentiment can become completely abject." Emma could not have said it better. But that "great historic body" had to be protected against "alien" blood. "Let it be admitted," said Eliot, "that it is a calamity to the English, as to any other great historic people, to undergo a premature fusion with immigrants of alien blood; that its distinctive national characteristics should be in danger of obliteration by the predominating qualities of foreign settlers. . . . I am all ready to unite in groaning over the threatening danger."[14]

Eliot did not advocate sending away those Jews who were "elbowing us in a threatening crowd," but "our best course is to encourage all means of improving these neighbors," she said, "and for sending their incommodious energies into beneficent channels."[15] Emma Lazarus was to propose this in her own polemic in 1882–83. "Improving these neighbors" was her objective for those East European Jews who had appeared on her doorstep. For those who remained in Europe, repatriation to re-nationalized Palestine was the only solution. Both Lazarus and Eliot saw re-nationalization, in an age when nationalism was a powerful new concept, as a transcending, cleansing experience for a people seriously flawed.

Although Josephine Lazarus asserted that the impetus for Emma's Jewish polemic came as a result of that "fatal juxtaposition" of her Disraeli essay and Ragozin's piece, her rejoinder just one month later exhibits a knowledge and understanding of East European Jewish history she could hardly have acquired "on the spot," so to speak.

Ragozin, a Russian expatriate living in the United States since 1874, addressed the "situation" in eastern Europe from a Christian point of view. In a most articulate way, she attempted to prove that the world at large was in error in blaming anti-Semitism for what she saw as the "mild" destruction of Jewish property in Russia. Ragozin used a Jewish convert to Christianity, Jacob Brafmann, as her authority, quoting from his highly questionable treatise *The Kahal*, an exposé of Jewish communal life. In short, it was Ragozin's contention that because the Jewish community was treated as a state within a state, Jews behaved as if it were one, structuring their community in such a way that the governing body, the kehilla, taxed and terrified its constituency. As a result, Jews in turn exploited their peasant neighbors, selling them spoiled meats, indulging the peasants' alcoholic tendencies with their breweries and inns, and coercing them into borrowing sums of money they could not repay. Therefore, the peasant attacks on the Jewish populace were understandable; the Jews deserved them.[16]

Lazarus refuted these charges, point by point, in her rejoinder, her second *Century* essay, "Russian Christianity versus Modern Judaism." Not only did she teach her readers about the dynamics of East European Jewish life, she took issue with Ragozin's whitewash of the brutal pogroms, discussing the means of torture and describing the wholesale destruction of Jewish villages. Nevertheless, she seems to have accepted Ragozin's description of the East European Jewish personality or character.

Ragozin described Russian Jews as "loathsome parasites," herding together in "unutterable filth and squalor, . . . a loathsome and really dangerous element," spreading "all kinds of horrible diseases and contagions." But this is not the reason they were hated, they were "loathed because their ways are crooked, their manner abject—because they do not stand up for themselves and manfully resent an insult or oppose vexation, but will take any amount and cringe, and go off with a deadly grudge at heart which they will vent cruelly, ruthlessly." Ragozin called for emancipation for Russian Jews so that they could dissolve their own system of government as well as their exclusive religion that had what she saw as archaic practices. Lazarus took issue with this idea in her rebuttal, pointing out the fallacy in the idea that emancipation would eliminate anti-Semitism. She cited West European countries as examples where emancipation and subsequent political power had caused anti-Semitic excesses.[17]

Lazarus felt that Jews must reform themselves both occupationally and religiously. This would not cure anti-Semitism, however. Only when Jews had a homeland of their own would anti-Semitism cease. She articulated these ideas in her lengthy treatise, *An Epistle to the Hebrews*. This series of fifteen essays appeared in the *American Hebrew* from November 1882 to February 1883. It has been described, with admiration, by one Lazarus scholar as her "mature confession of her faith, the most effective contribution she made to Jewish thought and policy."[18] The series is racist, derogatory, patronizing, apologetic, and harsh. Nevertheless, in these essays her call for a technical education for East European Jewish refugees in the United States, and a repatriation to Palestine for those remaining in Russia, has brought her enduring honor.

Emma Lazarus set herself up, as did Paul, from whom she borrowed her title, as a harbinger of Truth. The word "Hebrews" suggests that she was using Hilton's definition, designating her audience as so-called uptown Jews, many of whom were acculturated to the point of assimilation, as was she. Her desire in addressing her "fellow Jews" was to rouse them through study of their "glorious" past to join her in her mission for re-nationalization of their ancient homeland. For Lazarus, as for Mordecai Ezra Cohen, George Eliot's hero in *Daniel Deronda*, whom she quoted, Jewish Nationalism apparently was the ultimate charismatic experience. With Eliot, she endowed history with the power to create a conversion experience for all who would study the "full beauty and grandeur of her past, the glory and infinite expansiveness of her future."[19]

As in her essay on Disraeli, Lazarus described and explained the flaws of her "race," the result of centuries of oppression. Because they were now the focus of attention in the "present adversity," the persecution of her people in Russia was a chance, however, to "look into the mirror held up by well-wishers and enemies alike"; to investigate the situation "coolly, rationally, and impartially." Wherever a blemish was found, they must "shrink from no single or united effort to remove it."[20]

"Judaism," as Lazarus called it, was both a race and a religion with a divine mission to lift up "our own race to the standard of morality and instruction" in order to "promote the advancement and elevation of the Gentiles." With unabashed pride, Lazarus boasted that the Jew, with moral and intellectual eminence, would serve as a "beacon-light to others." She wanted a "nation of priests, . . . devoted servants of the holy spirit. What is needed," she said, "as George Eliot said, is 'the torch of visible community,'—that these few scattered workers be united and reinforced until they represent no longer an insignificant minority, but a resolute and homogeneous nation."[21]

Emma Lazarus' concept of "Judaism" was unorthodox to say the least. At that time, there were two branches of Judaism recognized in this country, Traditional and Reform. Traditional Jews observed the 613 commandments, or mitzvot, and believed that when the Messiah came, the land of Israel would witness the ingathering of all Jews, living and dead.

Orthodox Judaism had changed little in the almost two thousand years since the destruction of the Second Temple and the dispersion of the Jews of Israel. Reform Judaism was another story. German Jews who had migrated to the United States in the first half of the nineteenth century had been intensely patriotic in Germany, even though their position in the general community was fragile. When they came to the New World they brought their patriotism with them, embracing the United States with the fervor with which they had loved their homeland. They also brought their ideas about a modernization of their religion.

By the 1880s, Reform Jews had negated almost all of the significant concepts and practices of traditional Judaism in an effort to Americanize the religion. They proclaimed America as their homeland, removing all prayers addressing the return to Zion. They would become anti-Zionists and would hold that position until the Holocaust. They did away with most observances. No longer did they keep kosher, nor did the men wear headcoverings or prayer shawls inside the synagogue. They called their houses of worship temples rather than synagogues. For them, there was no need to return to Jerusalem. Paradise could be found, now, on American soil.

Reform Jews placed their emphasis on prophetic Judaism. They saw their role much as Emma had articulated, as a "light unto the nations." But Emma could not have become a member of a Reform Jewish congregation because of her position on Palestine. We know that Emma's solution to the Jewish Problem rested on the repatriation of Jews to their homeland, Palestine. Although she could agree with most of the tenets of Reform Judaism, her idea of a return to Zion would have been challenged.

We might say today that Emma Lazarus was an ethnic Jew. She would have been very uncomfortable with that definition if she could, in fact, have understood what it meant. Lazarus saw herself as a member of a race. But she had no intention of encouraging the perpetuation of the ethnic characteristics of that people. For a variety of reasons, she wanted the East European Jews to become as American as those Americans born here. On the other hand, she wanted American-born Jews not to become aware of their ethnic history, an ethnicity rooted in what she called East European obscurantism, but to become knowledgeable, through study, of their ancient heritage.

Lazarus contended that her race could be saved from the "chronic decadence" that resulted from "luxury, materialism and indifferentism [sic] by sedulously nourishing the sacred fires of historic memory at the same time that we emancipate and fortify our Reason to keep pace with the intellectual advance of the age."[22]

We know that Emma Lazarus was honored in the Jewish community as the premier spokesperson for East European Jews. Clearly, her immortal sonnet is addressed to "wretched" refugees. But, interestingly, she saw those from eastern Europe, these "pale and stunted pariahs," as "unfitted [sic] by nature and education for competition for existence under American conditions." She took literally the words of Darwin and Spencer, to whom she referred throughout the *Epistle*. She saw Russian Jews, who had emigrated to these shores, having lived for centuries in the "darkness of a superstitious obscurant religion, in the filth of poverty," as a group of people desperately in need of education. They must be taught the "Godliness of cleanliness, the dignity of womanhood, the delights of reason, the moral necessity of a broader humanity, the universal charity."[23]

Emma's aristocratic cast of mind informed her ideas about education for young Jewish immigrants. She bemoaned the "wretched quality of work performed by the majority of American mechanics and domestic servants," as well as the "false sense of pride that revolted at the very name of servant, as derogatory to the freeborn American." She admonished her co-religionists against shunning domestic work, which so many Americans did. And although she saw this as a national problem, she felt that it was an "unhealthy social tendency fraught with even greater danger for the American Jew than for the American Christian." Jews, Lazarus felt, lived more by their wits than by their hands, a function of years of oppression when all trades were closed save usury. Thus, if they were "as a rule a race of soft-handed, soft-muscled men," it was not their fault. Now they must return "instantly and earnestly" to the "avocations of our ancestors in the day when our ancestors were truly great and admirable."[24]

In an article published in the *American Hebrew* in October 1882, Lazarus spoke strongly for "employment and education." It was on both that the survival of the race depended.

> Mr. Spencer and Mr. Darwin, not to cite less authoritative names, have pointed out the positively maleficent effects of ignorant philanthropy, and the portentous evils of that short-sighted charity which neglects to take into account the laws of nature and of natural selection. In justice to future generations, in justice to ourselves, in justice to the objects of our sympathy, we must dispense only those gifts which strengthen the character and the mind, and we must study how best to avoid the rush of enfeebling the race by pauperization, and the artificial preservation of the vicious and idle.[25]

Emma Lazarus' crusade seems to have been uncomfortably frantic. She told East European Jews to reform themselves, and her passion was informed, one must suppose, by fear. The terrible problem for Emma Lazarus was the reality of collective guilt, imposed upon all Jews in a hostile Gentile community that continued to condemn them "as a race for the vices or follies of individual members." Lazarus knew this was inevitable, even for American Jews; they belonged to a "race whose members are unmistakably recognized at a glance, whatever be their color, complexion, costume or language."[26]

An Epistle to the Hebrews, a brutally honest assessment of the Jewish Problem as Emma Lazarus saw it, was reissued by the Federation of American Zionists in 1900, thirteen years after her death, and published again in 1987 as an annotated edition by Lazarus authority Morris U. Schappes.[27] The language and ideas are archaic and offensive to a post-Holocaust generation, but Lazarus' treatise is an artifact of her era. Placed in a culture where Darwin and Spencer were the interpreters of a world in which industrialization had run wild, her construct would make sense. With George Eliot as a resource, her words would be taken seriously.

In February 1883, Emma's third Jewish essay, "The Jewish Problem," was published. Thousands of Christian readers of the *Century* were edified by this chauvinistic appeal for sympathy. Throughout the piece, Lazarus quoted Christian clergymen for authentic historical accounts of Jewish persecution in Christian Europe. Early on, she referred the reader to Reverend Henry Hart Milman, Dean of St. Paul's, "if it be supposed that I am drawing too dark a picture of Christian atrocities and too partial a presentment of the innocence of my victims."[28]

The first part of the essay is a "brief history of the Jews from the Third Century before the Christian Era" to the present. Lazarus acknowledged her "indebtedness to a pamphlet written in 1881 by German Christian, C. L. Beck, entitled 'A Vindication of the Jews' " from which she had "freely quoted." Step by step she traced the litany of persecution in each country in Europe and was relentless in her description of the various methods of torture. Her pessimism, even after the emancipation of Jews in western Europe in the early nineteenth century, extended to her own country, where the word "Jew" was "in constant use, even among so-called refined Christians, as a term of opprobrium, and is employed as a verb to denote the meanest tricks."[29]

Interestingly, Lazarus had included with the corrected proofs of her essay a letter to Robert Underwood Johnson, one of her editors at the magazine. She thanked him for pointing to her errors in spelling and grammar, and then with sarcasm asked him to thank the appropriate party for the "charming" review of *Songs of a Semite.* She wished "he could be a Jew for only 24 hours," she wrote, "& he would then understand that neither materialism nor indifference prevents the Jews from decrying their provocateurs. They have never had a long enough interval of security or equality (if indeed they have *ever* had the latter) be able to utter a lamentation without risk of bringing down upon themselves again the immemorial curse."[30]

The second part of the essay dealt explicitly with the Jewish Problem. Emma Lazarus found a Jewish solution, similar to those of her fellow proto-Zionists in Europe, and agreed with her adversaries who proposed that Jews exit host countries in which they were unwanted residents. She told her Christian audience that Jews, "naturally a race of high moral and intellectual endowments," may have, however, "superficial peculiarities which excite the aversion of Christians, . . . the lingering traces of unparalleled suffering." But Jews, she said, have too long turned the other cheek. They have proved themselves willing and able to assimilate with whatever people and to endure every climactic "influence. But blind intolerance and ignorance are now forcibly driving them into that position which they have so long hesitated to assume. THEY MUST ESTABLISH AN INDEPENDENT NATIONALITY."[31]

"The idea formulated by George Eliot," she said, "has already sunk into the minds of many Jewish enthusiasts." Quoting both Daniel Deronda and Mordecai Ezra Cohen throughout the essay, she agreed with their concept of "an organic center," a homeland, for their "race." With a "heart and brain to watch and guide and execute, the outraged Jew shall have a defense in the court of nations, as the outraged Englishman or American."[32]

Emma Lazarus had a vision. Her treatment of the meaning of Exile, first articulated at the age of eighteen in her poem, "In the Jewish Synagogue at Newport," became a call to action as she came to know the meaning of Christian anti-Semitism. Her exaltation of "martyrdom" and "heroism" matched her need to recapture a time of grandeur for her people. But Emma lived in the real world where a "colossal experiment" involving masses of people in the organized chaos that was the nation's largest metropolis was being conducted before her eyes. In the midst of this ferment, she faced Jews of an eastern Europe ignored or at least passed by in the modernity of the hour. Her solution, repatriation of East European Jews, would be both realistic and romantic in the eyes of this late nineteenth century New Yorker.

Never in her wildest imaginings could Emma Lazarus have predicted the capacity of that city to accommodate the more than one million East European Jews who would emigrate there between the 1880s and World War I. She would have been astonished to see how rapidly those exiles would adapt their religion and their way of life to American culture.

Emma Lazarus had a great deal to say about the subject of exiles, as we know. But her position was contradictory. Not only was she drawn to Jewish exiles at an early age, she addressed the subject in one of her last published pieces, "By the Waters of Babylon," which appeared in the Century in 1887, shortly before her death. In the first of these poems, "Exodus (August 3, 1492)," she dealt with the expulsion from Spain, when all of Spain's Jews, Emma's ancestors, were forced either to convert to Catholicism or to leave. Interestingly, she treated these exiles with respect; when she wrote of exiles from eastern Europe, later in the piece, she saw them in a different light. These outcasts with "ignominious features," and "shuffling gait" wore "the sordid mask of the Ghetto."[33] And we will remember that when she was composing her famous sonnet, she was also working to keep alive her organization for the repatriation of Jewish exiles to Palestine.

Lazarus could rhapsodize over Jewish exiles in history, but those who would be settled in the neighborhood next door were cause for apprehension. We have seen the specter of anti-Semitism that threatened even well-established Jews in the late nineteenth century. Emma was dislocated from her security as a Sephardic Jew, so to speak. Furthermore, she had been dislocated, physically, in that rapidly changing Manhattan environment. Her family had to move uptown in 1877 when a furniture warehouse next door chased them out of their Fourteenth Street home where they had resided for twenty years. They lived on Fifty-seventh Street for only six years and then moved back downtown to Tenth Street.

Perhaps Emma was drawn to exiles because symbolically she was an exile herself. Not only was she uprooted geographically, her own identity was fractured. She was a woman for whom her father had grand professional ambitions, in a world where domesticity reigned supreme; a Jew whose relationship to her Christian friends was ambiguous; an "outlaw" among her own observant Jewish relatives; a northerner with southern connections; and a New Yorker whose close friends, Tom Ward and Rose Lathrop, were New Englanders. Where would she fit in?

We need to say, finally, again, that it is not clear, really, why this woman, who in 1880 felt herself relegated to "elf-music," would bond to a people with whom she had nothing in common save an opprobrious name. But the Darwinian geist of the era seemed to permit her to see the possibilities of a reversal of the "mutations" caused by centuries of persecution. Lazarus' chauvinistic and enthusiastic endorsement of Jewish history and her belief in man's capacity for change in the "proper" environment led to a self-anointed leadership of her people. She became an Ezra. Her vision of a Jewish state as a palliative for anti-Semitism came to fruition sixty years after her death.

Emma Lazarus was an American original. Born into the constraints of a nineteenth-century Victorian angle of vision, she was made aware of her talent at an early age. She knew that she was expected to take herself seriously. Her parents enabled her to meet the important American and European artists and thinkers of that time. And these intellectuals served to validate her as a young woman to reckon with. This patrician young Jewess found herself as comfortable in Concord or Newport or the capital cities of Europe as she was in Manhattan. But the "quaintness" of Concord, the superficiality of Newport, the dazzling differentness of Europe would never provide the environment demanded by her muse. Only in Manhattan, in the neighborhood of her birth, would she find the backdrop for her short life's achievements.

Emma Lazarus. *(Courtesy of the University of Virginia Library)*

Emma Lazarus. *(Courtesy of the American Jewish Historical Society)*

Rose Hawthorne Lathrop. *(Courtesy of Rosary Hill Home)*

Bronze medallion of Charles deKay by Olin Warner. *(Courtesy of the Century Association and Ormonde deKay)*

Richard Watson Gilder and Helena deKay Gilder. *(Courtesy of Helena Pappenheimer)*

Emma's friends *(left to right)*: Mary Hallock Foote, Helena deKay, Olivia Ward, Bessie Stickney. *(Courtesy of Evelyn Foote Gardiner)*

Moses Lazarus (1813–1885), undated. *(Courtesy of Henry R. Geyelin)*

Sarah Lazarus (1842–1910), 1869. *(Courtesy of Henry R. Geyelin)*

Josephine Lazarus (1846–1910), undated. *(Courtesy of Henry R. Geyelin)*

Emma Lazarus (1849–1887), 1866. *(Courtesy of Henry R. Geyelin)*

Agnes Lazarus
(1856–1905), 1874.
*(Courtesy of Henry
R. Geyelin)*

Emma Lazarus
(1849–1887), 1885 or 1886.
*(Courtesy of
Henry R. Geyelin)*

Annie Lazarus (1859–?), undated.
(Courtesy of Henry R. Geyelin)

Letter from Emma Lazarus to Helena deKay Gilder, 20 August, 1883.
(Courtesy of Rosamond Gilder)

Henry James (with doughnut). *(Stephen Crane Papers, Rare Book and Manuscript Library, Columbia University. Reprinted with permission.)*

"The Beeches," the Lazarus summer home, Bellevue Avenue, Newport, Rhode Island. *(George Champlin Mason,* Newport and Its Cottages *[Boston: James R. Osgood & Co., 1875]. Courtesy of the Redwood Library and Athenaeum, Newport, Rhode Island)*

PART II

The Letters

9

Helena deKay Gilder

T he letter was brief. "My dear Helena, Emma is at rest. She died this morning at 11 o'clock—quietly at the end but after a long agony. Sincerely yours, Josephine." On 19 November 1887, a brief but intense friendship had come to an end.

Helena deKay Gilder, daughter of Commodore George C. and Janet deKay, was the granddaughter of the poet Joseph Rodman Drake. She was born in New York City, where she met and married Richard Watson Gilder, who, in 1870 at the age of twenty-six, became managing editor of *Scribner's Monthly*. Not quite eleven years later, he became editor of the *Century*.

Richard and Helena Gilder were legends in their own time; their Friday night salons were legendary. Their friend Will Low wrote of them, "To the hospitable welcome of that modest dwelling everyone who came to New York in those days, bearing a passport of intellectual worth, appeared to find his way."[1]

In fact, the Gilder home, known as The Studio, was a converted stable that had been redesigned with hospitality in mind. One "great room" where they ate and lived with "sun-shine coming through the windows cut in the big stable doors" welcomed "artists and actors, musicians and writers" who mingled with a "varied collection of philanthropists, millionaires and penniless philosophers."[2]

The Gilders had a limitless capacity for friendship. Helena Gilder apparently had boundless energy. Her daughter Rosamond described her:

> She accomplished an astonishing number of things with an apparent ease and calmness. . . . Besides five growing children her household usually included at least one visiting guest or relative. During these busy years, she belonged to several clubs, the Fortnightly, the Music Club and others; she read widely in French, German and English, and all the while comforted, encouraged, and

kept alive that firebrand of energy and emotion, my father, who without her support, could never have survived the struggle on this metropolitan battlefront.[3]

Although his work has not stood the test of time, Richard Watson Gilder wanted to be known as a poet. His frail, ethereal looks belied, however, an ability to lead, to bring together diverse groups and ideas and organize them for publication first in *Scribner's* and then in the *Century*. The *Century* under Gilder's tutelage was unsurpassed. As one of his biographers wrote, "1880 to 1890 might well be called the 'Gilder Age.' For those ten years, the family magazine was the most powerful literary force in America, the best of these magazines was the *Century* and the ruler of the *Century* was Gilder." By 1887, the *Century* had come to possess "the largest audience that ever was gathered about any periodical of its class printed in the English language."[4]

Within a year after Gilder took command, the *Nation* called the *Century* "perhaps the most judiciously edited magazine in the world." Gilder is said to have had a "remarkable capacity for enthusiasm about people, music, works of art and the United States."[5] So many people wanted to publish in the journal that a huge backlog was inevitable. It took years before publication of some authors. Emma Lazarus held a privileged position; her articles, in most cases, were published immediately.

According to Gilder scholar Arthur John, Gilder's "good will and boyish good humor endeared him to a host of friends, from impecunious poets and artists to presidents of the United States and millionaires."[6] Andrew Carnegie reportedly told the publisher Henry Holt that he "had never loved any man as he loved Gilder," who became one of President Grover Cleveland's confidants.[7] Cleveland wrote his first inaugural address at the Gilders' summer home in Marion, Massachusetts. Later, Mark Twain lived for a time in the guesthouse on the Gilder summer estate, Four Brooks Farm. His daughter Clara was married there.[8]

Helena deKay Gilder was an artist of some note. She had studied with John LaFarge and Winslow Homer and at the Cooper Union School of Design for Women. She was a member of the first life drawing class for women that the National Academy of Design offered and was a founding member of the Art Students League in 1875 and the Society of American Artists in 1877.[9] In the next decade, her career became subservient to her role as wife and mother.

Helena and Richard Gilder were equal partners in their social enterprise. They were self-proclaimed arbiters of culture in an era when art and music were seen to have the same attributes for moral enlightenment as religion. They utilized the pages of *Scribner's* and the *Century* to communicate "the latest aesthetic news." The *Century* was the semi-official organ for the country's young painters. According to literary historians, the Gilders and many other editors of the time had entered into a "conspiracy to preserve the Victorian values in poetry":

> The liaison which the poetic idealists had established with editors and publishers was an intimate one; the strength of the continuing tradition of Victorian poetry was a result of the coordinated activities of the writers, editors, and publishers. Richard Watson Gilder of the *Century* [and other editors of similar magazines] early served notice of their respect for the ideals of genteel tradition and the type of poetry their magazines might be expected to welcome.[10]

Msgr. Maurice Francis Egan was a close friend of the Gilders. His impressions of them and of their effect on American culture are instructive. Father Egan says that the influence of the *Century* on the artistic development of the country "cannot be overrated. Nobody can appreciate it who did not live through the the reign of the Philistines that preceded it. And it would be difficult to overrate the effect of the Gilders on the clever group of men attached to the *Century* who surrounded them." He continued, "It seems to me that there could have been no pleasanter or more satisfactory society":

> The Gilders gave to it a tone of simplicity and an appreciation of real values that one found only among those old families in New York whose exclusiveness consisted in a dislike for the invasion of barbarians—barbarians with vulgar standards which they did not care to acknowledge. To these high ideals, the Gilders added genius, sympathy, tolerance and the finest powers of criticism of life. They discovered at once, talent, charm, high character, and drew it into their circle.[11]

The first known letter from Emma Lazarus to Helena Gilder is dated 24 July 1876. For the next decade, Emma shared her thoughts and her feelings about a number of people, places, and ideas. Although we have none of the letters Helena wrote to Emma, this one-way portion of the dialogue reveals a warm and enduring friendship.

Helena and Richard Gilder had five children, four of whom are mentioned in the letters: Rodman, Dorothea, George and Rosamond. Francesca was born after 1887. These children are mentioned throughout the letters but are identified infrequently in the notes, the glossary, and the index.

This volume includes letters from Emma's sisters Annie and Josephine. They began to write when Emma became mortally ill in 1886. These letters are a poignant record of her last days. After Emma's death, the sisters continued their friendship and their correspondence with the Gilders. Today, the progeny of the Lazarus/Gilder/deKay families continue to see one another with regularity.[12]

Emma Lazarus to Helena deKay Gilder
New York
July 24th 1876

My dear Mrs. Gilder–

I cannot tell you with what a painful shock of surprise, I heard of your trouble.[13] My heart truly aches for you– above all when I think how lonely and how far away from all help or comfort you must have been. I know only too well how little can be said or done by friends at such a time, yet I cannot but think that situated as you were you must have actually needed & vainly looked for many a little service that might have been offered to you. I am sure that you must take comfort in the thought of all that your innocent little darling has been spared by her early release– All the bitterness of the . . . is for you alone, and I trust your patience & strength will not fail you in accepting it as bravely as you may. I was deeply touched by Mr. Gilder's kindness in writing to me, and I send him my heartfelt sympathy and thanks.

If it can be in any way grateful to you, my dear friend, to know that I think of you with infinite compassion, pray believe in my sincere sympathy.

Your friend

Emma Lazarus

Emma Lazarus to Helena deKay Gilder
September 17, 1877

My dear Mrs. Gilder–

Your kind cordial letter was most welcome & delightful to me– I expect to return on Friday of this week to New York, but as I suppose I shall not find you there for several weeks, I shall send you from here my thanks & greetings before we get into the agonies of tearing up our household roots. I trust before now you have rid yourself of "restless" thoughts that were perplexing you when you wrote. I was so sorry to learn that Mr. Gilder's hard-earned holiday was interfered with by his indisposition– But I sincerely hope, now that you are feeling so much better yourself, that your whole horizon is brightening correspondingly. I am convinced that your baby is a beauty, in spite of your motherly modesty asserting that he is ". . ."[14] Even Cupid disguised in blue flannel would lose some of his radiance, & you subject your son to the most trying of costumes. When are you going back to the city? I am afraid we shall find the weather there oppressively warm, but my Father grows restless & anxious to leave Newport, as soon as September sets in.[15] We are talking of moving as far as 57th Street & Madison Avenue![16] I wonder how many visits a year you will pay me when we put all that distance between us. I am sorry for some reasons to go uptown (and you are one of them!) but our old situation is becoming really uninhabitable & I think a furniture warehouse that has planted itself next door to us will prove the "last straw." Colonel Higginson has left Newport– he has gone to Vermont for a short visit & will only return to prepare for a lecturing tour all over the West & South.[17] He came to see us before he went away, & talked with a good deal of simplicity & dignity about his position. He is so unused to freedom that he gave me the impression of a long-caged bird that wants to try its wings in short flights, before it can realize & make use of its liberty. I think he will be in New York during the Fall or Winter– perhaps you will see him. Appropros of unhappy birds, how is your fishhawk? I have been writing a story about a fishhawk this summer & should like to see yours– I have never seen one– I hope you are making a sketch of him– & I hope also it will be more successful than my story which I cannot summon sufficient energy to copy & give a magazine editor the pleasure of refusing. I must go back once more for a few minutes to "Virgin Soil."[18] I am sure Mr. Gilder has the same idea about it that I have. Why do you find it so sad & depressing? To me it is hopeful, not because it ends with a marriage & the chief characters in whom our sympathy is enlisted, turn out ardently happy, but because the whole book is so permeated with an atmosphere of aspiration & heroism. Whenever I look into it or think of it I am reminded of a verse in the Koran that promises to the faithful– "one of the two most excellent things, martyrdom or victory." Viewed in this light, even Nezhdanoff ceases to be a failure, & his suicide becomes a noble necessary act.[19] In that little band of enthusiasts of which he is leader, there is nothing mean.

[page missing]

. . . Will she not soon be able to go to her own home again? I think your brother went away from Newport a new man, after his little holiday. He looked & seemed so much better than when he arrived.

I am looking forward with so much pleasure, dear Mrs. Gilder, to seeing you again. Will you not drop me a line, if it be only a postal card, letting me know when you come to town? Please give my best regards to Mr. Gilder & thanks for his kind note to me– Trusting we see you very soon, believe me

sincerely

Emma Lazarus

Josephine says she is always happy to be remembered by you & sends her love & thanks.[20]

Emma Lazarus to Helena deKay Gilder
34 East 57th Street
August 18, 1879

My dear Helena

May I not call you so? by the name that fits you so harmoniously & represents you always to my thoughts? Your letter was a delightful surprise to me– for I understand so well how hard it is to find time or opportunity to accomplish the necessary family correspondence, even while traveling that I did not look for an answer to my own egotistical letters– I think of you with always fresh sympathy & affection & am always hoping to hear that your anxieties have been relieved. Perhaps the repose of English life will do more toward furthering the purpose of your trip than all the varied pleasures of your continental experiences– May not your natural impatience prevent you from seeing an improvement which must at first be very gradual & for a long time almost imperceptible. I do trust when you return here you will find this to have been the case & that both you & Mr. Gilder will have derived all possible profit from your vacation–[21] Thanks for your cordial sympathy about my father– he has been wonderfully well this summer, although he has not left the city & we have enjoyed a happy, peaceful season, unusually free from care. I have spent the greater part of July away from home, on the Jersey Coast in Ocean Beach– I suppose Julia who was there also for a few weeks has written to you about the place & the people–[22] There was an unusual number of agreeable women who made the time pass delightfully, for a habitual recluse like myself. Among them was an old friend & schoolmate, Mrs. George Biddle whom I had not seen since her marriage three years ago, & whom it was a . . . pleasure to be with.[23] There is something about the generous tender womanliness of her nature which reminds me constantly of you– though superficially you are very unalike. I am going to be with her again at Nantucket where I am going next week to stay till the 1st of September. Meanwhile, I have paid a visit to my wise, . . . old friend Mr. Emerson who treats me with an almost fatherly affection.[24] Ellen asked me to spend a few days with them in Concord, & I gladly availed myself of the invitation. I found Mr. Emerson very sadly changed & much older than when I saw him last but with the same wonderful benign dignity of expression & bearing & the same sincere wisdom of thought as ever. It is only his speech which seems to have failed– for his mind appears clear & unclouded– the connection is broken between the idea & the word. And the unconsciousness of his impaired faculties makes him silent & sensitive. What do you think of queer, crotechety people who gravitate toward Concord? This year there is a more extraordinary set than ever. Mr. Alcott has formed what he calls a School of Philosophy & Platonists & Hegelians & all sorts of learned pedants meet & discuss . . . there to an audience assembled from all parts & the way the most difficult problems of life are solved by these half-cracked theorists who dogmatize about the immortal soul is absolutely . . . & made me at least doubt my own sanity.[25] I met again your old friend & devoted admirer Mr. George Bradford– who inquired about you with characteristic quaint affection.[26] He was sadly disappointed not to have seen you the last time he was in New York in June & does not see anyone in . . . here at all– He was dressed still in the fashion of Lord Byron's Fay– in a waistcoat and large-buttoned blue coat & looking as if he had stepped out of an illustration to an old "keepsake" or "Ainsworth." I saw your brother Charlie the other day in town.[27] It was refreshing to see a Bohemian & pagan again after dwelling with the Puritans.

Do you know I have become an aunt since I saw you? My brother's wife has presented him with twins, two more Lazarus girls! The poor little things are very ill just now & I am afraid they will not be able to fight out the long unequal battle– They are only a month old– having . . . just long enough for the parents to become all-absorbed in their existence– I trust to see you very soon although I should rejoice with you if your holiday could be prolonged–

Do have a good photograph taken before you come home– And believe me with best regards for Mr. Gilder

Sincerely your friend

Emma Lazarus

I hear with delight of Rodman's success among the Italians & how beautiful he must look.

Emma Lazarus to Helena deKay Gilder
Feb. 23rd, 1880
34 East 57th St. N.Y.

My dear Helena—

I cannot begin to tell you how happy I was to receive your dear, welcome letter. How I long to see you once more & to hear from your own lips the account of the wonderful adventures & delights of your trip. The idea of coming home again & to that dreaded work seems already to be casting its shadow on your spirits; but your holiday has been prolonged by so much, & appears to have been such a perfect success, that I do hope all your misgivings are needless. The only thing you seem to have been unfortunate in is the weather, which must certainly do its share towards depressing the best spirits. Such a winter as we have had has rarely been known here— a succession of bright, mild sunny days, like late autumn or early spring, interrupted by but two snow-storms, the traces of which were erased within a week— I don't think Marie Oakey has the slightest idea of saying a word against your beloved studio to anyone— her only fear seems to be that you will want it back again— it evidently is a place everyone grows very much attached to.[28] There is no marked change in it that I see— except the necessary change of Maria's individuality pervading it instead of yours— I miss you constantly although I ought to get used to not seeing you there, for I am a great deal with Maria— But I am more constant than I have the credit of being (particularly with your family) & to me the place is always full of dear associations with you— I have been interesting myself in a great many things this winter, & have <u>lots</u> to talk over with you— I have enjoyed myself very much, & don't think I have been quite the same morbid, moping creature you remember— I have only twice lost my head musically— the first time about Joseffy, the Hungarian pianist, who has revived for me some of the old Rubinstein enthusiasm, & the second during this last week about Berlioz' "Faust"—[29] Now, don't laugh because it is Berlioz. Even his most pronounced opponents have been won over by the exquisite beauty & the marvelous orchestration of this extraordinary production. It has made a great sensation in New York, & I have heard it six times during ten days— each time with increased delight. I am eagerly looking forward to one more final hearing of it tomorrow evng. The last time I heard it I was with your brother, & if he could listen with delight & wonder for three hours to Berlioz, you may be sure it is no extravagant eccentricity on my part to be so enthusiastic about it. How I wish you had been with us! If you get a chance to hear it in Paris, where it was repeated 15 times last winter & 20 this year— don't miss it! What do you think of my having joined Mrs. Crosby's "Review Club?" & has anybody written to you of this ambitious & intellectual society—[30] The original design was for some 30 or 40 women to meet every fortnight & discuss the various topics of interest treated in the Reviews– but the "Review" part of it has been done away with & they select their own subjects.– I confess that although I joined it chiefly from curiosity, I have become very much interested in it, & have been very well entertained at the 3 meetings I have attended. In spite of its ambitious sound there is a real absence of pretension about it, & when you once muster sufficient courage to talk at all, which for me is a terribly formidable thing, it seems simply like a general conversation among bright, agreeable women & is at times quite animated & suggestive. The most agreeable among the women I have heard are, I think, Mrs. Charlie Post, Mrs. Lockwood, Mrs. Chapman, Mrs. Hobson, Mrs. Pellew, etc.– I don't know whether you will think it supremely absurd, or whether you will take an interest in it. Mrs. Crosby has spoken once or twice about you to me, & wished you were here to stay. It is a great deal pleasanter than it sounds– that is all I can say– so please defer your judgement until you come home & I tell you about it– what we talk of & how we talk.

I spent last evng. (Sunday) at the (S.G.) Wards'– where I was asked to meet young Mr. Julian Sturgis–[31] Did you ever hear of him or his light popular little novel– "John or Dreams"? It is strange you did not meet him in London, as he knows your sister, Mrs. Bronson, very well, & is an intimate friend of Mr. James.[32] How charming it must have been for you to see so much of the latter– As is rarely the case with me, I have acquired through his books for which I have no extravagant admiration (I think they are always lacking in force) a strong prepossession in favor of their author's personality– Everything about them is so refined, so graceful, so polished & at the same time so manly. And how do you find your old friend Mr. Nadal?[33] What is he working at? There is a charming style which should not be neglected– I am afraid you will think I am never going to stop writing, & I haven't said half of what I wished to say. Please give my kindest regards to Mr. Gilder– It is very good of him to be interested in my work. I have written a play which is awaiting a publisher, & with no immediate prospect of finding one.[34] I shall have one of my Jewish poems in one of the coming Scribner's.[35] You say Mrs. Gilchrist told you of my visit to Concord.[36] I wrote you a long account of it myself. Did you ever get that letter? I am so glad to hear of Rodman's beauty & bloom– He must look like an angel. Goodbye & take care of yourself– & believe in the love of your sincere friend.

Emma Lazarus

Letter 5HdeKG

Emma Lazarus to Richard Watson Gilder
Thurs. Evng.
Oct. 25 (1880)

My dear Mr. Gilder

How good you are to remember your promise to gratify my impatience in regard to "Hesperus!"[37] The poem makes on me the same impression as when I heard it read, & I heartily wish it the appreciation & success it deserves. Pray accept my best thanks for letting me have the advance copy–

I hope to see you in this ultima Thule on Sunday. Mrs. Gilder has held out a half promise to see us then, & I shall certainly look for you with her– As a mortification of the flesh & the performance of a difficult duty, a visit to us now is the next best thing to a [letter cut off here] . . . lovely when you get here, & I feel that I shall grow a thousandfold more unsocial, savage and hermetically sealed within myself in this delightful solitude than I have ever been before– When I feel the pressing need of the refinement of civilization & human intercourse, I shall make a raid upon the Studio– so beware! Do you know that I am such a slow dull sort of a person that it is only lately that the pre-Raphaelite simplicity of your picture of the sad poet twanging his golden lyre has been haunting me with a vague sweet charm– I wish I could see it again– Are you not going to publish it? Trusting to see you again soon, believe me with many thanks for the poem [rest cut]

Letter 6HdeKG

Emma Lazarus to Helena deKay Gilder
34 E. 57th St.
Friday morng
(Nov. 1880)

My dear Helena

Although I hope to see you on Monday, I must send you my thanks in advance for letting me see the charming & characteristic verses of Browning.[38] They seem to me more than ordinarily graceful for him, besides bearing the strong stamp of his individuality. How proud your niece ought to be to have inspired them, & how proud you ought to be to have such a niece! More than a thousand thanks for troubling yourself to send them to me– I congratulate you on the safe arrival of your new nephew– I am delighted to think you have been spared all unnecessary anxiety in regard to your sister-in-law– I shall <u>save</u>

up whatever I have to say till Monday– I am in the midst of reading five books & writing half a dozen poems with subjects ranging from the Middle Ages to the California Indians– inclusive & I have lots to tell you about all of my friends & I want your sympathy & interest about everything!

Meanwhile believe me impatiently your friend

Emma Lazarus

Letter 7HdeKG

Emma Lazarus to Helena deKay Gilder
34 E. 57th St.
Nov. 11 (1880)

My dear Helena–

Your information in regard to Oliver Madox Brown was very interesting– & made clearer for me a lovely poem of Swinburne's, which I suppose you know– a "Birth Song" for Olivia Madre Rossetti.[39] "What a spendthrift nature is–" (as somebody has said)– to create & destroy such rare spirits before they have accomplished their mission– And what an indescribable, strange feeling of personal loss comes over me in reading of the abrupt termination of his so rich in promise. It hurts– doesn't it?

I wish you would tell me more about Mrs. Stillman when I see you.[40] She would have a strong interest for me– even if it were only for her beauty– I am sorry, but not altogether surprised that you could not read Prince Hohensteil.[41] My own conversion to Browning is much too recent for me to accuse of "heresy" anyone who does not exactly share my enthusiasm– & I know too that the sudden stimulus & encouragement one occasionally gets from a work of art is greatly a result of accident– Perhaps some day the "Savior of Society" will appeal to you as intimately & forcibly as it did to me– & perhaps it never will– In that case, something else will– & it is all the same. I know of a woman whose whole moral complexion was altered by reading—Sainte Beuve—Can you imagine anything as emotional?

I can all the more easily understand your impatience with Browning when you tell me you have been reading Sophocles. The worst thing about reading the Greeks or the Orientals is that they make modern and Western poetry seem either clammy or cold. To go back to Browning, I rejoice heartily with you, in his admiration of "Hesperus." Genius is *not* self-supporting, whatever people may say or think– I have been struck lately in reading Shelley's Life with how completely even he was crushed & silenced from time to time by the want of popular, or rather sympathetic recognition– A generous, appreciative word from the greatest living poet to your brother outweighs many Atlantic Monthlys- & drivelling "Evening Posts." I am glad you recognize the importance of an audience– This is one of my chief bones of contention with Maria who seems to think artists can live on air– & accuses me of worshiping mammon & bowing down to vulgar Success, because I don't agree with her– No! I don't think Maria has the faintest suspicion that her brother Aleck is anything but the best & most brilliant of men–[42] If she looked badly when you saw her, I should attribute it to her anxiety at that time about little Bevan for whom she was much distressed. She is very variable in looks– some days she looks extremely young & pretty to me– & again for no apparent reason, haggard & old– Sophie Ward told me she was so much struck by the contrast between your appearance & Maria's– seeing you together– & still more so by Rodman's magnificent bloom as compared with the delicate little Bevan's–[43] Mrs. Aleck Oakey is well & happy & definitely in love with her illusion, so I don't think we need waste our sympathy on her– she seems like a very sweet little woman.

I had such a pleasant visit at Morristown last week where I spent a very bright summer day with your lovely friend Olivia Ward–[44] I envy you knowing each other so long & so well– what jolly times you must have had together– I am looking forward to seeing her tomorrow before she goes down to you– I am glad you enjoyed Mr. & Mrs. Tom Ward– I think there is something very sweet & real about Sophie particularly when you see her with her husband. Only she so often does herself injustice. I hope to see you again before you drag yourself to your friends & I want to see that splendid owl & that Persian rug! I am afraid you will be bored or tired by too many visitors– Josephine enjoyed seeing you so much yesterday but she feared it was too much for you to have so many at one time. I don't see why if I can't make buttonholes, I cannot be used for any other than purely ornamental purposes. If I come down again, why cannot I look over your Millet mss?[45] I have done so much of that sort of thing, especially with translations– & it would be a pleasure to me, & save Mr. Gilder some extra work. You have very little confidence in me! If I don't want to be like Tennyson's Brook, I had better stop now–

Affectionately your friend

Emma Lazarus

Of course I shall not go to see you without letting you know before hand–

The Editors of the "Literary Remains" of Oliver Madox Brown record that while in his 14th year, & before it had ever been supposed by his family that

he so much as understood the meaning of the word sonnet, this truly marvelous boy had produced a number of sonnets which he unfortunately destroyed
in a fit of morbid irritability or bashfulness caused by their being shown to a
few friends. One of these however written for a picture of Mrs. Stillman (then
Sparlati) & printed on the gilt of the frame has survived— It is as follows:

> Leaning against the window, rapt in thought,
> Of what sweet past do thy soft brown eyes dream,
> That so expressionlessly sweet they seem?
> Oh what great image hath thy fancy wrought
> To wander round & gaze at it? Or doth might
> Of legend move thee, o'er which eyes oft stream,
> Telling of some sweet saint who rose supreme
> From Martyrdom to God, with glory fraught!
> Or art thou listening to the gondolier
> Whose song is dying in the waters wide,
> Trying the faintly-sounding tune to hear
> Before it mixes with the rippling tide?
> Or dost thou think of one that comes not near,
> And whose false heart, in thine, thine own doth chide?
>   (by Oliver M. Brown)

Letter 8HdeKG

Emma Lazarus to Helena deKay Gilder
34 East 57th St.
Dec. 16th [1880]

My dear Helena—

   Are you able to read letters— particularly very badly written ones? & do you
care to know how your friends have thought of you, have sympathized with
your suffering, & rejoice now in your returning health & strength?[46] I have
heard frequently about you since you were taken ill, & always steadily improving account until finally a letter Maria showed me from her sister Kate, represented you as brave & almost as strong as ever. I think of you a great deal &
wonder how the long days & nights go by for you— Everyone speaks of the
courage & patience you have shown— What a comfort it is to have succeeded
in conquering ourselves to make trouble lighter for those we love. As soon as
I think you are well & interested enough to hear of what goes on outside of
your sick room, I shall write you <u>all my news</u>! I am looking forward to seeing
your Millet book, which I hear looks very prettily. Isn't it about time for it to
be out? I am afraid poor Mr. Gilder has been too occupied & anxious to feel

half the pleasure & pride he should have felt in the Second Edition of his Poems– Please give him my kindest regards– Forgive me if I have tired or bored you– believe in the warm affection of your friend

Emma Lazarus

Emma Lazarus to Helena deKay Gilder
34 E. 57th St.
December 29th 1880

I was delighted, dear Helena, to hear that you were so well as to be able to go downstairs for your Christmas dinner & enjoy it with your family. I trust you had a happy day & I wish you from my heart all that you can wish yourself during the coming year. Of course you have heard the surprising news of Maria's engagement.[47] Her friends can only rejoice that she has at last found what she needed to give her rest, stability & happiness. She is radiant with joy– as you probably know, for doubtless you will have seen her before you receive this. I wonder whether you will see Mr. Dewing at the same time. I think he is very attractive– handsome, young & with an air of refinement & intelligence. I don't know anything about his work– from all I hear I should imagine it was very much in the same direction as Maria's & their art-theories seem exactly in accord– Sarah Bernhardt above Salome, Chopin above Beethoven, & Tintoretto above everybody! They have not known each other two months & yet one need only see them together to be persuaded that they are not only sincerely in love, but have apparently been born & bred for each other. I have seen so much of Maria during the past year, & this engagement is so strange, so sudden that I have not been able to forget since it was announced to me on Christmas Day. I should love to talk to you about that & many other things– I miss you dreadfully from New York, & yet if you were here, I suppose I should not dare break in upon your own heavy troubles & beautiful resignation with my unhappy egotism. When will you have the strength to write me again? Please give me as much of your affection as you can spare– You don't know how much I need it– I am so lonely & discouraged–

fondly your friend

Emma Lazarus

Letter 10HdeKG

Emma Lazarus to Helena deKay Gilder
Monday
Jany. 10, '81

My dear Helena—

Rodman's letter was perfection! I could hear his rich, delicious little voice, as I read & especially could I hear him chuckle over the idea of an egg walking & sitting on walls! I wish you would please give him an extra kiss for me, & tell him I received his beautiful letter. If it had not been for the universal dissolution of the cloud, snow, mud & apparently even of solid sleet, I should have given myself the pleasure of seeing you today. I saw yesterday Olivia Ward who suggested that we should go down together & take you by surprise. But of course this weather puts it out of the question, & as she may not be able to come to town again for some time, our visit will have to be indefinitely deferred. I see that the Staten Island boats yesterday were stopped on account of the floating ice, so perhaps it is as well that we should not risk being "quartered" upon you— when you might not even be able to accommodate two at a time. I often think of your long, unbroken monotonous days which must be so full of sad thoughts,— & I wish so much I could go in & make a little change for you— I hope you felt better for your first drive in the open air. Long imprisonment in the house is almost intolerable to me.

The Oakey family had, as you supposed, a cruel shock in the death of poor Frank— What a sad, wasted barren life, it seems, through no fault or weakness of his own— To subject himself to a fatal climate & finally die among strangers— homesick & alone— for what? Even if he had succeeded in accumulating a fortune, what a mockery it would seem to set it in the scale against the rise of such a fate as he has met. Poor old Mr. & Mrs. Oakey bear up with great fortitude, though it is not only a terrible grief to them but one for which they were wholly unprepared. I have not seen them, nor Maria— her cousin tells me she is calm & composed— It is, as you say, a dark cloud upon her happiness, but on the other hand, her happiness enables her to bear it in a way which I scarcely think she could otherwise have done— In a certain way too, I think this misfortune reconciles her parents to her engagement— that which they looked upon a week ago as something to cry over,[48] & a personal loss to themselves, they now see as a source of consolation for them all— I am so delighted with Olivia Ward— Each time I see her I feel more strongly the influence of her sweet, rare charm— Perhaps it is because you have so often prepared me not to find her "intellectual," that I am agreeably surprised at her brightness, her good sense & her intelligent sympathy— but it is not for these that I like her– but for that indefinable magnetism & fascination about her personality which only one or two among all the women I have known, have exercised over me– That little French verse you repeated to me describes it exactly & I have often since wished to hear it again.– It would take a "great relief off my mind" (as I heard someone express it the other day) to talk to you of Maria. I am already quite used to the idea of her engagement, & not only think it the most natural thing in the world, but heartily rejoice in it– But I confess that my first feelings when I heard of it were so mixed with perplexity, amazement & discouragement that I did not know what to think. I know the world so little & have so few temptations myself, that I am afraid I often judge & condemn others with undue harshness– then I have reactions of remorse when I say to myself that in daring to judge I am infinitely worse than those who have done what I happen to disapprove of– then reappears my virtuous indignation– & the only thing I can think of is to state my problem to someone whom I trust & care for, & who can set me straight again. This is one of the reasons why I am so impatient to see you again– You have a particularly quieting effect upon me, & life seems to round & smooth itself when I am with you– I know this must seem stupid to you, because you have so many problems of your own, & have suffered so much. It is so, nonetheless– I cannot explain it– but I feel it all the same.

I saw your Mother the other day. I was surprised to find her looking so well. Though she said she had not all her strength yet, she did not seem as if she had been ill a day– she had color in her cheeks & looked pretty & young. Do you see that there is a new life of Fromentin out, which they say compares unfavorably with Sensier's delightful biographies.[49] I am eager to see the Rousseau.[50] Do you know Henri Regnault's correspondence?[51] I have it & will lend it to you if you wish– It is very charming– full of life & color–

Trusting to see you soon–

Affectionately your friend

Emma Lazarus

I am afraid from what I say about your Mother you may fancy she has been ill again– She has not, but I had not seen her since the last attack of asthma several weeks ago.

Letter 11HdeKG

Emma Lazarus to Helena deKay Gilder
34 E. 57th St.
Sunday afternoon
Jany. 23, [1881]

You cannot imagine, my dear Helena, how I enjoyed my two beautiful long, quiet days with you & how much better I felt for having talked with you. My family thought me half-crazy to have come to town in such a storm, but I did not want to tire you out & make you feel as if you never wanted to see me again, & thanks to Mr. Gilder's kind care of me, I reached home safely in spite of the elements. It <u>was</u> a terrible day– the worst I ever was out– the Island looked beautiful with its bowed down crystal trees & snowwhite ground– but New York! It would require a Dantesque vocabulary to give you any idea of the dirt, slime, frozen mud & glassy sleet & grime of our streets. I have not been out of doors since– as for the Review Club & the dinner to which I had promised to go, I was only too glad to give them both up & to stay under the shelter of my own roof– I gave your kind message to "those of my sisters who take interest in you"– & they were very much obliged & Sarah said she always took the warmest interest in you–[52] You need not have the slightest fear of being forgotten by any member of the family– I had a long visit on Friday afternoon with the author of the "Frivolous Girl"– Mr. Grant–[53] He seems like such a very earnest, simple & refined young man– quite untouched as yet by that dreadful "commercial spirit" which we spoke of the other evening as invading nearly all artists & literary men after a while– I wish you had read his little sketch of New York Society– I think it has such brilliant promise, though I am afraid now if you read it, you will expect too much & be proportionately disappointed. I have come home to <u>hard work</u>– finding three books to read & review by Tuesday for your sister-in-law. I fear the "Critic" will give me more employment than I am capable of.[54] I don't believe I have ever really worked in my life & as soon as I feel that a certain thing is expected of me by a certain time, I get a panic & don't know how to do anything. How anyone lives by writing I cannot imagine. I send you Regnault & Dominique– & hope you will tell me how you like them, as I think they will both please you greatly.[55] After you have read them, if you are still in need of books, & care to have them, I will send you another volume of Sully Prudhomme, & my translation of Theocritus which you said you had not read.[56] I trust you will not have the time to get very lonely or depressed again before you come up to town yourself where you will have plenty to occupy you & many to welcome you– I felt when I came home from your house as I imagine a good Catholic feels after Confession– why it should be such an immense relief to tell things I don't know– but it seemed as if your gentle sympathy had taken from me more than one of my fancied burdens. Accept a thousand thanks & believe me devotedly your friend

Emma Lazarus

Give my love & kisses to Rodman

P.S. Just as I finished the accompanying letter, came in "Tom" to take me out for a walk, in one of his guiltless & most amiable moods.[57] I wish you could have heard him talk about you! There was nothing too poetical & admiring for him to say & I only don't write it for fear of making your blushes uncomfortable. About Mr. Gilder, he went on in the same strain– his "warm humanity, his unselfishness & heartiness– the kind of man to put his arm around your neck & call you Tom!" "The most brotherly man he knew!" Do you mind my repeating all this? or is it not pleasant to you as it would be to me to know that you have the genuine sympathy of a man who rings so true himself? He is a Jingle Bell.

Fondly yours

Emma Lazarus

Letter 12 HdeKG

Emma Lazarus to Helena deKay Gilder
34 E. 57th St.
Sunday
January 30, 1881

My dear Helena,

I know you will not be surprised to hear from me so soon again– for as I love to write you & you like to receive letters, what could be more natural? Besides, I wish to send you while it is still fresh the enclosed clipping from the "Nation" which you may not have seen– about Mr. Nadal's article in Scribner's. I thought all that Mr. Nadal said was charming, shrewd, clever, wryly humorous, & with that delightful flair about its literary style peculiarly his own among writers of today & yet which always faintly recalls the best work of Lamb. The "reply" to it which I enclose is so flat, stupid & clumsy that it really enrages one to think a man who can write as tediously & diffusely as this shall dare to sit in judgement upon or attempt to compete with so graceful & delightful a writer as Mr. Nadal. Don't take the trouble to save it or return it to me– I only send it to you as a curiosity– not because it interests me. Olivia Ward has been here this week at the Johnstons'– She came up & spent the morning at my house & then we went together to the concert.[58] I find <u>learning to know</u> Olivia Ward one of the pleasures of my Winter. I expect to see her again this afternoon, & tomorrow she will go back to Morristown, but as she appears to have prospects for working with Mr. LaFarge, she may possibly be in town before long again.[59] Maria I have not seen since I was with you. She is <u>completely absorbed</u> besides being difficult to find at home, & I feel as if I had almost lost sight of her. I am afraid I am a hardened sinner! My Conscience has not even pricked me since I came up from Staten Island. What do you think about "Nimrod?"[60] I have read it many times, & never once without discovering new beauties in it. I have tried, most unsatisfactorily to myself, to write a review of it for the Critic. I am afraid I shall have to accept the world's opinion after fighting against it all my life– that personal friends <u>can not</u> fairly criticize each other's work. I half wished, for the moment, in my zeal for poetry that I had never known Mr. deKay nor you nor any of your family! Not at all because the fear of paining my friends made me unduly anxious to gloss over what I considered the blemishes of the poem, but from a far more cowardly reason– the fear that the sincere enthusiasm which I feel for the work & my exalted opinion of its weight & importance would be falsely ascribed to personal friendship– As it is I have not said all that I wanted to say & I suppose I have more than enough to give color to this imputation. Fortunately what I say or don't say in a newspaper notice is not of the slightest consequence to anybody but myself– if the poem is what I think it is. Did you enjoy your visit from Annie Holland?[61] I saw her on Tuesday & she told me she expected to spend the day with you—The only news with me is that I have been vaccinated & have a dreadfully lame area. It is exceedingly painful & disagreeable– but everyone seems to think it necessary. I hope Mr. Gilder's is all right by this time. If I dared I would send my love to Mr. Gilder & tell him how dying I am to know the decision about the *Scribner's Magazine*.[62] I do hope some conclusion has been arrived at & that he has a respite from such excessive work & dreary squabbling.

I am going this evng to Mrs. Sam Ward's– How I wish you were here to take part in some of the New York pleasures & brighten yourself up once more. I rejoice each week to think you are nearer coming back to your own home.

Affectionately your friend,

Emma Lazarus

Letter 13HdeKG

Emma Lazarus to Helena deKay Gilder
34 E. 57th St.
Sunday, Feby. 6, [1881]

You cannot imagine, my dear Helena, how delighted I was to get your interesting & affectionate letter– I am only sorry you should have been troubled by
anything you told me when we were together– I assure you that you cannot
only place implicit reliance upon my respect for your confidence, but upon
my wretched memory which has enabled me long since completely to forget
any details which you may regret having mentioned. As for the facts & the
mutual relations existing between all the persons you spoke of, I naturally
knew them all before– & if you have any affection for me, I wish you would
not regret having talked to me from your heart, or having told me anything
that would make me understand & love you better than I already did. I am so
glad you enjoyed Regnault as much as I thought you would– I have no idea of
translating his book– Evidently the same quality impressed you which chiefly
struck me– the wonderful <u>youthfulness</u> of the man– Did you ever meet with a
more exuberant vitality, a more delicious freshness of enjoyment? Every page
seems sparkling with color, health, the glory of being alive, strong & well-
equipped in such a magnificent world as this! And that unnecessary, cruel,
frightful death– it is one of the crimes of fate, that one cannot forget or resign
oneself to.[63] Let me know when you have read Dominique & Sully-Prud-
homme & are ready for the other books & I will send them to you at once– I
trust your vaccination has not been as painful as mine was. It is a great bore &
very troublesome & then there are always sceptics to say it is of no use after
all– I have only had a glimpse of Olivia since she was with you, but am looking
forward to her coming up this afternoon to spend the rest of the day with me.
She evidently enjoyed her visit to you as much as you enjoyed having her. The
more I see her the more I am struck by the contrast between herself & Maria–
It seems strange that they should be friends, & almost incredible that they
should belong to the same family– I am very happy at having recovered my
enjoyment of music once more– A song of Schubert's sung by Henschel was
the first thing to restore my blunted sensibilities & the Leonora Overture last
evng. made me once again realize that music is a good thing. Did you ever
hear Schubert's song– "Ganymeed"– & did you who don't care for Goethe,(?)
ever read the exquisitely beautiful poem of his for which the song is composed?
If you don't remember it– it is one of the semi-classical unrhymed poems–
please get out your Goethe– look over it & see what a great man he is– Read
too the "Prometheus" which immediately precedes it, & which I suppose of
course you know. The beauty & variety of melody & sentiment that Schubert

has put into that "Ganymeed Song" are like an enchantment. Last evng. I heard the wonderful Brazilian boy-violinist Dengremont–[64] Without making any allowance for his age, he is a charming & sympathetic artist. He has a noble little head which would, I think, fascinate a painter, & there is something very touching about his childish air & extraordinary talent. It is picturesque, to say the least, to see him stand up before the audience, in his little knicker-bockers & his boyish costume, his coat glittering with decorations– medals, chains & ribbons– swaying his little bow like a master while the old graybeard drudges of the orchestra look on in amazement– I am fast exhausting my paper, not to speak of your time & eyes, without having said a word about "Nimrod." I want to tell you how extravagant my father's opinion of it is– I don't believe you or Mr. Gilder or your Mother, who must all fancy yourselves biased somewhat by your affection, have any higher opinion of it than my father has who is naturally absolutely unprejudiced. He says it suggests to him in its power & beauty only the greatest masters & after his first reading of it, he not only raved about it just as I had done after hearing it in your Studio, but began immediately over again at the first page, & liked it better on a second reading than he had done at the first. I hope this is an earmark of the impression it is going to make upon greater authorities than he.

What do you think is my latest "discovery"! The School for Scandal! I went to see it yesterday for the first time in my life– It is admirably put upon the stage at Wallach's, & I had the daring inclination to make up my mind that it was a very clever play– I hope to see Salvini in "Macbeth" this week & am in a state of delightful anticipation–[65] The Review Club is in a very flourishing condition– This Friday meeting was particularly pleasant– "George Eliot's Writings" were the subject for discussion, & we had a very agreeable general conversation– I think you would get interested if you belonged to it– Don't think I am never going to stop– here I am at the end–

With kindest regards to Mr. Gilder, & much love for yourself

Affectionately your friend

Emma Lazarus

Josephine asked me when I wrote to give you the most affectionate message on her part– & wound up rather tamely by saying she had a "great respect for you!"

Emma Lazarus to Helena deKay Gilder
34 E. 57th St.
Tuesday,
Feby. 15, [1881]

My dear Helena–

I was delighted, as I always am, to see your beautiful <u>round</u> handwriting yesterday– if you only knew how eagerly I read again & again your sympathetic letters! What you say about "Dominique" is very true– he is a morbid & irritating character– but the book is written with such exquisite literary skill & in such a beautiful style, that it completely fascinated me– I don't think you will agree with me, but notwithstanding the great <u>superficial</u> unlikeness, I find many marked traits of resemblance between the hero of this novel & our friend Tom Ward– Some of the former's "Confessions" reminded me so startlingly of the latter, that the book (which he himself gave me) seemed almost like a confidence & a page torn from his own life– Please don't repeat this theory of mine to anyone– it is only that I know Tom Ward so well that I recognize some of his peculiarities even in this foreign disguise–[66] & I don't think he would like to hear that I seriously compared him with anyone who is so <u>unlike</u> him in many [sic] most important points. You say nothing about Sully-Prud-homme– but I send you another volume which I think you will like better than the first– & you can compare it to the volume of Coppee whom I do not find nearly as <u>strong</u> as Prudhomme though very graceful & poetical. Does not Coppee look like Mr. Gilder? Read especially in the Theocritus the XV idyll– I think that is the number– it is the conversation between Gorgo & Praxius– It is the most curiously modern thing I ever read. How the critics of the N.Y. Herald, etc– would pull it to pieces for its anachronisms if it were published now as a picture of the antique! The Second Idyll is my favorite– though it loses inestimably in a prose-translation– My little library is not yet exhausted & if you care for more after you have read all this poetry, I will be so glad to lend you whatever I have– I thought if all went well & the day were fair on Saturday & you did not expect Mrs. Carter this week, I should like to go down & see you & stay overnight if you could accommodate me?[67] I name Saturday because my sister is going down that day to see a friend of hers on the Island & it would be convenient for me to go with her– but of course, do not hesitate to let me know if it is <u>not</u> convenient for you– If I don't hear from you, & circumstances are propitious at home– I will go to you some time on Saturday– You cannot imagine how delighted I was to hear there was a chance of your coming to town yesterday for the Salvini Matinee– I do hope you succeeded in getting a seat & enjoyed him as I have– What did Mr. Gilder tell you about his "Macbeth?" It has haunted me ever since, not with horror, as I expected– for the chief impression it made, was of its magnificent pictur-esqueness. Such majesty of bearing & gesture, such gorgeousness of tawny gold in hair & beard & costume and such an imposing stature & proportions, combined to make up a picture that I will never forget. And what do you think of his voice? or rather his <u>voices</u>, for he has a complete orchestra of them– & I find that certain intonations remain in my memory like strains of music– I suppose Mr. Gilder has repeated to you all the "points" of this extraordinary performance, which I consider fully equal to the best of his roles– but it cannot be described & must be seen to be imagined– I am very sorry to hear of the death of Mr. O'Shaughnessy who must have been an ambitious & rather promising young poet.[68] It shocked me all the more that I had never before heard him spoken of in a serious tone! Do you know what a strange effect that produces? It is so strange to have comedy so suddenly change into tragedy. I had not heard of either of poor Mrs. Lathrop's afflic-tions & I can well understand how much you must feel for her–[69] Is Mr. Gilder really going to Washington & for how long? I have an invitation to go & could go at any time. It would be great fun to go there with him– Please tell him I wrote to Ellen Emerson yesterday & told her everything– "Money," "Scrib-ner's English reputation" & everything I could think of to induce her to yield up whatever papers her father may have– I think it is a most brilliant idea to get up such a number of the magazine & will look forward to it with eager interest.[70] What a fine cut that was of Regnault's head in the "Critic." My sister Josephine will translate his letters if there is any chance of publication– She has written to Mr. Osgood already–[71] I never see Maria anymore– All the time she is not making love, she is making dresses, & is rapt from the world. I was greatly surprised to hear that she is to be married <u>in Church</u>, with all possible ceremony, & "<u>Azaleas all around</u>." She has talked to me so emphatically, even violently against religious observances, that it scarcely seemed possible she would submit to any more ceremony of the kind than was absolutely necessary in her own house– I am such an idiot– I go on being surprised when no inconsistency in that quarter should any longer produce the slightest effect upon me. If you are thirsting for music, as you say, I wish you would come up to town some day & go with me to hear anything that may be worth going to– I should so like to be with you at any of the good matinees– though I don't know of anything at the moment to suggest– Perhaps we can arrange something when I see you– I have been seeing a good many people– for me-lately– lunching & dining out several times a week– & taking a great interest in life– I don't know when I have felt so happy, so satisfied with my fate (<u>for the time being</u>) & so interested in people, books, art, music– everything that is to be enjoyed– It seems like a silly thing to say– but I so often say just the reverse that I take pleasure in confessing it. Besides, I know well enough that neither the mood nor the circumstances can last long– so I want to make the most of both. I date my restoration to health & ordinary sanity from my visit to you– I had been in a dreadful frame of mind– Trusting to see you soon

believe me

affectionately your friend

Emma Lazarus

Emma Lazarus to Helena deKay Gilder
34 E. 57th St.
Wednesday
February 23rd, 1881

Were you dreadfully tired last evening– dear Helena– or did you not find the Obelisk Entertainment as utterly unsatisfactory, flat, unprofitable & muddy as I did–[72] The world was all "rind without the melon" for me when I came home– & I wondered how you succeeded in forcing your way through the crowd & slush back to your boy & your home– I am so sorry not to have had so much as a glimpse of you again even for goodbye– How old & ill poor Dr. Holland looked,[73] & how disgusted you must have been to be separated by him from Mr. Gilder– I want to congratulate you about the Hymn– I think it is perfect– written in so noble & simple a style that it leaves nothing to be desired & seems just fitted to the music of the stately old chorale– I think it one of the strongest & finest things Mr. Gilder has ever done– & when I realize the extreme difficulty of doing such a piece of work <u>on command</u>, I am the more impressed with its singular force & beauty.

Was it not a mistaken impression of mine that Mrs. Sidney deKay's "theatricals" take place on Monday evening?[74] She said the 1st of March– & that will be Tuesday– I am hopelessly <u>mixed</u> about it. But as I said I would go to you on Monday, (if I could go at all) I will, <u>unless I hear from you to the contrary</u>. One thing I <u>was</u> mistaken about—I told you Tom Ward had gone to Texas– I misunderstood Nina Howard to say so the other day—but she said a friend of theirs– (<u>Mrs. Todd</u>) had gone & I misunderstood. Tom is flourishing about New York as usual. With much love, believe me

Affectionately your friend

Emma Lazarus

34 East 57th St.
Wednesday

Letter 16HdeKG

Emma Lazarus to Helena deKay Gilder
Saturday
Feb'y. 27 [1881]
34 East 57th Street

My dear Helena–

Many thanks for your kind little letter & for your assurance of welcome to me "with or without philosophy," with or without theatricals. If I did as I felt inclined I would go to you again next week, but as there is now no sufficient reason why I should so soon again, & I don't expect on Monday to be in condition to move about very comfortably, I think I had best give up the idea– & wait until a more favorable opportunity or else until you come up to town, to see you– I am so much obliged to you for your lovely encouraging words about Annie–[75] I cannot tell you how proud & delighted she was when I read them to her– & how grateful to you for taking the trouble to say them. She is like me– very distrustful of herself & very dependent upon outside encouragement from people whose opinions she values. Before I plunge into either philosophy or poetry, I want to tell you that I asked the address of the man at the Battery who sells Japanese China. His name is Lewis & he is a gentleman– an importer– not an ordinary shopkeeper– his address is 44 Broadway. I believe he has a very beautiful stock– not only of Japanese & Chinese but also of East Indian wares, all of which he sells at wholesale prices.[76] I hope you will be able to find what you want there. I don't wonder you are tired after your day in town– No– I never pretended to have imbibed my philosophy at Concord or anywhere else– In so many ways I am so much duller than other people, especially in that of receiving & profiting by impressions– that if I didn't have a streak of talent in me (!) I would be generally considered what at present a few people know me to be, a Born-Natural. As I write this & don't say it– you know that it is true, & that I am not fishing for compliments. Apropos of Concord, please tell Mr. Gilder it is no wonder we don't hear from Ellen Emerson– What do you think she is doing? Giving a ball– in the Town Hall at Concord!! She is to celebrate her birthday (some time this week I believe) by receiving two or three hundred of her friends & acquaintances from country & city, at a "Calico" party.[77] It must be a great excitement for the quaint little village–

I think Mr. Gilder's Hymn is not only considered fine by the Connoisseurs, but destined for popularity as well. A very un-literary but fairly cultivated woman, who did not know I knew him, told me she had wanted to go to the

Obelisk celebration for nothing but to hear that "magnificent Hymn"– That was <u>her</u> idea of poetry & religion, & she did not know when she had seen anything that had made so powerful an impression upon her.– I am actually going to enclose for you a copy of the Hebrew Melody of Byron which I spoke to you about– As soon as you see it you will probably remember every word of it, but I think it is so beautiful that I want to recite it to you.– I went out on Thursday evng. to meet my "fate" and greatly to my disappointment he was not there & had not even been invited. My friend had given up the hope of inducing him to make even that much of an appearance in Society– so I have to resume my position of old maid <u>ad infinitum</u>– unless I inherit a fortune or turn out a genius like Miss Coutts or George Eliot– Maria's wedding has been postponed as late as the middle of April– She finds it impossible to prepare her trousseau before then. I have shamefully neglected her– but I don't believe she even knows it. I went yesterday to hear some good music with your brother Charlie– Handel's music & Milton's Allegro & Perseus & afterwards we saw some delicious Corots– The Concerts were bad, but the composition & the poetry made up for the poor performance– Don't forget that the first hint of anything else really good in the way of music is given here in the daytime, you have promised to come up. You must have had a delightful day with Mr. Eaton–[78] is he making a portrait of you? I am awfully sorry to give up the hope of seeing you & Mr. Gilder next week– Please give him kindest remembrances, & accept much love for yourself from your friend

Emma Lazarus

I have read Lewis impressions of Salvini & I don't think much of them. I had a nice letter this morning from Mrs. Gilchrist– who asks to be remembered to Mr. Gilder. She has been very ill with asthma & bronchitis, but is now better. I find the nightgown of mine which you like cost $2.25– I got some very nice ones at A Straus the other day for $1.95– they have others still cheaper & very good.[79] The $2.25 one was <u>handmade</u>.

HEBREW MELODY

Oh! Snatched away in beauty's bloom,
On thee shall press the ponderous tomb;
But on thy turf shall roses rear
Their leaves, the earliest of the year,
And the wild cypress wave in tender gloom.

And oft by on yon blue gushing stream,
Shall sorrow lean her drooping head,
And feed deep thought with many a dream,
And lingering pause, & lightly tread–
Fond wretch! As if her step disturbed the dead.

Away! We know that tears are vain,
That death nor heeds nor hears distress.
Will this unteach us to complain?
or make one mourner weep the less.
And then– who tell'st me to forget
Thy looks are wan, thy eyes are wet.
　　　　Byron

Letter 17HdeKG

Emma Lazarus to Richard Watson Gilder
34 East 57th St.
Thursday, Mar. 3rd, 1881

My dear Mr. Gilder–

It was only today that I received a charming letter from Ellen Emerson– I feared it was of little use to ask anything of the Sage of Concord for a New York magazine–[80] She tells me she has written to you, & received your note in return. She asks me to tell you in answer to this that she "thinks it pretty certain her father means to never publish anymore. He reached that decision more than a year ago." So your beautiful project is vetoed irrevocably– I am more than a little sorry for it was a brilliant idea– As I know you are interested in Mr. Emerson even if he <u>won't</u> subscribe to <u>Scribner's</u>. I will add that Ellen reports him in excellent condition– taking long walks, bravely enduring the cold winter & now very much interested in every memorial word that is written about Mr. Carlyle–[81] He is in daily receipt of English & American papers containing notices of Carlyle & these keep him occupied. She says he is no worse than when I saw him– I am delighted to hear it, as I had fancied in my usual gloomy way, that he was no longer capable of receiving new impressions. I am looking forward to seeing you in town <u>very, very</u> soon– & am very impatient– So the private theatricals are without me after all. I was dying to see them. Give my best to Helena & believe me your friend

Emma Lazarus

Emma Lazarus to Helena deKay Gilder
(March 1881)
34 E. 57th St.
Saturday

My dear Helena–

I hope you have not forgotten your promise to come to town & hear some music with me– Can you come on Friday & go to the Philharmonic Rehearsal at two o'clk? I am not <u>perfectly sure</u> of the programme, but I believe it is the same as that of the Brooklyn Philharmonic this week– which is exceptionally good– one of Berlioz' "Faust" music, a Schubert symphony, a Wagner overture, & <u>Joseffy</u>![82] I am very anxious to have you hear him, & he is going to play that beautiful Concerto of Schumann. Do make an effort to come– I am sure you will enjoy it– & please let me know as soon as you possibly can, so that I may lose no time in securing our tickets. If you can come, I will meet you at your mother's anytime you say, & spare your journey up to 57th St. Did you see the article in the "Nation" on Millet which I enclose? I would not believe the English language capable of having the whole meaning so utterly washed out of it as the Nation succeeds in doing. I don't understand one word of this notice, & I trust you will prove more discerning. I received a note from Mr. Gilder this morning. I am delighted at the prospect of his having something from Emerson after all.[83] Will you please thank him for it for me, & ask him if he cannot please send me on a postal card, the <u>number of pages</u> to which he wishes me to confine my article on Salvini?[84] I have no idea at present, & hate to work in the dark with a chance of having the ms. cut in two afterwards. Salvini wrote me a charming letter & has furnished me with ample material for an interesting article. I wish it could be illustrated by photographs of his great parts–

I have lots more to say but shall wait until I see you– I am so glad to hear you like your new home & am longing to see you in it. <u>Please don't say "no" about Friday</u>.

Affectionately your friend

Emma Lazarus

Letter 19HdeKG

Emma Lazarus to Helena deKay Gilder
Monday, March 14, 1881
34 E. 57th St.

My dear Helena–

I wanted to write you a long letter today, telling you how much I had enjoyed my visit to you, & what a happy self-oblivious time I had had with Carlyle in the boat & in the car[85]– & this morning, everything personal & near seems to be knocked into utter insignificance by the tragic news that fills the papers, of the poor old Czar's assassination.[86] Isn't it horrible to think of the two Liberators of their people in one generation, butchered by the very ones who owe them most gratitude? Any great public crime seems to shock me with double force since my own realization in my first youth, of such horrors– or, I wonder if everyone else has this morning, on reading the papers, the same sick feeling of pain & sympathy & terror that makes my iron heart so full– I found all well at home yesterday– nobody had thought anything of my prolonged stay, & would not have been surprised if I had waited on till today– But I knew I had done wisely to break away from your own & Mr. Gilder's sympathetic society– for I have a great deal to do this morning & an early engagement. I was not invited to the S. G. Wards' last evening– but did not care much for anything but Carlyle. The book is like a magnificent poem. I trust you will find your mother still in town today & will accomplish all you have to do. I cannot tell you how much good my little visits to you do me– Each time I go to you, I seem to get rid of all the little worrying trifles that prey upon me, & come home fresh & cheerful again– I suppose it is the perfect sympathy, the change of atmosphere & the rest- which have so strong an effect on me.

I was glad to know it was not my great . . . for your brother's . . . which made me sympathize so much with Mr. Gilder's touchingly beautiful poem- I read it to two of my sisters, on whom it made precisely the same impression it had on me- They thought it perfectly fascinating. I shall not show it to anyone else- as I don't know what Mr. Gilder wants to do with it . . . a thousand thanks, dear Helena, for all your loveliness to me, & the sincere affection of your friend

Emma Lazarus

Emma Lazarus to Helena deKay Gilder
Thursday,
March 17, 1881

My dear Helena–

   Don't be surprised at hearing from me so soon again– I did not half say all
I wished to the other day, because I was really in a strange excitement, & I
want to talk to you about several things. I am counting the days before you
get back to town– & do hope your arrival will not be again postponed. I was
very sorry to hear of your brother Sidney's being ill in your house– I trust you
have not had any cause for anxiety about him, & that he is well once more. Of
course you received your Carlyle which I returned to the office on Monday. I
bought a copy for myself at the same time, as it is a book I don't wish to be
without. I had not half finished it when I returned it & I am enjoying slowly
every word– It makes a singular impression upon me– as if it were a special
confidence bringing me into more intimate & personal relations with the
writer than almost any book I have ever read. I hate to think of ordinary
people– the people who think Carlyle a failure "because he was poor"– having
the privilege of reading it at all– though I suppose it makes no difference for
they won't understand it. Every now & then you knock up against a rock of
prejudice- as when he speaks of that "blackguard Heine" having "no real
wit," & of the folly of "nigger emancipation"– but the general tone is so noble
as to seem like an epic poem– rather than a prose account of a hard & rugged
life– With marked differences, there is much in his portraiture of his idolized
wife that suggests You– so that I have you constantly before me when I read.
I am sure you cannot help feeling it yourself when you read of her relation
to & faith in her husband. There is one sentence of hers quoted which I can
hear you say, "Years after her marriage when the world began to admire her
husband, she gave a little half-scornful laugh & said– 'They tell me things as if
they were new, that I found out years ago.' " It is good to read about people
like this, & I find myself in a peculiarly soft & melting & thrilled mood all the
time I have the book in my hands.– My dinner at the S. G. Wards' which did
not come off on Sunday, took place yesterday. I will give you a hundred
guesses and you won't guess who else was there. Maria & her fiance! You know
she has not been in the houses of her most intimate friends since her brother's
death– & expressed herself greatly shocked at meeting me, my sister Josephine & your brother Charles, all in evening dress. She thought she was to be
quite alone with Mr. & Mrs. W. though why she should mind seeing me whom
she knows so well more than Sophie W. & Tom & Lily Howard & Mrs. Thorn

who were sure to be there, I can see no reason. The whole thing was such a palpable farce that I don't see how I have the energy or think it worthwhile to sit down & tell you about it this morning. Mr. Dewing looked handsome, but delicate & was not at all brilliant, though he may have been very charming. Maria looked better than I have ever seen her, dressed in deep mourning. She is to be married on the 18th of April. In the evening, Mr. Eaton came in– with whom I regretted very much not having had any talk. I like him so much– Mr. White, your architect was also there– but was merely introduced to me, & before I had spoken to him, he was called away.[87] I did not see him again– What a bright, jolly looking man he is. In my usual fashion, I could not resist telling your brother Charlie about "Mrs. Sherwood" & himself– so you can speak of it, if you please– He is so far above any other feeling than that of amusement at such stupidity, that I could not help telling him. Was I inconsiderate? Another thing I have on my mind to set you, or rather Mr. Gilder right about. I told Mr. Gilder the other day on the strength of an impression I had mistakenly received from my Irish maid, that the name of the Virgin was Mary Lazarus– according to Catholic tradition. I was all wrong, please tell him. It was Mary Magdalen (or rather Mary McDillon as the maid calls her) whose name was Lazarus. I always get mixed on social subjects even when they are so far back as to be scriptural- so tell him to please forgive my carelessness. Goodbye– Trusting to see you soon, believe me affectionately your friend,

Emma Lazarus

Letter 21HdeKG

Emma Lazarus to Helena deKay Gilder
Sunday
March 22, (1881)

My dear Helena–

I enclose a picture painted from memory which I trust you will not fail to recognize. I wish I could do it justice! I knew you & Mr. Gilder would be so madly jealous if I celebrated either one in verse, that I cut the Gordian knot by singing the beauty of your wonderful boy–[88] All the more, as I have had that picturesque scene by the fire in my memory ever since I witnessed it, & wished to record it for my own sake. I don't know how insignificant the merit of the verses may be– but I know you will value them quite apart from any literary deficiencies, for their association & the sincere affection of their author for you & your household. I know how awfully busy you are– Don't think you have to write me an acknowledgment for I trust to see you very soon– Mr. Gilder took me partly over your new home yesterday–[89] I think it is fascinating– it gave me the feeling that I too wanted to <u>play at keeping house</u>– That way madness lies! Affectionately your friend

Emma Lazarus

I am so glad to hear Mr. Eaton liked my portrait. If it is accepted at the Exhibition I am going to hire a seat in front of it, & watch it all day long – a la Narcissus. I had no idea I was so loved.

Letter 22HdeKG

Emma Lazarus to Helena deKay Gilder
34 East 57th St.
March 24 [1881]

My dear Helena–

I am afraid you will vote me a bore, if my scratchy letters don't stop, even when they are unanswered – but this is on business, & I can't help it! I had hoped, as no doubt you did too, that you would be in town before now – & I ordered to be sent to your Studio a plain old chair which I found at Sypher's–[90] I suppose it will arrive there some time tomorrow, & I write so that you may know where it comes from, & that there may be some place found to stow it away in until you are established in your own home, yourself. I hope it will give you as much pleasure to accept as it gives me to offer it, dear Helena – & to feel that I have a part in filling one little nook at least of your home – It is very simple & old fashioned & as uncomfortable as all our grandmothers' furniture apparently was – but you must take it for what it is, – a souvenir of my affectionate friendship.

I am so sorry to hear your return to New York has been again postponed. Are you not worn out with impatience & the discomforts of moving. The weather is simply <u>hideous</u> in town– & there is no such thing as comfort or pleasure anywhere until the dust subsides.

With kindest regards to Mr. Gilder & a kiss for little "<u>Bacchus</u>"[91]

your friend

Emma Lazarus

Letter 23HdeKG

Emma Lazarus to Helena deKay Gilder
34 East 57th St.
Sunday, June 26, 1881

My dear Helena–

The next best thing to being among the roses & orchards of Milton is to put oneself in communication with somebody who is there– so I shut myself up in my big city room to think of you & talk to you & try to imagine what you are doing this soft Summer morning.[92] Perhaps you are, after all, at . . . which I don't know– but I cannot be grateful enough for having seen Milton– it was all that you described & a great deal more besides, & I would not give up my one day there & the memory of it for anything that could be offered to me. I hope you reached there safely & comfortably on Thursday– & read through Geisman & Petrarch both– Of course, as soon as I had left you I wished more than ever that I could have gone with you– the sail must have been delightful, & you know how much it is to me to be with you– When I told my family how near I had come to running away with you, they thought it would have been a most sensible & charming thing to do! However, I was right to resist– for I could not have returned in time without over-fatiguing myself by far too much. I have been dreadfully tired in the past few days, & I don't know what would have become of me if I had undertaken more than I did– Our dear Olivia appeared bright & early, fresh as a flower on Friday morning– We had a happy time together, talking, indefinitely walking about,– shopping, lunching at Pursell's– sitting in Madison Square– like two tramps– to admire Farragut's statue which greatly delighted her, & resting & lounging at home.[93] We occasionally mentioned you!– & I hope you fully appreciate having two such friends. You must know just what we said without my telling you, but I don't believe you half understand how much you are to both of us. She asked me to give you many affectionate messages & to tell you how happy she was that you were going to Bernardsville–[94] It is so strange to me the way her "charme-in-time" is lost upon people who admire the worldly & conventional type, & whose finer sense is blunted by having lived much among worldly people. To such she has neither beauty, "style" nor cleverness– We know what we know– don't we?

Your brother Charlie came up & dined with us & we three had such a nice evening till past midnight in the dark drawing room by the open window– I don't know what he thought about it– but Olivia & I agreed that it was one of the pleasantest evenings we had ever spent– She left me yesterday– We went down to the University & paid a little visit to Maria & Tom who looked worn out with work & heat & <u>each other</u>– I must tell you, the reason why Olivia had not accepted my invitation at once was because I said in my letter something "in case she could not come"– which she immediately interpreted as meaning I did not wish her to come!– I had yesterday a most pathetically grateful note from our friend Annie McKim– so I escaped the interception of my own.[95] She says she is "all aglow with my kindness"– & speaks of herself as formerly being like a "kitten before its eyes are open, unable to see & appreciate the beautiful people whom she might have gone near enough to know– but she knows better now"– etc.– Poor girl! She mentions you most affectionately & gratefully & tells me of her enjoyment of her evening with you at the Concert. How do you get on with my Heine?– or haven't you had a chance to look at it?[96] I had such a kind note from Mr. Stedman about it– He had gone himself in the midst of his work to the Tribune office to see its getting a prompt & sympathetic review.[97] He said he would write it himself if he only knew German– but this being impossible, he had <u>nearly</u> extracted a promise from Colonel Hay to write it– At all events, it would receive immediate attention. I enclose the little quotation from Stendhal which evidently was the occasion of Heine's poem the Asra– It is curious. Don't forget when you write me to tell me how the poor little bandaged feet are– I trust they will be better soon– How is Rodman– are his eyes & his knee better? Please remember me most kindly to Mrs. Foote– How does Mrs. Hallock look in her new shawl?[98] I should love to see her. This is enough bad scribbling for today. So goodbye & believe me with sincere affection

Your friend

Emma Lazarus

My address will be care of Mrs. W.H. Draper[99]
Lenox, Mass.

Letter 24HdeKG

Emma Lazarus to Helena deKay Gilder
September 2nd, 1881
Chestnut Hill. Phila.

My dear Helena–

I was delighted to get your little letter last week, as I could not account for your long silence, & had no idea where & how you were. I had hardly thought it possible for you to write me while you were at the Wards', but after that I had hoped you would give me some account of your whereabouts. You can imagine, therefore, how glad I was at last to get a word from you & to know that all is going well with you– I am sorry that camping out was not a perfect success, & should think it a most trying ordeal to be thrown with unsympathetic & disagreeable people in such close relations. I was amused at your confession of preference for the conventional luxury of the Lenox Establishment. How many hard names of "Cockney," & "Philistine" & "Epicurean" would be flung at me, madam, if I dared acknowledge such weakness on my part! I will be generous & will not take advantage of your confession for I understand it only too well.– I was at home for three weeks after I left you, & as the weather was very pleasant I did not find New York at all uncomfortable. I had one delightful day with dear Olivia who came to town, stayed with me overnight, & spent the next day with my father, Josephine & myself, at Long Beach– She has gone now to Newport with her father & mother to spend a fortnight at the Cliff House. Toward the middle of August, the weather was getting hotter & hotter, & my spirits were falling lower & lower, when suddenly appeared in New York, my friends George & Minnie Biddle, who dragged me out of my desperate solitude & carried me away with them to this charming place in the neighborhood of Philadelphia– Chestnut Hill.[100] It is a remarkably pretty suburban village, out in the midst of a thickly wooded rolling country– All the houses are of stone, whether large or small, which gives a very solid & singularly un-American look– Many of them are very spacious & surrounded by park-like estates & splendid trees– I have seen the country to great disadvantage, as it is suffering from a 5-weeks drought, & the heat has been very great– but I am charmed with it nevertheless, & think it must be one of the most attractive places in good weather in the Spring or Fall. The Biddles are delightful people– & I have enjoyed their companionship immensely. Minnie is one of the loveliest women I have ever known, & as she represents to me that class you describe as "the girls with whom one has giggled"– you can know what happy days we have had together. She has a dear little child & a thoroughly nice husband. I find that the little "French actress" we saw up at the Crossman House was a young bride, Mrs. Walter Biddle, nee Miss Lena Carter a Philadelphia <u>belle</u> married in June & up there on her wedding tour. She was educated in Paris, & they say speaks German & English as well as she does French. I have seen some very pretty pictures of her since I have been here– I have had a great fright about my father since I have been away from home– he was taken suddenly & violently ill, & I packed my trunk to return immediately to New York, when a reassuring telegram from my sister encouraged me to stay & told me that the danger was over– Since then I have had better news each day– & though he is yet ill & in charge of a nurse & doctor, I have hopes all cause for alarm has passed away & that I shall find him convalescing when I return on Monday next. I have been quite ill myself for the past two or three days, & today is the first day I have had the strength or spirit to answer your letter. Is not this prolonged heat depressing to you to say nothing of Annie Holland's engagement though I fancy you were more surprised than I was. I expected it when I left. I am <u>not</u> & improbable as it sounds, I <u>don't want to be</u>– I am dying to have that other pair of low shoes of yours, I cannot live without them. I have lots more to say, but don't wish to exhaust your eyes & patience. Give my most affectionate regards to dear Mr. Gilder– Write me again & believe me always your friend

Emma Lazarus

Letter 25HdeKG

Emma Lazarus to Helena deKay Gilder
34 E. 57th St.
Sept. 8, 1881

My dear Helena–

I write to thank you for your note & your promise of the shoes, which however I have not yet called for, for the same reason that I have sent you this extraordinary looking note paper– it is too terrifically hot to stir from the house unless a matter of life & death. I have never in all my life experienced anything like the weather during the past forty eight hours, & today has opened as badly as ever– & when I tell you that added to the usual discomforts of such a temperature, with the temperature 100 degrees by day & 90 degrees by night, we have much care & grave anxiety on account of my father's serious illness, you may know what a cheerful household we are– It seems almost useless to look for a change in his condition until there is an improvement in the weather, which is enough in itself to prostrate a strong & healthy man, much less one enfeebled already by pain & illness– I only trust the change will come soon enough for him not to find it too difficult quickly to recover his former strength. I was sorry to know that you too were "out of sorts"– I hope Newport has helped you up again– Of course you have seen Olivia who must also be there, & I trust & . . . has . . . you with affectionate & sympathetic companionship, for all the discord & cross . . . you have had among the . . . woods & at other places. I came home Sunday from Chestnut Hill, . . . refreshed in mind & body by my visit. Indeed, I feel as if it were in that change of scene & . . . air that enables me now to bear up with health & moderate strength under the depressive influences at home. I had a very quiet time, but was made happy by being spoiled . . . the top of my . . . The only time I went out anywhere else than among the Biddle relatives was to . . . family tea at Mrs. Owen Wister's where I met . . . friend, the editor of Lippincott's– Mr. Kirk–[101] . . . anyone so completely fossilized & petrified by work, so utterly embittered & soured by his life, I've never seen– & the more he whined & moaned about his hard fate & the dreadful tasks that were put upon him, the more I thought of the energy & courage & enthusiasm which Mr. Gilder puts into just the same kind of drudgery & so transforms it into a really enviable career. He almost made me vow (internally) never to moan or whine again myself. I was so disgusted & I saw more clearly than ever how happiness depends almost entirely upon ourselves & not upon our condition. He is in the same state about books as Mr. Dusel the Bostonian musician was in last summer about music, when he told me he was sick of the old (Beethoven, Handel & Haydn) & the new was unmitigated trash– Liszt, Wagner, Berlioz, . . . Mrs. Wister is a "person" in your sense of the word & impresses me more than ever in her own house. She looks like & has the manners of a princess, & is singularly agreeable & intelligent– I have never heard such musically spoken English, & I think she must inherit some of her mother's gift, although in most respects she is said to be a perfect contrast to Mrs. Kemble–

I had a letter the other day from young Herbert Gilchrist announcing the death of his sister Beatrice who was studying medicine.[102] She died from the effects of ether inhaled while she was carrying on some scientific analysis. Poor Mrs. Gilchrist! I feel very sorry for her under such a blow & such grief,– it must be terribly hard to bear. Have you heard lately from Bonnie Castle?[103] Annie writes that her brother's engagement is now announced, & also her cousin Miss Lampson's. It is just like the end of a good old-fashioned novel– is it not? I had to be there to keep up the average!

I have been reading a such wonderful book on "Russia" by Leroy-Beaulieu.[104] I feel as if there were nothing I did not know now on the subject! But I have talked to you too long to go into literary subjects now & will reserve them for the next chapter.

I am ever so much obliged for the shoes & will call for them the moment this heat abates. Is your mother with you, & how has she borne the summer? Trusting soon to have a good account of you

Emma Lazarus

My latest "discovery" is Demosthenes–

Emma Lazarus to Helena deKay Gilder
Sept 14 1882

My dear Helena–

I know you owe me one but I will be generous & not wait for it– all the more as I have something to ask you– Bessie Stickney was at my house the other day, & we entered into a partial agreement to go to the Philharmonic Rehearsals (not Concerts) together & decided that our party could not be complete without you.[105] Will you let me know as soon as you conveniently can whether you consent– for Bessie is to try & get the seats through the influence of a music critic whom she knows. I hope you won't be able to resist such a great temptation. I don't expect to go to the Concerts this winter, as it is too hard to get down in the evening in spite of all your kindness which made it just possible for me last year. I have kept the numbers of our very bad seats however– & if you wish to renew them, I can give you the cheques. You know that is the subscriber's privilege from year to year– I don't think, however, any seats can be worse than those we had.

I hope you are still enjoying your marine Arcadia– & keeping Mr. Gilder there as long as you can chain him away from the office. Dr. Edward Emerson asked my sister Annie if he (Richard) "was not one of the finest men in the world"?[106] The letters he had written to Mr. Emerson had given the Dr. this impression– He thought they showed the finest kind of a nature– he is very fond of the "New Day"– & particularly so of the "Sower"– which he always associates with Millet's, thinking it has the same qualities of mysterious & poetic power–[107] Was it not written before Mr. Gilder had seen Millet's picture I fancied it was. I am going on Monday [rest of letter missing]

Letter 27HdeKG

Emma Lazarus to Helena deKay Gilder
45 Half Moon St.
Picadilly
May 31st, 1883

Yes, my dear Helena, the miracle has come to pass & here I am happy as a queen, on the classic soil of England.[108] It is all a dream & miracle from beginning to end, & I don't know how to write you about it. Ever since I landed, I have thought of you in every nook & corner that we have peered into, so far, & have been simply dying to write to you– but I thought for your sake I would rechain my impatience until I reached London, when I might tell you something of your friends. I was really touched to hear that dear Mr. Gilder & Rodman had been driven in the pouring rain to see the "Alaska" off– & I never ever saw them, nor got a sight of the yellow roses but I appreciated nonetheless the kindness & <u>loveliness</u> of their coming, when I heard of it from my family. I can never thank you enough, dear Helena, for the affectionate interest you showed me before I left home– the way you helped & encouraged & urged me forward is something to be grateful to you for life for I did not find the voyage nearly as dreadful as I had anticipated– & never felt better than while I was at sea, except the first two days, when I <u>simply</u> slept <u>solidly</u> for 48 hours. After that, although the weather was cloudy & blustering, the greater part of the time, I cannot say that the days were absolutely devoid of a certain charm– & when towards the end of our trip, the soft, calm days came when the sea and sky seemed cut out of a single sapphire, I was enchanted. The sensation of "Land"– after a week of ocean-tossing, is certainly indescribable– What do you think of those ghostly Irish promontories looming up on the distant horizon, & the revolving star of Fastrict Point, & the mingled excitement & delight that they bring? It is a sensation never to be repeated or imagined & receiving it as I did in the glow of the most glorious afternoon light, it was worth living for– Our first visit in England was to Chester where we spent four days & with difficulty tore ourselves away for the goal of our pilgrimage– London. I have an impression that you did not go to Chester while you were here. If so, you must decidedly make another visit for that alone. It is just the place that you & Mr. Gilder would go wild with delight in. Every lane is a picture– every house ought to be sketched or painted & such quaintness, picturesqueness & old-time beauty I had never conceived. The walk around the town on the old Norman wall with its gates & towers is unique & gives the most enchanting glimpses into winding, queer old streets lined with houses where Shakespeare <u>might</u> have been born– & on the other side, across a beautiful green-velvet English landscape, miles in extent with the

River Dee winding through it, & bounded on the extreme horizon by the hills of Wales. Standing on an old bridge one evng. last week at twilight, & looking into one of the streets that seem to me to be like to *Wynds* of Edinburgh, we saw a detachment of the Salvation Army come along with drums & chanting of hymns, & disappear down another picturesque old scenic lane.[109] It was exactly like a scene in one of Scott's . . . novels. And then the cathedral! And the feudal castle, & the Duke of Westminster's Seat! All the most characteristic features of English architecture & life seemed revealed to us in one fascinating little town– & as we saw it with the rare advantage of bright sunshine & exquisite spring weather, we were quite beside ourselves with enthusiasm. When I tell you that I attended service in the Cathedral twice, you imagine how much I was impressed with the majesty & greatness of the Church of England accessories & local habitation. I was simply overwhelmed with the grandeur & beauty– & last Sunday evng. after the service, Annie & I were rewarded for our piety, by hearing an organ-recital of the most classic kind on the glorious instrument. The organist is a fine artist– a brother of the one in Westminster Abbey & always plays after services for the benefit of the music lovers in Chester. I think only a sense of duty brought us away on Monday to London– It is a great event to be here & I can hardly believe it is true– but I feel as if it were very homelike & familiar to me. As yet I have seen none of your friends but they have all responded cordially to the letters I sent. I received a note from Mrs. Gosse asking me to her house on Sunday– but as she tells me that her little boy has the measles, I am not going–[110] She writes very kindly & informally, & I hope to see her soon. Mr. Nadal has not been well & is not able to leave his room– but says he will call upon me as soon as he is out. Mrs. Procter is at Tunbridge Wells– but wrote me an extremely nice note, asking me to come to her house on Sunday week to meet Browning!![111] These are all the letters of yours I have presented so far– My own people– the Jews– receive me with open arms. A Jewish M.P. has called upon me this afternoon, & I am to meet Claude Montefiore on Sunday.[112] We are invited to a musical party at the Moscheles' on Tuesday evng. next–[113] Last evening we went to the Lyceum with some friends, & saw Irving in Much Ado About Nothing with Ellen Terry as Beatrice.[114] I was very agreeably surprised by Irving. I think he has much power & originality & although he is full of tricks & affectations there is something extremely interesting in the artistic & scholarly character of his work. The performance as a whole was the most complete & satisfactory I have ever seen. It was a series of pageants– such scenery & costumes I never imagined. We had Irving's box– a " . . ." which he had sent to my friend & were very fortunate as the house was packed, & seats were very expensive. Tell Mr. Gilder he must let me write about Irving in the Century when I come back–. The whole troupe will be in New York next winter. I haven't said a word about the National Gallery, Westminster Abbey, & the House of Commons, simply because I have no words. I am living in a dream– & every sense is quickened to enjoyment. And I must have tired you to death with my egotism– Please excuse my provincial enthusiasm. Write to me as soon & often as you can for I think of you all the time. I shall want to hear all about your new home in Marion. Tell me as much as you can, for every detail is interesting! With fondest love to you & all your dear household. Affectionately your friend

Emma Lazarus

Emma Lazarus to Helena deKay Gilder
(2nd Letter)
London
1883

My dear Helena–

Are you still interested in the travels of your adventurous friend & do you care to hear about my impressions & sensations in this extraordinary part of the world? If I could spread over a month in New York the impressions I receive here in a week, I should consider myself rich– as it is, I rush from one variety of pleasure or interest to another & hardly know what I am doing. Our visit to London, which I am sorry to say will end on the 3rd of July, has been all my fancy painted it. Since I wrote to you, I have "discovered" the National Gallery, which I cannot get enough of, & Westminster Abbey, of which I can sincerely say the same, & the House of Commons. I have dined with John Morley, & John Bright, & James Bryce, & Burne-Jones, and lunched with Browning, & shall dine with William Morris on Monday– & have met du-Maurier, & Andrew Lang, & the Gosses, & Montefiores, Goldsmids, Roth-schilds, Moscheles, Montalbas– your friends the Comyns-Carrs & alot of oth-ers whose names you do not know.[115] I am in a state of bewilderment as you may imagine– simply dying to see you & tell you all about it. Mrs. Procter has been out of town ever since my arrival– but I hope to see her on Sunday & shall dine with her at Lady Goldsmid's that day. She has sent me two delightful notes, & I am prepared to fall in love with her. I agree with you about Mrs. Smalley (<u>confidential</u>).[116] I agree with you about Comyns-Carr– & Miss Strut-tel–[117] I am disappointed in Browning in spite of fancying that I was fully prepared. I am delighted with Mr. Gosse who is all simplicity, kindness &

cleverness– also with Burne-Jones against whom I had been prejudiced– also with William Morris whom I am to dine with at Burne-Jones'– also with DuMaurier who has asked me to his house today to meet Anne Thackeray and her husband. I think of you all the time & wish you were with me to enjoy all this– for it is just the kind of thing you love, & I am seeing just the people you would care for. My dinner with John Bright was quite an event– for I had the honor of sitting next to the great man who talked to me most amiably & agreeably about Cobden & our war & his own Parliamentary career & opinions about people & things. It was at Lady Cunliffe's– the wife of Sir Robert Cunliffe, member for some Welsh county.[118] Both very charming people, who seem to know a good many Americans. Among others Clarence King (who also dined there)– & the John Hays & Adams, & Henry James, through whom, of course, I know them.[119] Mr. Lowell called upon me a day or two after my arrival– he spoke most affectionately about you & Mr. Gilder.[120] I have seen very little of Nadal– he comes in occasionally in the evng. & has sent us passes for Westminster Abbey & the Chapel Royal– he is very "gay"– very discontented & homesick & amusing as can be– but enough to throw a damper upon the wildest enjoyment with his blasé cynicism. I predict that when once he gets back in America he will not be able to live without the amusements & entertainments which he thinks he despises here. Mr. Gosse has been simply perfect to us both– We had a delightful Sunday evng. in Delamere Terrace– & he showed us his books, & pictures & mss. It was the only time we have seen Mrs. Gosse who went out of town the next day– but will be back on our last Sunday in London which we are to spend with them. She was very kind & hospitable, & I am very, very much obliged to you for making us know them. Yesterday we dined at the Bryces'– where there were a good many people. It was very pleasant & Mr. Bryce charming as usual. We lunched with Mr. Browning at Mrs. Schlesinger's– Oh! Oh! Oh!

Mrs. Lillie's interrogatives have been very useful to us.[121] The Moscheles have been extremely kind, & we have heard the best professional music at their house. The Henschels are here, & took us to a glorious concert the other evng. The best orchestra I ever heard, led by Richter the famous Viennese conductor. We have heard Henschel two or three times- he sings delightfully as ever, & he is going to take us to Sir Frederick Leighton's studio on Sunday.[122] Tomorrow night we are going to hear Patti & Scalchi in the Rothschilds' box at the Royal Italian Opera.[123] So we are in good luck. Don't fancy that we are being feted by the Rothschilds for we are not– but yesterday I met Lady Nathaniel, the wife of the head of the house here–[124] & she was very sweet & offered us her box for tomorrow night. I am bitterly disappointed in not seeing the slightest prospect of marrying Sir Moses Montefiore[125]– as I had hoped. He is approaching his 99th birthday & has not made any advances to me & I fear there is no time to be lost. We go from London to Surrey to stop with some very kind & agreeable English people, to whom Maria Dewing introduced us– & from there with them, to Oxford. Oh, how I am going to bore you when I get back!– this letter is a ridiculous apology for one– There is no use in attempting to rave about the <u>places</u> & <u>things</u> I have seen– especially the pictures which I enjoy more than I ever imagined myself capable of doing– All I can do is to give you a faint idea of some of the people we have seen here– who are of special or general interest to you. Don't think I am as bad as Browning in mentioning so many names. When we leave London, we don't expect to see or know a soul. Do write to me as soon as you can. I am hoping to hear from you– I met Mr. Edwin Story the other day who said he never would forget your kindness to him.[126] How nice he is!

With ever so much love, believe me

affectionately your friend

Emma Lazarus

Don't let Mr. Gilder forget me. What <u>do</u> you think of Westminster Abbey? July [sic] 21. Howells is here. I don't know him.[127]

Letter 29HdeKG

Emma Lazarus to Helena deKay Gilder
Fairfield Surrey
July 4, 1883

My dear, good Helena–

Your letter received yesterday was a perfect delight to me– & I cannot tell you how deeply I appreciate the interest and sympathy with which you and Mr. Gilder follow my enjoyment here. If I were not thoroughly sure of my own unworthiness, I should begin to be quite spoiled by having the very people I care most for, so awfully kind to me. I left London yesterday & was really overwhelmed by the kindness & marks of positive attention which I had received– & then when your letter came– & I felt how rich I was in friends at home, I almost cried, myself, to think how happy I was. A thousand thanks for Rodman's photo– it is, as you say, a bad print, but it can't help being beautiful & I am delighted to have it with me. I have not seen or heard of Mrs. Stillman, since I have been here, neither have I seen the Peacock Room.[128] But I have seen so many beautiful houses & Studios, & been admitted into such

Sacred places including Browning's study & Morris's home– that I am bewildered. I am quite happy at finding that I am capable of enjoying pictures fully as much as music or poetry or anything else. Annie & I have spent every spare moment in the National Gallery- & yesterday after receiving your letter, we went to say goodbye to the beloved pictures & give a special greeting for you to the Doge (!!) & the Anunciation. But Oh! the Rembrandts & the Titians, & the Rubenses, & Caracci's two . . . & the Moroni portraits & the solitary gem of Leonardo da Vinci, outshining everything else, & the Veronese "St. Helena," & the sad knight of Velasquez, & the Dutch landscapes & the Turners– aren't they the things worth living for? My enjoyment of them has been more intense than I ever could have imagined– The first time I went there with a guide, I hadn't an emotion but the second & the third & the fourth times, it grew greater & greater, until now I love it more than any other spot I know– & I am satisfied just to sit there & remember where I am. But I must tell you of our two great days last week. Annie & I became great friends with Browning– I sat next to him at dinner on Friday, a 3 hour dinner, when he talked with the most wonderful eloquence & picturesqueness– a stream of wit, reminiscences & anecdotes– music, poetry & fun- He gave me in the most vivid way his recollections of Kean, Mendelssohn, George Sand, W. S. Landor, & of his intimacy with the Byron family, & talked in the frankest way about a hundred topics of deep interest to me. He is a great enthusiast of the Jews, & I think this may be the secret of his immense kindness to Annie & myself. He did for us what his oldest friends say he has never done to them– he asked us to spend the afternoon on Saturday with him & his sister, & he would show us his books, mss., relics of his wife, pictures, etc. Well, I hardly need say we went, & I had a most memorable visit– They live in a lovely little house by the Canal near the Gosses'– & he seemed altogether a different man from the Browning of Society. A sad, joyless, old man– living only in the past, for himself, & in the future for his son– whose art-work is his greatest pride– He grew more & more pathetic, as he took out his wife's precious little souvenirs & treasures, her Greek & Hebrew books with marginal notes & comments in pencil upon every page, his mss., letters & everything he thought could interest us– He gave me his photograph, & wrote under it an affectionate inscription in Hebrew, & after blessing & shaking hands with us again & again, said goodbye. It was a most curious & intimate revelation & we were almost as much surprised as touched. Please don't repeat this account of my visit indiscriminately, as it is not the kind of thing I wish to tell generally. But our greatest delight in the way of a personality has been Morris. I don't remember whether I wrote you about our dinner with him at Burne-Jones'. As I am afraid I did, I will not repeat the way we were both taken off our feet by his tremendous force & genius, visible in every word, look & gesture– He asked us to his house on

Sunday, & we spent two enchanted hours there. Helena, you would go simply wild in that house– just on the edge of the river, on a little avenue planted with magnificent oaks, & looking out in the rear on a garden such as you read about in the Earthly Paradise.[129] And the house itself is so different from everything else you have ever seen or imagined– there is not the commonest article of household furniture in it that is not original in shape, color, & design. And yet all is perfectly simple & very beautiful from its exquisite taste & appropriateness. Mrs. Morris is very beautiful & exactly like all the Rossetti pictures– she wore an esthetic dress of dark dull red, with a garnet necklace & cross & looked like an old Italian portrait.[130] Morris received us in a blue blouse, & looked, as usual, like a cross between an English sailor & a Scandinavian god. He is good enough to take an interest in our trip through England, & is so anxious that we should see the places he knows & loves best, that he took out a dozen maps, & marked out a route for us– writing down not only the names of the towns & villages, but just where we were to stop, & where we should find the best stained glass, & the best churches & castles, etc. etc. He has even held out the hope to us that we may visit him in his own home in Kelmscott, which is said to be the loveliest house in England. He will probably go there with his family in August, & if we are in the neighborhood of Gloucestershire at the same time, he has made us promise to come. At all events, we are going over this Friday to see his work-shop in Merton Abbey.[131] I shall have a million things to tell you about when I come back.

It is true that we saw a great variety of people in London, considering the short time we were there. Among the Jews, those that I liked the best were Mr. Frederick Mocatta, Lady Rothschild, Lady Goldsmid, & Claude Montefiore.[132] Lady Goldsmid is particularly interesting– a kind, plain little old lady, with the sweetest of English voices, a highly cultivated mind, & very gentle, highbred manners. We lunched with her on Sunday, & met the original of George Eliot's Mirah– a very handsome Jewess–[133] On Friday evng. we went to a party at the Dowager Lady Stanley's of Alderly– where poor old Lord Houghton was presented to us in the last stages of decrepitude.[134] He is a sad wreck. We have visited Sir Frederick Leighton's, Watts', Thornycroft's, & Du Maurier's Studios besides our dear friend Burne-Jones'– Our visits to his house have been the most delightful thing we have done in London. Did you see or know him? You would love him I am sure– he is like a medieval saint, so gentle, kind & earnest, & so full of poetry & imagination, that he shines out among the people I have seen, with a sort of glamour of his own. I have grown very much interested in his work– the cartoons of the Sleeping Beauty & of the Perseus Myth in his studio are wonderful for beauty & suggestiveness. But I will go on babbling forever if I don't stop soon– I am sure nothing would make Josephine happier than to go to your house– She is less fussy than I am, by long odds, &

thinks I am a terrible grumbler– so you need not be afraid of her– I am so glad to hear about your stone studio. It must be palatial– Tell Mr. Gilder that I met Thomas Hardy the novelist & discovered that he began life as a <u>Stonecutter</u>– it is a great vocation![135] I spent last Sunday evening at Gosses'– they have been very, very kind to us– Mrs. G. will see us Monday at the Alma-Tademas'.[136] I have seen Mrs. Procter & dined thrice with her (not at her own house). She is a wonder– There is not a day passes without my thinking of you & wishing you were here. I am so glad Mr. deKay is better & hope he may turn up here before I leave. I am now in Surrey stopping with some pleasant English people– the Pyes– friends of the Oakeys– On Monday next we go to Paris for a fortnight– to do some shopping, sight-seeing, & to see <u>the</u> Jews. Then we return to dear England to follow Morris' route. I am amazed to hear the Dewings are here– & expect to see them today. We are only 20 minutes from London– write when you can– I think of you so much. My best love to you & Mr. Gilder if he will take it. Annie is very grateful for your kind message & is following all your advice– A kiss to the children & hundreds for yourself from your friend Emma Lazarus. My address is always care:

Baring Brothers

London England

Letter 30HdeKG

Emma Lazarus to Helena deKay Gilder
July 17, 1883
(Paris)

How is Olivia?
What do you hear of Rose Lathrop?

My dear Helena–

Although I am so tired I can hardly sit up, & it is past bedtime, I am not going to leave Paris without sending you a line about my valuable impressions– & this is my last chance as I shall be dreadfully busy all tomorrow, & the next day at seven a.m., I start on my return to England– I have been here a little over a week & although I have of course seen & done many interesting things, I have not for a moment been able to reconcile myself to the life, the place, or the people. Take away the Louvre & the pictures & the statues, & I should never wish to see it again– What with the horrible associations connected with every street & building, & the childish frivolity of the people amidst these ruins & decayed splendor, it is the most depressing place I have ever seen. I cannot imagine where people find the "gayety" of Paris & the good "taste" of the Parisians. How anyone can walk through these streets & squares that have been torn & defaced & convulsed by the Revolutions & the Commune & call them cheerful is more than I can understand– The more the old holes are stopped up with new buildings that look as if they were made of sugar-candy they are so white & <u>filigreed</u>, the more they are plastered over with "Liberty, Equality & Fraternity," & dubbed with new names & washed & decently cleaned up, the more suggestive they are to me of the agonies they have witnessed & the ignorant fury of the people who inhabit them. As for the good taste, I am at a loss to find it– either in the vulgar & tawdry shops, the gilt & the glass of the decorations, or even in the very cemeteries where the helplessly bad taste of these frivolous people covers the most sacred graves with wreaths of brass & wire that make even the dead ridiculous. Yesterday, I went to Montmartre to see Heine's grave– it was pitiful. But you must not think I am morbid, or that I have neglected what I could find to enjoy. In the first place there are the pictures– I cannot describe to you the pleasure I have taken in them– Everything surpasses my expectations– that is to say everything upon which I had built my greatest hopes of enjoyment. I know we shall agree about the old masters & I am longing to talk about them with you– & look over your photographs. Today, I went to a most interesting loan-collection for some charitable purpose, gathered from the best private collections in the city– It is called the "Cent Chefs d'Ouvres" & is worthy of its name– It consists chiefly of modern pictures– & I wish to say just here (as I once told you that I never could appreciate Rousseau) that I saw for myself today, why & how he is by all odds the greatest among all the great moderns. There are some land-scapes of his in this little gallery that are enough to drive you wild. Oh, if you could only see them! Among the other pictures are Fromentin's "<u>fantasia;</u>" Decamps . . . 4 Millets, Daubigny, & the best Rembrandt I have ever seen– I have been twice at the Theatre Francais– the first time I saw Coquelin in a play of Dumas fils– the second time was a gala performance in honor of some Hungarians who are visiting Paris– so I saw Mounet-Sully in "Ordife Roi," & one act of "Le Roy J . . . , Got & Delaunay in an act of "Le Menteur," Got as Tribouley, . . . Lumay, & Coquelin in "Les Précieuses Ridicules." Did you ever in your life see anything equal to Coquelin's comedy? I cannot imagine anything finer, & have to laugh to myself whenever I recall his scenes. He kept the audience screaming with laughter from the way he appeared– Mounet-Sully is very <u>stagy</u> & exaggerated, but interesting & romantic– especially in his love making. Delaunay & Got were each perfect in their way, & the evening was a memorable one. Saturday was a great fete-day– the anniversary of the Bastille– We were out at Versailles all day– As soon as I got out of Paris & saw the beautiful country, & the picturesque peasants, & the fascinating old stone farmhouses & foreign looking courtyards & dazzling sunshine I began to feel happy again, & think I might like the French people– But what a place Versailles is! Did you ever see anything so sumptuous & so audaciously luxurious & extravagant– It is worthwhile for them to keep it in such a perfect state of preservation to explain the Revolution– It was curious & suggestive to see on the fete day of the Republic the crowds of common people in blouses & peasant dress, & swarming through the private apartments of the proud monarch, & the gorgeously decorated halls. In the evng. the city was illuminated & it was indeed a sight worth seeing– the Place de Concorde was a mass of intertwined ribbons of fire, the bridges & quais & river & arches were jeweled & outlined with the most brilliant flame– It was really like an enchantment– & I could not have believed it would be so beautiful. There was not an inch of space between the lights– all along the bridges & buildings & boats & reflected in the water– & that glorious Arc de Triomphe with a single band of flame around the top was something never to forget. I have hardly seen my people in Paris, as I have had too many other things to do even to deliver my letters of introduction. I was greatly surprised just before I left England to see Maria & Tom Dewing– We passed two very pleasant days together in Surrey– I took him to Burne-Jones' studio– where I expected Tom Dewing would be entranced as his own painting appears to be modeled on that of Burne-Jones. But on the contrary, he was very critical & severe. Maria looked & seemed well & ecstatically happy. I met your friend, Mrs. Middlemore & she was extremely kind to me. I lunched at her home. She has a very nice husband whom I met last summer at lunch at Lenox. Oh Helena, William Morris! I shall have a million things to tell you about him– such a day as we had with him down at Merton Abbey where his works are– He is a saint – and is the only man I have ever seen who seems to be as good as Emerson– & I don't know but that he is better– for he is more of a republican & not an aristocrat as Emerson was– But I must stop & go to bed– Forgive this dull letter– write soon– I am going out to Canterbury & shall be truly grateful to get back to England. Much love to you & Mr. Gilder from your devoted friend

Emma Lazarus

I suppose you think I have not seen your Notre Dame! Only think of one possibly, or probably, going to stay with William Morris in his country home– the prettiest house in England.

My latest discovery is Philippe de Champagne.[137] Why didn't anyone ever tell me about him?

Letter 31HdeKG

Emma Lazarus to Helena deKay Gilder
Sunday
August 5, 1883
Stratford on Avon

The sprig of jasmine is from Anne Hathaway's cottage

My dear Helena–

Although I am beginning to be seriously exercised as to why you don't send me . . . answers to my last two letters to let me know how things are going with you, I cannot resist writing to you from Stratford-on-Avon. The very sound of the name has magic in it, & as for myself, the broad sunny . . . & cheerful little town & dear little church with the most sacred dust of England in it. If I remember rightly, you came here but didn't take the walk to Shottery & Anne Hathaway's cottage which . . . did take & from which Annie & I have just come home. We started in spite of a heavy threatening sky, & are . . . by not having the rain fall until night as we re-entered our inn, & by seeing the most picturesque & appropriate old cottage, & having the loveliest walk in England. . . . Greenwich & beautiful . . . without the machine. Oh how I want to see you & Mr. Gilder, to talk it all over & compare impressions & sensations. What did you think of Shakespeare when you made his personal acquaintance here? The perfect naturalness, simplicity & humanity of the man, the absolute fitness of those cheerful, healthy surroundings, the quaint essence of everything that is English. There doesn't seem to be a shadow in the landscape– everything is so broad & bright & laughing– no Byronic gloom or Dantesque horrors– all simple, sane & utterly wholesome. Didn't you find it so & aren't you glad to know the place he was born in & must have loved? Of all the places in England I have yet seen, it is the one I should most like to spend a summer in– & I admire the good taste of an American friend of ours, Mrs. Wylie Pomeroy (May King of Newport) who has leased (or bought, I don't know which) Hidstay Hall, a beautiful country . . . that winding between . . . & . . . I cannot imagine a lovelier home– unfortunately I have not seen the inside as they just happen to be away for a week since we are here. I went to church again this morning. I go nearly every Sunday now! Last Sunday in Oxford & the week before in Canterbury– but there is always some paramount attraction & today as you may imagine it was just for the pleasure of sitting in that truly consecrated entrance for a few hours. How bright & cheerful the church is & how picturesque the old churchyard sloping to the town, & how lovely the approach through the . . . of . . . trees. Do you remember or didn't you see it?

We drove nearly all the way from Oxford to Stratford– & I only had the conscience to spend so much money as it required. I would more travel in England in . . . any other way. We followed the route laid out for us by William Morris, & it led us through the Cottswolds, through part of Glousceershire, Oxfordshire & Worches'shire, stopping at the most . . . and delicious old villages, supping, sleeping or lunching at the most primitive little inns, in places with the most . . . names (fancy Burford on the Windnish, & Stow-on-the-Word & Bourton on the Hill) & finally driving into Stratford-on-Avon & putting up at the sign of the "Golden Lion"– Isn't it like a fairy-story? & fairy-like as it sounds, you who know what the English country is, know that it doesn't begin to sound as fascinating as it really is. When we returned to England from Paris, our first stopping place was Canterbury– the Cathedral was more beautiful than I could have dreamed, & my first visit to it gave me one of the greatest sensations I have had since I have been abroad. We reached it on one of those afternoons that come once in a lifetime– We had to wait under an elaborately carved gateway– the Pilgrim's Gate, until a shower passed by– & then without . . . as the sun came out in full splendor illuminating the falling raindrops & making a vivid rainbow over the marble spires, as . . . crusaders in the Cathedral . . . , in the midst of rich turf & architecture as you cannot imagine. We wandered for almost an hour or two till the sun went down, in a state of perfect ecstasy. The inside of the Cathedral was magnificent– & I could not tire sitting or roaming about the stately nave & looking into the chapels with their alabaster tombs & faded, riddled old bones, while service was going on within– the choir & the organ & . . . rolling in to us. The stained glass alone is worth the visit to Canterbury– much of it dates from the 13th century & is like the richest kind of jewels. I need not tell you how delighted I was with Oxford even during the long vacations– & the Colleges & the Parks & the . . . & the . . . Ruins, & the old streets & the fascinating bookshops are there whether the students & Dons be present or about & it was all of the most intense interest to me. In the library of Christ Church College they have some good pictures– I have . . . , . . . the Virgin & St. John at the foot of the Cross– I know you would love it– It is nothing but two heads– St. John in full face & Mary in purple & the whole tragedy is told in their expression. When are you going to make a tour through England with me? Do write & give me some news of you & your family, or I will think your interest in my travels is on the wane. Not a day passes without my thinking of you & longing to see you– I have lots to say but refrain out of compassion.

With much love to you & Mr. Gilder–

Affectionately your friend

Emma Lazarus

I have just a word about the most enchanting visit yesterday to Warwick and Kenilworth. Oh this England! I love it too much. I am going tomorrow to . . . Abbey.

Letter 32HdeKG

Emma Lazarus to Helena deKay Gilder
London
August 17th, 1883
45 Half Moon Street

My dear Helena–

Many thanks for your welcome letter which reached me in Exeter– You did not seem to be in the happiest frame of mind when you wrote it– & I am afraid the surroundings of your life this summer have not been inspiring– And yet, as you say that all is well with you, & you have your new stone studio & Rodman & Dorothea to amuse you, I am in hopes it is only my imagination that makes me fancy you somewhat depressed. I am sorry to hear that your brother Charley is not yet well again– I wish he could have come over for a sun-bath in Venice– it would have done him more good than anything. Give him my kindest remembrances & tell him I don't agree with him about Europe! I am delighted to hear the book looks so well– & heartily wish it all success–[138] I am back in London as you see– but only for a few days, & for the last time– I have got to that point now, when it will tear my heartstrings to leave England! I begin to think London the most beautiful city in the word, & to agree with Mr. Lowell that a London fog is better than sunshine anywhere else– Nobody is in town. Picadilly is a picture of desolation as compared to what it was when we were here before– but I am revelling in the thought of a few days of solitude here in which to take my last look at the National Gallery & Westminster Abbey, & to see the Kensington Museum pictures. All the time we were in London during the Season, we never saw the latter.[139] I shall not see a human soul while I am here– so I am sorry to say I cannot find out anything about Ellen Terry for you– All my brilliant acquaintances of the "Season" are out of town & even if they were not, I have said goodbye to everybody, & could not dream of presenting myself again. Burne-Jones and William Morris are things of the past for me already!– How can I break gently enough to you the fact that I am going to chaperone Miss Strettel on the way home? I know how you love her, & that you will be therefore truly delighted to hear she is going to make another visit to America– She will sail with us on the "Alaska," & I have naturally promised to do what I could for her. My opinion of her is very much the same as yours– but when I think of my own helplessness in coming here, & the kindness I have received from the English, I am glad to reciprocate some of it even upon Miss Alma Strettel– I did not grow to like Paris any more all the time I was there– but I find myself getting more dangerously attached to England every day. How I wish you had seen some of the Cathedral towns we have. Salisbury, the last one we were in, is in many respects, the most beautiful of all– You would simply die if you could see me sitting through high service of the Church of England, nearly every blessed day of my life, & sometimes three a day! I cannot get enough of these majestic buildings– & just to sit in them & hear the organ & look about me at the infinite beauty & variety of the architecture, is an inexhaustible pleasure. Theologically, I am so stiff-necked a heretic as ever– perhaps even more so, on such intimate acquaintance. And besides I have just <u>discovered</u> the Athanasian Creed![140] I nearly died laughing over it–

Did you see Tintern Abbey when you were in England? We had such a divinely beautiful day there– & a drive from there a short distance into Wales which made me feel like giving up everything else in the world & just planting ourselves among the Welsh hills. It is the most romantic country I have ever seen– & as we drove through it in weather which was like one brilliant early October, among the most magnificent wooded hills & ravines fairly dazzling you with the intensity of their green, we received impressions that we never shall forget. It was really like fairy land. We have since been among scenery of a very different character– equally fine but not so interesting to me– We went to the coast of North Devon, and drove twenty miles from . . . to Lynton– where one gets sea & mountain views combined. It is really magnificent– but I hate the sea & was glad to get away from it– When are you going back to New York? I hope to be there the last week in September & shall be wild to see you. I feel as if I had grown ten years since I started. I look dreadfully ugly, have <u>no clothes</u> & have lost two or three of my pet illusions. Nevertheless, I have been intensely happy, & have enjoyed my trip more than I dared to hope. I will not bore you with another letter– so good-bye until we meet again. Please don't expect anything of me & like me a little still when I come back. Annie sends her love– Give mine to Mr. Gilder & believe me in the devoted friendship of yours always

Emma Lazarus

P.S. I had a nice letter from Molly Foote just before she went to Idaho– & wrote to her from Stratford– What a sad breaking up that seemed & how sorry I feel for dear old Mrs. Hallock–

Letter 33HdeKG

Emma Lazarus to Helena deKay Gilder
45 Half Moon St.
London
Aug. 29, 1883

My dear Helena–

I did not intend to bore you with another one of my scrawls but as I have succeeded in gaining the information you asked for about Ellen Terry, I write again in case you should need it before I come back.[141] I don't think you would care to have her at your house– She is a double divorcee & very much of a friend of Irving for whose sake a few respectable Irving maniacs receive her– As you know how I hate scandal, you will understand my not writing anymore– I will tell you what I have heard when we meet– meanwhile, I only send this . . . word. London with the people away, & the pictures & Westminster Abbey steadfast in their old places, is more delightful than ever– Annie & I spent three hours at the National Gallery on Saturday & made up our minds that we had not begun to see it. We are going to . . . this morning to it again. They have just had a new treasure bequeathed to them– supposed to be a Velasquez– one of the most extraordinary & beautiful pictures imaginable– all in grays & pinks & blues– It represents a martyr tied to the stake, a little child in a light blue gown praying for him with the most divine expression of face & figure, & a guardian angel standing behind. It is called the "Power of Prayer"– & is almost sensational in its originality of color & composition. I went yesterday to Mr. Watts' studio again & saw the artist & his work– I think I told you of him before– his pictures disappoint on a second visit– he himself is an interesting & agreeable person– but does not give you the idea of much power. There was a lady in our party who is a great friend of Modjeska, a Miss Ethel Coxon.[142] Do you remember my going last Christmas with Modjeska to bring her Christmas presents? Wasn't it funny that here in London I should see again one of the "Cards" I went with her to select at the Decorative Art Association? The world is small! Miss Coxon is an interesting woman, only 26 but looking older, having a very large frame, & a handsome face full of character & expression. She writes novels & stories which have a fair success, I believe– She is longing to go to America, & seems to live upon the "Century" magazine. The "Century" seems to be a great bond between the two countries– I see it in nearly every house I go into & everybody loves it. I have a million things to do this morning, & so will stop this bosh– What is the use of writing & talking? I get more disgusted with all forms of expression every day– & think I will take a vow of eternal silence soon– It is the only <u>decent</u> thing.

Affectionately your friend

Emma Lazarus

Emma Lazarus to Helena deKay Gilder
Saturday, [February 17 or 18, 1885]

My dear Helena–

Thanks for your note & the Reviews. I am so sorry about the face-ache– it is such a misery– Do be careful not to catch cold in it– I hope it is being relieved.

My father has suffered terribly all day with acute pain as well as weakness–[143] Yesterday he was comparatively comfortable– & now he is back farther than ever– What a queer dream of yours! I don't wonder that you dream of us, for you are so full of sympathy & thought for our trouble all the time– I don't think I have either of the French Reviews you asked for– but I will look & see tomorrow, as I cannot very well get at them tonight– I have an impression that I was not a subscriber on those dates– If I find them I will send them to you– Josephine sends her love & says she was going to send some of the books she promised you– but I have prevented her, as I told her you had more reading than you could manage just now. I cannot forgive myself for my stupidity in lending you the Heine Vols.– out of order– No wonder you have lost all interest– It is a pleasure to me to think of you enjoying the George Eliot– & I follow your progress as if I were rereading it myself. Thank you so much for your kindness on Wednesday about Dr. Damrosch's funeral–[144] I couldn't have gone– I hope you were not belated by coming so much out of your way.

With much love,

Fondly yours

Emma Lazarus

Letter 35HdeKG

Emma Lazarus to Helena deKay Gilder
18 West 10th St.
[1885]

My dear Helena—

Thanks for your kind note— I should be glad to meet anyone who is original enough to "want to know" such a stupid old fossil as I am— although I cannot make out your friend's name— If possible I will go to you tomorrow but it is more than doubtful that I can— I have not the energy or spirit to leave home at all, & have not even had my daily walk of late. We do not expect any sudden changes in my father's condition, but he is so evidently growing weaker every day, that it is pitiful to see him— & the gloom seems to deepen around us each day. It is all very strange & awful— but I shove off the thought of the inevitable as much as possible, & knowing that I shall need all my strength to bear it when it comes—

I have been reading George Eliot's life— up to a certain point, it is like being on top of a mountain— such intellectual & moral greatness combined, I have never known equalled in anyone brought so close to us— But the second marriage is a terrible blow! I should like to know what you think of the book—

Always affectionately yours

Emma Lazarus

Letter 36HdeKG

Emma Lazarus to Helena deKay Gilder
[1885]

My dear Helena—

Here are the books I promised you— We are in great trouble here— Dr. Draper came yesterday & gave us no hope whatever. A possible alleviation of suffering by anodynes is all we have now to look forward to— Don't come, dear Helena, for there is nothing more to hear & I cannot see even you—

With fond love

Your friend

Emma Lazarus

It was so good of your mother to come yesterday with Julia. Please thank them both

    Tuesday

News clipping enclosed:[145]

They were prefaced however by remarks by Dr. W. T. Harris, and the reading of the following sonnet for its author, Miss Emma Lazarus.

TO R.W.E.

> As when a father dies, his children draw
> About the empty hearth, their loss to cheat
> With uttered praise and love, and oft repeat
> His all-familiar words with whispered awe
> The honored habit of his daily law
> Not for his sake, but theirs, whose feebler feet
> Need still the guiding lamp, whose faith less sweet
> Misses that tempered patience without flaw–
> So do we gather round thy vacant chair
> In thine own elm-rooted, amber-rivered town,
> Master and father! for the love we bear,
> Not for thy fame's sake, do we weave this crown,
> And feel thy presence in the sacred air,
> Forbidding us to weep that thou art gone.

Letter 37HdeKG

Emma Lazarus to Helena deKay Gilder
Gersonia Hotel
Chester
May 30th 1885

My dear Helena–

    Here I am in England again feeling about twenty years older than when I was here last, trying with all my might & main to get back a healthy, natural way of looking at this beautiful world of ours. But before I give you any of my impressions, let me thank you & Mr. Gilder most affectionately for your delightful greetings in mid-ocean– the lovely crape *[sic]* fan is far too pretty– It is just what I needed, & I was touched at the thought of your giving it to me. Richard's letter began in a very ghastly way– How would he have felt if I had actually gone to the bottom & he had never rec'd an answer! But towards the end, he was much too kind to me– & I blush to think how undeserving I am of such a good opinion. Our mail bag was a great success at sea & the only thing that relieved the tedium of the voyage. Do you know that that kind brother Charles of yours, actually got up the morning we sailed to see us off? He was a little late, so that I could only see him in the distance as we steamed away from the dock– but I thought it was so very, very kind in him, & I wish you would tell him so with my thanks. We had a beautiful start, & a beautiful arrival. Our last day on shipboard off the Irish coast was very rough but very grand to look at– a green & snow white tumbling sea with the colors of Niagara in it– & a brilliant sunlight. The approach to Fastrict was really exhilarating– & I know of nothing more delicious than the change from the strong salty winds of the sea, to the warm, soft earthy smells of grass & flowers that reach you there from the Irish hills. We found letters at Queenstown, & letters of friends awaiting us at Liverpool, & had such a welcome that we almost felt as if we had come from one home to another. Although we landed at Liverpool on Sunday evng. we could not leave that detestable town till Tuesday, owing to the Bank Holiday & Whitsuntide. Since then we have been luxuriating in delightful old Chester. I spent a good part of my days in the Cathedral where the music is the best I ever found in England. I suppose you Italian swells would sniff at this Cathedral & I confess even after my limited experience, I find it rather insignificant. But the woodwork of the choir would be worth going many miles to see at home– & is indeed unrivalled here– It is very old & rich & delicate as lace– then the cloisters are delightful, & after all a Cathedral is a cathedral, & one gets a sensation in it that no parish-church could give. Chester itself is unusually picturesque for an English town– with its old wall & its "Rows," & its beautiful old gabled houses, some of them decorated with the richest & most elaborate carvings in black oak– they are a study in themselves, & you would find something to sketch at every turn. We are going on Monday to London– having given up our trip to Wales– we are too tired & too <u>poor</u> (!) to travel. I don't expect to see a soul in London– I can't say that I wish to. So don't expect any interesting letters or exciting news. Josephine writes me that you are so kind to her– & have taken compassion on her loneliness. I am afraid to think of our empty house at home. I hope you are feeling better– & taking all possible care of your dear self. Give my fond love to all your family, & to your mother & Julia. Tell the latter her slippers are the joy of my life. I use them every day. Write soon, dearest Helena.

Your loving friend

Emma Lazarus

I forgot to say that my Harriet Martineau gown was the admiration of the whole ship–! I wore it every day, I am taking it to London to be presented in.

Emma Lazarus to Helena deKay Gilder
London
June 17th 1885

My dear Helena–

Never in my life have I felt so utterly stupid & blank about letter-writing–
Nothing that I do or think seems worth repeating & added to this mental
incapacity, I have been much troubled by my lame finger which has hampered
me a great deal. I have been so very sorry to hear of the general indisposition
of your family– & fear you have had your hands overfull with Rodman &
Richard suffering, besides your own weak & uncomfortable condition to upset
you.[146] I trust, before now, you are installed at Marion, & all feeling better for
the change & rest. Nothing could be quieter than the life we are all leading
here– we go absolutely nowhere & see nobody. I have not told any of my
former acquaintances that I am here– so even if they wished to show me any
hospitality– (which I think is doubtful on a second visit!) I don't give them
the chance– I have not seen the Gosses nor Miss Stillman nor any of your
friends so can give you no interesting news– Poor Henry James is detained at
Bournemouth by his sister's illness– & I may not see him at all. Miss James
has been more than usually ill all through the late Winter & Spring & he has
been nursing her, & is waiting for her to be well enough to move to Malvern
in July.[147] Did you know that old Mrs. Procter has lost her daughter during
the past year?[148] She (Mrs. P.) lives quite alone now, & is, they say, much
broken & aged, but still receives on Tuesday & Sunday & tries to keep up the
same show before the world.
London has a peculiar fascination for me yet– in spite of its ugliness, & of
my being outside of all its real life & charm. The National Gallery & the
Abbey are my chief standbys & I never tire of either, nor of wandering in the
neighborhood of Parliament Square & gathering there the full impression of
the massiveness & age & <u>imperial</u> quality of the great old town. The bridges &
rivers, the towers & trees & parks & huge solid buildings & rich <u>historic</u> air
about it all, makes me think it the only really beautiful spot in London– Hyde
Park with its Marble Arch seems in comparison a clumsy imitation of Paris–
There is much excitement here just now over the political crisis, & on Monday
when we walked along the Embankment from the Temple to the Abbey, we
found Parliament Square one mass of people waiting to greet the new Prime
Minister.[149] They were all perfectly quiet & well-behaved. Politics are in a terrible muddle & not much if any, more edifying to the looker-on than our own–
The defeat of the Government seems to be generally considered a trick played

by the Liberal party themselves in order to get out of office & Gladstone's position is anything but dignified or creditable– though he makes a good show today of refusing an Earldom– the scramble for place & power, & the predominance of self-seeking petty motives, seems to be equally great & are fully as disgusting as among our home-politicians– Tomorrow we are all going over to Cobham to dine & spend the night at the Arnolds.[150] It seems like an invasion of the Goths for us all to go at once into their tiny house– but Mrs. Arnold came to us herself, & was so urgent & hospitable, that we could not easily decline. Next week we hope to make some short day-excursions to Cambridge, St. Albans, Oxford, etc. I don't think we shall leave London till the 21st of July when we are going to Yorkshire. We have such comfortable lodgings & are so much interested that it seems hardly worthwhile to make an experimental move. I am so glad I did not attempt in my present frame of mind to see Italy. I only hope I shall be able to find a little more glamour over things when the autumn arrives! And yet I am very well & very glad to be here rather than in New York. Please write whenever you can muster strength & energy– I am hoping to hear from you. Much love to Richard, also to your dear Mother & Sylvia & from your friend

Emma L.

Tell your brother Charlie to write to me!

Letter 39HdeKG

Emma Lazarus to Helena deKay Gilder
London
July 1st
Thursday '85

Dearest Helena–

I suppose you are fully aware that you are treating me very badly– but when I take into consideration all your past goodness & your recent anxieties, I am not going to resent it, & am going to bore you with letters just as if I had heard from you every day.[151] The only trouble is, they will be still more egotistic than usual– for not knowing anything about you, I can write of nothing but myself! I am so comfortable & so much at home in London, that I have given up all idea of leaving it till the end of this month when we go to Yorkshire for August. Annie has begun to "Copy" at the N. Gallery– which is another motive (or excuse) for staying on– She is at work on a Boy's portrait by Isaac van Blade, &

is deeply interested– & I go & sit with her, & wander about the rooms, or sit & read Fromentin while she works, for hours– You may imagine how contented & happy we are– I don't think this portrait was here when you were in London– It is a gem– a lifesize picture– nearly profile & taken to a little below the waist– the boy is very dark with straight brown hair falling over his brow & down to his shoulders, & he wears a big felt hat trimmed with fur & carries a sable muff– I heard accidently the other day how it came to the Gallery– It was owned by a Dutch lady who had a passion for England & sold it for £300 to an Englishman, after having refused any price from Paris– Of course you saw the Dulwich Gallery when you were here?[152] We went there one day this week & <u>discovered</u> it. Naturally I had no idea of its existence until I was taken there, & to my amazement, found myself in rooms filled with the most dazzling Cuyps, Reynolds, Holbeins, Van Dycks, Velasquez & Rembrandts– to say nothing of Gainsborough & lesser stars. The collection of Albert Cuyps is, I believe, the best in Europe– & they make the walls radiant with their color– Dulwich is a picturesque place, with an interesting College through which we were shown by the young Headmaster who gave us luncheon in his luxurious rooms– It has been less invaded by the "spreading of the hideous town" than any other suburb of London– & is a pretty place of soft green, & tall elms, & embowered cottages & fragrant hedges overgrown just now with masses of wild rose & honeysuckle– Another white or rather golden day– we had lately at St. Albans– such weather as fancy can not be had out of America or Italy in June– a sky of intense & cloudless blue & the most transparent, crystalline air. And under these conditions we saw the Cathedral– one of the most beautiful we have yet found– massive, venerable, Norman, with such a play of color inside & out, & such dignity & severity of line, & such vast & magnificent propositions as must be seen to be believed– I never can understand what it is that makes one Cathedral a breathing thing of life, & another one, equally renowned, cold & dead– A few days before we had been at Winchester, & had vainly tried to get up an emotion over these faultless regular Gothic arches– but the minute we entered the warm, glowing atmosphere of this solemn old Norman Abbey, we were touched & subdued & entranced. How painfully stupid the English are about these treasures of theirs. This one fell into the hands of the "restorers" some centuries ago, & the result is a nave whose Northern arches are the purest simplest Norman, & whose southern wall is the most elaborate Decorated Gothic! But still worse than this, the whole Cathedral is now given over with <u>Carte Blanche</u> to "restore" & putter at it, to a certain Sir Edward Bechelt, who has offered to expend a fixed sum annually on it for permission to do as he pleases. And the consequence is a West front such as would be a disgrace to the Roman Catholic Cathedral in Fifth Avenue.[153] We are still living in absolute seclusion– Today for the first time,

Annie & I have promised to go out to dine– We are going to the Burne-Jones' where there will be nobody else but William Morris– We only let Mrs. Burne-Jones know late last week that we were in London– & she welcomed us as affectionately & warmly as if we were her oldest friends. She asks us to go to her tonight as if "we were going to our own home"– & we have not wished or cared to decline– On Tuesday, I saw for the first time Henry James– He had come to London for a couple of days to see about lodgings for his sister– & came at once to welcome me– He was <u>so</u> nice! he looks quite handsome & much better than when I saw him last– all the better for his absence from London dinners & late suppers– He seems however very anxious about his sister– who must be very ill & who though somewhat improved– is still too ill to see anyone– I don't know what is the matter with her– Her friend Miss Loring is with her now– Mr. James is going to bring her to London in about ten days– & I hope then to be able to see something of him– Did I tell you that poor Mrs. Procter's daughter had died last August? I left my card for Mrs. P.– & got such a pathetic note from her– She said she had never been separated from her daughter until last March when they wrote to each other for the first time– & were parted only for a few days– And now she is left quite bereft & lonely. She keeps up a brave show & sees all her friends as formerly– but they say she is really broken hearted– Do send me a line– if only a line– to let me know how you all are– & remember how far away I am, & how much I love you–

fondly your friend

Emma Lazarus

Letter 40HdeKG

Emma Lazarus to Helena deKay Gilder
Richmond-York
August 22nd [1885]

My dear Helena–

Many thanks for your satisfactory letter giving me news of you and all of your family. I was so glad to get it, & it seemed to bring me quite near to you to have details of each separate one. I am sorry to hear Richard has been so overworked & trust he has been persuaded to take a little more rest before now– I wish you had given me Mrs. Burnaly's address– of course I should have been delighted to see any friend of yours in London– but I am going to be there only for a few days in September, & I fear now it is too late to hear from you again before I leave town. My present plan is to go to Cambridge, Sept. 1st & stay there for two or three weeks– & then after some days– (possibly a week)– in London, to go to Holland. That would bring me to about the first of October. My curiosity is fully aroused about the Netherlands, & I am looking forward with a great deal of interest to the trip. I grew to love so the Dutch pictures in London & Dulwich & am eager to see all I can of them. However, I am not impatient to leave England where I feel so much at home– You know how lazy & unadventurous I am, & can imagine how I shrink from rousing myself out of the little rut I have found here– Richmond continues to be the prettiest place I have ever seen– there is more variety of lovely views– hillside, meadow, woodland, river, town, castle & ruins– than I have ever found combined in one place before– The walks are inexhaustible & their beauty inspires me to great pedestrian achievements– Fancy my walking six miles in an afternoon, & Annie 14 miles in one day! The weather has been perfect, clear, transparent atmosphere, brilliant sunshine & gorgeous cloud effects, like our October skies under which the English green has looked more vivid than ever, & the town on the hillslope with its crowning tower & castle, like an enchanted vision. It was a favorite place of Turner's, & I believe he has painted a good many pictures of it–[154] I have never seen them but he alone could do justice to the romantic splendor of the whole thing. I don't know whether I told you that within ten minutes' walk of our house, we have the ruins of a delightful old Abbey untouched by the restoring fiend, & undiscovered by tourists. It is just by the river's edge which is literally enamelled with turf, so rich & green is it– & magnificent old birches & oaks spring up between the arches & doorways where they have taken root, & over shadow the ruins. Anything more characteristic, more melancholy & beautiful, you cannot imagine. We walk about the whole neighborhood of Richmond as if we owned it– in the oldest & shabbiest of clothes, never meeting a soul & enjoying absolute independence. I have never had such perfect freedom & quiet in my life, & hate the very thought of giving it all up. I went to York one day to see the Minster & the old stained glass once more– which is the finest in England– In the Cathedral I met your friend Mrs. Schuyler Van Rensselaer who very kindly came up & spoke to me–[155] She is going in September– to live with her mother in New York– She looked ill, but said she was better, & was very agreeable & attractive as she always is. We had quite a little talk there & at the hotel– & she seemed much interested in the work she was doing for the "Century." No– I have not read "Anna Karenina"– but I am ready for it! When I go to Paris, probably after Holland, I shall try to get it in French, as I cannot enjoy it in German–[156] Josephine sent me the article from the "Evng. Post"– which has made me impatient to get at the book– The English seem so stupid about any literature outside of their own– It is a rare thing to find anyone who knows Tourgenieff even & I suppose it will take another generation– to wake up to Tolstoy. Here, we are surrounded by Tourgenieff's books– as we introduced them to our friends the yr we were in England before– & now they cannot move without them. I am so glad to think of you reading the "Memoires d'un Chasseur"– which is always before me here on the drawing-room table– it seems to bring us together. I know it well & love it all.

About the "Women's Club"– <u>between ourselves</u>, you must have $50 handier than I have if you think of joining. I have declined. I really don't see any "raison d'etre" for such a thing & can see no object promoted by it, except more useless "talking out of one's mouth"– of which there is more than enough already. As for meeting one's friends, reading reviews, etc.– I should much rather do these in my own home than at a club room– However, my main reason for declining is that I don't expect to be in New York again for over a year, & I prefer to spend the initiation fee in Italy! I should not like to influence you one way or the other about it– especially in opposition to the voluble Mrs. Bales Smith.

Tell Richard I am going to cut him out with the "Filibriges"– if I go to Provence on my way to Italy. My friend Mr. Mocatta of London has given me a letter of introduction to Mistral–[157] & I hope to make use of it when I get to Avignon. This however is all in a very dim future. Give much love from me to your brother & Julia when you write or see them. Tell the latter her slippers are the staff of life. As you can probably see, my spirits have been much better since I have been in this lovely spot– such beauty & peace are a very great refreshment. I wish I could think of you as having a little more rest & quiet. Who is going to write & tell me about you, when you are no longer equal to it yourself. I shall be so anxious. At all events, keep on as long as you can & believe me your loving friend

Emma Lazarus

Letter 41HdeKG

Emma Lazarus to Helena deKay Gilder
Cambridge
Sept. 6 1885

My dear Helena–

As I am thinking about you this quiet, beautiful day I see no reason why I shouldn't write to you, although you owe me a letter. I know however that your present condition doesn't "lend itself" very conveniently to letter writing.

So I shall not stand upon ceremony. My last days in England are drawing to a close– & I shall leave it this time with a greatly modified upset– for I confess I am impatient for something different, & especially for <u>Italy</u>– That however still seems very remote for I shall not dare to go within the cholera latitude– for many months– especially as I intend to get to Italy by way of the South of France &. . . . Meanwhile I am looking forward with eager interest to Holland– My nerves & spirits have been sufficiently <u>healed</u> by this long, quiet summer in the midst of such foreign associations, to make me quite ready for new scenes & sensations– & in the light of what I expect from the near future, Cambridge, which looked so beautiful to me two years ago, seems somewhat tame. It is very elegant & refined & our cozy little apartments command a beautiful view of Chapel & Gateway & College– . . . –but it all seems cold & lifeless to me with everybody away for vacation– & I made up my mind that here, as in most English towns, the English themselves are the main point of interest. Certainly, there is little else here, to attract one for long, though I can imagine few more interesting places when everything is in full swing. I appreciate so well your constant sense here of the absence of art. Yesterday morng. I spent at the FitzWilliams Museum, a hideous structure with two or three good Dutch pictures, & rooms full of <u>atrocities</u>– where English art (represented by Stanfield) that seemed as if it could go no further in crudity & stupidity was being <u>copied</u> by students, in a way that showed there was yet a further limit to British philistinism. Since then I have been reading Ruskin on Venice & Story on Rome–[158] I have come to the conclusion that for mere travelling purposes, Italy <u>must</u> be a better country than England! You see, at this distance even, the usual Italian mania is coming on– & I only hope I shall have strength of mind to control my enthusiasm & not inflict my school-girl dithyrambs on you or any of my friends when I once find myself in Arcadia. I had hoped to see Waldstein in Cambridge– but as you doubtless know, he is in America–[159] Gosse also is away– On Thursday we are going to London– where we shall be obliged to stay for a few days at least, in order to prepare for our winter campaign. We shall take the steamer from Harwich to Rotterdam, early the following week. I remained faithful to Richmond to the last, although our quarters were anything but comfortable. I have never seen such beautiful country as it was– the richest & most varied landscape– & everything architectural in keeping with the beauty of the scenery. Unfortunately our last weeks there were marred by very dull & cold weather which would have quite destroyed the charm of any less lovely place. Here we have had the most brilliant sunshine, & cloud effects as fine as our own in October. Over these elegant Colleges & dignified avenues of beeches & limes, & rich green lawns, the lights seem magical. Have you ever read Matthew Arnold's essay on "Falkland?" I have read it since I have been here– in his volume of "Mixed Essays."[160] If you don't know it, do get it & enjoy it– it is the most exquisite & <u>classic</u> English style & will delight you from beginning to end. In the same vol. the Essay on George Sand in wonderfully fresh & charming & <u>good style</u>– Two such chapters of those would justify his reputation– & make one forgive or forget his stupid reiteration & dilettantism & "<u>ach Britische-Beschranktheit</u>" as Heine calls it– When I next write, it will be from your dear, curious Dutchland– Please write to me whenever you can muster up the energy– You don't know what a delight home-letters are from the few people one really cares for–

Lovingly yours–

Emma Lazarus

Letter 42HdeKG

Emma Lazarus to Helena deKay Gilder
Hotel de Bellvue
The Hague
Sept. 21st 1885

My dear Helena–

I wrote to Mr. Gilder about a week ago– as soon as I heard of the sad crises you had been through– I think of you with deep affection & sympathy– & wonder how you kept up your strength & spirit during this trying summer after the long strain of the Winter– But I hope soon for good news of you from someone– if not from your dear self, & meanwhile I will try & give you a little of the brightness that is around & cheering me just now– Thank you so much for your reiterated injunctions to come to Holland! It has already thrown its spell over me, & every moment is rich in enjoyment. We left England last Tuesday Evng. & came by way of Harwich to Rotterdam– It was a calm, fine night & I took a special pleasure in the thought of rocking to sleep upon <u>Heine's</u> North Sea– Rotterdam itself was a dreadful disappointment– a nightmare of dirt & squalor & hunger & home-sickness & confusion. But we left the next day by the first train for The Hague where I should be quite satisfied to take up my abode permanently. What an enchanting town it is, with its entanglement of shipping & trees & canals & palace & dear little old gabled houses! Do you remember it all? The rich chocolate color of the soils, the <u>limpidity</u> of the canals, the brilliancy of the green reflected in them, the <u>Park</u>, that glorious old forest, the <u>Binnenhof</u>, the old gateways & the <u>picture gallery</u>![161] What a collection of jewels it is in this beautiful faded pink Maurits-huis.[162] I suppose you will despise me when I say that I cannot even look at

Rembrandt's Lesson of Anatomy– it is too horrible; & I shut my eyes as I pass it. But I make up for it in my enjoyment of the other pictures, & the more I see of the Dutch painters the more I love them. Do you remember in the old German room, a small woman's portrait by Holbein with a cream white kerchief of folded linen about her head, her hands folded in the usual Holbein style, & the most saintlike but human expression of resignation, patience & simplicity– the figure is relieved against a peacock blue background. Do you remember Van de Helit's portrait of Paul Potter & the two Reynolds, & the Rembrandt portrait, & Rubens' two wives & the Nativity & Adoration of the Magi & Annunciation of Hunscherck Van der Veen? Perhaps the mere names will recall to you a past delight– & so I go over a few of them, although it is all useless. Annie is going to "copy" there tomorrow. The days are not long enough for all we wish to do & see here– Yesterday, the weather was glorious, & we spent the whole morning walking about the fascinating streets, along the canals & over to the other end of the town to see the house where Spinoza lived & died, & his statue nearby– The court instrument maker lives there now– & the house which is a very comfortable one, is decorated with the armorial bracings of the state, & a tablet with an inscription about Spinoza– The statue is interesting & represents him seated thinking with a pen in his hand– a heavy, grave, noble-looking head with very curly hair– In the afternoon we drove through the Park which was beautiful as fairy land, with its soft carpet of autumn leaves, & its thick foliage & mostly bright green trunks– all lit up by broken patches of struggling sunshine. Today we had another great morng. in the picture-gallery– & on coming out found the city swarming with crowds of people– We found it was the opening day of Parliament & everyone was waiting to see the King– So we had chairs brought out on the steps of the Mauritshuis & from this commanding height, we reviewed the whole pageant. It was extremely picturesque– The streets & the Pleiu beyond were a compact mass of people– & on our right was that delightful old carved stone & brick gateway– (the Gevanspaport) leading into the Binnenhof– the only historic part of The Hague–[163] Through this archway, just like a scene on the stage, came prancing first the richly uniformed trumpeters on horseback, then the court carriages with scarlet velvet trappings & gold decoration, & then in a coach all crystal & gold, drawn by eight magnificent horses, surrounded by a long guard, the King of Holland– a grey-bearded old man bowing to his people– On top of the carriage was a huge gold crown placed on a crimson velvet cushion– As I had never before seen a king in my life, off a playing-card or the stage, you may imagine how full of interest & excitement the whole thing was. There was very little enthusiasm, & much less noise than at a Socialistic meeting which crowded all the streets yesterday. We completed our day by taking the steam train that passes the door of our hotel, & going in 15 minutes to spend the afternoon on the Scheveningen Beach–[164] The sun-shine was glorious, the sea every color of the peacock, enlivened with a long line of Dutch fishing-boats standing out against a silver sky– & the long stretch of beach was brilliant with groups of well dressed city people & still better dressed Scheveningen peasants with their lovely caps & fichers & their fishing baskets in their hands. It was too delightful & I sat & read Amicis & drank in the glorious air, & looked at the gay & beautiful sight in perfect content. We expect to stay here a week or ten days longer at least– since we are all so comfortable & find so much to enjoy– & we are perfectly independent & need not leave until we are ready. I am reading Fromentin's (for the dozenth time) & Maxime de Camp's "En Hollandc," & Amicis' "Olande"–[165] The last two I got here– at the bookshop which is chiefly French & Dutch, I was shown a copy of the American (Petrean) edition of Amicis'– which they evidently think much of with its pretty illustrations & nice get up. Fromentin's descrip-tions remain the best– not only of the pictures, which of course he deals with en maitre– but of the places & impressions. I had a charming letter from Henry James the other day from Paris– & he said– "I envy you Holland– dear, damp flat little country with its russet towns"–[166] Isn't the word "russet" one of his perfect touches & doesn't it give exactly the tone of these red-brown bricks? I hope to see him in Paris– he is always kind & friendly. His sister I never saw in London, as she was still too ill. But I believe she is getting well– At all events, she is much better– I saw her friend Miss Loring. (Olive Chancel-lor?)[167] I must finish this egotistic scrawl– Agnes asks me to give you best love– Accept much for yourself & for Richard from your . . . friend

Emma

Emma Lazarus to Helena deKay Gilder
Paris
Nov. 17th '85

Please thank R. for his note

My dear Helena–

Ever since I read your welcome letter a month ago, I have been daily & anxiously awaiting news of you– & feared to write lest my letter should reach you inopportunely. I am so happy to hear of your happiness & congratulate you most warmly on the safe arrival of your boy–[168] It is the only good news I have heard for a long time & I am truly grateful for it– I trust all is going well with you– Please give my love & congratulations to Richard– who must be as happy as yourself. When you are able to write tell me all about the "little stranger"– how big he is & what you are going to call him– I hope your spirits will come back with your strength & that life will look brighter & gayer than it has for the past melancholy year–

If I write to you at all, I must write to you about myself– though I don't know whether it will interest you– I suppose Joe has told you that I am delighted with Paris– All the ghosts of the Revolution are <u>laid</u> this time– I don't know why or how– At all events, I have taken a fresh pleasure each day in the brilliancy of the city– old & new– the rivers & the quays, the book shops & the churches, & the inexhaustible Louvre. Here, I have spent so many hours that I am at last really familiar with the things I care most for– My Dutch craze is still on me in rabid form– & I am not ready for Italian art. I suppose I shall feel differently after I have been in Italy– & you know I am never ashamed to be inconsistent. We leave for the South on Dec. 1– stopping first at Avignon– then Marseilles, Mentone, Genoa, Pisa & Florence– which we hope to reach by the 12th or 13th. I suppose it will all be an enchantment– but I am in no haste to leave Paris– where I have not had a moment of loneliness or ennui– Henry James was here when I first came– but he has gone back to his sister in London– He was kind as usual– & came occasionally to see me, but he was soon called back by her increasing illness. From what he told me, I should think her condition was critical, & she must be a terrible sufferer– I felt very sorry for him too– he seemed so nervous & anxious. He looked well– but no longer young. He told me such a contemptible story about that cowardly Aleck Oakey– but like everyone else, expressed sympathy with Maria.[169] What a tragedy it is, & how I pity that sweet little wife of his & his poor parents– It is reported that he is in Venice– I don't know with what truth– Since I have been in Paris I have read "Anna Karenina"– which is an event. I am quite insane on the subject. I went one evening to hear a "conference" about it by Mr. Francisque Sarcey– but he was not a critic, & simply raved in a schoolboy fashion & vulgarized it all a la francaise– & the lecture was very dull.[170] We have been living in a very Russian atmosphere as the only other boarders in the house (except one) besides ourselves are a Russian lady & her husband– bride & groom. She is excessively pretty with golden red hair & beautiful coloring– & Annie has been painting her portrait. This has brought them much to our rooms & she has told us a great deal about Russian life & people & books. She says Levine is a portrait of Tolstoi himself– & also that the pictures he paints of corruption & brutality of Petersburg society are exact. What an impossible country it must be to live in & how melancholy even the least serious Russians seem to be!– Mrs. Lockwood has been & gone– She spent ten days here, & I saw her often but not satisfactorily, as she was overwhelmed with shopping. I hope to rejoin her in Florence– These few are the only people I have seen– Our lives are of the quietest, & of course we don't know even what is going on in the theatre or the opera or concerts. But the sunshine, & the looks of Paris, & Notre Dame, & the Louvre, are quite enough for me, & my days have never seemed more full & satisfactory. We have not seen any of the young artists' studios, except Mr. Sargent's. He was in London at the time but we saw his last two pictures– one the portrait of Mme. Gautreau which made such a scandal at last year's salon–[171] It seemed to me masterly– perfectly original & as full of character & expression as an old portrait. If she is a fast, immodest looking woman– it is not his fault. He has painted her in her ordinary ball-dress– a black satin, decollete down to her waist nearly– <u>without sleeves</u>– the courdage attached or rather just kept from slipping off her by two thin silver chains over the shoulders. As she is a lady of the Grande Monde, her friends are shocked not by her, but by the artist! The strength of the picture lies to me in the wonderful way he has shown by her pose & expression the real character of the woman– & <u>in the bold</u> & brilliant technical treatment. I haven't seen any other modern work. I hear Donnat is making rapid strides. I have written more than enough & haven't said anything– as usual. Once more let me tell you how grateful I am to know your boy is born– Don't let it be too long before you make the effort to write a line– Agnes & Annie send their best love & congratulations

Always fondly yours

Emma L.

Emma Lazarus to Richard Watson Gilder
Paris
Nov 21st
(1885)

My dear Mr. Gilder–

I had a delightful surprise last evening, in receiving fresh from the press the new edition of your poems– for which I send you my warmest thanks.[172] How good you were to remember me & send them to me– It was like seeing a friendly old face in these foreign parts & gave me genuine pleasure. The form is charming– & this morning I have been reading some of those which are new to me– I find them quite worthy to stand beside the older ones– & these keep all of their familiar charm. The volume is quite imposing in size– I had

no idea you had written so much! I wish them heartily all success & appreciation. I hope that Helena is gaining strength & that the new baby is no less
lovely & wonderful than Rodman & Dorothea. How busy you all keep over
there– & here I am, dilettanting along & watching my own life flow past me
like a useless stream. Just now it sparkles a little, so I am content. Paris is very
beautiful– & within little more than a week, I hope to be in Italy. It is a great
event, & fills me with an almost frightened sort of expectation. We go by way
of Avignon, where I shall think of you & your troubadour friends– I have a
letter of introduction to Mistral, but I feel so <u>shy</u> & unequal to seeing people
that I don't expect to deliver it. I live in complete solitude– animated only by
my sisters & the great pictures & books of the world. I see men & women in
the street passing like amusing sort of phantoms, but they have no real existence for me. The only trouble about this life is that it is too luxurious & is
making me so savage that I shall soon be unfit to speak to anyone. Fortunately
for me I care a good deal for my old friends– & when I think of you & Helena
I become almost human again– With sincere thanks & much love to Helena–

Your friend

Emma Lazarus

Letter 45HdeKG

Emma Lazarus to Helena deKay Gilder
Florence
Dec. 16, 1885

My dear Helena–

It was a real joy to me today to get your bright, happy letter with its good
news of yourself & your family. I am quite prepared to fall at the feet of George
Coleman deKay Gilder if he is anything like his brother & sister in appearance–
At the same time with yours came a letter from Ruth Draper telling me she
had just seen your Dorothy who was the most "exquisitely beautiful little
creature" she had ever seen. Thank you for your kind thoughtfulness in sending me the introduction to your sister. I don't expect to go to Venice before
the Spring– but I am glad to look forward to the pleasure seeing her in her
own home.

Richard's book did arrive safely– I found it awaiting me in Genoa– I had
already recd a copy from Josephine– & thought it was from him– so he must
have been surprised at my premature letter of thanks. Please thank him
again, & tell him how doubly valuable it is to me coming from him. What can

I say to you about Italy! I should not be writing to you at all on a glorious sunny day in Florence, & if it were not that I have made myself ill already with excitement & enthusiasm, & impatience & after staying in bed all yesterday with fever & fatigue, am positively <u>forced</u> to keep to the house today. I am all right again now & only exasperated at being obliged to stay indoors– But how can anything feel calm & well in a place like this? I am perfectly crazy & you need not expect any thing coherent or sensible from me in the way of a letter while I am in Italy. I will try to begin at the beginning however. The Valley of the Rhone was my first <u>sensation</u>. The trip from Lyon to Avignon was a day stolen from paradise, & I shall never forget the splendor of the flaming Provencal landscape– all purple & scarlet & gold in an atmosphere like that of the middle of May. You may imagine the effect of Avignon on me– & of the views from the Papal palace of the Rhone & the Durance– & my first glimpse of olives & oranges & frogs & lizards & December roses in that gorgeous Southern sunshine. I did not see the <u>filibres</u>– I had a letter of introduction for Mistral– but somehow or other I hadn't the courage to present it– & then we were there for such a short time, it seemed scarcely worthwhile to impose myself on him. After Avignon came the Riviera & Nice & Genoa, with all of which I was so painfully disappointed that I began to think there was some essential lack in my nature & that I wasn't going to appreciate Italy! But all doubts vanished when I came to <u>Pisa</u>. Oh Helena! isn't it divine? I was just <u>drunk</u> with beauty when I saw that little jewel of a town in an atmosphere like a Claude Lorraine glass,[173] & wandered all day by the Arno, through the dear, heavy-eaved Italian streets with their intense lights & shadows & saw for the first time the Cathedral & the Bapistry & the Campo Santo & Campanile! There they all stood as fresh as April, looking as if nobody had ever raved & exhausted their adjectives over them before– What is the use of talking about those frescoes in the Campo Santo– or about those cypress standing in the green quadrangle– or about the miracles of that Cathedral or about anything! I have never dreamed of such wealth & radiance of beauty– & I can only make a fool of myself if I begin to talk– Well, we tore ourselves away from Pisa with a firm conviction that we should never see anything so beautiful again– & we came through the Garden of Eden to <u>Florence</u>. Isn't it ridiculous & do you wonder that after three days of trying to grapple with the Pitti, & the Uffizi & Santa Croce & Masaccio & Luca della Robbia, & Leonardo & Michael Angelo, I collapsed & had to send for a Doctor? I am trying now to work myself down to a proper frame of mind for seeing things calmly & decently. The Doctor this morning, a nice young American, told me he had police officers stationed at various palaces & picture galleries to keep his patients out of them. I said it was all very well for him who had been here for years to take things so calmly, but what had he done when he first came? "Oh," he said, "I made a fool of myself then!" So it does seem inevitable.

I saw Mrs. Lockwood in Paris for a week & again here, where she waited a day over before starting for Rome, so that we might at least <u>meet</u> in Florence. She was lovely– all kindness, forethought & consideration, & had filled my room with roses & anemones. Her two girls are exceedingly attractive & interesting & it was a pleasure to see them too. I hope to rejoin them in Rome where we shall probably be at the same hotel.

From all that Mr. James told me, I don't think his sister's illness has touched her mind in the least.[174] He gave me a good many details & did not refer to that– it is some trouble with the spine, I think, together with nervous dyspepsia & general weakness– but I don't believe there is a word of truth in the report that her mind is affected. I had a cheerful letter from him yesterday, saying she is much better, & so far promises to have a very comfortable winter. I am so sorry to hear of Mrs. Henry Adams– I know what an interesting & intelligent person she must be.[175] Thank you so much for giving me the good news of Maria Dewing. I am delighted to think of her happiness. As for you, I am proud of the way you have behaved yourself, & I trust you will keep brave in spirits & energy now that this difficult ordeal is past. I shall think of you all at Christmas & wish you much merriment– I suppose the Tree will be more splendid than ever. Do write whenever you can spare the time from your numerous family & remember what pleasure it gives me to hear, & to see your handwriting. I sent you a little Christmas card which I hope has reached you safely– I have got Italy "very bad"– & trust you will excuse this rambling & idiotic letter. Your loving friend

Emma Lazarus

Letter 46HdeKG

Emma Lazarus to Helena deKay Gilder
Florence
Dec. 24 [1885]

Dear Helena–

Although you despise photographs, I send you one I had taken in Paris. I hope you will like it a little for my sake, while I am not there to bother you in its place. I also copy for your special benefit a translation of a little Russian poem by Mikeassef– which my new Russian friend in Paris put into French verse for me, & which I am sure will touch you as it did me. Life is still a dream to me– & Florence grows more bewitching each day. Directly opposite my window is Bellosguardo & if you could only see it pink & gold in the morning bathed in rosy mist– with pale blue shadows,– & a mass of black shadow at sunset standing against a sky of solid gold, with its cypresses pointing upward– you would know how I love it, & how I am already dreading the time when I shall have to leave it.[176] On Sunday I climbed to the top– & saw the silver olives against such a sky as I never imagined, & looked down upon the vision of splendor that is Florence– What a sight it is– & how in spite of all one hears or reads beforehand, the reality finds one wholly unprepared! It looks like a city of jewels– & yet so exquisitely delicate & poetical, & soft in its atmosphere & rosy-purple– that it seemed ready to melt into air at a breath. I am just dazzled by everything– & cannot get used to the beauty on every side. Almost my greatest art sensation here is Luca della Robbia–[177] I knew I should like him, but I had no idea I should find him so inexorably lovely– He seems always equal to his best work, which I have found the case with almost no other artist– except possibly Rembrandt– What do you think of Dante's death mask at the Uffizi– Why didn't you or anybody else tell me that Italy wore a veil of roses & gold? That is the most surprising thing to me– & it is that that makes everything here seem an enchantment. We are going to Rome on the 15th of Jany. to stay (I hope) six weeks, if we all keep well. Then I am happy to say, we shall come back to Florence– I don't think I will go to Naples, or indeed venture any further South– I hate the sea, especially the Mediterranean, & know I should not enjoy that kind of thing. Pompeii is the only part I shall regret, & I will have other compensations here & at Venice. Everything away from Italy seems cold & gray & hard– How I wish you could be with me in this heavenly spot! I must go out now so goodbye. Shall I go this morning to San Lorenzo or San Mario? I can't decide!

Much love to you all from your friend

Emma Lazarus

Emma Lazarus to Helena deKay Gilder
Rome
Jany. 25 '86

My dear Helena—

If I can collect my scattered wits for the space of half an hour before going to the Palace of the Caesars, I must & will write you a few lines & let you know that I think of you & should dearly love to have a talk with you— I am simply wild with the excitement of this tremendous place & after being torn between the Papacy & Paganism for the first few days, I have come to the conclusion that I will not attempt to do more than see Pagan Rome in the few short weeks I have to stay here, & will give up all the churches & their music, & all the Popes & all the Renaissance— My first hour in Rome was a sensation never to be forgotten. My first view of the Coliseum thrilled me more than anything of the kind (if there be anything else of the kind I had ever seen) & each moment is so full of emotion & excitement for me with every step I take through these eloquent streets, that I do not know myself at all. I can't imagine what people mean, or what they are made of, when they talk of disappointment with the first impression of Rome— To me, it is so overpoweringly beautiful, strange & significant, that from the very first instant I was crushed by it, & have continued to feel the spell of it all, more & more profoundly with each hour of my stay— The first few days I was ill as I was in Florence, from sheer nervous excitement & too great mental stimulus of so many impressions at once— But I have managed to control my enthusiasm since then & take things a little more quietly. Mr. Story[178] asked me if I was enjoying Rome— or suffering from it? & I suppose there are just as many enthusiasts to do the latter as the former. I am not alone in taking it so hard! I don't know why it is, but I cannot remember whether you came here with Mr. Gilder— I associate you so entirely with Florence & Venice that I don't see you here at all— were you here? & if yes, how did you feel? I am sure you must have come, & yet I don't see how I could have forgotten if you had talked of it to me, as you did of other things in Italy. I have been here a week & have seen the Vatican & the Capitoline Museum & the Sistine Chapel & St. Peters, besides the ruins in the streets & on the hills & the graves of Shelley & Keats— It is all heart-breaking— I don't only mean those beautiful graves overgrown with acanthus & violets— but the mutilated arches & columns & dumb appealing fragments of the wreck looming up from the desolate Forum & on the Palatine & Capitoline hills. I spent yesterday afternoon at the Protestant Cemetery as lovely with its green-black crowding cypresses as when Shelley's luring eyes saw it— for the sun was shin-

ing thru' the tree trunks & the <u>Roman blue</u> sky hung over it all morning. I was
in the Capitoline Museum– what a gallery! Do you remember the one small
room where the Dying Gladiator is? Each separate thing in it would make the
fame of any other collection in the world. I am so out of humor with the
pictures here, that I have not even had the curiosity to see Raphael's frescoes.
A bit of broken stone or a fragment of a bas relief, or a Corinthian column
standing out against the Lapis-Lazuli sky, or the tremendous arch are the only
things I can look at for the moment– except the Sistine Chapel. How gigantic
this is– & how thoroughly un-Roman! But even here it forces itself upon you
with an unequal might. There is really nothing to be said about Rome– Just to
go over the names of the places one sees in a day is enough to give anyone
who knows them an idea of one's feelings & impressions– & no idea can
possibly be given to those who don't. My friend Mrs. Lockwood is here in the
same hotel with me– & I have enjoyed very much going about with her– She
cares for so many of the same things, & is always so affectionate & lovely to
me– She has had a great blow lately in the news of her niece Miss Bagned's
death– She sees nobody now & we have been thrown much together. I have
seen also Nelly Barlow who is settled in delightful apartments very near me– &
is as thoroughly acclimatized & self-possessed as if she were in New York or
Staten Island.[179] She looks well & pretty & very sweet– & is going to be presented at Court next week– Here as elsewhere I live absolutely by myself– Even
if I were going about I should not care to do it in Rome– where the sensations
of a single day's mere living are enough to wear me out mentally & physically
without the miserable little strain of one's faculties that society always brings.
The one exception I shall make will be to go to the Storys who have welcomed
me most hospitably & kindly– & who ask me to dine with them entirely en
famille. I was invited one day last week to go back to Florence & spend a day
under the same roof with Liszt– but I was not equal to the effort & thought I
had best content myself with Rome– By the way, will you please tell Mr. Gilder
that if at any future time he should receive a mss. on some musical subjects
from the Countess Resse of Florence, that I hope he will give his attention to
it– as she is a fine musician & I should think very competent to write about it.
It was she who invited me to meet Liszt. She was an American widow named
Mrs. Pearsall who has married an Italian Count & who lives in the most delightful way in a villa just outside of Florence– She is a great friend of your
friend Mrs. Stillman's & told me Lisa had been such a great success in London
Society last season– Fancy an Italian villa where Liszt & Rubinstein stay as
familiar guests, a villa overlooking Fiesole & Vallombrose, fitted up in ancient
Florentine style & possessing a genuine & most beautiful <u>Botticelli</u>! The "Italian Count" sounds badly, but is on the contrary the best of the whole– a
cultivated, charming & handsome man– For <u>one day</u> I came very close to

envying the Countess her "luck"– but it didn't last when I found out that there too were closets full of skeletons! Since I received your letter, I have been delightfully surprised by receiving Mr. Gilder's photograph. It is perfect & most interesting & poetical looking– I feel as if I should write him a special letter of thanks, but I know he will be a great deal better pleased if you will tell him how grateful I am for it, & how very much I admire it. I hear of you as going to grand dinners & looking very handsome & having a beautiful boy– besides Rodman & Dorothy. Oh, I must tell you that while I was in Florence I saw a little boy playing about one day on top of Bellosguardo who was so exactly like Rodman at the age of six, that I could not stop staring at him, & felt as if the dial hand had moved backwards. He was a beauty– with the same peach-like bloom, dark eyes & golden hair– an Italian of course– It is an age since you have written to me– have you forgotten all about me or do you intend to let me hear from you sometime? We shall be in Rome until March when we go back for a visit to Florence– Forgive me this long, dull letter & believe me always affectionately your friend

Emma Lazarus

Who took Mr. Gilder's photo? It is decidedly the best I have ever seen of him & I am delighted to have it. I enclose for him a daisy from his beloved Keats' grave. Am reading Mrs. Foote's story of John Rodman.[180] Isn't it fresh & charming?

Letter 48HdeKG

Emma Lazarus to Helena deKay and Richard Watson Gilder
Rome–
Feby. 23rd '86

My dear Helena (& Richard!)

Please don't hate me for answering your delightful letter the very day I receive it, but I have been so long waiting to hear from you, & it is so much more like a little tete a tete talk, if I "talk back" at once! Of course I forgive you for not writing with all your daily cares & duties & pleasures & with George Coleman & Rodman & Dorothea besides– but you know what a pleasure it is to me to hear from you & have your sympathy– I am grieved to hear of poor Mr. Eaton's sorrows & trust his own strength will prove equal to the trial. How lovely the Wards must have been– they are truly the salt of the earth & I am always proud to think of them as among my friends. Bessy von

Schoenberg has just come to Rome & has been most kind & affectionate with me–[181] I have quite lost my heart to her for she seems to me to have all the Ward force & intelligence together with her mother's sympathetic charm– She is a most interesting woman. So you joined the "Causeries" & I can only say you have my deepest sympathy![182] In a rash moment I was persuaded to enroll myself among its members two years ago, & it has been the bane of my existence ever since– It is quite the biggest bore I have ever been associated with, & I have already sent my resignation in three times with no perceptible result. Please don't breathe these sentiments of mine to anyone, least of all to Mrs. J. Boorman, Jr. who got me in & seems to think it a galaxy of genius! I have never seen Edith Story Peruzzi so I cannot say whether you look like her–[183] She does not live in Rome but in Florence where I shall doubtless see her when I go back. I have seen her picture & her bust at her mother's house, & they are certainly very <u>un</u>like you– Mr. & Mrs. Story have been more than kind to me here– & have been the one outside element in my life. I like them both extremely– Mrs. Lockwood has been in the same hotel with me till yesterday when she returned to Florence– so I cannot give her your message till we meet again. She was greatly overcome & upset by her repeated shocks– but did not break down physically or mentally– & before she left, she had recovered a great deal of her usual courage & spirit. She has a strange, keen restless mind– repose seems an absolute impossibility to her & her nerves are always overstrung to the last degree of tension– but she is made of noble stuff & it shines through all her eccentricities. It has been a great comfort to me to have her in the house– all the more as Agnes had a very tedious attack of bronchitis, & Mrs. L. was all kindness & affection to me & to her. I will <u>not</u> give her your message about Clarence King– as I heard, (tho' I don't know how true it is)– of a very bitter passage at arms between them last Spring apropos of Ellen Terry– in which Mr. K. had the last word & a very cutting one! Did you like him? I have only met him twice, at dinner– once in U . . . & once in London– but I thought him very agreeable. I have seen the R.U. Johnsons[184] two or three times in our hotels and in galleries, etc. They are very happy & enthusiastic– They came to see me on Sunday evng. He was going to Athens the next day– He has discovered the greatest of all painters in - - - Domenichino! Don't you think this is curiously characteristic? If he had selected one who was downright bad, it wouldn't have seemed so funny– But how anyone can stop at Domenichino & not go any farther after getting so far, is a most puzzling phenomenon to me. All this nonsense I have written & not said a word about Rome– Well if I thought it was great the first day, I have gone on in a wild crescendo & enjoyed it more thoroughly & profoundly with each day of my stay. As Florence Lockwood says "First it knocks you flat, & then it <u>grows upon you!</u>" I am glad & grateful to know that you have seen it– if only for a fortnight– a lifetime isn't enough, but a single day is better than nothing & gives you an impression beyond everything else. And above all, I am glad to think you have seen the Sistine Chapel! One hasn't seen anything until one has seen that. I have spent as many mornings as I could there & each time it is a fresh & strange sensation of wonder & awe! What do people mean when they say it is hard to see? Except for the agony in the nape of one's neck (which is a slight matter) there is nothing to find fault with. I had expected a dark, dingy room with a blackened ceiling covered with almost invisible figures– but the freshness of that divine colouring, & the distinct plastic outline of each separate figure was a perfect revelation to me. The whole thing seems to dwarf so entirely all else in the way of painting, that it is only by forgetting it & putting it altogether out of mind, that you can look at other things. From a different standpoint, how lovely, lovely, lovely the Botticelli & Luca Signorelli are. My only consolation is to fly from the Chapel to the photographics and from the photographics to the Chapel & get groups & "details" & compositions in every shape. This is the only thing in the way of painting that I enjoy in Rome except a few things in the Colonna Leber– I am completely swallowed up by the Greek art of the Vatican, the Lateran & the Capitol– & I consider myself very wise in having just eliminated from my list of sights to be seen the Guernicos & the Guidos & the Raphaels & given all my time to Ancient Rome & the Sistine Chapel. There are so many things I haven't seen at all that everybody goes to see– & on the other hand I have had such glorious hours in the Vatican, & in the Coliseum reading Coriolanus & Julius Caesar & Marcus Aurelius as if I were in my own little den at home– & just drinking in with every sense the spirit of the antique world, & the beauty of life. We are in the midst of Spring– the almond trees are in perfect blossom– the violets & anemones are thick in the villa grounds– it is a perfect intoxication. Last Friday I went to San Orofino, the Church where Tasso is buried. It stands on a hill in the midst of an old orchard & garden. The day was like May at home– Around me were the greenest of slopes, planted with vegetables & pink & white flowering almond trees– at my side on an old cream-colored Italian wall with orange trees leaning against it loaded with fruit– On the heights were cypress & stone pieces against the radiant sky, & at my feet was all of Rome surrounded by the Campagna & the purple Alban & Sabine hills! Isn't it all a glory & an embarrassment. Did you have time to see the Villa Medici where the lucky "prix de Rome" students are. It is as green & as lovely (almost) as the park at The Hague– & there too I have had long hours of beauty under those overarching ilex trees. Did you see the Palatine Hills & wander among the ruins of the Caesars, & did you love it all as I do? I wish you would tell me what you most care for, & what you did most often– & who were your favorite gods in the Vatican. We are going to leave on the 4th March– next Thursday, & if it weren't that I am determined to come back if I live I don't know how I could do it. We are going to Florence & shall stop by the way at Orvieto, Peruggia, Assisi, & Cortona. I have got the usual infatuation for the Italians, & am willing to give my last franc for one of their smiles! I was so proud of a compliment I had this morning from one of the dirtiest, most miserable old mechanics in a trunk shop. I bought a trunk, & he asked me to make a pencil mark on it to be sure he sent me the right one– & I laughed & said I "wasn't afraid of him"– whereupon his whole face beamed & then he seized my arm & stretched it & said in the most enthusiastic tone– "Grasis Signera– e una vera parole romana– Lei e brioria!" To say that I felt like Volumnia, & the mother of the Gracchi & the wives of all the Caesars, doesn't express my sensations. Don't say anything about it, as I have no plans whatever– but I feel sorely tempted to delay going home for the sake of another winter here– There is so much to stay for & so little to go home for– except a few good friends who will like me none the less if I come home improved. However, this is the merest possibility as yet– I may not be able to carry it out. I am interested to hear of Mme. Grenville– but I had fancied her more attractive. I am longing to see George Coleman– he must be an angel. Don't let Rodman go to college before I come home– Give my love to your mother & Julia– & with lots of love for yourself believe me proudly yours

Emma Lazarus

Nellie Barlow lives near me & I see her very often– She is very sweet & looks so pretty. P.S. I have heard it positively that your sister Mrs. Bronson is engaged to be married to Robert Browning– is it true?[185] I heard it here at the table d'hote from a lady who didn't know I knew of you– or that the item would have a special interest for me– Apropos of K.B.– I have met here Miss Constance Fletcher– author of "Kismet," etc.–[186] I only saw her once– but thought I should like her– She lives in Venice where I hope to see more of her– We expect to be in Venice in April. I find Mr. Gilder's photograph most poetic & satisfactory. Why didn't you speak of mine? Do you think it bad?

Emma Lazarus to Helena deKay Gilder
Florence April 7 '86

My dear Helena–

It is a long time since I have heard from you, but I go on trusting you have not forgotten your foreign friend & that your silence is only caused by the superior claims of George Coleman, Rodman & Dorothea. I hear from home that you are looking well & <u>handsome</u>, so I shall indulge myself in the luxury of a morning's talk with you.– Well, I have seen the Spring in Italy & I agree with all the poets & all the fools about it– the only trouble is they never said half enough. The pink & white orchards & the olive groves & budding green of the hills about Florence have made it a perfect paradise for the last fortnight or so. Last week I went on a little three days' excursion with Florence Lockwood to Siena & San. . . . The latter place disappointed me, but I enjoyed Siena immensely. Did you see it? I found it more picturesque than any other town I have yet seen– with its grey old palaces & "tigre striped" Cathedral & Campanile & its glorious outlooks over the wide sea-like valley. The Duomo is a world in itself. Do you remember the "Genffiti" on the floor & the interminable intricacy of those great old columns? & the delightful Petrucchios in the Chapel and the famous Todelanos? Did you care much for Todelanos? I was disappointed in him & enjoyed the Pinturicchios more, as well as some old altar pieces in the Academy. In matters of art, I go through the most extraordinary revulsions of feeling from week to week– I pass through such rapid "phases" that I can scarcely understand my enthusiasms of a month ago. What did I mean, for instance, when I raved so to you about Luca della Robbia? When I came back from Rome with the Greek sculptures & bas reliefs fresh in my mind, it was hard to believe he had ever made such an impression on me. And yet there are some of the Renaissance men that a love of Greek art makes one only admire more– especially & preeminently Botticelli– Leonardo– Donatello– & a few others. It is absurd to talk much less to write about these things when one is as ignorant as I. I only wish I had you here with me to exchange opinions about each individual master. One thing more I must say– Why did you ever tell me I would care for Raphael when I got in Italy? The more I see of him the less I care, & so far I have seen nothing of his I like as much as the little "Apollo & Marsgas" of the Louvre. I am reading Italian books and trying to follow Italian politics & trying to learn to <u>speak</u> Italian– all under the greatest difficulty & impedimenta. There is an Italian novel here that has made a great sensation, by a man named Fogassara– It is called "Daniele Cortis"– I was much interested & delighted with the beginning but found it tedious towards the end, & very unequal. Have you seen it? Carducci is the only poet– & a very genuine one– if not a giant. I think I told you that I hope to stay abroad & spend another winter in Rome. The R.U. Johnsons are in the house with us & Nelly Barlow & her family– Nelly is looking very pretty & is very sweet & affectionate. Mrs. Lockwood & her family have gone today. Strictly between ourselves, alas! alas! Some of my poor little old rags of illusions have gone with her! We have fortunately had none of the usual fellow-travelers' quarrels, but her pedestal has crumbled beneath her. It was my fault, as it always is, to have placed her on one. Don't say anything about this to anyone, including my family– only I am a shade more disappointed & cynical than I was before. I take refuge from the cruelties & trivialities of life, in art, nature & books– Thank heavens, they don't fail me here!– Yes, Mme. Peruzzi is startlingly like you. I suppose partly on that account I find her peculiarly attractive & interesting. I don't know her at all well & have not seen much of her– I should think she would be a slow person to get to know– like everybody else who is worth knowing– but she makes the impression of singular earnestness & sweetness– & I cannot resist the wish to know her better– She has three lovely children & looks some years older than you. I have met here also Miss Violet Paget– otherwise known as "Vernon Lee"–[187] She is clever & brilliant though not personally attractive. Our friend Miss Mary A.F. Robinson of London is staying with her just now.[188] I saw her yesterday– She has a good deal of charm, I think.

Of course you know that the larger part of my family expect to join us in June– I shall be glad to have my brother here & am looking forward to our summer together in England. As for Joe, we have had such distracted letters from her at the mere thought of undertaking the journey, that much as I wished for her, at first, I hope now she will not be persuaded to come– the voyage at best would be a great risk for her, & if she comes so reluctantly I feel sure she would only be homesick & wretched. I heard indirectly that your brother Charley was coming abroad this month. Is it true? It would be such a pleasure if he turned up in Venice. We are going there next week– on the 16th & hope to stay a month. I feel as if I had a great deal in store for me.

I have just finished "John Rodman's Testimony"– which seems to me full of beauty– not only good & artistic in itself but rich in capacity of future development. I hope it will have the success it deserves– I think it is so superior to the majority of stories that appear every day by writers who ought to know better! But I suppose I have no right to talk– I don't do anything myself, & feel as if I never should– All motive, ambition & capacity (such as it was) seem to have left me. The mere thought of writing paralyzes me & overwhelms me with painful memories– Are you going to Marion? I wish I could think of your taking a holiday from housekeeping this summer. Do tell me something of your plans & don't neglect me altogether. I had a good laugh over Mr. Gilder's . . . hoff" letter to Mr. Johnson written from the office. . . . read it to me & it was . . . amusing. I am reluctant to send this dull letter but it is only to let you know that I think of you warmly & constantly.

Your friend

Emma Lazarus

Letter 50HdeKG
[New York Public Library]

Emma Lazarus to Richard Watson Gilder
London
May 23, 1886

My dear Mr. Gilder:

Is there any of the "Feel" of Venice in the accompanying rhymes? If you think so, & if you care to find room for them in the "Century" I shall be glad– if not, please let me know their fate. I never <u>could</u> do much & I can do even less than ever now– so, I shan't be surprised if they prove worthless. This ought to be only a business letter, but I must add a line to ask where & how you are & why you & Helena & your ". . . full of children" to speak Biblically, cannot be here with me in the beautiful . . . fog & murk at the moment. I had no idea England was so beautiful until I came back to it full of foolish misgivings & fears after the splendors of Italy. But it is lovelier, fresher, greener & softer than ever, & I feel as if I were at home– London is huge & interesting as usual– Annie & I are chiefly preoccupied just now with the Rubinstein concerts– but politics are wildly exciting & the whirl of London-life all around us seems as dizzy & distracting as ever–[189] A friend of mine described the political situation to me by repeating what a "membre" had first said to her– "It's a crisis when an honest man can change his opinion every night!" So you may fancy the heat of the excitement– I haven't seen anyone except Mr. James who came yesterday to welcome me but I shall try to pick up again my stray acquaintances here– Today, being Sunday, I am going to Mrs. Procter's where I shall probably see the great Robert. Mrs. P. is more active & younger than ever– according to Mr. James, with a cute "Indian Summer" bloom– I suppose you know that my sister Agnes is going to be married here on the 17th of June.[190] Before then, I expect all my family (except Sarah) over, so we shall present a very solid front. I saw your friends the Johnsons last at Bulaffio. They were well & happy. Give my love to Helena & tell her this doesn't count– I am going to write her very soon– although she owes me lots of letters. What do you say to coming over & spending next winter in Italy– with us? We shall be in Rome. Don't forget me, please– even if I do stay abroad longer than I should. It is so easy here & life is so short.

Sincerely & faithfully your friend–

Emma Lazarus

Letter 51HdeKG

Emma Lazarus to Helena deKay Gilder
London
May 30, '86

My dear Helena–

I have just had such a delightful afternoon with your friend Mrs. Stillman, that although you owe me half a dozen letters I am not going to resist the impulse to write to you all about that & lots of other things. It was the first time I had seen her– Annie having only yesterday sent word to her Liza that we were here– & she (Liza) came over the first thing this morning, to ask us to lunch with them. We went, & I quite agree with you that Mrs. S. is the most beautiful woman I have ever seen. I could not take my eyes off the magnificence of her hair & her eyes– & the perfection of the whole woman, head, face & figure– She was most amiable & charming to us & spoke with much affection of you– She was dressed in black which was very becoming to her– but I suppose anything would be– Liza looked very well & very handsome also– & the third daughter, Effie, is equally beautiful.[191] The second, Bella, though not as handsome, is a fresh, attractive-looking English girl, more winning in her manners than the other sisters, by her great simplicity & frankness– She is studying hard for the Cambridge examinations & seemed like a most charming & interesting girl. I found the whole household much better appointed & regulated than I had expected– a pretty home with delightful artistic work in every direction– & in a word, I could quite understand all your enthusiasm & admiration in talking of that exquisite creature & her family.

London is more interesting than ever– I had an eventful morning before going to the Stillmans'– having spent it with the great Rubinstein–[192] Mrs. Moscheles who knows him very intimately, came yesterday to ask if we would not go to his hotel with her this morng– to see him as she had not yet been– & he takes it quite amiss if his friends (ladies especially!) don't go on his reception morngs to see him– As we knew him in New York, we gladly went with her– & found him so simple, affable & agreeable that we were more than ever enchanted. He invited us to breakfast with him for one day this week, & you may imagine how we are looking forward to it. His personality is one of the greatest I have seen– & the sense of power is never missing, whatever he may talk about. We talked of course, a great deal about Russian literature & authors. Tolstoi is an intimate friend of his– though he considers him on the road to insanity, as he thinks anyone must be who goes into mysticism. It was a great disappointment to me to hear that Tolstoi has given up nothing except the dress of the world, wearing always the peasant's costume– but living as comfortably as ever with his wife & children in his fine, rich house. Rubinstein expects to spend next Winter in Rome where he gave us the hope of really getting to know him. He speaks perfect English & is interesting in all subjects. As for his music, I can give you no idea of what it is like– fortunately you have heard yourself, so it is not necessary. All I will say, is that your most enthusiastic & exaggerated recollection falls far below the reality– for much as I have thought of him during the 14 years since I heard him last, I could not have believed his art was so phenomenal as I found it. It is a revelation of what music should be. What a crazy world this is! While we were there, a half-cracked German came in to see him with a very serious proposition. He was a flute-player, & he wanted Rubinstein to accompany him in perpetuity. He had already asked Liszt, but he had refused, & there was no one in England capable of doing it. He also thought Rubinstein might be of help to him in exterminating the Catholic religion! If you had seen the perfect seriousness on both sides in this extraordinary interview & the courtesy with which he was received & dismissed, & had heard Rubinstein's great hearty laugh when he got rid of him, you would have enjoyed it as I did. I have seen your brother Charley here, one day last week– looking the picture of health & good humour– I was so glad to see him, & in such full enjoyment of everything around him. He shared our miserable lodging-house dinner with us, & we exchanged our travelling experiences & it was quite refreshing to see him in such spirits– Your sister I have not seen– I was glad to get good news of you from your brother– & oh, how I wish you could have come with him! How many things we could enjoy together!

I went to Mrs. Procter's last Sunday– She is more wonderful than ever & was very cordial & nice to me, remembering every detail of our last meeting three years ago, which I had quite forgotten. I did not see Browning as he had just left, & I have been nowhere yet, so that I have not yet met him elsewhere– Lowell is here, as you doubtless know & Dr. Holmes is being made very much of by everybody, from the Duke of Westminster to little Gosse–[193] Please tell Richard I have just heard that Gosse is responsible for the suppression of my Morris article– & I am accordingly furious with him & the whole editorial staff.[194] As King Lear says– "What my revenge shall be, I know not yet!" I don't know whether I told you that I have seen Henry James who seems very well & prosperous– & his sister is almost well– She has gone to the country with Miss Loring. I saw the "Salon" while I was in Paris a fortnight ago– & found it full of interest. There was a quantity of brilliant work & much that was beautiful. The best pictures there, were American– Donnat's Portrait of his mother, Melchior's "Dutch Church"– & a big rural scene of Pierce's. But the general level of the work was so high & there was so little in the enormous collection that was really poor, that I was amazed– My experience of contemporary exhibitions having been previously limited by New York & London, I was quite unprepared for so much talent. I have not yet been able to screw my courage to go to the Royal Academy– nor even to the Grosvenor Gallery. The English are so hopelessly stupid about art. Sargent's work this year in Paris is very poor– I hear he makes a better show here– & you know he has come to live here altogether– I must not begin another page– so I will stop. Nearly all my family are on the Atlantic, & I am anxiously looking forward to their arrival. Agnes is going to be married on the 17th. Do write to me sometimes & believe me with constant love

Your friend

Emma Lazarus

Letter 52HdeKG

Emma Lazarus to Helena deKay Gilder
London
June 21st '86

My dearest Helena–

I have only just heard of your poor brother's death– & I know what this must mean to you & your dear mother & family. I hope it came quietly & painlessly– but I know no particulars having heard of it indirectly through Agnes who is in Paris and saw the brief newspaper announcement. Although you cannot . . . at the release from a life that was nothing but mental & physical pain– yet I feel that you must suffer from a thousand thoughts that will not be put aside– It is hard to acquiesce & hard, hardest of all to understand– but I hope that you struggle against morbid ideas as bravely as when your poor brother was attacked with his mortal illness. He has found rest & peace at last– There is nothing but comfort in the thought & so for you, dearest Helena, I think of you with deepest affection & sympathy– I only wish I could be with you, for I . . . my part in whatever trial or sorrow touches you–

I fear I shall leave London without seeing your brother Charles again, as we go to . . . in a week, on the 5th July– & he has only just gone to Holland. The Johnsons whom I saw yesterday, had seen him in Paris a few days before & I know very well that when he gets to the enchanted land of dykes & . . . he will not be able to tear himself away for the sake of . . . hot London in July. I have been very much preoccupied with my own family. Agnes' wedding took place ten days ago– an unusually picturesque & solemn ceremony in the Synagogue here– Almost the only guest present besides the two families, whom I had asked the privilege of inviting was Browning.[195] He had never seen a Jewish wedding before, & seemed much moved & impressed by the services which he said were the most beautiful he had ever seen– We were glad to have anything so simple & solemn & only wished all our friends could have been with us. Of course you have heard how well Josephine bore the voyage– She has not been so well since she arrived as the London climate does not suit her. Yesterday was our first summer day– but the doctor does not appear to consider her case at all serious, & evidently does all he can to prevent her from becoming an invalid and becoming ". . ."– She does not take as kindly to England & the English as I did, & I am disappointed to find how slight her interest is in the things I care for so much– but I suppose this has a great deal to do with her state of health. We are going to Malvern on her account by the doctor's advice– & we shall probably spend the greater part of the summer there. I had a long visit yesterday with Henry James– He is over-worked, & over-dined and over-bored & over-everything. He neither looks well nor seems well– but you know he always interests me & it is always a pleasure to me to see him. Your lovely friend Mrs. Stillman has been most hospitable & kind to us– & we have seen her & Liza several times. Liza is looking very beautiful. She talks of you with the most loyal affection & I believe her when she says she would gladly cross the ocean (which she hates) for just two or three days with you– if she had to come back by the same steamer. I was glad to hear her speak of you as she did– for without knowing her well, I had never given her credit for depth or constancy in friendship but the more I see of her the more I find to like & admire in her & this is in a very objective & personal way– for our own relation towards each other is a very slight one. Her mother has every charm & I don't wonder at all you have said about her. Annie & I dined with them last week– just in their family– they are so generous & simple in their hospitality. Waldstein is in London & has come to see us– He is more brilliant & attractive than ever– He seems to be on top of the wave as far as success goes, but is very cordial & nice to his American friends. He begged us to go down to Cambridge for a day, & there is nothing I should enjoy more– but I am afraid we shall have to leave London before he goes back. I have also seen your friend Mrs. Middlemore (Nina Sturgis). She looks very badly & much changed. I believe she had a painful illness some few months ago. She is going to Spain in the autumn & talks of going to America next winter. She is attractive & amusing still, & has a remarkably nice husband– I saw a curious ceremony on Thursday in the prorogation of the Parliament. Mr. Bryce sent me a ticket for the House of Lords & I went with his sister– The Medievalism of the whole thing, the wigs & scarlet gowns of the Lord commissioners, the old Norman French of the Clerk's proclamations "La Reine, la Viult" (pronounced 107 times badly) & "So it facit comme il est désiré"– the extraordinary imperial tone of the Queen's speech– all in the first person, speaking of "my Parliament," in "my city of Westminster," & of "releasing them from their duties" when she has in reality so absurdly little to say in the matter– all this was most curious, theatrical & interesting to me. I went the day before to a debate in the House of Commons– it had no special interest, the only question being of course in abeyance now. I hope you won't find this a very selfish & boring letter, dear Helena– but I write what I have been doing, thinking it may amuse you– I heard from Bessie Stickney the other day that you were at Northampton–[196] What & where is that & how do you like it? How I wish I could see you over here– there are so many things we could enjoy together. Did you see . . . House when you were here? I spent two hours there the other day. It is one of the best collections in the world, as well hung & lighted as a public gallery. Not even in Holland have I ever seen more glorious Rembrandts, & finer Van Dykes, . . . etc. Every master is represented by masterpieces. Do write to me when you feel able & can snatch a half hour– & believe always in my loving sympathy & my love to Mr. Gilder

Your friend

Emma Lazarus

Sunday

Letter 53HdeKG
[New York Public Library]

Emma Lazarus to Helena deKay Gilder
Sunday, London, June 29th, '86

My dear Helena–

Our letters have crossed each other and though I wrote you a very long one on Sunday, I must write again to thank you for yours rec'd last evening and to answer all your questions. I knew without your telling me how you must have suffered, and I could indeed feel with you and for you in all you went through. You must never mind, dear Helena, sending me a "gloomy" letter and writing just as you feel– It is such a relief sometimes to be able to write openly and fully– almost better even at moments than it might be face to face, when we dare not express all our pain and bitterness– Only remember that I have the deepest sympathy with all your sorrows and your joys– and every word you write is dear to me– I hope you have no cause for anxiety about your mother and that she too has been able to meet her grief with patience and resignation, seeing it chiefly as a blessing and relief to the poor sufferer.

What are you doing in Northampton and why did you select such an extraordinary place of refuge? Is it pretty or bracing or convenient or what is the charm that can compensate for being surrounded by the ". . ." and infirmities of every kind? You asked how I like the Scotts and Johnsons–[197] The former I saw only twice– once at "Bulaffio" and once the other day at the National Gallery– so I don't know much about them– Mr. S. seemed rather nice to me– not interesting but frank and sensible. As for the Johnsons, they were by no matter of means always "round." I managed to protect myself too well for that. One hates to say such unkind things about such kindly people, but strictly between ourselves, he represents to my mind the ideal Bore– and she though a little more alive bears a striking resemblance to him in this respect. But we always meet pleasantly and are the best of friends and I would not for the world have them think that I have other than the kindest feelings toward them– as indeed I have not– we have really only met at tables d'hote and in railway carriages– I have carefully avoided seeing "sights" or pictures together. I don't doubt I bore them just as much as they do me and they are equally heroic in giving no sign. As for "little Gosse," I must altogether disclaim the charges of having done him an "injustice." I happen to know exactly what his action was in regard to my article on Morris so the fact of its appearance in the August "Century" does not change my opinion in the least! I have heard the whole story from some English friends. I have not seen him at all. Mrs. G. invited me twice to her "Sundays" but I have declined not on account of the magazine article as you may imagine, but because I had a great many other more interesting things to do, so I think they have not been very cordial in not coming to see me all the time I have been here. I have just rec'd. a photograph I sent for from St. Petersburg of Tolstoi– such a disappointment. A great coarse face with a bushy, most objectionable beard– that does not hide a coarse and disagreeable mouth– huge projecting ears and the general look of a vulgar politician or social "agitator." I try to think it is a bad photograph, or perhaps they have sent me by mistake Tolstoi the politician instead of Tolstoi the poet. But I am afraid I shall have to reconcile myself to recognizing in this unattractive type, the author of "Guerre et Paix." It is all the worse to me as Rubinstein had raised my hopes by telling me he was such a magnificent looking man. I suppose he has the colossal build of the Russian. This is not visible in the photograph. I should very much have liked to see your sister Kate while I was in London but we have not come together. I took it for granted that if she cared to see me she could easily find my address through Mr. deKay– and as neither she nor her daughter ever returned my call in New York, I did not wish to bore them with any more advances. Of course, for your sake and that of the rest of the family, I am very sorry– but there is nothing for me to do about it. I should love to see your Eaton portrait.[198] Bessie Stickney writes me that it is so good and artistic, though an unusual aspect of you. This old National Gallery here keeps getting better every day. Each time I go there, I am astounded by the brilliancy and splendor of the collection. There is certainly nothing more complete among the galleries I have seen so far. I am going there in the morning for a final p.p.c. Much as I love London I shall be ready for the country next week. The last few days have been oppressively hot and the dust and noise and the incessant organ grinders have made life a burden– I am longing for the green again, and the blue sky and open air, all of which we go in search of to Malvern next Monday. I am hoping the climate will have a bracing effect on Josephine– She is so depressed and homesick– (though you must not tell her I said so). Of course her weak condition must have something to do with her lack of spirit and interest but I can plainly see all this new world would never have been the revelation it has been with me. My own curiosity and interest are insatiable– and I think with a shudder of the empty dreariness of Tenth St. Nevertheless, for some very substantial reasons, I want and intend to go home. If all goes well, I shall probably be back a year from this coming autumn. I miss you very much and constantly out of my life & there are a few other friends and a vague general sense of Duty to take me back– but if I let myself go, I might drift on indefinitely until I am summoned for the Long Voyage. Here too I begin to have friends who interest me exceedingly– but they don't take the place of the old. Meanwhile I rely on you to keep a little corner warm for me.

   With fond love to you and all your household,

Your friend,

Emma

I am so glad Jenny Gilder has had a holiday![199]

Letter 54HdeKG

Emma Lazarus to Helena deKay and Richard Watson Gilder
(To Marion Mass.)
Malvern
Aug. 17th '86

My dear friends

I must send you a double letter in return for your two delightful single ones rec'd a few days ago. I am of the opinion that people who stay abroad so long are unmitigated bores, with their perpetual claim for letters, & I am only surprised that you continue to be so good to me– It is a great comfort to me when I get "low in my mind" (As I sometimes do, even in the enchanted land of ruins & Cathedrals) to think of that warm chimney corner waiting for me, & even that porcelain bath, & Buzzards' Bay. I am most grateful to you both for your constant sympathy & interest.

I should love to have seen the theatricals & I wonder how they came off. To think of Rodman already an author! What a veteran it makes me feel! Do you know that I have not a sign of a photo of any of the children but Rodman & his are now several years old– Is there nothing of Dorothea you could send me? Everyone confirms the report that she is bewitching– & I want to know how she looks before I go home & find her a grown-up young lady.

Your little P.S. about Gosse, dear Mr. Gilder, made me regret more than ever the inability of making oneself understood across 3000 miles of ocean. I am no more "offended" with him than with you– I thought it a joke that I should have accidently found out one of the business mysteries of the Editor's Cabinet–[200] & although I was impatient of the long delay, it never entered my head to take offense with him or anybody else for it. At the same time I am a little sceptical about the height of his regard for me, when he never called on me during the two months I was in London– nor Mrs. G. either. Any coolness that may arise between us, would spring from this cause, but <u>not</u> from my literary susceptibilities. Please don't think I would be foolish enough to carry these into my personal relations with anyone whom I regarded as a friend! Malvern is quiet & restful & increasingly beautiful as the days go by– but it lends itself surprisingly little to letter-writing. I do a great deal of reading– chiefly old favorites– & occasionally make a little day excursion to some of the interesting places near us– In this way I have seen Gloucester & Tewkesbury– two of the noblest churches in England– They are all the same in photographs or in description– but what infinite variety there is in the <u>real</u> effects when you enter one of these splendid old monuments & find each one with its special secret of beauty that cannot be communicated or repeated. The more

I see of them, the more I love them & I feel as if each new <u>great</u> one were so much added to my life. Of course, they don't all affect me equally— & Hereford, which I saw for the first time the other day, gave me no sensation whatever. Out of the 22 cathedrals in England, there are only three now that I have not seen— & I am going to lessen this number still by going next week to Litchfield, with Mr. & Mrs. Middlemore (Nina Sturgis). They are stopping with his parents just out of Birmingham which is very near here— & I shall spend a couple of days with them there. I have seen them a little lately, as they have been house-hunting in Malvern— I believe he has given up all his connection with the Saturday Review, & they wish to live here instead of in London— They are going to America on Sept. 30th— for a 6 weeks' visit— so you will probably see them. I like them both— though I don't know them well— She seems kindly & amiable & clever in her way— & he, an intelligent, serious, straightforward sort of man— It has been especially pleasant to see them here, as we lead the most isolated life. If it were not for my brother & his family who lodge not far from us, I don't know what we should do for a little human companionship.

Where did you get Tolstoi's "Children & Youth"? They are slower here about translating foreign books than we are, & I have not seen it advertised anywhere— I shall look for it when I go back to Paris in October— Of course you saw "Sebastopol Sketches"— Some of them were published in the "Revue des Deux Mondes"— but not all— They are as fine as anything he has written— If you would like to have them, <u>let me know</u>, & I will send them to you from Paris. I am sorry to send you such a dull letter— but I know less of what is going on in the world, here in Malvern, than you do at Marion— Tell me how that wretched Aleck Oakey affair was patched up? I hear he has gone back to his wife—

With affectionate regards

Sincerely your friend

Emma Lazarus

I find I have not acknowledged Mr. Gilder's "business" letter for which many thanks.

Emma Lazarus to Helena deKay Gilder
London
Sept. 10 '86

My dear Helena–

   All I can say about the accompanying little table-cover is that it comes from Rome, which gives it a glamour in my eyes, as I hope it may in yours. When I bought it, I thought it was pretty– but now, I don't know anything about anything– so please accept it with my warmest love, as a little souvenir to refresh your memory of me till we meet. I take advantage of Joe's going home to send it to you.–

   I am in London, in the midst of the sordid part of travel– packing & unpacking; storing & shopping & calculating time-tables, expenses & everything horrid. An occasional hour between whiles at the National Gallery or with a good book is enough to set things straight again. The N. Gallery is brillianter than ever– & I come back to it with more devoted affection each time. As for books I have just got hold of 3 vols. of John Morley's Essays– Have you read them? They are the most delightful reading– Do you know Shelley's prose-writings? I have only now made their acquaintance & have been treading on the clouds. They are <u>divine</u>! I am off for Holland in a week. I must see Haarlem, & The Hague once more. I hope to be there two or three weeks. Do write whenever you can spare the time– the longer I stay away, the more I miss my friends & the less they miss me! Such is life!

fondly yours

Emma Lazarus

Emma Lazarus to Helena deKay Gilder
Mrs. R.W. Gilder 103 15th St. NY
The Hague
Sept. 23rd '86

My dear Helena–

   You may imagine how shocked & pained I was when in taking up yesterday's "Herald" here, I saw the announcement of your sister-in-law's death– Though I think of you & Mr. Gilder so constantly, yet when trouble comes to you it seems as if I only then realize how much you both are to me, & how I should love to see you & be with you again. Indeed, I often <u>dream</u> of longing to go to your studio which is just around the corner from me, & yet being prevented by some indefinable thing from working my way to you! Do let me hear how you all are when you can find a moment to write– Poor Mr. Gilder must be grateful that his mother was spared this cruel pang– Where is Jenny Gilder? Still over here? This is a sad ending to her first holiday– I wonder if you are back in New York & how Marion has treated you this summer. I had a letter from Olivia not long ago, who said she had not for years seen you look so well & so handsome– All my family except Mary & our faithful Ellen left Annie & myself last Saturday & sailed on the "Auramia" & we are anxiously awaiting news of their safe arrival.[201] We took the night-boat to Rotterdam & hope to spend two or three weeks in this friendly spot. It is as pretty & attractive to me as on my first visit, & I am glad to be here again– all the more as I left Haarlem unseen– & Amsterdam half seen before, & wish to complete & fix my impressions– We have . . . & golden mornings in the Park & blue & silver afternoons on the Scheveningen Beach– & the whole town looks just as it did to me before a lovely little . . . seen through a Claude-Lorraine glass. We shall go from here to Paris & as early as we dare, to Rome– that however will not be before December– as we are none of us in very robust condition, & I am afraid of that enervating climate unless we are perfectly well– Please give all kind messages of sympathy & friendship to Mr. Gilder from me & with very fond love to yourself

believe me

affectionately yours

Emma Lazarus

Letter 57HdeKG

Emma Lazarus to Helena deKay Gilder
Paris
30, rue de Bassaret
Oct. 5th '86

My dear Helena–

As usual I find myself writing to thank you for your long and most welcome letter the very day I received it. I always pounce so eagerly upon every word from you the moment I see your handwriting & although this letter brought me such sad news, yet I was especially glad to get it for I had been anxiously waiting to hear how you all– & especially Richard– had borne the shock. Thank you so much for writing so fully about all your family– I have thought of you with so much sympathy– & had partly guessed what harrowing experiences you must have had– I am grateful to think you keep up your strength– for everyone writes me how well you look– & as to your spirits, I don't doubt you are even able to make a brave show with them,– for this is always possible with a woman of your temperament when those you love have need of your cheerfulness. Dear Mr. Gilder! Does he really imagine I was "hurt" with him? I fancied I was showing him the greatest kindness when I didn't enter into a correspondence with him on the strength of his letter to me– & only answered it by writing jointly to you both. Perhaps you never got my double letter? As for explaining the measuring of my "poem," I thought his asking it was merely a delicate way of telling me that the verses wouldn't do!– & I accepted it as a failure– Besides, even if I hadn't, I don't believe in "explained" poetry– do you? Please give him my affectionate remembrances– & tell him I always think of him with admiration & true friendship– Talking of poetry– real not pretend– have you ever read Browning's "Inn Album?"[202] I have just made its acquaintance– to my infinite delight. It made a ten-hour railway journey fly by as "a watch in the night"– so to speak– What a great, great man he is! We came here from The Hague on Saturday & after three days of abject misery in a French hotel, we have moved & installed ourselves today in the most delightful apartments of Miss Ellis' pension– It is a typical, conventional American thing to do– but everyone finds their fate, & there is no escaping it– Our rooms are so pretty, cheerful & attractive, & we have such a sense of privacy & cleanliness, that we are enchanted with it all– The weather is unseasonably warm & I am longing for an autumn breeze– In the quarter where our hotel was, the noise & bad smells made the city most unpleasant– We were just out of the Rue de la Paix in one of those nasty, narrow, reeking little Parisian streets– but here, near the Champs Elysees, the air & the sky have an altogether different quality. We hope to stay here till we go to Rome– which will not be until the cold weather & until we all get in better physical condition than we are in now. While I was in Holland I went to Haarlem & gratified my long-standing wish to see the Hals pictures–[203] There are only eight of them, but they well repaid me for the journey– & far surpassed all I had expected of them– The photographs that Braun has taken of them in detail & in ensemble, for sale here just drive me wild– I looked over them yesterday & ventured finally to ask the price of the whole "album" of Hals– I found I got it for 593 francs! Nothing in Paris tempts me as much as these big Braun photos– They are a perfect triumph in their way, & almost seem to reproduce the colours of the original– Do you know now that the Louvre has devoted a special cabinet to them? I am happy to say that the first <u>fever</u> of foreign life is passing away with me– & I think I shall be glad to go home after all– I hate knocking about & can only stand a certain amount of it– If it were not for Rome– I think I should be now ready to go back– but I do want a little longer draught of Italy, before I put the cup down– Paris is bright & beautiful but I shall never love it– I should have been glad indeed if Olivia would have come to see me– but of course, I had little hope of it when I wrote– The bribe was such a big one– that I took the one chance in a thousand of its tempting her, & wrote– but I was not surprised at her answer– There are so few people one would really care to have in travelling, that I wished to show her she was one of those very particularly few. You will be back in 15th St. when this reaches you– How I wish I could look in on you! With ever so much love to you & your household–

fondly yours

EL

Letter 58HdeKG

Emma Lazarus to Helena deKay and Richard Watson Gilder
26 Ave. Friedland
Paris
Jan. 4, 1887
(dictated by Emma Lazarus)

My dear friends:

I should like to write you both a long letter in return for all your kind and affectionate ones which have touched me very deeply– I wish I deserved half of the good things you say to me which make me blush all the way across the Atlantic! My strength is so very limited that I can only say what I <u>must</u>, however, & not what I wish.

An English friend of mine, Mrs. Yates Thompson, is going to America with her husband next month. She is a charming woman & I should very much like you to know her– <u>but</u>– her husband is the Proprietor of the Pall Mall Gazette– & as you may have objections to receiving him, I write to ask if you can possibly let me know by return mail whether it would be agreeable to you. I gave them letters of introduction to you. I rely upon your answering with <u>perfect</u> <u>frankness</u>. I shall easily understand your objections, if you have any, & if you haven't I shall be glad for Mrs. Thompson's sake & yours to bring you together, for I am sure you would like her.

I was so much interested to hear of the Millet-Rousseau paper for the "Causeries" & am longing to see it.[204] How warmly you must have thrown yourself into such a sympathetic subject– & I know of no one who could treat it with surer knowledge– I am ill– as you know. My strength comes back very slowly, if at all– I spend my days & nights on my back, & can't even write a letter. All my dreams of returning to Italy are dashed to the ground,– & I don't believe we shall leave Paris till we go home, which will probably be as early in the Spring as we can make it– I hope the children are all well again. I was so sorry to hear what a siege you had had– but Sarah brought me good news of your health & looks & beauty (this last sentence is for Helena)– Write whenever you can to your broken-down old friend

Emma Lazarus (per A.L.)

Letter 59HdeKG

Annie Lazarus to Helena deKay Gilder
26 Ave. Friedland
Jan. 22nd 1887

My dear Mrs. Gilder

It has been a great temptation to me for some time to take upon myself the answering of some of your letters to Emma & the arrival of your last long one (which I have heard parts of) proved too great a one to resist. Poor Emma is so distressed at not being able to write to you herself– there is nothing she enjoys as much as a good, <u>fat</u> letter from you & I really believe it is the hardest part of her sickness to <u>her</u>– that she cannot write to any of her playmates at home. I had hard work holding her down this morning– when she came to your generous offer of the Mino da Fiesole Madonna– she would have taken the first steamer that sailed & she said to tell you it was the greatest inducement she had yet had to go back to New York– that is if you <u>really</u> meant it. The studio news is all of such interest, I try & make Emma read me every word she will. It seems like looking in upon you for a moment– I can hardly imagine Dorothea a big young lady– that is the only unfamiliar part of the scene– But I can well believe she is as lovely as ever in her new capacity.

S.L.'s[205] impressions of Paris would fill several large volumes– I don't see how I can begin to tell you any of them. I have to act as courier to the newly imported sisters. So I have every means of studying the various effects. The funniest development in Sarah is that she hasn't been able to buy a thing she needs in the Paris shops. I had thought it was a good city for shopping if for no other purpose but as she seems only to need unlimited supplies of pins/ safety & otherwise/ & the latest Macy & Daniell improvements, she is utterly disgusted with the poverty of the shops. I feel just the other way about it of course & am always distracted and amused by a walk along the quays among the old book stalls & bric a brac shops. I wonder if Joe ever asked you what number you wear in gloves. I want to take you home some– that is if you care for them. Perhaps you will send me a message by her & tell me if you have as many as you need or if you don't care for them something else instead. If you want me to take you any paints– will you please make out a list of the colors you use & the make you prefer. I haven't touched paint in so long that I don't even remember the names of the colors. Talking of painting I heard yesterday that Mrs. Bronson has had a miniature made of Robert Browning's eye & wears it as a ring set in diamonds. This is a very original kind of devotion– don't you think so? I think Salome chose a more beautiful eye than his– even if he couldn't write poetry. The account you give of the little Japanese was most interesting. Emma, with her usual scepticism, says he must be a "Djimn"– but I believe him to be a real man & should love to look through the crack of the door at him.

I have nothing of the slightest interest to tell you. One day is just like an-other– sometimes worse but never better. I steal a few moments of fresh air every day & occasionally try to see a few pictures– but not often. Tomorrow, I am meditating accepting a most tempting invitation to hear Joachim[206] at the Chatelet, but it is hard to find the heart to do anything now. Emma wants me very much to go & I think it may interest her to hear of so I shall probably go. Charlie Forbes wants to take me to Madrazo's studio & I may try to do that as I believe it is interesting.[207] I shall soon be back in 10th Street & then these little distractions will not be possible. I don't look forward a day though, for it frightens me too much– but only try to live on without thinking of anything. Alice has written several times of having seen you– & "lost her heart"– of course! I hope you like her a little. She has been like the most devoted sister to Emma & we both have a special affection for her. I am frightened at having come to another page. Please forgive me for scribbling in this way to you– about myself. I know it is very wrong but I can't help it. I wish I could see the little book of poems you have decorated with flowers; how delightful to be able to do it; I am fonder of flowers than any I know– & long to see a whole book of them. You hear all there is to know of Emma I suppose, from Joe, so I shan't try to give you any details. There isn't any good news to send unfortunately– I am so glad to hear of your looking so & being so well. What a comfort to have the measles over at last. Please give my kindest greetings to Mr. Gilder & with much love for yourself & the children whether they remember me or not–

Always affectionately yours

Annie Lazarus

Annie Lazarus to Helena deKay Gilder
Feb. 1st, 1887

My dear Mrs. Gilder:

Emma wants me to send you the best thanks for your letter of Jan. 19th & for sending such a prompt answer to her question. She fully understands your own & Mr. Gilder's position about the introduction & says she would have been surprised if you had answered otherwise. She felt however that it was due to Mrs. Thompson, who had been exceedingly kind to her, to take whatever chance there might be of your feeling differently–

She is very grateful to you for all your affectionate wishes– & offers to nurse but she says that if you had any idea of how old & sick & miserable she is, you wouldn't suggest taking a hand in it. Your letter arrived late last even'g– when she was tossing & groaning before taking her anodyne for the night– but she had the lights brought at once & read every word with the greatest interest. So you see even at this distance you can make her forget her pain.

We are having the dreariest days imaginable. I shan't talk to you about them for you are always so full of sympathy for others, that it would make you unhappy– This is only to be a little note– & not the long volume that my last letter was–

With much love from Emma & myself– to you all ever affectionately yours

Annie Lazarus

What an extraordinary woman you are– living in a world full of <u>Mina</u> <u>da</u> <u>Fiesoles</u> & <u>Luimis</u>!! Won't you please give us the secret of converting New York into a medieval Italian town?

Letter 61HdeKG

Annie Lazarus to Helena deKay Gilder
26 Ave. Friedland
April 9th [1887]

My dear good Mrs. Gilder

You don't know what a comfort your letters are & I don't suppose I shall be able to tell you– but whether you wish it or not I must send you my poor little mite in return– that is a very shakily written letter– from a dark gloomy sick room in the Ave. Friedland. Your beautiful letter came this morning & I read every word of it to Emma after which we indulged in a prolonged rhapsody on the subject of the writer which must have set all your ears tingling– or perhaps they are so used to tingling that you don't feel it anymore! I know just how hard a task it must be for you to write us everything & I am more grateful than I can say– so I might as well not try anymore but you will believe me that the days I hear from you seem easier to get through & indeed it seems as if your good influence could find its way over any number miles of sea or land– & make life better for us all–

Emma holds her own wonderfully in spite of all her afflictions– every possible one I should say that can come to us in this world. Her face is very much paralyzed now– one ear is quite deaf & her eyes are both going very fast. The well one began to trouble her last week & now she can't bear a ray of light in the room & has to wear a patch besides– In spite of it all her spirits are as good as ever & she talks with all the interest she ever had– of people & things– It is wonderful how we accustom ourselves to any condition, however unbearable it seemed in the beginning Now I find that my one hope is for this to last– the blessing of her not knowing the truth would be so great that I cannot complain as long as she is peaceful & unconscious of what is happening– It seems as if this weather must put life in her– If she could only bear the sunlight that pours into these rooms– You can't imagine anything more spring like than today– All Paris smells of fresh flowers & little warm gusts of air blow in at the windows. Our salon is filled with beautiful pink & white azaleas– & you see we are trying very hard to keep cheerful– I am glad you have given up your black gowns & are beginning to make the effort to go out. I hate black as much as Mr. Gilder possibly can & I don't see why anyone should wear it. Still I do wear it for I haven't anyone to ask me not to! Your designs for the new book of poems sound very lovely, & I envy you working over a Parisian flower. How I should love to be able to paint one– I have tried so often & never could. Do let us see them as soon as they appear–

I like Toche's work– extremely though you don't seem to believe me. The work was so brilliant & startling that perhaps I should have gone oftener to study it more closely– But sometimes it seems as if first impressions might be better than others– & there is no reason why the first shouldn't be as true as the second or third– French art is less distasteful to me than it used to be– So you see I am just the other way around. Of course I know the "quality" you speak of in French art– but it was altogether absent, I think, in Toche's art as it always is in the best of the French artists.

. . . one of these days– I seldom get a chance now to go even to the Louvre– my last visit was with Sarah– to introduce her to Leonardo & Titian & the other gentlemen there– but she didn't warm to them & I think a good old wooden portrait of Washington crossing the Delaware would have been more to the point. This is not meant to be wicked– it will only tell you that she is still dreadfully homesick– & she sees no charm in any of the things . . . for here. I wonder how you liked Mrs. Thompson– You must surely have found her attractive didn't you? I had a pathetic little note from Mrs. R.U. Johnson who is over here in miserable quarters I should say– far out on the Avenue de la Grand Armice– where it looks like Harlem more than any other place & all her children sick. Mrs. Robert U. is very kind to ask about us– & to remember me in the bargain! I read Daniel's Journal at the time it came out & liked it very, very much, but I should have to know Mr. Johnson better to see any resemblance between the two men– Please forgive my dispirited letter– Emma sends you a great deal of love & says it is always a pleasure to hear from you. With warmest thanks & love to you all believe me ever fondly yours

Annie L.

Letter 62HdeKG

Emma Lazarus to Helena deKay and Richard Watson Gilder
Paris
July 11th '87

My dear friends (H & R)

Your two overwhelming letters from Marion have just reached me– Keep on saying such kind things to me only I warn you before hand that I don't deserve one word or one syllable of them, & blush to receive them, pleasant though they may be. I shall reserve all my answers until I see you for I write now to say that we are to sail for home on Sat. 23rd by the "Gascagne."

Of course I have regained much of my strength to be able to undertake the voyage, but I am still very ill & weak & you will find me dreadfully changed. I have no use of my eyes yet & have to be written for and read to. Under these conditions I do not allow myself to think of the excitement of going home & seeing you all again– but you may imagine how eagerly I look forward to it–

I am so glad to hear of the new edition of the poems– how lovely they must be. I am sure I shall not be contented with less than both forms– but I am shocked dear Mr. Gilder at your audacity in asking me to write a love-poem for you to "Frankie" Cleveland.[208] You, the Anacreon of America– do you intend it as satire or do you only dare to express by . . . the depth of your admiration? If your affairs are not already too entangled, I advise you to ask Amelia Rives[209]– How delightful her love poems are and what a fiery creature she must be. Dear Helena, you say nothing of your health so I hope you are better than when you last wrote. I long to see you in your Marion studio, but fear I shall be crippled for many months to come. I think of you constantly & am more than grateful for your affection & sympathy– but have no strength to write more– This is only to let you know I am coming– fondly yours– Emma (A.L.)

I am Annie & I am coming too– so don't forget all about me before the ship gets in. Thank you dear Mrs. Gilder for your always kind & gladdening messages. What a pleasure it will be to see you again. I am sorry to have always forced my shocking hand-writing upon you– but Emma uses me for want of a better secretary. This time it is partly the fault of a d . . . pen– My love to you–

Yours–

Annie

Letter 63HdeKG

Josephine Lazarus to Helena deKay Gilder
18 W. 10th St.
July 24th [1887]

My dear Helena–

I have no idea what part of the world you are in– your last letter was . . . in its "Itinerary" if you know what that means. I write principally to tell you that Emma sailed yesterday, on the Gascagne for home & that we shall look for her arrival next Sunday, a week from today– I wish some of her friends were in town & that we could make something of an ovation for her– But perhaps it is best as it is– The voyage may be hard for her, but we shall hope for the best. We had a letter last evening in her own handwriting– the first in how many months! But it is yet an unexplained mystery. For the present course I am rooted to Tenth St.– I have no idea what the moves or plans of the family will be. Petersham has faded out of existence– & after all I shouldn't have had much good of you up there. I too hate to travel & New York has its compensations– The weather is lovely to be sure but it was pretty nearly as hot in Westchester where I spent a week & mosquitoes thrown in– Sophie Ward is improving but not a sight have I had of her or of him– Sarah is very well & giving herself to the pleasures of life. She says soon she will not be able to walk she is so fat– & I don't think she will. Agnes has gone to Newport– with the baby who is sweet & a prodigy of size. Sarah has fallen a victim of it & misses it dreadfully. Did Mr. Gilder send me the Critic with part of his college address? If so please thank him for it– It was nice & he was nice for sending it to me. What are you reading or are you too busy to read? The donkey arrival must have been an excitement. You write me charming letters, Helena dear, & I wish I could do as much for you– I am actually engaging servants at this time of the year– Do not I have my share of the amenities?

Fondly & faithfully yours–

Josephine Lazarus

Letter 64HdeKG

Josephine Lazarus to Helena deKay Gilder
18 W. 10th St.
Sat. Aug. 6th [1887]

My dear Helena–

Emma arrived last Sunday morning after a terrible voyage as you may have seen by the papers– the waves dashed over the deck cabin that she had so that she had to keep the port hole closed. She was of course completely prostrated & has been very very poorly ever since. Today she is worse than she has yet been– too weak to lift her head or speak or have a word spoken in the room– She looks dreadfully– At first she was able to talk a little & keep up her spirits somewhat– but for my part I think she is intensely discouraged now. She said to me, "It is useless trying to struggle any longer"– but don't say this to anybody. Annie went yesterday to Newport for a week with Agnes. She is very well– wonderfully so when you think what she has been living through. Mary is also well & still faithful to the bedside. Emma has a Bon Secours nurse & is so pleased with her– I have been in a whirl with housekeeping & so many things to think of. I hope you are enjoying life & your friends– Write when you can. Emma may be able to hear about it– but don't kill yourself. The weather is still most trying.

Always yours faithfully

Josephine L.

Annie says you were an angel– you wrote them <u>such</u> letters!

Letter 65HdeKG

Josephine Lazarus to Helena deKay Gilder
18 W. 10th St.
Nov. 2nd, 1887

My dear Helena–

What Mrs. Cleveland has done is so far "above my station" so to speak that I don't know what to say to you or to her–[210] I must trust you to tell her what we all feel– that such a sweet and gracious act is beyond thanks. It is easy to see why she wins all hearts. Although Emma's days have been more wretched than ever, she was able to look at the flowers & feel refreshed by them & above all of the gentle sympathy they expressed– She told the doctors with great pride from whence they had come. Are we to see you today? I hope you are feeling quite well. Emma is decidedly worse & the doctors say she is failing.

With fondest love

Josephine

Letter 66HdeKG

Josephine Lazarus to Helena deKay Gilder
18 W. 10th Street
Nov 19, 1887

My dear Helena,

Emma is at rest. She died this morning at 11 o'clock– quietly at the end but after a long agony.

Sincerely yours,

Josephine

10

Thomas Wren Ward

Emma probably knew Tom Ward as a child. Her correspondence with him seems to have begun in 1876. Five years older than Emma, he graduated from Harvard College in 1868, having taken a year off to participate as an aide to Louis Agassiz on a botanical expedition to South America. Although his first love was science, he subsequently joined his father's banking firm in New York City.[1]

Emma spent time in the summers with Tom's parents, Samuel Gray and Anna Barker Ward, at their rather palatial cottage in Lenox, Massachusetts. Her letters to them are published in the Schappes volume, *The Letters of Emma Lazarus*.[2]

Samuel Gray Ward is one of those hidden figures in history with an interesting background. Born in Boston, he met Ralph Waldo Emerson and Margaret Fuller, among others, while attending Harvard College. Fuller is said to have been in love with him, but he married the legendary southern beauty, Anna Barker, from New Orleans. Ward was a member of the early Transcendentalists and wrote for the *Dial*. He settled in Manhattan to join his father's banking house, which was the American representative for the London banking firm Baring Brothers. Samuel Gray Ward is said to have been one of Emerson's closest friends, although he was some years younger than the master.[3]

Tom Ward roomed with Emerson's son Edward at Harvard. His close friend was William James. Although he was a member of that tight-knit Concord community, he, like Emma's friend Rose Hawthorne Lathrop, would eventually convert to Roman Catholicism.[4]

The first record we have of Ward's correspondence with Emma Lazarus is a letter from her dated 2 April 1876. Interestingly, her sisters continued to correspond with Ward and his wife, Sophie, until their deaths.[5]

Letter 1TWW

Emma Lazarus to Thomas Wren Ward
36 West 14th Street
Sunday, April 2nd 1876
Thomas Ward, Esquire

My dear Mr. Ward

I have just finished reading the remarkable poem of "Olivier" which you so kindly gave me the other day, and I feel as if I must renew my thanks to you now, for the great pleasure it has given me. You have here introduced me to a new poet, and I find his work as artistic and finished in expression as it is original in design. I had heard and read of this latest development of French poetry, with its realistic pictures of nature and sketches of character, but I had not yet seen any of its productions, and I have been truly charmed with this. I should be only too happy to be able to gratify you by writing like Mr. Francois Coppee–[6] and I trust the study of so sincere and original a poem may have some visible result upon my own efforts. I know now what you meant by your remark about the loss of friends the other evening, though I did not quite understand at the time.

With all kind regards for Mrs. Ward and yourself believe me

Very sincerely yours

Emma Lazarus

Letter 2TWW

Emma Lazarus to Thomas Wren Ward
36 West 14th Street
May 30, 1876

My dear Mr. Ward–

I am afraid you have given yourself far too much trouble to afford me the great pleasure of reading "Joseph and His Brethren."[7] I cannot imagine how you have succeeded so soon in getting it, or where it comes from, but I can only sincerely thank you for the result. I intend to be as dilatory as my predecessors in this borrowing line, and keep it all summer, if you will kindly allow me. I am delighted with the little I have already read– half of the first act– and find that it fully comes up to my extravagant expectations. You seem to object so to <u>goodbyes</u>, that I did not tell you last evening how sincerely I wish you and your dear family a happy summer– Let me do so now, and with love for Mrs. Ward and best thanks and regards for yourself believe me

faithfully yours

Emma Lazarus

Letter 3TWW

Emma Lazarus to Thomas Wren Ward
Newport
July 19th 1876
Thomas Wren Ward, Esquire

My dear Mr. Ward–

I return by today's mail your copy of "Joseph and His Brethren" with my best thanks for the pleasure it has given me, and sincere regrets for the inconvenience I must have caused you by keeping it so long. I did not imagine you would expect it till we met again in New York– so pray accept my apologies. I have enjoyed it beyond measure, as have also my Father and all my sisters.[8] And I really feel as if you had put me in your debt by bringing to my notice so noble a work. Mrs. Ward's bright, charming letters have kept us posted about you and your household during the summer– I am glad to think you have all been well and enjoying a moderate degree of coolness.

Believe me sincerely your friend

Emma Lazarus

Letter 4TWW

Emma Lazarus to Thomas Wren Ward
Newport
September 7th, '76

My dear Mr. Ward

I do not know anybody but yourself generous and thoughtful enough for others, to have sent me the two volumes of Coppee's poetry which I received yesterday afternoon. I have examined every square inch of the paper they were wrapped in, & of the books themselves, to try to find some clue to the kind friend who has enriched me with them– but there is no trace anywhere. So falling upon probabilities, & remembering your casual remark to me last Spring about letting me see these poems some day, I think I may give myself the pleasure of sending you my warmest thanks. Please let me know if I am right in believing that it is to you I am indebted for this most delightful surprise. I know I shall enjoy any poems by the author of "Olivier" with which I was so greatly pleased– & I shall study them carefully & diligently for the sake of their exquisite workmanship.

I have only been home a few days from a charming week at Concord. I suppose Mrs. Ward has told you that I have been staying with the Emersons.[9] Nearly everybody I met there asked me about you– & although I know you do not feel comfortable in thinking that people set a high value upon you, yet I am sure you could not help being pleased to hear how many friends you have there, & how much they think of you & wish you back in their midst. Your old friend Mr. Channing[10] made himself particularly agreeable & kind to me– He spoke to me quite sadly the last evening I was in Concord of your having promised him to come every year & make your favorite excursion with him to the top of Monadnoc–[11] &, he said, that was many years ago & he had never seen you since– He seemed to fear you were faithless to your old worship of Pan.– If I did not fear to offend you I would give you messages from Ellen & "Edward"[12] & all Concord, but I will wait & tell you all about your friends when I see you– We expect to return to New York on the 14th. When does the Rockaway establishment break up?

Meanwhile let me thank you again & again for your beautiful gift, & believe me with kindest regards for yourself & your household,

Sincerely your friend

Emma Lazarus

Bellevue Avenue
Thomas W. Ward, Esquire

Emma Lazarus to Thomas Wren Ward
Thursday, November 16, [1876]

My dear Mr. Ward

Do you want to read, or have you read already, a truly admirable charming & touchingly sincere page out of real life? I refer to the "Souvenirs d'Enfance & de Jeunesse" of Ernest Renan,[13] in the last number of the Revue des Deux Mondes for November 1st. I have this moment laid it aside, & as for some unknown reason, I have been thinking vaguely of you all the time I was reading it, I write to claim your sympathy or to direct your attention to it, now that I have finished it. What a deliciously poetic prose that man writes, & what a study it is for us clumsy lumbering Saxons. I read these Recollections immediately after Scribner's monograph on Charlotte Bronte which is pitched throughout in the key that one would <u>scream</u> in & the effect of the softly flowing harmonious music of this exquisite French prose was something indescribable. If you have the time in your present homeless condition, to bury your self in the ideal for a little while, & forget furniture & truckmen & decorators & housecleaning, I know you will thank me for pointing out to you anything so lovely.

Your friend

Emma Lazarus

Emma Lazarus to Thomas Wren Ward
36 West 14th Street
December 3rd 1876

My dear Mr. Ward—

I am sorry to hear you have given yourself any uneasiness in regard to the French Book which you lent me, & I hasten to relieve you of all uncomfortable feeling about it by telling you that I only read two or three of the stories, & that in these there was absolutely nothing objectionable. As I found them however very dull & unpleasant I returned the volume to you without so much as glancing at the rest. Even if I had come across anything disagreeable I should only have blamed myself, for the leaves of the book were uncut when you sent it to me, & you told me you did not know what was in it. I owe you nothing but thanks for the pure & healthy enjoyment which I have derived from the books you have given me or brought to my notice, so please do not waste another thought on this. With kindest regards to Mrs. Ward and yourself believe me

Sincerely your friend

Emma Lazarus

Emma Lazarus to Thomas Wren Ward
August 25th, (1877)
Newport

My dear Mr. Ward—

If, as I imagine, you are quite alone in 25th Street during these hot, depressing August days with no more substantial luxury than that of <u>dreaming</u> of the top of Monadnock or the Lenox woods or the Newport beach, I flatter myself that even a letter from me may have been an encouraging influence, bringing as it does the assurance of constant friendship & regard. I am afraid you will think me very unreliable but I never got any farther with my Coppee article. When I first came to Newport, I was interested in the completion of a little story I had begun in New York, & then I was still in suspense as to the fate of my Heine essay, & did not at all know whether I was capable of that sort of literary work.[14] As the Heine article however has turned out to be a success & been accepted, perhaps I shall yet go back to the other. The story is also finished and will appear in Scribners.[15] I don't think you will like it, if you even read it. I should think you, with your partiality for Socialistic subjects, would be deeply interested in Tourgenieff's last novel. I find it by long odds the greatest of his works, without any of the unhealthy passion that mars some of his earlier stories— noble in design & as far as my poor judgement goes, flawless in execution. As a representation of certain features of Russian Society it seems to unite the art of a great picture with the accuracy of a photograph. When I first read it, as I had already received several marks of kindly regard from Tourgenieff, I took the liberty of sending him my thanks & impressions, & about a week ago I had the honor of receiving a friendly letter from him in return.[16] Even my gratitude & enthusiasm must have been acceptable to him, for he writes in a spirit of marked disappointment about the poor success with which his great labor has been rewarded. Have you read any of Rudolph Lindau's stories?[17] There is a new one in the last number of "Nord und Sud" (edited by Paul Lindau) which I think very fine. It is called "Der Scher." The two numbers I have seen of this new magazine make me think it is one of the best periodicals I have ever met with. I don't see how such a standard of excellence can be kept up. Paul Lindau himself writes in a masterly style of criticism about Victor Hugo. What a wonderful family those Lindaus are. I hear often from our mutual friend Mr. Leopold L. who has sent me these & a quantity of other good things this summer. Was it you who took the trouble to send me the "Nation?" If so, please accept my thanks– It came very opportunely, when my mind was very much exercised by the Railroad Strikes and Communism in general, & while I was in the midst of reading "Felix Holt the Radical."[18] Don't you think there is something essentially unjust about the whole theory of Communism? I shall never believe in it as long as there are such natural inequalities in the minds & capacities of men. As for Richepin,[19] the suffresard poet, I suppose he is the necessary result of the reaction from the artificial school of Gautier & Coppee– but would not something between the two be far more excellent than either? I have never seen Newport looking more beautiful than it does this year, & I have enjoyed my summer immensely. I wonder what deep problems you are meditating just now. I live from day to day, & do not allow myself to think of anything serious. I imagine a summer in town is a very depressing sort of thing particularly to anyone who is fond of an outdoor life. I trust you do not indulge any morbid fancies, but retain a brave faith in yourself & your friends– Do not be too much surprised at receiving this long, egotistical letter. I know you will understand why I have written.

Sincerely your friend

Emma Lazarus

Letter 8W

Emma Lazarus to Thomas Wren Ward
34 East 57th St.
November 20th 1877

My dear Mr. Ward–

I return with many thanks Browning's "Agamemnon" which I cannot read. I knew I did not understand Greek, but I did think I understood English until now. I would rather take the original Eschylus with a Greek dictionary & spell out word after word, than attempt to unravel the hopeless intricacy of this extraordinary patois. If the purpose of a translation be, as I have always supposed, the interpretation of a foreign work to the minds of people unacquainted with the original language, I do not see how this "translation" can be called anything but grotesque. From one point of view it is a genuine <u>tour de force</u>– It is a rendering of the poem which makes it unintelligible to both Greek & English. What do you think of this passage, page 26.

> "And so, upsoaring as to stride sea over,
> The strong . . . voyager & all for joyance
> Did the gold-glorious splendor, any sun like,
> Pass on, the pine-tree, to Makistos' watch place,
> Who did not tardy, caught, no wits about him
> By sleep, decline his portion of the mission.

Here is Mr. Fitzgerald's version of the same–

> The Torch of Conquest, traversing the wide
> Aegean with sunbrown-stretching stride.
> Struck up the downy watchers on Makistos';
> Who flashing back the challenge flashed it on
> To those who watched on the Nussafian height.[20]

I must not omit to thank you heartily for the opportunity of comparing the two versions. I appreciate Mr. Fitzgerald better than ever now. I have been trying to reduce to practice your politico-economical views, &, I think, with success. You can have no idea how much you helped me on Sunday.

Please give my best love to Mrs. Ward, and believe me with kindest regards & thanks for yourself

Your friend

Emma Lazarus

Letter 9TWW

Emma Lazarus to Thomas Wren Ward
34 East 57th St.
Friday [June 1879][21]

My dear Mr. Ward–

I return with best thanks "Les Frises Temporaires"– I agree with you as to the admirable skill with which the story is written, but the subject is to me a very uninteresting one, so that I cannot share your enthusiasm about the book. I am glad however to have read it & very much obliged to you for remembering to send it to me. You cannot imagine how much good your visit did me the other day– & how grateful I felt to you for your kind & sensitive advice. I have really taken it to heart & hope to profit by it– I have not been depressed since I saw you,– nearly a week ago!– & I have taken steps to begin a series of <u>furious</u> studies– Perhaps I shall go out of town after all– for a week or two in July, to be with some friends by the seashore, while my father is at Saratoga.[22] Before then however there will be lots of bright evenings and beautiful June sunsets, for the Park–[23] & I wish you would come up again & repeat our pleasant walk. Even my finger is better since I saw you, & I am once more using my right hand.

Believe me sincerely your friend

Emma Lazarus

Letter 10TWW

Emma Lazarus to Thomas Wren Ward
Lake Minnewaska House
New Peltz, Ulster House, N.J.
August 17th 1880

My dear Mr. Ward–

I am perched on the top of a mountain overlooking Lake Minnewaska– & I find it so much more beautiful than I had anticipated, & I think you would enjoy it so much, that as you spoke of the possibility of your coming up here, I write to urge you to do so– I am sure you would find the visit would refresh you– even if it were only for the sake of your geological studies– for the rock-formations are so curious that they attract many geologists to the place–[24] It is very accessible– My sister & I left New York at 8:45 & reached the hotel a little before 4– It is so beautiful & the walks are so romantic & the lake at all hours of the day & night so enchanting, that I find myself wishing constantly that you who appreciate & are in such sympathy with Nature, could see it all– The weather is perfection & the air like early October– & you can be as independent as you choose, for the hotel is admirably kept. I shall be here till the end of the month & do wish you could get here before I leave. I have not heard a word from Lenox for some time– I trust all my dear friends there are well– & that Sophie takes care of herself & gains strength. Give my love to them all– & come here if you can– & believe me

Sincerely your friend

Emma Lazarus

I have a poem in next month's Scribner's which I want you to like if you possibly can.[25]

Emma Lazarus to Thomas Wren Ward
Saturday
34 E. 57th St.
[before or during November 1880]

My dear Mr. Ward—

Is this beautiful book of Sonnets really for me? It seems too handsome to accept, & you are far too generous & kind to think of me & associate me in this way with your literary pleasures. The Collection appears to be a remarkably rich one, & it is a delightful shape to have many of my old favorites in, & to make the acquaintance of so many beautiful new poems. Of those that were familiar to me, Sir William Drummond's make the strongest impression— there are fortunately a good many of his quoted— most of which are very fine. Accept my warmest thanks for the volume— Please do not forget to look at my little Critique of Browning in the November Scribner's—[26] I think it is the best piece of critical writing I have yet succeeded in accomplishing. What do you think? Did you see that our friend Mr. Gilder has the honor of being quoted in this English "heresy?" A whole sonnet of his is given.

Pray believe me in the thanks & friendship of yours

Most sincerely

Emma Lazarus

Emma Lazarus to Thomas Wren Ward
Wednesday [sic] Dec. 9, [1880]
34 E. 57th St.

My dear Mr. Ward—

A kind fairy has sent me today a beautiful present in the shape of a French book— Causeries Florentines— & as I take it for granted you are in league with this generous spirit, I write at once my sincere thanks. You are altogether too good to me, to think of me so constantly & to give me the rare pleasure of associating with my enjoyment the thought of your generous & sympathetic friendship.

I feel as if it were an age since I have seen you— I know how much your time & thought have been occupied— & am only now however, beginning to look for you again. I have fallen in love– & want to tell you all about it– with Miss Bessie Minturn.[27] Have you seen her since her return? She is "stunning"– She looks remarkably handsome, is very simple & sweet in her manner, & gives me the impression of so strong & solidly equipped a mind that it is a delight to talk to her. I saw your new home on Monday– it is really beautiful– I need not tell you how sincerely I wish you & your dear family all happiness within it. It is provokingly far from us, but I suppose that is our fault!

Once more accept my thanks, & believe me your friend

Emma Lazarus

Letter 13TWW

Emma Lazarus to Thomas Wren Ward
Saturday, Dec. 11, [1880]
34 East 57th St.

My dear Mr. Ward–

I have just finished the "Causeries Florentines" & I must once more write you my thanks & tell you how much I have enjoyed them. The design of the book seems to me an admirable one & is executed in such a charming way that one half forgets how much scholarship it has required. How clearly the author has drawn the subtle distinction between the <u>love</u> of the troubadores & the "gay labor" & that profound passion of modern dramatic & lyric poetry, whose first note was struck in Romeo & Juliet– Isn't it strange how in the study of life & literature, all roads lead to Shakespeare.– I am still hoping to see you again one of these days– to talk on all I have learned since I saw you last!

Meanwhile believe me sincerely your friend

Emma Lazarus

Letter 14TWW

Emma Lazarus to Thomas Wren Ward
34 East 57th St.
December 23rd 1880

My dear Mr. Ward—

I am so delighted to hear that you cared for Cherbuliez' "Noirs & Rouges."[28] I was perfectly fascinated by it— How touchingly, how exquisitely it is written! It is long since I have seen in any work so beautiful & lovable a figure as Soeur Marie— & I am interested to know what kind of a <u>pendant</u> it is going to make in the treatment of religious questions, to "Daniel Rouchat."[29] Of course, to my mind it is much more sympathetic than Sardou's play— but I am afraid Cherbuliez is going to err in the opposite direction, & give an unfair picture of the religious people— Mere Amelie is painted in cruel colors—[30] When you get the second part (Dec. 1) after you have read it yourself, may I ask you to lend it to me? I fear I shall not see it otherwise as I don't subscribe to the "Revue."

Sincerely your friend

Emma Lazarus

Letter 15TWW

Emma Lazarus to Thomas Wren Ward
Tuesday [December 28 1880]

My dear Mr. Ward—

I did not have a chance yesterday to thank you for so promptly and kindly sending me the Revue des Deux Mondes which I herewith return. The second part of Noirs & Rouges does not please me quite as much as the first— but I am still greatly interested & anxious to follow the story. I was more touched than I could tell you by your gift yesterday of the "Sonnets"— It was the first and only proof I had had this Christmas that anyone remembered me with pleasure or friendship. Accept my earnest thanks and believe me your friend—

Emma Lazarus

Emma Lazarus to Thomas Wren Ward
Tuesday [January 1881]

My dear Mr. Ward–

If you continue to spoil me to this extent by paying such immediate attention to the expression of my slightest wish, I will soon be demanding a chariot-&-four, or a house & lot or something equally impossible. I am a thousand times obliged for the "Revue" which I will read as quickly & return as promptly as I can– I am disappointed to see that Cherbuliez's story is not concluded in this number– I hear you recognized my style in the "Critic"–³¹ I am glad to hear it, as I did not know I had any style. Are you sure you guessed right?

I never see you anymore, for which I am very sorry, but I go on thinking of you as my friend whether you will or no! I am going away from New York next month and then you will miss me– With best thanks,

Sincerely yours from

Emma Lazarus

Emma Lazarus to Thomas Wren Ward
34 East 57th Street
Monday, Feb. 7 [1881]

My dear Mr. Ward–

I did not have half a chance to thank you the other day for bringing me the Revue which I herewith return. I am glad to have finished Noirs & Rouges.³² I have never read a more utterly disappointing, false, stupid & ridiculous novel– I fancied from the opening chapters that for once Cherbuliez was going to give us something as charming & sympathetic as it was clever– but the story has gone steadily downhill ever since, & with the exception of a few shrewd epigrammatic sentences & observations, culminates in downright trash. I have been much interested in Therriet's impressions of Douarnenez in the same number– they are very fresh & full of the open air & the sea– a delicious contrast to the hothouse style of Cherbuliez– George Sand's correspondence this month is exceedingly entertaining. At least we see the woman as she really was– No longer the moralizing philosopher, Saint & prude of her own Memoirs, but the most curious combination of genius, force, cleverness, generosity, . . . , vanity, vulgarity & immorality ever seen. One's eyes open in amazement to read in a magazine that makes a tour of the world, her letter to a young man of 20, describing her quarrel with her husband, published by her own son! I have many things to talk over with you– When shall I see you? Have you ever read Regnault's Letters?[33] If not, I want to lend you my copy, for I know they will enchant you.

Your friend

Emma Lazarus

Letter 18TWW

Emma Lazarus to Thomas Wren Ward
Wednesday [before December 19, 1878]
34 East 57th Street

My dear Mr. Ward–

I have just received the magnificent Atlas you were kind enough to send me, & I hasten to thank you for your friendly interest & the trouble you have taken for me. On your suggestion, I spoke to Mr. Lindau about Colorado, & he has asked me to go to the Library & examine their books on the subject– & as they have duplicate copies of all, he has kindly offered to lend me anything I think might be of service to me.[34] So as far as outside material goes, you see I am well provided for– Now where is the inspiration? I don't think I ever should have thought of applying to Mr. Lindau, if you had not mentioned him. Only see how stupid I am! Among the books you have lent me, I find the Powell Expedition the most interesting and most useful– the other by Lt. Ives, seems already a little out of date– the Pacific R. R. has made so many changes & the towns have sprung up so rapidly since then.[35] As for Bayard Taylor, he remains true to his reputation of having traveled more & seen less than any other man living.[36] Where & how he is to get his meals seems to be his only thought. I have read "Mark Twain"– it is rough & common– I really don't know how to thank you for the interest you have shown in me & my work– If I could only accomplish something witty, that would be the only adequate return.

Trusting to see you soon,
believe me

Sincerely your friend

Emma Lazarus

Emma Lazarus to Thomas Wren Ward
34 East 57th St.
April 20

My dear Mr. Ward–

I have read "Mauroy" & true to my promise I will tell you what I think of it– How pleasant it would be in life if we could sharply define the good from the bad, & as you suggested I should do with this novel, positively classify things under one head or the other. But that is impossible– "Mauroy" is neither good nor bad– & while it is gracefully written & contains some shrewd observations & nothing positively objectionable, the impression it leaves is such a weak one, that I am sure I shall forget tomorrow that I have ever read it. The only use I can imagine for books of this kind is to wile away the tedium of a Convalescence– When one is not strong enough either to feel or think profoundly– In perfect health, they seem to me tiresome, "stale, flat & unprofitable"– They were not original enough to be either amusing or instructive– & yet one is carried lazily along from beginning to end by a Curiosity to know the denouement of the various entanglements. It is like hearing alot of society gossip & leaves one very unrefreshed. I trust to see you this evening.

Sincerely yours

Emma Lazarus

Emma Lazarus to Thomas Wren Ward
34 East 57th St.
Monday

My dear Mr. Ward–

I have never seen the "free will" problem stated in a most satisfactory way than in a translation I lately read of an Indian poem. As I have not such an unconquerable repugnance as you to writing, I transcribe it for you– & <u>when I see you again</u>, if you remember it you can tell me how it strikes you.

> "Man follows the bent of his will, subdues or is led by his passions, respects life or ruthlessly snaps it, bows to the law of his conscience or willfully lives in rebellion. He says to himself, "I am free!" He says true; he <u>is</u> free to grow noble, he is free too to work his undoing. But let him act as he will he is a

tool in the hands of Destiny, used to perfect the fabric of life. There are sons of the night & their portion is blackness; there are sons of the Dawn & the daylight is theirs; both are workers for Destiny– from the labors of both issues harmony. But of evil comes good, but not for the doer of evil; he has earned for himself sorrow, that he did freely; he has worked for the good of the universe,– that he did blindly in obedience to the hidden pleasure of Destiny!"

Au revoir!

Sincerely your friend

Emma Lazarus

11

Rose Hawthorne Lathrop

R ose Hawthorne Lathrop (1851–1926) was the daughter of Nathaniel Hawthorne. She led a tragic and martyred life. Her only son, Francis, died in 1881 at the age of four and one half. Her marriage to George Parsons Lathrop at the age of twenty-one was not happy. Lathrop, who was assistant editor to William Dean Howells at the *Atlantic Monthly* and later editor of the *Boston Sunday Courier*, became an alcoholic. After several separations, the couple converted to Catholicism in March 1891. They separated finally in 1895, when Rose decided to enter the convent of the Gray Nuns, hoping to prepare herself for life as a nun.[1]

In 1896, Rose began her work with the incurably ill at the New York Memorial Hospital. In 1901, after she had entered the novitiate as Sister Mary Alphonsa, and founded the order of the Servants of Relief for Incurable Cancer, the Rosary Hill Home was opened in Sherman Park (later called Hawthorne), New York, a hospice still in existence today. For the remainder of her life, Mother Mary Alphonsa lived there, training novices and ministering to the incurably ill. She died in 1926.

It is said that Rose Hawthorne Lathrop's decision to care for the incurably ill was occasioned, in part, by the death of her friend Emma Lazarus at the age of thirty-eight. Emma and Rose had become friends in 1881. Interestingly, Rose would later write to their friend Helena Gilder, asking if Emma had converted to Catholicism.[2]

The letters included in this collection are the only record of the friendship of these two women.

Emma Lazarus to Rose Hawthorne Lathrop
Sunday

My dear Mrs. Lathrop

If to be "cheerful" is to send you a delighted acceptance of your charming invitation, I will indeed be cheerful. You are so kind to have thought of me, & to wish me to be among your family & one of your two chosen friends. I shall be with you as early as I can– somewhere between six & half past six. I cannot think however of taking advantage of your kindness in proposing to bring me home– which is so very far out of your way. And as I have been three Fridays in succession at Helena's,[3] & do not wish to wear out my welcome at her most hospitable home, I will come home from Martinelli's in a Cab. I was so disappointed to miss seeing you again yesterday– & awoke this morning wondering what I could do to arrange a positive meeting with you. You have anticipated me most kindly. My sister sends her regards & was also sorry to miss you.

Sincerely yours

Emma Lazarus

Emma Lazarus to Rose Hawthorne Lathrop
34 East 57th St.
May 11 [1881]

My dear Mrs. Lathrop–

You must not think me ungrateful for your more than kind & welcome letter– but I have waited until you had time to get to Concord before I have attempted to answer & thank you for it. I trust you left your brother-in-law quite better, & that you found yourself strong to meet the sorrowful associations that must now be inseparably connected with your Concord home– I am sincerely glad to know that you are not to remain there– for I feared your courage would fail you & the inevitable loneliness of your life there would be almost unbearable to you.[4] I hope you will let me hear from you again & tell me of your future plans– I cannot feel as if you were a stranger to me– for the impulse of sympathy was so strong & so rapid that it seemed to bring me quite near to you in a very short time– You are so kind to suggest that I should go abroad with you– & I know you mean it seriously.[5] But although I cannot imagine anything more delightful, my life is circumstanced just now in such a way that I could not think of carrying out my wish. Believe me, I appreciate none the less your tempting offer, & am glad to think you cared enough for me to make it. I have seen Helena several times, & I gave her your message & the news of your change of plans, which she was delighted to hear– I dined with her last Thursday when we were both in hopes that you might come in during the evng. but Mrs. Stedman explained to me how you had been pre-vented, & I was to be disappointed in my hope of seeing you at all again before you left New York. I was very sorry, but it was a real & deep pleasure to me to have met you, & I feel as if we might still be something to each other– as far as human beings can– for a sincere sympathy has brought us together. I feel almost as if I have been defrauded of a right– when you say you would like to write me a long letter, & then give me a brief note. I shall be so glad to hear from you if you will only write when & however you feel inclined– It might do you good to talk a little about yourself– & I will send you all the news I can of the city & our mutual friends. Meanwhile believe me sincerely your friend

Emma Lazarus

Letter 3RHL

Emma Lazarus to Rose Hawthorne Lathrop
34 East 57th Street
January 8th, 1882

My dear Mrs. Lathrop–

I was very much surprised & greatly disappointed to learn from your brother-in-law on Friday evening, that you had settled in Philadelphia for the winter & had given up your plan of coming to New York– I had been looking forward so confidently to seeing you from one week to the next, & wondered why you had not already appeared, or at least let me hear from you– However, I am not going to allow you to forget me so I take advantage of the beginning of the year to send you all kind wishes & affectionate regards, & to beg you from time to time to let me know how you are & where you are. Are you living very quietly, or do you care to see people? I should like so much to make you know (if you do not already know her) a very dear friend of mine who lives in Philadelphia & who I am sure would make your stay there pleasanter. She was a Miss Rodgers of New York (a half sister of our mutual friend Mrs. O'Sullivan), & is now Mrs. George Biddle.[6] She is a woman of about my age, bright, sympathetic, and thoroughly charming, & has a husband, nearly, if not quite, as delightful as herself. I am sure you would mutually enjoy each other– May I not ask her to call on you? I have had, thus far, a very pleasant winter. The weather has been mild & beautiful, & I have seen some interesting people, & enjoyed music & Rossi. I have subscribed to the Philharmonic Concerts– with Helena & Richard– & so enjoy them double. I spent last Friday evening at the Studio which is decidedly becoming a Salon! I wish you could be here, to add to its interest. Will you not please let me hear from you, & tell me that you care to hear from me occasionally. I shall be glad if you will know my friend.

Believe me

Sincerely yours

Emma Lazarus

Letter 4RHL

Emma Lazarus to Rose Hawthorne Lathrop
Jany 14 1882
34 East 57th St.

My dear Mrs. Lathrop–

I am afraid you do not expect to see my bad handwriting so soon again but you must not send me such suggestive letters, if you do not wish me to answer immediately. I was so glad to hear from you, to know what you were doing & feeling & thinking about, & I feel as if I had so much to say in regard to your discussion with Mr. Leland,[7] that I can resist no longer– I have <u>not</u> seen Oscar Wilde[8] & have little or no curiosity to see him– I do not agree with Mr. Leland that "he is beneath contempt"– intellectually– he has written together with alot of trash & verbiage, some charming & some manly verse– "Ave Imperiatrix" is I think a fine poem, & could only have been written by a man of genuine imagination & talent– But for the very reason that he is <u>not</u> a fool, & knows so well what he is about, I think he is the more to be despised & shunned by all sensible people, for making such a consummate ass of himself. This bare-faced courting of a vulgar notoriety, in a man with well-founded pretensions to good birth, good breeding, & an intelligence conspicuously above the average is, I really do think, something "beneath contempt"– & the only excuse I can find for it is that he will know more when he grows older–

He is very young. Do not let us waste our time talking about such a mass of egotism, affectation & nonsense. But for the other questions to which your conversation about Wilde led you, I am altogether with <u>you</u> & opposed to Mr. Leland. Especially do I want to shake hands with you about Shelley. I, too, have always revolted against this apotheosis of Shelley as a hyper-moral man– a blameless saint, a sinless angel, too pure, too spiritual, too exquisite for this gross world of ours. I have never been able to see, in reading his life, on what his admirers set up this preposterous claim to superhuman virtue. I think of him as a misguided, unbalanced, dangerously fascinating man of very low principles in regard to women & money– the two things which hightoned men are supposed to have honor about. A Philanthropist who did not remember to pay his tradesmen's bills, & a saint who deserted his wife & children– That he had noble aspirations, a soft heart & dazzling genius I freely admit– but I think the thing I resent about him is his being set up as a pure & lily white contrast to the "wicked Byron"– who was a better son, <u>quite as good a husband</u>, a more faithful lover to the only woman who really sympathized with him, a kinder master to his servants, & a far more practical worker for the cause of humanity in his devotion to the Greek cause, than was ever Shelley with his agitation pamphlets & his advocacy of Free Love– Can it be possible that Mr. Leland said– "All works based upon crime or un-health are pernicious & <u>unliterary</u>?" What is the theme of Hamlet, but of murder & insanity, of Macbeth, of Othello, but crime & brutal crime? Is "Faust" unliterary? Are the Greek tragedies (some of them based on unnamable sins) pernicious? The true difficulty I think, is in keeping our sense of proportion & putting things in their right places, as only the one or two masters of the world have been able to do. That cool sanity of judgement & vision, is I think, the greatest thing about Browning, who deals with such tragic passions & yet never loses his own intellectual balance & philosophical spirit. But any theory that would banish crime from fiction would be about on a par with one that would banish shadows from painting. I am delighted to think you have work to do that interests you– I am going to write to Mrs. Biddle in spite of what you say, to give her the pleasure of knowing you. My belief is that when we feel least inclined to see strangers, we <u>need</u>, most to see them– the more we indulge our sad thoughts & our love of solitude, the more do these tyrannize over us.

This is not the kind of letter I wanted to send to you but it is too late now to make it any better– & I do not dare to make it any longer– Please forgive me if I have bored you– & write to me when & as often as you can.

Sincerely your friend

Emma Lazarus

Emma Lazarus to Rose Hawthorne Lathrop
34 E. 57th St.
August 23, 1882

My dear Mrs. Lathrop

"Anger" was not exactly the correct word to express my feelings toward you while I did not hear from you– but since it has brought forth such a delightful letter from you, I will let it pass, & pretend that I really was seething with indignation. No, I was only a little impatient to get some news of you, & to hear whether you were philosophizing or rebelling against Fate. Your letters are always so satisfactory & suggesting– they are the kind I wish to reply to the moment I receive them which is, to say the least, inconsiderate on my part! But I have an excellent excuse for answering this at once– for I wish to thank you heartily for your charming invitation. Indeed, I would love to see you in your own home & visit dear old Concord again– I have a peculiar affection for it– but– as usual there is a but, I cannot promise now that I shall be able to be away from New York in October– In September (probably the middle or later part) I hope to go to Lenox & if I could combine that visit with a few days with you in early October I should be quite happy– But I may have imperative duties recalling me to New York in connection with work for the Russian Jews–[9] & it may be impossible to prolong my holiday beyond the fortnight I have promised to my Lenox friends– I appreciate so much your kind thought in asking me to go to you, & I should so like to do it, that I tell you exactly how I am placed & try to leave the invitation open– But if this puts you in the slightest inconvenience, dear Mrs. Lathrop, please let me know & I shall regretfully forgo at once the possible pleasure. My sister has written to me of the pleasure she had in meeting you & your kindness to her– for which I also thank you.[10] She is my great friend in our enormous family, & I am glad to have you know her. I have not heard a word about Mr. Stedman's "Night in Venice"– What do you mean? I have had only one satisfactory letter from Helena all summer, & don't even know where she is now– I think Mrs. Bronson is returning to Europe these days, & I suppose after the great event is consummated, the deKay family will gradually return to their friends. Poor Helena had been absorbed with her mother & her baby, both of whom had been ill– when she wrote. I trust no news is good news & that she & Richard are enjoying a holiday now. Did you know that you & I were at Newport at the same time? I had no idea of it until my sister told me, the other day– I should have loved to see you there– but we were the whole length of the island apart. I was only there for a few days. I have had a very bright & happy summer & feel eager for work again– I am going to undertake the study of Hebrew in the Fall with a very learned & intelligent old Orientalist who has offered to teach me all he knows![11] The Jewish Question which I plunged into so wrecklessly & impulsively last Spring has gradually absorbed more & more of my mind & heart– It opens up such enormous vistas in the Past & Future, & is so palpitatingly alive at the moment– being treated with more or less ability & eloquence in almost every newspaper & periodical you pick up– that it has about driven out of my thought all other subjects– I have reached a point now where I <u>must</u> know Hebrew, & I am constitutionally so indolent, that very systematic study is a little alarming to me. One of the most interesting contributions to this topic is Laurence Oliphant's paper in the last "Nineteenth Century." Have you read George Sand's correspondence? It is wonderfully beautiful & throws a splendid light upon her personality– She looms up as a truly great & noble woman, whom with all her faults, one must love & admire. Goodbye & believe me with kind regard to Mr. Lathrop & much love for yourself

Affectionately yours

Emma Lazarus

Letter 6RHL

Emma Lazarus to Rose Hawthorne Lathrop
34 E. 57th St.
Sept. 9 1882

My dear Mrs. Lathrop–

I have deferred answering your more than kind letter, in the hope that I could soon give you a definite answer to your invitation. But I find now I shall not be able to do this, until I get to Lenox. So I will not wait any longer to write, & at least thank you for your considerate offer to keep the first week in October "clear" for me. You may be sure I will make every effort to avail myself of your hospitality– for I feel that it would be the most satisfactory way of seeing you & I should dearly love to find myself once more in Concord– I will let you know definitely as soon as I possibly can whether I can go to you– in the meanwhile please don't let my uncertain visit interfere with any other arrangements you might make. My sister returned ten days ago in fine health & spirits from her visit to Massachusetts. She had enjoyed so much seeing you & asked me to tell you that she was only in Concord a day or two after she had spent the evening at your house. She went to Gloucester before she came home, & thus she was deprived of the pleasure of seeing you again, which she very much regretted. She says you were so kind to her, & she sends her best regards to you & Mr. Lathrop. I have had a delightful, satisfactory letter from Helena since I heard from you– You need not distress yourself about her children as she and they are in excellent condition– They are having an Arcadian time up in the neighborhood of Buzzards' Bay where Mr. Gilder has been taking his holiday & Mrs. deKay has joined them & the babies are thriving, & Helena has had a studio "fitted up" in the ruins of a dilapidated oil-factory![12] Stone walls of substantial masonry, & the blue sky overhead– does that not give you a romantic picture? They will return to the city in the latter part of this month.

Poor Mr. Stedman! That was a truly pathetic story you told me about his Venetian, or rather his non-Venetian experience.[13] But there is no use in trying to be a poet & a stockbroker– putting Pegasus in harness with a Bull or a Bear– these are the penalties! You seem to think I am attempting something very formidable in attacking the Hebrew language– But it is not so very difficult as it has the reputation of being, & if I were not stupid & lazy, I should have learned it long ago. It is easier than Greek & infinitely easier than Russian. To be sure, I don't know a word of either of these languages, but I only mention the fact to prove to you that I am not undertaking such a colossal achievement as you appear to think.

I have gone through a course of George Eliot lately & have been rereading most of her novels this summer–[14] What a mine they are!– I am doing all I can to try to keep myself from being utterly absorbed in a single thought & a single work. As you say, it may, & probably will, fill my life. There is so much to be done & my strength is so little, & my experience less– I will write to you from Lenox where I go on the 18th– meanwhile believe me

Sincerely your friend

Emma Lazarus

Emma Lazarus to Rose Hawthorne Lathrop
34 E. 57th St.
Sept. 30, 1882

My dear Mrs. Lathrop–

I am indeed grieved to think of your being again in the midst of trouble, & can imagine only too well how much you suffer with those you love. Many thanks for writing to me at such a moment. I have only just returned from Lenox, & find so much work awaiting me, that in spite of my disappointment in not seeing you, I am more than ever convinced that I did wisely not to prolong my holiday. My little book of "Semitic" poetry is at last out,[15] & I send you herewith a copy with my affectionate regards. It is sombre & tragic, but I hope you will care for it a little for my sake.

I saw Helena & her babies yesterday– all in fine condition. Rodman is as handsome as ever– the baby strong & promising but <u>not yet</u> beautiful. Her eyes are like Helena's & are consequently lovely– The heat & the equinoctial storm marred a good deal of my enjoyment of the country, but the woods were already beginning to put on their paint & war feathers as I left Lenox. Today the fine weather seems fairly inaugurated. How beautiful Concord must look! I hope you get all comfort out of the trees & skies & everlasting hills– or do you live much indoors? I found out after all what the Emersons thought of my little paper on Mr. E.[16] Ellen very kindly went over it word for word with my sister in order that she might repeat to me exactly the family opinion which was highly gratifying. Wasn't it good of her, & characteristic? Let me hear from you when you can– I trust your brother and sister-in-law are bravely enduring their trouble & that you will yield as little as possible to your sad thoughts & associations.

Affectionately yours

Emma Lazarus

Emma Lazarus to Rose Hawthorne Lathrop
Wednesday, April 16, 1883

My dear Rose–

I have received a list of addresses & prices from Lady Mandville which I send you without delay. The only trouble is that Lady M. says these are "out of the Season" prices, & that everything is a great deal dearer during the London "Season"–[17] & she suggests that we should make our first visit to Paris– However, I am in favor of going first to London & if we find things too dear, after a week we can leave & return later. At Roth's Hotel, 4 Clarges St. Picadilly– a room on the 3rd floor for one person is $5.25 a week. The other charges are Attendance 50 cts– Lights, 12 cts. Breakfast 30 cts. Lunch 50 cts. Dinner $1.25. Ten dollars would more than cover our living expenses for a week at this rate. (Without allowing for "Season" rates.) Lady Mandville highly recommends this hotel. As you gave me permission to act on her directions, I have written without delay to the Landlord, & asked to secure two rooms for the latter part of May. I have requested him to send our answer to Queenstown on board the Alaska. I have other addresses in case this should fail. I hope you are well & keeping up your courage stoutly! Every day makes me more eager to go. Let hear from you if you can find time to write– & please acknowledge this if only by postal card– Annie joins me in much love to you. Give my love to Ellen Emerson & to Mrs. Emerson if you see her.

fondly yours

Emma Lazarus

Emma Lazarus to Rose Hawthorne Lathrop
April 19 [1883]
34 East 57th St.

My dear Rose–

I was so sorry to miss you yesterday! Please keep me posted as to your movements & whereabouts. I am not quite sure, as you said you were going "away" whether you meant to your brother's or to Concord– When will you return to New York? I made a mistake in my calculations in my note written yesterday which you will probably find awaiting you at Concord. I said our living-expenses at Roth's Hotel recommended by Lady Mandville would be less than $10 per week. But I forgot that the incidental expenses of board, lights, etc. are $2.49 per <u>day</u>– so though the room is very cheap ($5.25 per week) yet the account mounts up to about three dollars a day. Well, we will try it for a week, & if we cannot get along, we will change our quarters or go to Paris, or do something else. I wish if you are not too busy you would write to me & let me know what you are thinking of all this. Direct to me here until Wednesday the 25th when I hope to be in our other house 18 West 10th St.

Always affectionately yours

Emma Lazarus

Letter 10RHL

Emma Lazarus to Rose Hawthorne Lathrop
London,
August 22nd, 1883

My dear Rose–

How good of you to write & to send such a kind, affectionate letter. Indeed I have thought of you very many times during my happy summer in England, & if I had only known your address would have written to you long before now– As it is I sit down to answer your letter the very moment I receive it, to thank you most sincerely for sending it. I have wished so much to know how & where you were, & whether there was any chance of your getting here this Season after all– In Stratford & Oxford above all, you were constantly before me, & I could not help feeling that to you & the impulse you gave me I was indebted for the greatest pleasure of my life. My trip to England has been one unclouded enjoyment– & I am now thinking of our approaching return as we have only three weeks more in this enchanted country. I spent five weeks in London during the Season, & in a quiet way, saw many interesting people–[18] The English are so kind & hospitable especially to Americans, when these are once well introduced, that it would be impossible not to enjoy such an experience. Browning, I saw (comparatively) a good deal of– he was particularly kind & friendly to me– William Morris was the most interesting man I met, & I had a charming afternoon at his house, & a delightful day at the old Abbey with him where he established his factory. I met a great number of the literary & artistic Londoners, also several interesting members of Parliament including John Bright & John Morley– & saw in a word most of the noteworthy men whom I came to meet. Then the Abbey & the National Gallery & the House of Commons & the huge town of London itself were each a "sensation" of the most exciting kind to me– & I did not know a moment's weariness or ennui. We have been travelling through the South of England for the past six weeks, & have seen many of the Cathedral towns as well as Oxford, Stratford & North Devon– Tomorrow we go to Cambridge & hope still to see Ely, Lincoln, York & Durham before the 15th September, the date of our sailing for home. I have no words with which to tell you of my enthusiasm for the English country– & the <u>Cathedrals</u>! I never imagined I could enjoy them so much– Do let me see you if you can, when I arrive in New York– Remember my new address– 18 West 10th St.– Accept a thousand thanks for your lovely letter & much love from Annie & myself from your friend

Emma Lazarus

Letter 11RHL

Emma Lazarus to Rose Hawthorne Lathrop
18 West 10th St.
Wednesday [December 1883]

My dear Rose–

Please let these fresh flowers say to you what you know I feel & should like to say myself– if I only knew how– Of course I am sorry not to see you today– but I quite understand your feeling unable to come to me & shall look forward to seeing you very soon again. I hope your sister will be well again before long– & that you will be cheered & strengthened by your visit to your brother's family.[19] With much love, & sincere wishes for your peace & welfare,

Affectionately your friend

Emma Lazarus

Emma Lazarus to Rose Hawthorne Lathrop
18 West 10th Street
Jan'y. 1– 1884

My dear Rose–

I have put off writing to you, not only because I hate and despise letter writing (not letter-<u>receiving</u>!) but because I have hoped from day to day, & from week to week that you would fulfill your promise of coming to New York & letting me see you– What has become of you, & why have you not carried out such a praiseworthy & delightful purpose? I will no longer delay telling you how impatiently I look forward to seeing you once more– & at the same time offer you my affectionate greetings for the New Year. May it be a happier one to you than the last has been– & restore the brightness & peace that the old one took away. Whatever may be said about a living trouble being worse than a buried one, yet there is always at least the hope of comfort & renewal of joy, with the one, while the other is irretrievable. And so, I cannot help trusting dear Rose, that I will once again see you smiling & cheerful. I have had a quiet & rather busy winter– studying & writing as usual. I continue to take infinite pleasure in recalling every moment of my English experience– How I should love to talk it all over with you– & to compare notes as to our relative enjoyment of places, people & Cathedrals. How can any American who has ever trodden that dear Mother-soil cease to love & cling to it? Did you see or hear Matthew Arnold while he was in Boston? He is to deliver his Emerson lecture here on Friday Evng. & I am very curious to hear it–[20] Opinions have been so violent in regard to it, especially in New England that I can form no estimate of its real value– I rather fancy that with all my intense admiration & gratitude for Mr. Emerson, I shall find much to agree with in Mr. Arnold's critical estimate of him.– However, I cannot tell & I may be as indignant as the most outraged Bostonian. I see Helena as usual, & we often speak affectionately of you– Her baby Dorothea is plump & rosy & <u>coquettish</u> to the last degree– Rodman is unchanged– except that he grows larger & taller; & more boyish every month– & keeps all his childish beauty. Helena is better than I have seen her in years, & looks very handsome. Do come in & see us all– I am sure it would do you good, however much you shrink from the thought. Your photograph, which I brought you from Paris is still awaiting you. With much love & all good wishes for 1884,

Believe me

Affectionately your friend

Emma Lazarus

Emma Lazarus to Rose Hawthorne Lathrop
18 West 10th Street
Jany. 29 [1884]

My dear Rose–

I had every intention of answering your welcome letter the very day after I read it– but I have been so busy that twenty days have slipped by, & while it has not gone out of my mind ever since, yet I have not been able to acknowledge it– I am delighted to hear that you are at last coming to New York, & shall look forward to many a good long talk about yourself, & myself & England & America– I am afraid you have had a sad & lonely time of it since I saw you last Spring– but for the "smallness of your resources" of which you complain, there are few of us who are not "appalled" when set face to face with their fate– & I am sure you have shown as much pluck & fortitude as the best. An acquired interest in outside things is one of the most difficult things to get– especially when one is bruised & stunned– But I doubt not, it will come to you gradually, & you will once again laugh & take pleasure as the days go by. You ask me about Matthew Arnold's Lecture on Emerson–[21] I heard it with great interest & enjoyment– While I did not agree with some of his opinions yet I admired extremely the well-ordered thought, the fluent, graceful style, & the charming tone of the whole. I am disposed to value Mr. Emerson's poetry far more highly than Arnold does– but in most other respects, I found myself fully in accord with him– especially in the main point of considering Emerson rather as a moral & spiritual influence than as a so-called <u>literary</u> man. Helena's "Friday Evngs." grow more & more brilliant– last Friday she had about 50 people, literary, artistic, social "lions" of all kinds. I have heard very little music this winter– there have been fewer concerts than usual, I think. Just now I am interested in helping to get up a series of free Concerts for the Working Classes– to be conducted by Theodore Thomas–[22] A rich philanthropist who lately died, bequeathed a legacy for this purpose– & it is desired to form a permanent organization for future seasons. I have been trying to write a brief record of one of the interesting episodes of my trip to England last Summer– an account of my visit to Morris' workshop while I was there.[23] I thought nothing would ever induce me to follow the usual American fashion & "report" it for the benefit of the public– But the scribbling instinct is irresistible, & I am doing the very thing I despised & abjured! My only excuse is that I have got Morris' consent to do it, & his promise to correct & authenticate the M.S. So I am in hopes it will have a certain value & it is such a delight to live over again those beautiful happy hours! I have just finished it, for it is uppermost in my thoughts– but please don't mention it to anyone else– Write to me when you can, & tell me when I may hope to see you– & when you will be in New York. I hope it will be soon. Meanwhile believe me always affectionately yours

Emma Lazarus

Emma Lazarus to Rose Hawthorne Lathrop
Thursday
18 West 10th Street
[black border] [After 9 March 1885] [24]

    I must thank you for your letter & beautiful words– What you say goes to my heart more directly than almost any words that have been said or written to me in my trouble. I will take your letter with me to England where I shall wish to read it many times again– & I have little doubt that your cheering prophecies will come true under the influence of that lovely country & climate. I hope you will let me see you before I go– I do not sail until the 6th of May on the "Servia" & I may be away for a long time– possibly eighteen months. I should be so sorry to go away without seeing you again– I am at home almost any time– morning or afternoon. Come in the morning if you can– I am very well & busy enough with stupid little preparations for my journey, not to have time for brooding or even thinking much– Our experiences seem to be <u>all</u> <u>pain</u>– & I dare not allow my mind to dwell on it– Once more, dear Rose, I thank you from my heart for your loving note.

Always your friend

Emma Lazarus

12

Edwin Robert Anderson Seligman

E dwin R. A. Seligman was the son of Joseph and Babette Steinhardt Seligman. His father, an immigrant from Germany, was the founder of the international banking firm of J. and W. Seligman and Company. Seligman and his eight siblings were tutored by Horatio Alger. He graduated from Columbia College in 1879, second in his class, and received a double M.A. and LL.B. in 1884. He received his Ph.D. in 1885.

Seligman was still a graduate student when Emma tried to interest him in her cause. He was twelve years her junior. These letters are the only record of their friendship. Interestingly, her sister Agnes' granddaughter Nancy-Joan Marks married Madron Seligman, of the British branch of the family. He is a member of the European Parliament in Strasbourg, France.[1]

Known at his death as the "Dean of the profession," Seligman began his teaching career at Columbia as a lecturer on economics in 1885 and remained there until 1931, when he became professor emeritus in residence at the school. In 1886, Seligman originated the *Political Science Quarterly*. He was a prolific writer on economics and taxation and is said to have reorganized Cuba's economy in 1932.

Seligman's library of more than fifty thousand volumes, which he began accumulating at the age of twenty, included all of the writings of Alexander Hamilton on economic subjects, and a large number of Marxist manifestos. He sold the collection to Columbia University in 1930 for $500,000.[2]

We do not know when or how Emma met Edwin Seligman, but she may have felt that he would be interested in her scheme to reform and resettle East European Jews because of the Seligman-Hilton incident in Saratoga. In short, Joseph Seligman, a leading Jewish American banker, was refused rooms at the Grand Union Hotel because he was a Jew. The incident received national attention.[3]

Emma Lazarus to E. R. A. Seligman
34 East 57th St.
Feb. 1, 1883

Dear Mr. Seligman–

Will you give me the pleasure of calling at my house next Monday evening at 8 p.m.– to meet Professor Rice and Mr. Daniel DeLeon[4] to discuss the question of Jewish Colonization in the East? I shall be very glad to see you & to hear your views on the subject, & I need scarcely repeat to you that you will not be considered as allying yourself to my party, or pledging yourself to any principle by coming. We shall simply have an informal talk upon a subject that must necessarily be of deepest interest to us all. Trusting you are not already engaged, & that you feel sufficiently interested to come, believe me very truly yours

Emma Lazarus

34 East 57th Street

Emma Lazarus to E. R. A. Seligman
Feby. 6, Tuesday [1883]

My dear Mr. Seligman–

I was extremely sorry to learn the cause of your absence last evening. I need scarcely say that we were all greatly disappointed not to have you with us. As Mr. Rice tells me that you cordially approve of our plan as represented in the little paper which he showed you, I write to give you the results of our first meeting– so that if you are able to join us at our second, you will know just where we stand. We agreed that the Re-Colonization of Palestine was the only solution possible of the Jewish Problem of Eastern Europe.[5] And being desirous to extricate our unfortunate co-religionists from their present untenable position, we decided that the first step would be to draw up a Circular, as briefly as possible– consisting of little more than one paragraph, stating that "we, the undersigned" have formed an association for the purpose of promoting this project, & that we seek co-operation, aid & advice from the Community, Jewish & Christian alike. Mr. Rice, Mr. DeLeon & I have each promised to try our hand upon the composition of such a paper– & we should very much like to have you, too, try to put it in the most condensed & forcible shape that presents itself to your mind. At our next meeting (Tuesday Evng., the 13th) we will compare our papers, take what is best from each of them, & decide upon later action. Meanwhile we shall each endeavor to secure the sympathy & interest of one or two persons whom we discussed last evening, & who we thought would be desirable collaborators. Now, does all this sound very incendiary? I detect in your note a lingering spark of mistrust– & I can most sincerely reassure you that no slightest grain of political purpose under-lies or is in any way connected with our scheme. Mr. DeLeon & Mr. Rice would be as thoroughly opposed to anything in that direction as you are your-self– & I am certain that all such misgivings would have forever vanished from your mind if you could have been with us last evening. May I expect you next Tuesday at 8 p.m.– to meet Mr. Rice & Mr. DeLeon only? If you do not feel inclined or prepared to write the little paper– this need not interfere with your coming to talk over the subject– I cannot help thinking that one conversation (without the accompaniment of waltz-music, as we had it before) would bring about a clearer understanding than many notes, though they be as long as this. Can you come to see me this week, before meeting the other gentlemen here? If Thursday or Friday suit your convenience, & you will let me know, I will be at home, & shall be glad to see you upon either evening. I trust you will have no further trouble with your eyes. Believe me, very truly yours,

Emma Lazarus

Letter 3ERAS

Emma Lazarus to E. R. A. Seligman
February 11, 1883
34 East 57th Street

Dear Mr. Seligman–

According to my promise, I send you the titles of the few publications which I think necessary to read if you wish to understand the possibilities of Palestine Colonization. These are– 1) "The Land of Gilead" by Laurence Oliphant; 2) an article of his entitled "Jewish Tales" in Blackwood's Magazine of November 1882, 3) & another by him in the Nineteenth Century for August 1882– headed the "Jew and the Eastern Question"–⁶ I send you these names without delay, in the hope that even if you cannot use your eyes, you may find someone to read them to you– The two Essays together could be read within an hour, & the book itself is not long. I need scarcely say that I shall await with a certain amount of impatience the result of your study– trusting that it may induce you to take the same view of the Question as I take myself,

Believe me very sincerely yours

Emma Lazarus

Emma Lazarus to E. R. A. Seligman
Feby. 14 [1883]

Dear Mr. Seligman–

Professor Rice and Mr. DeLeon met at my home last evening, as agreed, & they were both so struck with the wisdom of your course, that we have adopted it as the basis of our own future action! We have determined to write, with as large & influential force as we can muster, for the very purpose for which you have retired– or rather withheld yourself– viz: to gather information as to the chances of ultimate success for a Colonization plan. Relying upon your sympathy which you have so cordially expressed, I send you the little paper we agreed upon last even'g– which states the aim & purpose of our association. We shall endeavor by communicating personally with Mr. Oliphant & the representatives of the Alliance,[7] to post ourselves thoroughly as to the prospects & difficulties of the scheme. If it be within the bounds of human power to accomplish it, we shall contribute our united energies towards its promotion. If, on the contrary, we find that this plan also, no less than the plans for Emigration to America or Internal Reform for Russian Jews, contains in its very essence, insuperable difficulties– well, we shall be wise in time & give the whole thing up.[8] On these terms, will you not be with us? Do you not think you could inform yourself better in conjunction with us, than alone & independently? I shall write about half a dozen others to meet here on Monday Evng. next, the 19th, punctually at 8 o'clock– & I shall be sincerely glad if you will join us– As you see, we only wish to form the nucleus of a preliminary organization for complete investigation of the subject– I am sure your suggestions would be of benefit to us all. I am going to ask your cousin, Mr. DeWitt Seligman, to join us on these terms, & the others whom I shall write are Dr. deSola Mendes, Mr. Nathan Bijur, Mr. J.J. Frank, Mr. Ullmann, Mr. deLeon, Mr. Rice– & Mrs. Alfred Louis.[9] I have been already assured of the sympathy of all these– with the exception of Mrs. Louis & Mr. Ullmann, whom I have every reason to hope that I will be able to interest without difficulty or delay.

If this were not a scheme in which I know you have at least as much at heart as much as I have myself, I would almost feel that I owed you an apology for pressing it so upon your notice– But I am sure that it needs no excuse in the mind of any generous & intelligent member of our race– I trust you no longer suffer from the effect of the operation upon your eyes. Believe me very sincerely yours

Emma Lazarus

Letter 5ERAS

Emma Lazarus to E. R. A. Seligman
April 12 [1883]
34 E. 57th St.

My dear Mr. Seligman–

I am sorry that last Friday evening was the last on which Mrs. Gilder promised to be at home– to her friends. It was too bad you could not have been there as it was very pleasant and there were a great many people. If you wish to see her, however, I think there is more likelihood of your finding her at home on Friday Evening, than on any other.[10] So you might take your chance, if you felt inclined– The only difference is that she does not formally receive, & there is no <u>certainty</u> about it. You are very kind to suggest sending me any tickets for the Berlioz Concert– and if you can spare me a couple without inconveniencing yourself I should be delighted to go. The programme is very tempting. Since I last saw you, I have decided to go abroad early next month to spend the Summer in England with a friend.[11] As we are about to move downtown am in great confusion– but I hope to see you before I sail.[12] I shall also call another meeting of the Society[13] if possible, for I wish to combine as much work for the Cause with my pleasure-trip as I can. I am sure you who know Europe so well can give me some advice about representative English Jews. With thanks for the tickets.

Yours

Emma Lazarus

Emma Lazarus to E. R. A. Seligman
Thursday [n.d. 1883]
34 East 57th St.

My dear Mr. Seligman–

I have just posted a note to you about tomorrow in case the weather be storming. I am very much obliged for your offer to call for me in a carriage, but I should prefer not to have you do so. I would rather go in the cars– if we are obliged to drive at all. I trust however the day will be pleasant & that nothing may interfere with our original appointment. Please do as I have asked you in my first note of this morning– if you can.

I have not seen Martineau's Spinoza– the only life of Spinoza I have ever read was by Frederick Polrack– & I do not want to read anything more <u>about</u> him, until I can get at the man himself & study his philosophy at its source. And I have so many other things to do that I do not know when this will be.

I am glad you sympathize with the Podolian Ghetto.[14] Too many critics– both Jewish & Christian– see nothing in it but a cause for shame & ridicule.

Sincerely yours

Emma Lazarus

Emma Lazarus to E. R. A. Seligman
[n.d.]
Friday

My dear Mr. Seligman–

Thank you very much for your note which does relieve me of my perplexity. As it threatens to be storming this afternoon, I will be very glad if you will be at my house at 4 (<u>rain or shine</u>)– and we will start from here and go down in the Madison Avenue Car.[15] If it had been a fine day, I had many little things to do downtown– But as it is not, I have no occasion to go out before the hour of our appointment– so I shall look forward to seeing you at four o'clk– I hope you do not think me very dictatorial. I will explain to you why I am so decided, when we meet–

Sincerely yours

Emma Lazarus

Emma Lazarus to E. R. A. Seligman
18 West 10th St.
Oct. 9th 1883

My dear Mr. Seligman-

A meeting of the Society for East European Jews[16] will take place at Mr. Rice's house, 106 East 62nd Street on Wednesday evening, October 17th at 8 o'clk. May I beg that you will be present without fail? I am anxious to have a full session as I shall present the Report of my inquiries abroad & their result upon my own views– & I think we shall then take action in regard to our future Course. I am anxious that we should get to something practical with as little delay as possible.– I regret to say that I was prevented from seeing your relatives while I was in London– notwithstanding the kindness of your uncle[17] who in response to your note invited me most cordially to Clapham– But a previous engagement obliged me to decline his hospitality and I had to leave England without seeing him.

Believe me very truly yours

Emma Lazarus

Emma Lazarus to E. R. A. Seligman
April 22 [1884]
18 West 10th St.

My dear Mr. Seligman–

Please find enclosed the amount of my own and my sister's dues to the S.I.C.E.E.J. Alas! alas! I fear the Society will never rise from its ashes– & it makes me sad to think of the high hopes with which I organized it a year ago. I am still awaiting a promised letter from Mr. Kann[18] in reference to Baron Hirsch–[19] But even this, I am afraid would now be insufficient to resuscitate our dispirited energies. The only thing we have proved is that the Western Jews have hard enough work on their hands in taking care of themselves, & that the Eastern Jews will have to look out for their own interests!

Believe me always sincerely yours

Emma Lazarus

Emma Lazarus to E. R. A. Seligman
18 West 10th St.
December 24 [1884]

Dear Mr. Seligman–

I thank you for your note, but hasten to say that an apology on your part is altogether uncalled for– There was not the slightest "intrusion" in your visit of a few weeks ago– On the contrary, I should have been glad to have had you stay longer as I was interested in your plans & ideas. A very old friend of the family, & the Sea-Captain who had carried us twice across the Atlantic, had been dining with us– & the servant was quite right to tell you that I was at home and disengaged. I am sorry you should have given yourself a second thought about it.– I, too, was unfortunately prevented by the stormy weather, greatly to my regret, from going to the meeting at Mrs. Louis'. So much time has elapsed in inaction, that I fear it will be excessively hard to bring the members together again or even to persuade them that something serious is to be done. I am going to make one more effort however, & have asked to have the meeting called for Thursday of this week at my house. But I don't know yet whether or not Mr. Bijur has sent out the notices. I have received from Mr. Kann (one of the Directors of the "Alliance") a very important letter containing a proposition from Baron Hirsch which <u>must</u> be laid before our Society with as little delay as possible– & after which the existence or dissolution of our Society, I think, depends. For if we cannot agree to carry out Baron Hirsch's plan, which is not only excellent but is couched in the most generous terms & does not involve the expenditure on our part of a single penny– I think we had better disband at once as incompetent <u>talkers</u>– & nothing more. At Mrs. Louis' there were besides herself, three present last Wednesday– Prof. Rice, Mr. Ullmann and Mr. Bijur. Of course nothing was accomplished, & they broke up in complete discouragement & uncertainty. I hope if the meeting is definitely fixed for this Thursday Evng. that you will surely come to my house– for as you see, it is a question of grave importance. How do your "Cooperative" projects[20] thrive? An intimate friend of mine– a lady– has become extremely interested in the subject & is anxious to devote her time & means towards making it a practical success. I should like to bring you together as I think you could help each other.

Trusting to see you soon

Sincerely yours

Emma Lazarus

Letter 11ERAS

Emma Lazarus to E. R. A. Seligman
Monday [n.d. 1884]
18 W. 10th St.

My dear Mr. Seligman–

When I spoke to Professor Adler yesterday about the Committee Meeting, I learned that he was Chairman of the Committee–[21] He did not seem to wish me to take any initiative in calling the meeting so I shall be relieved of the necessity of sending out the notes. He also preferred the afternoon to the evening– but wished to defer the whole thing till after a fortnight– He will let us all hear when he is ready for us to meet– I thought there were several disagreeable "hitches" in the Concert arrangements yesterday. After you left, the babies became such a nuisance, that Thomas had to stop the orchestra & wait until the sixth & last infantile disturber of the peace had been ejected.[22] The ushers don't seem to do their work well. I trust the whole thing will go better and then some. I understood that there were to be notices of yesterday's Concert in several papers– Yet as far as I am aware, the few lines I wrote myself & sent to the "Sun" were the only ones that appeared.

Believe me

Sincerely yours

Emma Lazarus

13

Henry James

In the summer of 1882, Henry James told his sister, Alice, that he "met and fell in love with Emma Lazarus: a poetess, a magaziness, and a Jewess. . . . She told me," he said, "my works had converted her from pessimism to optimism."[1] From that time until her last illness, Emma Lazarus and Henry James enjoyed a warm and reciprocal friendship. James and Helena Gilder had been childhood friends in Newport. His novels were serialized in the *Century*. It is probable that Emma met him at the Gilder home, perhaps at one of their famous Friday Evenings. Her friend Tom Ward may have made the introductions. The Ward and James children were friends in Boston and Newport. Emma seems to have known William James also, although we have only one letter written to her by the philosopher-psychologist.[2]

Letter 1HJ

Henry James to Emma Lazarus
131 Mt. Vernon St.
May 9, [1883]

Dear Miss Lazarus–

I congratulate you on your definite purpose of . . . yourself of the other half (as it were) of our little world-ball. I send you with great pleasure a note to Mrs. Procter, who is a most delightful & wonderful old person & a great friend of mine.[3] She doesn't "entertain" in the usual sense of the word—i.e. give dinners, etc.; but she receives eagerly every Tuesday & every Sunday afternoons. She lives in a "flat" on top of a high apartment– . . . as her address. Send her my note by post & send a word with it, saying you will present yourself on the nearest Sunday or the nearest Tuesday as the case may be, without waiting to be "asked." On Sunday afternoons you will be sure to find Browning there; go as often as you can. I will write to Mrs. P. myself & ask her to make you acquainted with Lady Goldsmid, whom I think you will find it pleasant to know. Kindly send me your prospective London (banker's) address that I may send you one or two notes more in case I don't find time to do so before the 15th, which I probably shall. Take everything easily, amuse yourself largely & discreetly & believe me ever faithfully yours

Henry James

Letter 2HJ

Henry James to Emma Lazarus
131 Mt. Vernon St.
Sunday [1883]

Dear Miss Lazarus

You are so much more than . . . fully grateful that I feel feeble & ashamed. Here however is a letter to Mrs. G.W. Smalley, the wife of the London correspondent of the N. Y. Tribune & a very charming woman. Also a very good friend of mine, whom I should like you to know. She has a very pleasant house to which many persons go, & is at home every Thursday afternoon. Go to her at once. I write to her also about you, & you will be wise to fraternize with her. I was going to give you a letter or two, but the persons I had in mind (women) are also good friends of Mrs. Smalley's, & I shall instead write to her to put them in relation with you. I shall also ask her to introduce you to the Montefiores, with whom she is intimate– She, her husband & her children (who are charming) were great cronies of Leonard Montefiore.[4] I have written this morning to Mrs. Procter to put you into communication with Lady Goldsmid (not the younger, but the widow of the late Sir Francis, a most kind & charming woman).[5] Sur ce bon Voyage!! Be comfortable at any hazard & write me a line if you have time, to let me know of your well being. Don't go off to London without having gotten a promise of lodgings in advance. You will arrive at the very crowded moment. Go to 18 Pelham Crescent North Kensington for rooms– unless you want something very "smart." Tell the woman I sent you thither– The only thing is that I put Howells there last summer & he seems to have engaged the place again. Excuse the brevity & haste, & believe me ever yours

very truly

Henry James

Henry James to Emma Lazarus
September 3rd [1883]
Picadilly

Dear Miss Lazarus–

I have an idea you will be back in England about this time & beg you to let
me know when the event occurs. Then I will explain to your satisfaction (possibly) why I never found time & opportunity to answer the very charming
letter you sent me from ½ [sic] Moon St.– I shall now call at that address, by
the way, & see if you have reappeared– My summer in America was full of
cares & preoccupation and the letter to you that was never written, was constantly nipped in the bud, after just being about to be begun! Then I was pretty
sure I shld. see you here, & have a chance to tell you in spoken words what
pleasure it gave me to hear that you were prosperous & happy. I was so sure
that you would be that had I written to you, my letter would even have surrendered too much of the triumphant "I told you so!"– which wouldn't have
been civil. I lose no time at last in communicating with you now– for I arrived
in London only last night, having sailed on the 22nd & landed on the 29th– a
wonderful . . . – after which I gave myself the luxury of waiting over in Liverpool till yesterday to see some friends off. I am to remain in London for the
present, though with occasional short absences. Do let me hear from you as
soon as you get this.

Very faithfully yours

H. James

Henry James to Emma Lazarus
Paris Feb. 5th [1884]
3 Bolton St. Picadilly

Dear Miss Lazarus–

Your friendly appreciation of my article about Turgenieff gives me real pleasure, as it does also so to get such direct news of you. Your other letter never
reached me & inquiry at the Army-Navy Club has elicited no traces of it. I am
very sorry to have missed such a gratification & I have never yet reconciled
myself to having arrived in England just at the moment you were sailing– or

arranged things so as not to have been able to talk over your impressions with you. But evidently you have given your pledge to reappearance in the stately (or at any rate friendly) limit of England. If I haven't been able to talk with you I have at least talked of you & everyone you saw asked me for news of you & expressed the most attached sentiments. You appear to have done more in three weeks than any lightfooted woman before; when you ate or slept I have not yet made definite– You may imagine indeed how I miss that dear, delightful human all-feeling, all-perceiving Turgenieff now. I crossed to this place but three days ago (to spend 2 or 3 weeks) & it has been already made clear to me that for all these years, seeing him was much the most interesting thing that Paris held for me– was indeed the only opportunity of much value. The place looks dull, empty & colourless, & this aspect accords with my own view of it– London is the same old London– whose worst fault is that it has a little too much of all things. It is too humorous, too promiscuous, too stupid (sometimes) & too a great many other things. But I love it well, for all that, & the proof of my affection is that I am homesick the moment I leave it. I hope you have had a fruitful winter. New York looks to me in retrospect like a bright high-pitched heterogeneous Tiffany city– as if some big Tiffany had made it. Excuse my blasphemy & give my love to Mrs. Lockwood.[6] No Tiffany made <u>her</u>.

Very faithfully yours,

H. James

Letter 5HJ

Henry James to Emma Lazarus
Liverpool
November 15, 1884

Dear Miss Lazarus–

Very welcome your kind & appreciative letter of the 24th October. I am always extremely glad to have news of you & I hope you will abide by your excellent resolution of letting me hear from you from time to time, without standing too much on the order of the answers– or unanswers– you may receive from so bad a correspondent. I grieve to hear of your recent illness, & hope that it has now quite faded into the limbo of things that might <u>not</u> have been. Don't you think that another journey to Europe is what you need to complete your convalescence? I shall be very glad when I next hear that such a project is taking form. In regard to the winter Atlantic, you must not think from my momentary whereabouts that I actually have designs upon it & you must excuse my vulgar paper– the first that comes to hand. I came hither five days since to meet my sister's landing from Boston, & she disembarked and made the worst for her voyage that, having little strength at best, she has had to wait here to pull herself together.[7] But we start today for London, or thus she goes– for the present to the south of England. I thank you cordially for your friendly words about my books. If one doesn't turn affected then one makes light of one's own productions. I should say that they are far from being what I shall (I hope) have done de miseries. I am doing two novels (one to commence soon in the Century, the other somewhat later in the Atlantic)[8] which I think will be more important than anything of the kind I have hither to published. (I don't mean that I am doing both at once, but one on top, as it were, of the other.) What do you read? You read everything I know & my question is idle. The last 2 vols. of Thomas Carlyle are of the deepest, most disagreeable interest.[9] What a black-hearted invidious man of genius he was & what an incomparable writer & pointier. Your mention of the "saraphio" Mrs. Lockwood refreshes me; if the seraphs have inferior spirits who . . . & adore them, as they do the highest, I am one of those. This makes me out a kind of angel, which I didn't intend but only to be yours very faithfully,

Henry James

P.S. London is the same old London: interesting, fascinating & fatiguing & brilliant & stupid, both rewarding & disappointing curiosity. I am only fond of it but it . . .

Letter 6HJ

Henry James to Emma Lazarus
St Alban's Cliff
Bournemouth
June 4th 1885

Dear Miss Lazarus–

Your note from Hempstead has been forwarded to me from London & I am very sorry it finds me at such a distance from your present perch. If I were in Bolton St. I should promptly give myself the pleasure of coming out to see you, but I fear that though the Atlantic no longer rolls between us, we shall for some time to come be divided by space. I am down here for rather an indefinite period (& have been for the past 2 months) looking after my poor sister who has spent the latter part of the winter & the spring here & who, though the place now much disagrees with her, is too ill to be moved. She is however now gathering strength by very short inches, & by July 1st will probably be able to go to Moderno for a different sort of air. After that in <u>July</u> I shall probably be in town, though not for long, & my entire plans are vague. I greatly hope however that your visit to England is not this time an affair of simple . . . so that my meeting you will be a question of no very long delay. I heard with much interest & sympathy of the death of your father, & am very sorry indeed to learn that you have been traversing this painful ordeal. I can well imagine that your loss for the time colours the world but don't think me particularly . . . if I say that– from my own experience– you will find, as life goes on, that you are glad he is out of it– that the things that successively happen to you don't touch or trouble him more. That is <u>my</u> principal feeling about my parents– I rejoice in their exception, immunities, liberations. Aren't you free now to stay in a country you so much appreciate? I hope to hear so, & that you will learn to really know London. I have been owing you a letter in answer to a kind one of yours– for two or three months, & my excuse for not having written it is that, since I have been with my sister– & indeed all winter– my correspondence has been doubled. I have had to write her letters as well as my own– She is too ill to manage letters. I hope you are in health & your sisters whom I suppose to be with you. Cultivate the philosophic mind (which you possess) & believe me yours very faithfully–

Henry James

Letter 7HJ

Henry James to Emma Lazarus
15 Esplanade
Dover
Sept. 9th [1885]

Dear Miss Lazarus–

Your note, which I was very glad to get, for I was on the point of writing for news of you (and this is not a figure of speech, but literal). Your friendly note finds me on the eve of leaving England for a couple of months. I am not, however, going further than Paris– & am to spend such a period as that there. I don't yet know at what address, but anything sent to 3 Bolton St. will instantly be forwarded to me. I have not been in London (to take . . .) since I saw you there & have been spending the last 5 weeks at this place, trying to work in extreme retirement. I have wondered about you & now wonder if you are not to turn up in Paris in the course of the autumn? If you do please notify me punctually– I envy you Holland: dear little damp, flat country with russet towns & brick that would be mossy if they didn't clean & air; which . . . a charming tone– And Mrs. Lockwood? is she coming out? I earnestly hope that isn't a . . . vision. Any light of this contingency could be very interesting to me. I hope you have enjoyed your summer & seen & done & tasted & recovered your equilibrium. Also that you are not, invidiously, going home within any calculable period. One always does leave too soon. My sister is better, relatively, (though still very infirm). She will be after Friday at Fischer's Hotel Clifford St. Bond St. I do hope that if you are in Paris you will be in London later; the winter there paradoxical as it may appear, is far the best time.

Believe me, very faithfully yours,

Henry James

Letter 8HJ

Henry James to Emma Lazarus
Bolton St.
Picadilly
December 9th 1885

Dear Miss Lazarus

I have longed to answer your note sent me just after I left Paris, that I must now send these few lines to Baring Bros., being convinced (. . . indeed the wish is father to the thought) that you will by this time have quitted the Rue de Chaillot and have located as they say in our dear mother-land, somewhere south of the Alps. The winter has by this time set in sharply here, & it is now for those who must do so in vain, a kind of consolation to dreams of Italy– of sunny windows & sunny walls. To you, therefore, who are apparently able to put your visions into actions.[10] I hope your substantial pleasure has come. I found my sister in urgent need of me when I got back here– but she is ever so much better now & is having a very comfortable winter– or beginning to have as far as one can tell. The country has been plunged in a barren electoral turmoil, the dirtiest, most uncandid, most self-seeking & continually abusing strife of party-politics.[11] A new parliament has been brought into existence with the aid of the just- enfranchised . . . ; but the only thing certain about it is that it will speak on the huge apparently quite insolvable Irish Question. Parnell is the most potent person just now, in the world. It remains to be seen whether from the King of Ireland he will also be King of England. I . . . you don't see Mrs. Lockwood, if she is in Rome & you on the Arno. But I trust you have good news of her & also that you are well & have . . . apartments to . . . ones– . . . sweet . . . of Italy.

Very faithfully yours

Henry James

NOTES

GLOSSARY OF PROPER NAMES

BIBLIOGRAPHY

INDEX

Notes

1. The Statue

1. At Emma Lazarus' death, the *American Hebrew*, an Anglo-Jewish weekly in New York, published a memorial issue to the poet. Of the numerous tributes, only that of Constance Cary Harrison mentioned her sonnet. Harrison had been chairperson in charge of the Literary Portfolio to be auctioned at the opening of the Art Loan Exhibition, and had solicited from her friend Emma the contribution of a sonnet to the Statue. She recalled this incident in her memorial. *American Hebrew* Memorial Issue, 9 December 1887, Emma Lazarus Scrapbook, American Jewish Historical Society Archives (hereafter cited as *AH*); James Russell Lowell to Emma Lazarus, 17 December 1883, Ralph L. Rusk, ed., *Letters to Emma Lazarus in the Columbia University Library* (New York: Columbia University Press, 1939), 74. Ignatius Donnelly wrote Emma Lazarus in 1885, praising her poem, which he had seen in the *New York World*. Donnelly to Emma Lazarus, 25 July 1885, Minnesota Historical Society Archives.

2. Georgina Schuyler, a member of the historically significant Hamilton Schuyler family, contacted Richard Watson Gilder, some time before 23 May 1901, asking him to help her with her "scheme." Two years of roadblocks by Emma's family and others are recorded in correspondence between Schuyler, Gilder, and Emma's sister Josephine. See Richard Watson Gilder Papers, Statue of Liberty Collection, New York Public Library.

3. Oscar Handlin writes that only after 1903, when the tablet was placed within the Statue, was the "connection" established. Handlin, *The Statue of Liberty* (New York: Newsweek, 1971), 60–61. Cecil D. Eby saw the first four lines of the second stanza as the "best articulation" of the image of America as "an asylum for the oppressed and the homeless of the Old World." Eby, "America as 'Asylum': A Dual Image," *American Quarterly* 14 (1962): 483.

4. *Inauguration of the Statue of Liberty Enlightening the World by the President of the United States, October 28, 1886,* issued under the authority of the committee (New York: D. Appleton, 1887), 32.

5. *New York Magazine* published a special edition honoring the Centennial of the Statue of Liberty, in May 1986. Twelve "accomplished New Yorkers" wrote about the Statue's "meaning to the nation's sense of destiny, to their lives and ours." Former immigrants

Isaac Bashevis Singer and Jerzy Kosinski heard the Statue speak. Singer called her "My Yiddishe Lady" and imagined as a child in Poland that the Statue spoke Yiddish. Kosinski "went to the Statue" shortly after he got his first job. "Imposing, the Statue greets me with a smile," he wrote. "I smiled back. It's a lovely scene—the two of us, two exiles, she from France and I from Poland." *New York Magazine* (May 1986): 48, 70.

6. The Statue of Liberty has been used in protest, not only by immigrants, but by such groups as the Gay Activists Alliance and the National Abortion Rights Action League (NARAL). In a flier, "Walk for Choice," the Statue is pictured striding, torch held high, in a pair of tennis shoes. *New York Times,* 6 May 1974, p. 39 (hereafter cited as *NYT*); Pro-Choice Columbus, a chapter of NARAL of Ohio.

7. In 1944, Irving Berlin put the last stanza of "The New Colossus" to music in his Broadway play, *Miss Liberty.*

8. Novelist Pete Hamill was one of the New Yorkers asked to contribute to the Statue of Liberty issue of *New York Magazine.* His descriptive phrases are used in this study, as they are most appropriate words to describe the Statue. It is interesting to note that Hamill, who was not an immigrant, saw the Statue as unreal, "too huge, too grand, to exist in the real world. It seemed to belong more properly," he wrote, "to that imaginary world where King Kong lived or giants roamed the earth. Liberty was a female Gulliver rising among the Lilliputians." *New York Magazine,* 44.

9. The history of the Emma Lazarus Federation of Jewish Women's Clubs was furnished by Morris U. Schappes in a letter to the author, 1 October 1983. Insight into the ideology of the organization came from conversations with Rose Rubenstein, who, at the age of eighty-two, and as a resident of Borman Hall, the Jewish Home for the Aged, in Detroit, Michigan, still frequented monthly meetings.

Inspired by her visit to Merton Abbey, William Morris' factory for decorative furniture, run on socialistic principles, Lazarus wrote a lengthy essay that was published in the *Century* in 1886. Overlooked by "Progressive" Jews like Rubenstein by whom she is revered is her statement that because in "America, avenues to ease and competency are so broad and numerous, . . . the intelligent American is apt to shrink with aversion and mistrust from the communistic thought." Emma Lazarus, "A Day in Surrey with William Morris," *Century* 34 (July 1886): 395. The sentiment in Lazarus' poem "Progress and Poverty" was evoked on reading Henry George's treatise by the same name. It appeared in the *New York Times* on 2 October 1881 on page 3.

10. Publicity pamphlet, June 1986, American Jewish Historical Society Archives.

2. The Chronology

1. Emma's five sisters were Sarah; Josephine; Mary, who married Leopold Lindau and moved to Germany; Agnes, who married Montague Marks, editor of *Art Amateur;* and Annie, who married expatriate artist John Humphreys Johnston. *NYT,* 10 March 1885, p. 2; 20 November 1887, p. 16.

2. For Nathan and Lazarus genealogies, see Malcolm Stern, *Americans of Jewish Descent* (Cincinnati: Hebrew Union College Press, 1960).

3. Membership Roster, Union Club, and Membership Roster, Knickerbocker Club, New-York Historical Society Archives.

4. In 1866, H. O. Houghton and Company published, for private circulation, Emma Lazarus' *Poems and Translations, Written Between the Ages of Fourteen and Sixteen.* One year later Hurd and Houghton published a second edition, adding a second year of poetry. It is not certain when Emma and Emerson first met, but it was some time before Emerson's first letter to Samuel Gray Ward, dated 24 February 1868. See Rusk, ed., *Letters to Lazarus,* 3.

5. The *Newport Mercury* reported on 5 November 1870 that "a house [is being] built for Moses Lazarus on Bellevue Avenue, 33 × 41, two stories, French roof amf L20 × 30, to cost $17,000." The house was sold on 17 June 1878 "for $1 and other valuable considerations." Newport Deed Book, 48/4, Newport Historical Society Archives.

6. "The Town and Country Club," *Newport Journal,* 17 September 1874, typescript; *Town and Country Club Officers, Members and Rules* (Newport: James Atkinson Printer, 1878), Newport Historical Society Archives.

7. *Westminster Review* (October 1871): 563; *Athenaeum,* 23 September 1871, pp. 395–96.

8. Ivan Turgenev to Emma Lazarus, 2 September 1874, Rusk, ed., *Letters to Lazarus,* 17. Emma corresponded with Turgenev through Hjalmar H. Boyesen, whom she knew in Newport and New York. See *AH,* 9 December 1887; *Lippincott's Magazine* (June 1874): 774–75.

9. *NYT,* 23 February 1867, p. 2.

10. *Critic* 1 (June 1881): 163; *Century* 23 (March 1882): 783–86.

11. In addition to *Lippincott's,* Lazarus published in the *New York Times, Scribner's, Galaxy,* and the *Jewish Messenger* before 1882.

12. See Rusk, ed., *Letters to Lazarus.*

13. Herbert F. Smith, *Richard Watson Gilder* (New York: Twayne, 1970), 13; Marian Moore Coleman, *Fair Rosalind: The American Career of Helena Modjeska* (Cheshire, Conn.: Cherry Hill Books, 1969), 166; Rosamond Gilder, ed., *Letters of Richard Watson Gilder* (Boston: Houghton Mifflin, Riverside Press, 1916), 212.

14. One of the most startling discoveries in research for this study of Emma Lazarus is the suggestion of her relationship with Charles deKay. Lazarites have always characterized her as an "old maid." Wallace Stegner, whose novel *Angle of Repose* is the thinly disguised story of the friendship between Mary Hallock Foote and Helena deKay, states in the work that Emma and Charles (Dickie Drake) were in love but the liaison was discouraged by deKay's family because Emma was Jewish. Stegner based his assertion on letters between Hallock and Foote. Wallace Stegner to the author, 6 April 1974. Charles deKay's grandson Ormonde suggested in two letters that Emma and "grandpapa" were lovers. Ormonde deKay to the author, 25 July 1983, September 1984.

15. The Society of American Artists, founded as the American Art Association, was organized in 1877 in protest against the judging practices of the Academy of Design. For several years, young artists had felt that the Academy was too conservative and too selective in its annual exhibitions. When sculptor Augustus Saint-Gaudens' work was rejected in 1877, he met with Richard and Helena Gilder and others to form an organization that would "lend a helping hand to the younger men, not offending the veterans of the guild." *NYT,* 30 October 1877, p. 4; Rosamond Gilder, 79–82. The Authors' Club was established in November 1882 for "better acquaintance and social intercourse." It was all male. Charles deKay and Edmund Clarence Stedman were two of the nine members of the Executive Council. Members included Emma's friends Vincenzio Botta, H. H. Boyesen, Richard Watson Gilder, and Edwin L. Godkin. *NYT,* 24 November 1882, p. 8.

16. The Metropolitan Museum of Art was opened in 1870. In 1880, it moved to its permanent home on Fifth Avenue in "the Central Park," as it was called. The Metropolitan Opera Company was established in 1883 when the Metropolitan Opera House was opened. Charles Lockwood, *Manhattan Moves Uptown: An Illustrated History* (Boston: Houghton Mifflin, 1976), 310–11. The New York Philharmonic Orchestra, led by Theodore Thomas, the New York Symphony Society Orchestra, led by Leopold Damrosch, and the Brooklyn Philharmonic played to packed houses. Both Thomas and Damrosch, arch-rivals, were friends of Emma Lazarus. See George Martin, *The Damrosch Dynasty, America's First Family of Music* (Boston: Houghton Mifflin, 1983).

17. "Emerson's Personality," *Century* 24 (June 1882): 453–55.

18. *AH,* 9 December 1887.

19. The best-remembered protest meeting was held on 2 February 1882 in Chickering Hall. Chaired by William Evarts, it included as a speaker the Reverend Howard Crosby, whose wife, Margaret, was one of Emma's good friends. *NYT,* 2 February 1882, p. 8.

20. Emma's so-called conversion experience in seeing Jewish refugees at Ward's Island has been a subject of controversy in Lazarus historiography. Was it an evolutionary process, or did she change dramatically, overnight, as her sister Josephine and others suggest? This issue will be discussed later in this study. Several contemporaries point out the role Lazarus played in the formation of the Hebrew Technical Institute. See Philip Cowen, *Memories of an American Jew* (New York: International Press, 1932); "Miss Lazarus' Life and Literary Work," *Critic* (11 December 1887): 293; James H. Hoffman, "From the President of the Hebrew Technical Institute," *AH,* 9 December 1887.

21. The following "Jewish" essays written by Emma Lazarus were published in the *Century* from April 1882 to February 1883: "Was the Earl of Beaconsfield a Representative Jew?" (April 1882): "Russian Christianity versus Modern Judaism" (May 1882): and "The Jewish Problem" (February 1883). The *American Hebrew,* an Anglo-Jewish weekly whose readers were so-called uptown Jews, became the vehicle for Lazarus' polemic. Not only did *AH* publish her treatise, *An Epistle to the Hebrews,* a series of fifteen essays expounding her thought, but her contributions including letters to the editor were given priority status.

22. Edwin Robert Anderson Seligman Papers; Rare Book and Manuscript Library, Columbia University (hereafter cited as ERAS).

23. Emma Lazarus to Helena deKay Gilder, [June] 1883, 4 July 1883, Letters of Helena deKay Gilder [HdeKG], private collection of Rosamond Gilder Estate, Tyringham, Mass.

24. Henry James to Emma Lazarus, Paris, 5 February [1884], Letters of Henry James, Rare Book and Manuscript Library, Columbia University (hereafter cited as HJ).

25. Emma Lazarus to Helena deKay Gilder, Paris, 17 July 1883, Letter 30HdeKG.

26. We don't know just why Lazarus failed in her attempt, but on 22 April [1884] she wrote Seligman, "Alas! alas! I fear the Society will never rise from its ashes—& it makes me sad to think of the high hopes with which I organized it a year ago." Letter 9ERAS.

27. The Nineteenth Century Club was founded in January 1883 by Courtlandt Palmer and others "on the idea of universal tolerance." The meetings were hosted by the Courtlandts in sumptuous surroundings. *NYT,* 24 January 1883, p. 8. An invitation, signed by Emma in 1884, is among her memorabilia in the American Jewish Historical Society Archives.

28. Emma wrote to her friend Rose Lathrop that she was "just now . . . interested in helping to get up a series of free Concerts for the Working Classes . . . & it is desired to

form a permanent organization for future seasons." Emma Lazarus to Rose Hawthorne Lathrop, 29 January 1884, Rose Hawthorne Lathrop Papers, Rosary Hill Home, Hawthorne, N.Y.

29. In January 1887, Annie Lazarus sent a letter dictated by her sister Emma from her sickbed in Paris, to the Gilders. This is the first established evidence of her illness. Both Annie and Josephine sent letters from Paris and New York describing their sister's final days. See Letters 58–66 HdeKG.

30. John Greenleaf Whittier, *AH*, 9 December 1887.

31. For contemporary criticism of Lazarus' work, see Cyrus L. Sulzberger's review of her essay on Disraeli, *Jewish Messenger*, 26 January 1883, p. 4; and "The Restoration Fallacy," *Jewish Record*, 23 February 1883. In 1882, Solomon Solis-Cohen, who would later marry Emma's cousin, prefaced his reading of her celebrated play *The Dance to the Death*, at a meeting of the YMHA in Philadelphia in October 1882, by saying that she was the "greatest Jewish poet of the nineteenth century and the greatest living poet of America." *Jewish Record*, 21 October 1882.

32. The Memorial Issue of the *American Hebrew* of 9 December 1887 included contributions from the following: Henry Abbey, Hjalmar H. Boyesen, Robert Browning, John Burroughs, Mary M. Cohen, S. S. Cox, Charles A. Dana, Anna Laurens Dawes, Mary Mapes Dodge, Edward Eggleston, Joseph P. Gilder, E. L. Godkin, Samuel Greenbaum, Constance Cary Harrison, John Hay, James H. Hoffman, L. S. Metcalf, Claude G. Montefiore, John Boyle O'Reilly, Benjamin F. Pexiotto, Jacob H. Schiff, Edmund C. Stedman, Henrietta Szold, Maurice Thompson, Charles Dudley Warner, John Greenleaf Whittier, and James Grant Wilson.

33. *London Jewish Chronicle*, 25 November 1887, p. 4.

3. The Myth

1. The term "fictionalized crystals" was first used in an undated letter from Norman Mailer to the author in reference to a proposed biography.

2. Morris U. Schappes, ed., *The Letters of Emma Lazarus, 1868–1885* (New York: New York Public Library, 1949).

3. [Josephine Lazarus,] "Emma Lazarus," *Century* 36 (October 1888): 875–84.

4. Ibid., 874, 877.

5. Ibid., 877.

6. Ibid., 879–80, 882–83.

7. Ibid., 883.

8. Ibid., 884.

9. Ibid.

10. Annie Lazarus to Bernard G. Richards, 25 February 1926, Papers of Bernard G. Richards, Jewish Theological Seminary Library.

11. *Appleton's Cyclopedia of American Biography* (New York: D. Appleton, 1888), 644.

12. *National Cyclopedia of Biography* (New York: James T. White, 1893), 25; Willard, Emma, ed. *Women of the Century* (New York: Mast, Crowell and Kirkpatrick, 1897). Reprinted as *American Women*, 2 vols. (Detroit: Gale, 1973), 452.

13. *NYT*, 7 May 1903; *New York Tribune*, 7 May 1903.

14. Henrietta Szold, "Emma Lazarus," *Jewish Encyclopedia* (New York: Funk and Wagnalls, 1904), 7:651–52.

15. Allen Lesser, "Emma Lazarus, Poet and Zionist Pioneer," *Menorah Journal* 26 (April–June 1938): 212, 217.

16. Ibid., 224, 225, 226.

17. *NYT*, 24 July 1949, p. 10.

18. Morris U. Schappes, review, *American Literature* 21 (1950): 506–8.

19. Heinrich E. Jacob, *The World of Emma Lazarus* (New York: Schocken Books, 1949), 27–28, 59.

20. Ibid., 59.

21. Arthur Zeiger, "Emma Lazarus: A Critical Study" (Ph.D. diss., New York University, 1951), 195.

22. Ibid., 86–87.

23. Ibid., 193.

24. Dan Vogel, *Emma Lazarus* (Boston: Twayne, 1980), 16.

25. Ibid., 15, 16, 75, 91.

26. Ibid., 18.

27. Solomon Liptzin, *Generation of Decision: Jewish Rejuvenation in America* (New York: Bloch, 1958), 113; idem, *The Jew in American Literature* (New York: Bloch, 1966), 61, 63.

28. Harry Simonhoff, *Saga of American Jewry, 1865–1914, Links of an Endless Chain* (New York: Arco, 1959), 131–32.

29. Carole S. Kessner, "From Parnassus to Mount Zion: The Journey of Emma Lazarus, on the Centenary of Her Death," *Jewish Book Annual* 7 (1987): 143, 145, 148.

30. Ibid., 149.

31. Patricia Dunlavy Valenti, *To Myself a Stranger: A Biography of Rose Hawthorne Lathrop* (Baton Rouge: Louisiana State University Press, 1991).

32. Papers of Thomas Wren Ward, (TWW) Houghton Library, Harvard University.

4. The Experience

1. For a comprehensive treatment of New York demographics, see Lockwood, *Manhattan Moves Uptown*.

2. The first Academy of Music opened in 1854 and seated more than 4,500 people. Its stage was among the largest in the country. The scarcity of private boxes, however, was a subject for constant complaint. This led, finally, to the establishment of the Metropolitan Opera House. Steinway Hall occupied the second floor of the Steinway and Sons Piano Company building and was the site of concert performances. The Metropolitan Museum of Art was at the home of the late Douglas Cruger, the so-called Douglas Mansion at 128 West Fourteenth Street. In 1880, the museum was moved to Fifth Avenue. Fourteenth Street was not only the home of high culture; popular restaurants, stores, and amusements found the street hospitable as well. By 1880, the street hosted at least fourteen saloons, oyster houses, bakeries, and restaurants, among them, Pursell's Ladies Restaurant. R. H. Macy's had its beginnings on Fourteenth Street in 1858 and acquired ten more adjacent properties to build in 1880 a "great arcade 150 feet along Fourteenth Street, extending back some 200 feet toward Thirteenth Street." For circus events, the Hippotheatron opened in 1864 across

from the Academy of Music. Made of corrugated iron, it housed 1,700 people and rose 75 feet in height. Tammany Hall was built next door to the Academy of Music in 1868. For documentation, see M. Christine Boyer, *Manhattan Manners: Architecture and Style, 1850–1900* (New York: Rizzoli, 1985), 43–101.

3. In December 1859, a "Great Union Meeting" filled the Academy of Music, spilling into the Square. And in 1861, more than 250,000 people filled the Square after the Confederacy fired on Fort Sumter. Later, in April 1864, the United States Sanitary Commission Fair raised money to support relief work, sanitary inspections, and hospital and nursing services offered to the Union army by the commission. Boyer, *Manhattan Manners*, 85–86.

4. Emma Lazarus to Helena deKay Gilder, 10 January 1881, Letter 10HdeKG.

5. Letters 50, 4HdeKG.

6. Letters 14, 12, 13HdeKG.

7. Letters 16, 22, 23HdeKG; Letter 1RHL; Letters 4, 3HdeKG. Emma probably visited Bonnie Castle before December 1881, when her poem "Among the Thousand Islands" was published in the *Century* (23 [December 1881]: 288–89). In addition, Helena deKay Gilder refers to Emma's visit to the Hollands there in an undated letter to Rose Hawthorne Lathrop (in the Rosary Hill Home collection).

8. Letter 16HdeKG; Letters 1, 4TWW; Letters 5, 10ERAS.

9. Letters 7, 11, 19, 23, 4HdeKG.

10. Letters 15, 23HdeKG.

11. Emma Lazarus to Ralph Waldo Emerson, 27 December 1874, Rusk, ed., *Letters to Lazarus*, 323.

12. Letter 3HdeKG.

13. Mary Hallock Foote to Helena deKay Gilder, 15 November 1876, Papers of Mary Hallock Foote, Stanford University Library; Emma Lazarus to Ellen Emerson, 16 November 1876, Schappes, ed., *Letters*, no. 7; Ivan Turgenev to Emma Lazarus, 23 October 1876, Rusk, ed., *Letters to Lazarus*, 18.

14. Emma Lazarus, *The Poems of Emma Lazarus*, 2 vols. (Boston: Houghton Mifflin, 1889), 1: 337–42.

15. Emma Lazarus, *Songs of a Semite: The Dance to the Death and Other Poems* (New York: The American Hebrew, 1882).

16. Emma Lazarus, "Salvini's King Lear," *Century* 26 (May 1883): 89.

17. Ibid., 90.

18. Ibid.

19. Even more to the point is the fact that Emma's brother Frank was married to a non-Jew at that time.

5. The Work

1. The poem was written in October 1880 and was not published until 1944, when Morris U. Schappes included it in his collection of Lazarus' work. Morris U. Schappes, ed., *Emma Lazarus: Selections from Her Poetry and Prose* (IWO Jewish American Section, 1944).

2. For a fine explanation of these pieces and Emma's response, see Vogel, 107–8.

3. Lazarus, "American Literature," 164. She wrote a letter to Stedman some time before December 1881, when Stedman's article "Poetry in America," which Lazarus discusses, was

published in *Scribner's*. For Lazarus' letter to Stedman, see Schappes, *The Letters of Emma Lazarus*, 24A.

4. Letter 2HdeKG.

5. Lazarus, *Poems and Translations*, 63–118.

6. Emma Lazarus, *Admetus and Other Poems* (1871; reprint, Upper Saddle River, N.J.: Literature House, Gregg Press, 1970), 86.

7. Ibid., 123–27.

8. Ibid., 132.

9. Emma Lazarus, "Outside the Church," *Index*, 14 December 1872, p. 399.

10. Vogel, 87.

11. Emma Lazarus, "An Epistle," in *Poems* 2:45–58, quotation on p. 45.

12. Ibid., 45, 47–53, 57.

13. Ibid., 57–58.

14. Emma Lazarus to Gustav Gottheil, 3 October 1882, Schappes, ed., *Letters*, no. 37.

15. Emma Lazarus, *Alide: An Episode of Goethe's Life* (Philadelphia: J. B. Lippincott, 1874), 152.

16. Letter 20TWW. Interestingly, Emma's sister, Josephine, wrote a similar letter to Ward, transcribing the same poem, apparently unaware of Emma's letter. Josephine Lazarus to Thomas Wren Ward, n.d., TWW Papers.

17. Lazarus, *Alide*, 153–54.

18. Vogel, 102.

19. Lazarus, *Alide*, 102–103.

20. Emma Lazarus, "The Eleventh Hour," *Scribner's* 16 (June 1878): 252–56.

21. Ibid., 256.

22. Ibid.

23. Letter 7TWW.

24. Lazarus, "The Eleventh Hour," 256.

6. Jewish Themes

1. Emma Lazarus, "In the Jewish Synagogue at Newport," *Admetus*, 160.

2. For Emma's thoughts about Longfellow, see her "Henry Wadsworth Longfellow," *AH*, 14 April 1882, pp. 98–99.

3. Heinrich Heine, "Donna Clara," trans. Emma Lazarus, *Jewish Messenger*, 18 February 1876, p. 1.

4. Emma Lazarus, "Don Pedrillo," *Jewish Messenger*, 18 February 1876, p. 1.

5. Emma Lazarus, "Fra Pedro," *Jewish Messenger*, 18 February 1876, p. 1.

6. Ibid.

7. Emma Lazarus, "Rashi in Prague," *Independent*, 25 March 1880, pp. 27–28; idem, "The Death of Rashi," *Independent*, 8 April 1880, p. 27. Rabbi Shlomo ben Isaac lived in the latter half of the eleventh century. Born in Troyes, France, he established an academy there, where he remained until his death. He was the first of the Jewish scholars in western Europe to write commentary on the whole of the Hebrew Scriptures. His greatest accomplishment was his commentary on the Babylonian Talmud. His work more than any other would be used in medieval Jewish scholarship and after the expulsion of the Jews from Spain. See

Joan Comay, *Who's Who in Jewish History after the Period of the Old Testament* (New York: David McKay, 1974), 328.

8. Lazarus, "Rashi in Prague," 27.

9. Judah HaLevi, "Longing for Jersualem," trans. by Emma Lazarus, *Jewish Messenger*, 1 February 1879, p. 1.

10. Zeiger, 43–48.

11. Lazarus, *The Dance to the Death*, in *Songs*, 20–21.

12. Ibid., 32.

13. Heinrich Heine, *Poems and Ballads of Heinrich Heine*, trans. with an intro. by Emma Lazarus (New York: Hurst, 1881).

14. "Miss Lazarus's Translation of Heine," *Century* 23 (March 1882): 785–86.

15. [Josephine Lazarus,] "Emma Lazarus," 879.

16. Emma Lazarus, "The Poet Heine," *Century* 29 (December 1884): 210–17.

17. *Heine*, trans. Lazarus, ix.

18. Ibid., xiv.

19. Ibid.

20. Lazarus, "The Poet Heine," 210–11.

7. A Jewish Identity

1. "Miss Lazarus' Life and Literary Work," 293–95.

2. Ellen Tucker Emerson to Edith Emerson Forbes, 26 August 1876, in Edith E. W. Gregg, ed., *The Letters of Ellen Tucker Emerson*, 2 vols. (Kent, Ohio: Kent State University Press, 1982), 2: 225.

3. David deSola Pool and Tamar deSola Pool, *An Old Faith in a New World: Portrait of Shearith Israel, 1654–1954* (New York: Columbia University Press, 1955), 503.

4. Ibid., 502.

5. Mary Thackery Higginson, ed., *Letters and Journals of Thomas Wentworth Higginson* (New York: DcLapo Press, 1969), 266.

6. Gregg, 2: 225.

7. Mary Hallock Foote to Helena deKay Gilder, 15 November 1876, Papers of Mary Hallock Foote, Stanford University Library. Mary Hallock Foote and Emma Lazarus would become friends in the ensuing years. See The Letters section in this book as well as the Letters of Mary Hallock Foote to Helena deKay Gilder.

8. Charles deKay, "Sibyl Judaica," *AH*, 8 February 1889, pp. 4–5.

9. Ibid.

10. The Seligman-Hilton affair was covered extensively in the *New York Times*, 19–24 June 1877.

11. *NYT*, 20 June 1877, p. 1.

12. Joseph Seligman obituary, *NYT*, 27 April 1880, p. 2.

13. Judge Henry Hilton obituary, *NYT*, 24 August 1899, p. 1.

14. *NYT*, 23 July 1879, p. 1.

15. Their business was "Rectifier of Spirits" in 1845 and "Sugar Refiners" in 1865. New York Business Directory, 1845–85, and New York City Directory, 1840–85, New-York Historical Society.

16. The best source for information on Bradish Johnson's background is Harnett T. Kane, *Deep Delta Country*, ed. Erskine Caldwell (New York: Duell, Sloan and Pearce, 1944), 42–44.

17. "Death in the Jug," *NYT*, 22 January 1853, p. 2.

18. Ibid.

19. *NYT*, 12 July 1863, p. 3.

20. For the complete report of excesses on Johnson's plantation, see Lieutenant George H. Hepworth and Chaplain Edwin N. Wheelock to Major General Nathaniel Banks, 9 April 1863, Nathaniel Banks Papers, Library of Congress.

21. New York Business Directory, 1845–85; New York City Directory, 1840–86.

22. Doreen Bolger Burke et al., *In Pursuit of Beauty: Americans and the Aesthetic Movement* (New York: Metropolitan Museum of Art and Rizzoli, 1987), 23.

23. Lazarus, "Progress and Poverty" 2 October 1881, p. 3. Henry George's work (of the same title) was published in 1879. His "single tax" paradigm was seen as so original that George became a political force, running for mayor of New York City in 1886 on a Reform platform. Emma and George had mutual friends—Leopold Lindau, who would become the husband of her sister Mary; and Daniel De Leon, who supported George in 1886.

24. Emma Lazarus, "The South," *Poems* 1: 178–79.

25. Ibid., 180.

26. Ibid., 179.

27. Letter 5RHL.

8. A Jewish Polemic

1. For more information on Wilhelm Marr, see *Encyclopaedia Judaica* (1972), 2: 1015.

2. Emma Lazarus, "The Crowing of the Red Cock," *Jewish Messenger*, 19 May 1882, p. 1.

3. Emma Lazarus, "The Banner of the Jew," *Critic* 2 (18 June 1882): 164.

4. The three *Century* essays were "Was the Earl of Beaconsfield a Representative Jew?" (April 1882); "Russian Christianity versus Modern Judaism" (May 1882); and "The Jewish Problem" (February 1883). The fifteen essays in the *American Hebrew*, included in her *Epistle to the Hebrews*, ran from November 1882 to February 1883.

5. Zeiger, 109.

6. Georg Brandes, *Lord Beaconsfield: A Study* (New York: Charles Scribner's Sons, 1880).

7. Emma Lazarus, "Beaconsfield, a Representative Jew?" 941.

8. Ibid., 942.

9. Ibid., 940.

10. Ibid.

11. Ibid., 941.

12. George Eliot, "The Modern Hep! Hep!" in *The Works of George Eliot: Adam Bede, Theophrastus Such, Essays* (New York: Thomas Y. Crowell, n.d.) 124–43, quotation on 135.

13. Ibid., 132.

14. Ibid., 136, 137.

15. Ibid., 141.

16. Zénaide Ragozin, "Russian Jews and Gentiles, from a Russian Point of View," *Century* 23 (April 1882): 905–20.

17. Ibid., 918, 920; Emma Lazarus, "Russian Christianity," 52.

18. Zeiger, 111–12.

19. Emma Lazarus, *An Epistle to the Hebrews* (New York: Federation of American Zionists, 1900); ed. Morris U. Schappes (New York: Jewish Historical Society of New York, 1987): 7.

20. Ibid., 9.

21. Ibid., 9, 13–15.

22. Ibid., 15.

23. Ibid., 19, 74.

24. Ibid., 17, 19–20.

25. Emma Lazarus, "The Schiff Refuge," *AH*, 20 October 1882, p. 114.

26. Lazarus, *Epistle to the Hebrews*, 79.

27. See n. 19.

28. Lazarus, "The Jewish Problem," 605.

29. Ibid., 608.

30. Robert Underwood Johnson Papers, Rare Book and Manuscript Library, Columbia University. Lazarus' letter is undated.

31. Lazarus, "The Jewish Problem," 608–10.

32. Ibid., 610.

33. Emma Lazarus, "By the Waters of Babylon: Little Poems in Prose," *Century* 33 (March 1887): 801–3.

9. Helena deKay Gilder

1. Low quoted in William Webster Ellsworth, *A Golden Age of Authors: A Publisher's Recollection* (Boston: Houghton Mifflin Company, Riverside Press, 1919), 148.

2. Rosamond Gilder, 213.

3. Ibid., 213–14.

4. Herbert F. Smith, *Richard Watson Gilder* (New York, Twayne, 1970), 13, 25.

5. John Arthur, *The Best Years of the Century: Richard Watson Gilder, Scribner's Monthly, and Century Magazine*, 1870–1909 (Urbana: University of Illinois Press, 1981), 113.

6. Ibid.

7. Carnegie quoted in Herbert Smith, *Richard Watson Gilder*, 13.

8. Rosamond Gilder to author, July 1980.

9. For an excellent account of Helena deKay's professional life, see Burke et al., 418–19.

10. Herbert F. Smith, 41.

11. Maurice Francis Egan, *Recollections of a Happy Life* (New York: George H. Doran, 1924), 188.

12. Ormonde deKay correspondence with the author, 1983–1987; Nancy-Joan Seligman telephone conversations with the author, 4 February 1993.

Letter 1

13. Helena and Richard Gilder's first child, Marion, was born on 12 December 1875 and died less than one year later. Rosamond Gilder, 76–77.

Letter 2

14. The Gilders' first son, Rodman, was born in 1877. *NYT*, 1 October 1953.

15. The Lazarus family spent summers in Newport at their family home, "The Beeches," on fashionable Bellevue Avenue. For more information, see Rosamond Gilder, 213–14.

16. The Lazarus family moved to 34 East Fifty-seventh Street in 1877. At that time, the "fashionable elite" were settling on Fifty-seventh and Fifty-eighth streets between Madison and Fourth avenues. The Lazarus home was probably a five-story townhouse. See Boyer, *Manhattan Manners*, 145.

17. Colonel Thomas Wentworth Higginson (1823–1911), author and critic, was raised in New England and became one of the most outspoken abolitionists before the Civil War. He went on in 1862 to lead the First Regiment of South Carolina volunteers, the first slave regiment in the Civil War. His book *Army Life in a Black Regiment* is a highly readable accounting of that experience. He was a prolific writer—his complete bibliography, as listed in his wife Mary's biography of him, fills twenty-six pages. Stanley J. Kunitz and Howard Haycraft, eds., *American Authors, 1600–1900: A Biographical Dictionary of American Literature* (New York: H. W. Wilson, 1938), 336–37. Higginson met Emma in Newport in 1872.

18. Written by Ivan Turgenev, *Nov' (Virgin Soil)* was published in 1876. A story of a group of young Russian revolutionaries whose goal it is to incite the peasantry to rebellion, the novel met with less than enthusiastic reviews. Emma praised the novel to the author himself. For his reaction, see Ivan Tourgenieff [*sic*] to Lazarus, 1 August 1877, in Rusk, ed., *Letters to Lazarus*, 19.

19. Nezhdanoff is the central character in the novel. The illegitimate son of a "great noble," he is described by one reviewer as "the inheritor of artistic and sceptical leanings which prevent him from sympathizing thoroughly with the party. He is ashamed of his doubt, however, and though he does not believe in the movement, he tries to throw himself into the 'revolutionary intrigues.' " When he can no longer stifle his skepticism, he commits suicide. Review of *Nov'*, *Athenaeum*, 17 February 1877, pp. 217–18.

20. Josephine Lazarus (1846–1910) was the second oldest of Emma's sisters. She was an essayist of some repute; her work appeared after Emma's death.

Letter 3

21. The Gilders started on their first trip to Europe in March 1879, going first to London, then to Paris, and on to Italy. See Rosamond Gilder, 89–98.

22. Julia deKay was Helena Gilder's sister.

23. Emma's calling her friend Minnie Biddle her "schoolmate" is instructive. Until this time it was assumed that she had tutors at home and never attended school.

24. Until the discovery of these letters, the assumption was that Emma visited Emerson only once in 1876, and that their friendship cooled in the following years.

25. The Concord School of Philosophy, founded by Bronson Alcott in 1878, remained in existence until at least 1884, when Emma's poem to Emerson was read at the opening session. (See *Critic* 5 [2 August 1884]: 55–56.) Of interest are Louisa May Alcott's and Ellen Emerson's impressions of the school. According to Alcott biographer Martha Saxton, "Louisa was glad to see her father in such good spirits, but felt rather tart about the whole thing. She would have preferred a conference of philanthropists. She thought that speculation

'seems a waste of time when there is so much real work to be done. Why discuss the unknowable till the poor are fed and the wicked saved.' " Saxton, *Louisa May: A Modern Biography of Louisa May Alcott* (Boston: Houghton Mifflin, 1977), 349. Ellen Emerson saw the philosophers and heard their "unintelligible introduction to [the] lecture." It gave her a "queer sensation to hear my native tongue and receive no clear idea when one evidently was expressed." On the questioning of the lecturer, Ellen asked, "Did these questions really mean anything? What learned men! Where did they dig up the amazing words they used? Did they understand themselves?" Gregg, vol. 2, 354.

26. George Bradford (1807–1890) was a former Brook Farm member and a bit of an eccentric.

27. Charles deKay was Helena deKay Gilder's brother. He became Emma's close friend. See p. 223, n.14.

Letter 4

28. Maria Richards Oakey (1842–1927), painter and decorative artist, was a good friend of Helena Gilder when both were students at Cooper Union School of Design for Women. She studied with John LaFarge and William Morris Hunt, among others. Oakey participated in the establishment of the Art Students League and was an early member of the Society of American Artists. Although this generation of artists seems quite conservative in retrospect, they saw themselves as a vanguard of artists who protested against the policies of the inflexible National Academy of Design by conducting exhibitions of their own. Maria Oakey is noted for her treatment of flowers, a favorite subject in that era of interest in oriental and decorative art. Burke et al., 419–20.

Emma maintained her friendship with Maria, who married artist Thomas Wilmer Dewing in 1881, all of her life. Her sisters continued the friendship through the turn of the century. See Susan Hobbs, "Thomas Dewing in Cornish, 1885–1905," *American Art Journal* 17 (Spring 1985): 3–32.

29. Rafael Joseffy made his American debut in New York's Chickering Hall on 13 October 1879. He was a great success. His critics knew that he would be heard "with an interest that very few pianists have ever excited in New York." *NYT*, 14 October 1879, p. 5. Russian virtuoso pianist Anton Rubinstein made his American debut in New York in 1872. Emma was introduced to him at that time. See Letter 50HdeKG. On 14 February 1880, Berlioz's *Damnation of Faust* was performed in New York for the first time by the New York Symphony Society Orchestra, and the Oratorio and Arion Society Choruses, led by Dr. Leopold Damrosch. It was rated as the "most important musical event of the season," and was repeated five more times that spring and "thrice" in December. *NYT*, 15 February 1880, p. 7; Martin, 55.

30. Margaret Crosby was the wife of the Reverend Howard Crosby (1826–1891), pastor of Fourth Avenue Presbyterian Church in Manhattan. The reverend was the son of well-known philanthropist William B. Crosby, who had inherited a great deal of choice Manhattan real estate from Colonel Henry Rutgers. Known for his generosity of spirit and for his work with the poor, he was chancellor of the University of New York from 1879 to 1881. *NYT*, 30 March 1891, p. 1.

31. Expatriate Julian Sturgis was a well-known art critic and writer. *NYT*, 14 April 1904, p. 9.

32. Helena Gilder's expatriate sister Katherine deKay Bronson lived in Italy and was friendly with such fellow expatriates as Henry James.

33. Ehrman Syme Nadal (1843–1922), an essayist of some repute, was second secretary to the London legation from 1877 to 1883. Kunitz and Haycraft, 554–55.

34. Most probably Emma was referring to her tragedy, *The Dance to the Death,* a dramatization of Richard Reinhard's prose narrative, "Der Tanz zum Tode" (1877). It is the story of the martyrdom of the Jews of Nordhausen, Germany, who were burned alive during a pogrom in 1349. The play was published in 1882 and is used, erroneously, to prove the assertion of Emma's "sudden conversion" to her Jewishness in 1882.

35. "The Guardian of the Red Disk" appeared in the September 1880 number of *Scribner's.*

36. Britisher Anne Gilchrist, widow of Blake biographer Alexander Gilchrist, read *Leaves of Grass* in 1869 and immediately fell in love with Walt Whitman. A correspondence ensued, and seven years later Anne went to Philadelphia to consummate her love. Unrequited after two years, she traveled to Concord, Boston, and New York before returning to England. During that time, she met, among others, Emerson in Concord and the Gilders and Emma Lazarus in New York. Anne Gilchrist was a close friend of Dante Gabriel, William, and Christina Rossetti, who helped her complete her husband's comprehensive work on William Blake. See Herbert Gilchrist, ed., *Anne Gilchrist: The Life and Writings* (London: T. Fisher Unwin, 1887); and Philip Callow, *From Noon to Starry Night: A Life of Walt Whitman* (Chicago: Ivan R. Dee, 1992), 329–45.

Letter 5

37. The title poem in *Hesperus and Other Poems* (1880) was written by Charles deKay. The volume consists of 300 pages and some 92 poems. Although the work as a whole was criticized roundly, the poem "Hesperus" was treated more generously. For a review of this work, see *NYT,* 16 August 1880, p. 5.

Letter 6

38. Robert Browning met Helena's sister Katherine deKay Bronson in Venice in October 1880. And on 14 October he wrote the poem, which Emma mentions, to Katherine's daughter Edith. For a full treatment of the Browning-Bronson relationship, see Michael Meredith, ed., *More Than Friend: The Letters of Robert Browning to Katherine deKay Bronson* (Houston: Armstrong Browning Library, Baylor University, and Winfield, Kansas: Wedgewood Press, 1985), xxiii–lxxviii.

Letter 7

39. Oliver Madox Brown (1855–1874), son of Ford Madox Brown, half-brother of William Rossetti, was a precocious author and artist. His collected works, entitled *Literary Remains,* were published in 1876. *Biographical Dictionary and Synopsis of Books* (1896: reprint, Detroit: Gale Research, 1965), 13.

40. Maria Sparlati Stillman was known for her great beauty. She was a Pre-Raphaelite artist who had studied with Ford Madox Brown and was used as a model by Dante Gabriel Rossetti. In 1871, she married an American, William Stillman, a widower with three daughters. Stillman, a former member of the Transcendentalists in New England, met John Ruskin and the Pre-Raphaelites in 1849. Having returned to New York in 1850, he published a Pre-Raphaelite art journal, *The Crayon*. It failed. Stillman was made U.S. consul to Rome during the Civil War and consul to Crete immediately thereafter. He became a foreign correspondent for the *London Times* in 1870. Edward Waldo Emerson, *The Early Years of the Saturday Club, 1855–1870* (Boston: Houghton Mifflin, 1918), 130.

41. "Prince Hohenstiel-Schwangau, Savior of Society" was written by Browning in 1871, shortly after the downfall of Napoleon III, and is the author's lengthy rendering of the French ruler's career.

42. Architext Alexander Oakey worked for Frederick Law Olmstead, Richard Morris Hunt, and Louis Tiffany, among others, before founding his own firm. We have discovered no information to clarify the inferences in this letter, but some years later he was involved in another incident. See Letter 43HdeKG.

43. Sophia Ward was the wife of Emma's close friend Thomas Wren Ward.

44. Olivia Ward, cousin of Maria Oakey Dewing, was an artist and a friend of Helena Gilder's. As far as can be determined, she was no relation to Thomas Wren Ward.

45. Helena Gilder's translation of Alfred Sensier's life of Jean François Millet, the first full-scale treatment of the French peasant-painter, was illustrated by his own distinctive landscapes and figures, and was serialized in the *Century* during a five-month period in 1880. Richard Gilder wrote the introduction to the book. John, 82.

Letter 8

46. Richard deKay Gilder was born and died in December 1880. Emma is probably talking about Helena's recovery from childbirth. Rosamond Gilder, 135.

Letter 9

47. Maria Oakey and Thomas Wilmer Dewing (1851–1938) were engaged on 27 December 1880. They met soon after Dewing came to New York in October 1880. See Susan Hobbs, "Thomas Wilmer Dewing: The Early Years, 1851–1885," *American Art Journal* 13 (Spring 1981): 4–35.

Letter 10

48. Maria Oakey was six years older than her husband, Thomas Dewing. Perhaps this is the reason her parents felt their engagement was "something to cry over."

49. Eugène Fromentin (1820–1876), French painter and author, was best known for his pictorial scenes of Algeria. Emma's essay "Eugene Fromentin" appeared in the December 1881 number of the *Critic*.

50. This probably refers to work by the painter Henri Rousseau.

51. Henri Regnault (1843–1871) was a French painter of some note who was killed in the Franco-Prussian War. Emma's "Regnault as a Writer" was published in the February 1881 number of the *Critic.*

Letter 11

52. Sarah Lazarus (1842–1910) was Emma's oldest sister.

53. Robert Grant, author of *The Confessions of a Frivolous Girl* (1880), wrote a number of satires on society. In addition, he would become a distinguished attorney and juror, reviewing and finding for the defendants in the notorious Sacco and Vanzetti case. *NYT,* 20 May 1940, p. 17.

54. The *Critic,* a monthly devoted to literature and the arts, was established in 1881 by Jeannette and Joseph Gilder, brother and sister of Richard Watson Gilder. Emma was a contributor to the magazine in the early years of its existence.

55. *Dominique* by Eugène Fromentin was serialized in the *Revue des Deux Mondes* in 1862. A confessional novel, it is an autobiographical story of a young man's love for an older and married woman.

56. René François Armand Sully Prudhomme (1839–1907) was a French poet and philosopher who would win the Nobel Prize in literature (1901). Theocritus (310–250 B.C.), Greek poet, was the creator of pastoral poetry.

57. Emma may be referring to Thomas Wren Ward.

Letter 12

58. German-born British singer George Henschel (1850–1934) made his American debut at Steinway Hall in December 1880, appearing in, among other concerts, *The Damnation of Faust.* According to critics, he failed to live up to the reputation that preceded him. See *NYT,* 8 December 1880, p. 5.

59. Noted painter, stained-glass designer, and decorator John LaFarge (1835–1910) was a friend and colleague of the Gilders' and a contributor to the *Century.*

60. Emma's review of "The Vision of Nimrod," a poem written by Charles deKay, appeared in the February 1881 number of the *Critic.* As expected, she praised the poem's "splendor of description, the vigorous originality of thought and imagery, and the powerful realism of the half mythic figures." The *New York Times* was not so flattering, calling deKay's technique "exquisitely awkward." The reviewer noted that in 256 pages, there were "nearly 200 bad rhymes, some of which are execrable." *NYT,* 14 April 1881, p. 6.

61. Annie Holland was the daughter of *Scribner's* and *Century* editor Dr. Josiah G. Holland.

62. We have no information about this statement. In October 1881, at the death of *Century* editor Holland, Gilder, who had been associate editor, became the editor. For more extensive information on the *Century,* see John.

Letter 13

63. As mentioned in the notes to Letter 10HdeKG, Regnault was killed in the Franco-Prussian War; he was twenty-eight. Emma Lazarus, who was to die prematurely herself,

seemed continually to notice those who died young. See her comments on Oliver Madox Brown (Letter 7HdeKG) and the British poet Arthur O'Shaughnessy (Letter 14HdeKG).

64. At the age of fifteen, Maurice Dengremont made his first public appearance in the United States on 11 January 1881 at the Music Hall in New York City. His reviewer cited him as a "boy who seems to have sprung like Minerva from the head of Jupiter to the foremost rank . . . an embodiment of rare genius" with "charming manners and youthful modesty." *NYT*, 12 January 1881, p. 4.

65. Emma had first written about Italian Shakespearean great Tommaso Salvini in 1873 on the occasion of his debut in the United States. She would write two additional essays about him, "Tommaso Salvini," *Century* 23 (November 1881): 110–17, and "Salvini's King Lear" *Century* 26 (May 1883): 89–91. Salvini became Emma's personal friend. A record of their friendship can be seen in his letters to her from 1881 to 1885. See Rusk, ed., *Letters to Lazarus*, 36–37, 41–47.

Letter 14

66. Emma is probably referring to Tom Ward's well-known moodiness.

67. Susan Carter was the head of the Cooper Union School of Design and a good friend of Helena Gilder's.

68. British poet Arthur O'Shaughnessy, who worked as a copyist and ichthyologist for the British Museum's Department of Natural History, was born in 1844 and died in 1881 at the age of thirty-seven, another premature death.

69. Emma was referring to Rose Hawthorne Lathrop, who would become her close friend. Lathrop's only son, Francis, died from diphtheria on 6 February 1881. See Valenti, 64–65.

70. On the occasion of the death of Emerson's longtime friend Thomas Carlyle, *Scribner's* would publish a piece titled "Ralph Waldo Emerson's Impressions of Carlyle in 1848" (in the May 1881 number).

71. James Osgood was the American publisher of Henry James, among others.

Letter 15

72. The Egyptian obelisk known as Cleopatra's Needle was installed in Central Park in February 1881. Transported to New York, it was paid for by William Vanderbilt and given, formally, to the city on 22 February 1881. At the ceremony, Emma's friend the Reverend Howard Crosby gave the invocation. The combined choruses of the Philharmonic Societies of New York and Brooklyn and the Chorus of the New York College of Music sang Richard Gilder's hymn written for the occasion. *NYT*, 23 February 1881, p. 8.

73. Dr. Josiah G. Holland, editor of *Scribner's*, may have been ill at the time. He died in October 1881.

74. Mrs. Sidney deKay was the sister-in-law of Helena deKay Gilder.

Letter 16

75. Annie Lazarus, born in 1859, was Emma's youngest sister.

76. Japanese design in home furnishings was quite popular at that time. See "Japanism" and "Anglo-Japanesque," in Burke et al.

77. Ellen Emerson gave a ball in honor of her fortieth birthday on 24 January 1881. For more detail, see Gregg, vol. 2, 407, 411.

78. Wyatt Eaton was, according to one source, artist-in-residence at *Scribner's* and a close friend of the Gilders. A portraitist, he was a founding member of the Society of American Artists. See Coleman, 282.

79. A Straus is the department store Abraham & Straus.

Letter 17

80. Ralph Waldo Emerson was known as the "Sage of Concord."

81. Thomas Carlyle died on 5 February 1881. Emerson's fifty-year friendship with Carlyle began in 1834, on a visit with him at his home in England. Emerson died a little over a year later, on 27 April 1882.

Letter 18

82. The Brooklyn Philharmonic on 4 March 1881 was reported to have rehearsed the repertoire Emma described. *NYT,* 5 March 1881, p. 5.

83. See Letter 14, note 70, above.

84. Emma's essay on Salvini appeared in the November 1881 number of the *Century.* She corresponded with him from 1881 to 1885. See Rusk, ed., *Letters to Lazarus,* 36–37, 41–47.

Letter 19

85. The first volume of Thomas Carlyle's *Reminiscences* was edited by Froude and published after his death. Emma must have had a review copy.

86. Alexander II, Czar of all the Russias, was assassinated on 13 March 1881. It is ironic that Emma was so sympathetic to the czar that she wrote a poem, "Sic Semper Liberatoribus: March 13, 1881," for *Scribner's,* when one considers that just a year later she would write so passionately against Russia's historic treatment of Jews. See *Scribner's* 22 (June 1881): 178.

Letter 20

87. The talented Stanford White, with his partners, Charles Follen McKim and William Mead, designed (among other edifices) the Washington Arch in Washington Square, the Farragut Statue in Madison Square, the Church of the Ascension at Fifth Avenue and Tenth Street; the Adams Memorial in Rock Creek Park in Washington, D.C.; and numerous residences and clubhouses. He is also known, unfortunately, for his murder by Harry Thaw on 25 June 1906. See Paul R. Baker, *Stanny: The Gilded Life of Stanford White* (New York: Macmillan, 1989).

Letter 21

88. The reference and the poem are to Rodman Gilder, Helena and Richard's first son.

89. The Studio, the Gilder home, was remodeled according to Stanford White's design.

Letter 22

90. Sypher's was an upscale home-decorating shop.

91. "Bacchus" refers to the Gilders' son, Rodman.

Letter 23

92. Milton, Massachusetts, a little village on the headwaters of Buzzards Bay, was the "inconspicuous and out of the way" location for the Gilders' summer home for ten years. Rosamond Gilder, 139.

93. Pursell's Confectionery and Restaurant was located along Broadway's fashionable "Ladies' Mile."

The bronze statue of Admiral David Glasgow Farragut was unveiled on 24 May 1881 in Madison Square. The statue, a tribute to Admiral Farragut for the role he played in the Civil War, was designed by Stanford White and Augustus Saint-Gaudens and modeled and executed by Saint-Gaudens in Paris. The unveiling was an event, according to the *New York Herald:* "The attending circumstances were brilliant, the crowd great, the stands filled with the best citizens of the Metropolis." Incidentally, the Gilders hosted a dinner party celebrating the occasion that night. Richard Gilder is said to have boasted that he posed for Farragut's legs. For fuller discussion, see Louise Hall Tharp, *Saint-Gaudens and the Gilded Age* (Boston: Little, Brown, 1969), 153–57.

94. Bernardsville, New Jersey, was the home of the mother of Mary Hallock Foote. See note 98 below.

95. Annie Bigelow McKim was the first wife of Charles Follen McKim, architect partner of Stanford White and William Rutherford Mead. Annie deserted her husband in 1878. They were subsequently divorced.

96. Emma's volume, *Poems and Ballads of Heinrich Heine,* was published in 1881.

97. Edmund Stedman had written to Emma on 23 June 1881, congratulating her and telling her of his trip to the *Tribune* office. Rusk, ed., *Letters to Lazarus,* 33. For Emma's reply, see Emma Lazarus to Edmund C. Stedman, 25 June 1881, Schappes, ed., *Letters,* no. 20.

98. Mrs. Foote is probably Mary Hallock Foote, one of Helena Gilder's closest friends. Foote was an illustrator and an author who would live in the West. Mrs. Hallock is Mary's mother. For a fictional treatment of the Foote-Gilder friendship, see Wallace Stegner, *Angle of Repose* (Greenwich, Conn.: Fawcett Crest, 1971).

99. She was the wife of Lazarus family physician William Henry Draper, who was professor of clinical medicine at Columbia University.

Letter 24

100. See Letter 3HdeKG, note 23.

Letter 25

101. Sara Butler Wister was the daughter of the British actress Fanny Kemble and the mother of the author Owen Wister. John Foster Kirk (1824–1904), an American historian, was editor of *Lippincott's* from 1870 to 1886.

102. Anne Gilchrist's son, Herbert, had accompanied his mother to the United States in 1876, where he met Emma.

103. "Bonnie Castle" was the name of Josiah G. Holland's summer home in the Thousand Islands. Emma visited there and wrote a poem about it, "Among the Thousand Islands," which appeared in the December 1881 number of the *Century*.

104. French historian Leroy-Beaulieu published the first two volumes of his history of Russia, *Empire des Tsars et les Russes,* in 1881.

Letter 26

105. Bessie Stickney was a good friend of Emma, Helena Gilder, and Mary Hallock Foote.

106. Dr. Edward Emerson was Ralph Waldo Emerson's son. Annie Lazarus visited in Concord in August 1882 and saw him. See Gregg, vol. 2, 478.

107. "The Sower" was a poem in Richard Gilder's collection of poetry, *The New Day* (1875). Emma is referring to a well-known picture of the same name by Jean François Millet.

Letter 27

108. Emma had originally planned to go to Europe with her friend Rose Hawthorne Lathrop. See Letter 8RHL.

109. It is interesting to note that the Salvation Army was founded in 1865 by William Booth as a religious and philanthropic group, but by 1878 it had spread past London and was reorganized on a quasi-military basis. It began operations officially in the United States in 1880.

110. Emma is referring to the wife of Edmund Gosse (1849–1928), British poet and critic, who was one of Henry James' best friends. Their friendship, according to Leon Edel, was "one of the most literary-gossipy friendships in Victorian annals." Gosse had been assistant in the Department of Printed Books in the British Museum and translator for the Board of Trade. He became Clark Lecturer in English Literature at Trinity College, Cambridge, in 1884. He was a sort of cross-cultural middleman, bringing "foreign literature" to British readers. He was a gossipy go-between for his literary friends. According to Edel, "He knew the secrets of the literary generation and he was an artful exchanger of confidences. If Henry praised a certain book he quietly passed the praise along to the author; if an author praised Henry, Gosse discreetly communicated the praise." For further discussion, see Leon Edel, *Henry James: The Middle Years, 1882–1895* (Philadelphia: J. B. Lippincott, 1962), 83–84. Mrs. Gosse (Nellie Epps) was the sister of Mrs. Lawrence Alma-Tadema (Laura Epps). They were known as "Grateful" and "Comforting" and were the daughters of a "famous cocoa manufacturer." See Rayburn S. Moore, ed. *Selected Letters of Henry James to Edmund Gosse, 1882–1915: A Literary Friendship* (Baton Rouge: Louisiana State University Press, 1988).

111. Henry James had written a letter of introduction to Annie Benson Procter, widow of the poet Bryan Procter, whose pen name was Barry Cornwall. Mrs. Procter was one of his favorites, "the best talker" he had ever met in London. According to James, she had known "almost everyone of importance during the nineteenth century. . . . She had once

made a list of her famous friends and it filled two closely covered sheets of notepaper in double column." Leon Edel, *Henry James: The Conquest of London, 1870–1881* (Philadelphia: J. B. Lippincott, 1962), 353.

112. Claude Joseph Goldsmid-Montefiore (1858–1938) was the great-nephew of Sir Moses Montefiore. A lay theologian, he was the leader of Liberal Judaism in England. Emma knew of Montefiore's thought and had critiqued his essay, "Is Judaism a Tribal Religion?," published in the *Contemporary Review* in September 1882. See letter 2 in *Epistle to the Hebrews*, 11–16.

113. Felix Moscheles was the artist son of piano virtuoso and composer Ignaz Moscheles.

114. For information about Shakespearean great Henry Irving and his leading lady Ellen Terry, see Letter 33HdeKG and note 141.

Letter 28

115. Viscount John Morley of Blackburn (1838–1923), journalist, statesman, and member of Parliament, was editor of both the *Fortnightly Review* and the *Pall Mall Gazette*. He was elected to Parliament for the first time in 1883. John Bright (1811–1881) was a Liberal member of Parliament almost continuously from 1868 to 1882. Bright was seen as a champion of the middle class. In fact, Henry James said that Bright gave him the impression of "sturdy, honest, vigorous, English middle-class liberalism, accompanied by a certain infusion of Genius." Leon Edel, *Henry James: A Life* (New York: Harper and Row, 1985), 235. Viscount James Bryce (1838–1922) was a jurist, historian, and politician. He is best remembered in the United States for his seminal work, *The American Commonwealth* (1888), published after his American tour.

Artist Sir Edward Coley Burne-Jones (1833–1898) was a member of the Pre-Raphaelite Brotherhood. His friendship with William Morris led to partnerships in business and close family ties. Georgina Macdonald Burne-Jones (1840–1920) was one of the Macdonald sisters who made such illustrious marriages. Alice Macdonald married John Lockwood Kipling (1838–1911). Kipling, an artist of note, was curator of the Lahore Museum in India, where the family resided for many years. Their son, Rudyard, is best remembered for his tales of India and Burma as well as his children's stories.

Interestingly, Rudyard's son John was a close friend of Emma Lazarus' great-nephew Philip Marks. Marks' daughter, Nancy-Joan Marks Seligman, was named for John Kipling, who was killed in World War I. Philip Marks was wounded in that war and recuperated on the Kipling estate. Correspondence of Nancy-Joan Seligman with the author, spring 1987.

Georgina's sisters Louise and Agnes were married in a double wedding ceremony. Louise married "morbidly religious industrialist" Alfred Baldwin. Their son Stanley became prime minister of England. Agnes married artist Edward John Poynter. See Ina Taylor, *Victorian Sisters: The Remarkable Macdonald Women and the Great Men They Inspired* (Bethesda, Md.: Adler and Adler, 1987).

British illustrator George du Maurier (1834–1896) was a satirist for *Punch* and illustrator for *Cornhill Magazine*. As an author, he is perhaps best remembered for *Trilby* (1894).

Scottish scholar and author Andrew Lang (1844–1912) was known for his works on Scottish, French, and classical history and as the author of very successful fairy tales for children.

The Montefiores, Goldsmids, Rothschilds, Moscheleses, and Montalbas were all distinguished members of the British Jewish community.

Joseph and Alice (Strettel) Comyns Carr were good friends of Henry James'. Joseph Comyns Carr was an "eager champion" of the Pre-Raphaelites and director of the Grosvenor Gallery. He wrote plays, edited magazines, and was at one time the head of the Lyceum Theatre. Alice, a talented artist, was a costume designer as well. She was well known for her striking design of Ellen Terry's costume for Lady Bacbeth in Irving's production of the play. Stanley Olson, *John Singer Sargent: His Portrait* (New York: St. Martin's Press, 1986), 117–18.

116. Emma is referring to the wife of G. W. Smalley, London correspondent of the *New York Tribune*. Edel, *The Conquest of London*, 273.

117. Alma Strettel later would marry artist L. A. (Pete) Harrison (1853–1935). A close friend of John Singer Sargent's, she was painted by him four times. They were both so passionate about Richard Wagner they "earned themselves the self-imposed titles of 'maniac' and 'co-maniac.' " Olson, 126. A gifted woman, Strettel was seen by her friend Henry James as the bohemian member of the Broadway group of artists and writers in London. Henry James, *The Letters of Henry James*, Vol. 3, 1883–1895, ed. Leon Edel (Cambridge, Mass.: Belknap Press, 1980), 94, n3.

118. Sir Robert Cunliffe, a member of Parliament, was a close friend of Henry Adams'. For a letter dated 11 June 1883 from Lady Eleanor Leigh Cunliffe to Emma Lazarus, see Rusk, ed., *Letters to Lazarus*, 60.

119. It is interesting that Emma mentioned Clarence King, John Hay, Henry Adams, and Henry James in the same sentence. They, with Adams' late wife Marian Hooper Adams, were almost inseparable friends, calling themselves the "Five of Hearts." Adams and Hay lived in adjoining houses in Washington, D.C. See Patricia O'Toole, *The Five of Hearts: An Intimate Portrait of Henry Adams and His Friends, 1880–1918* (New York: Clarkson Potter, 1990).

120. James Russell Lowell (1819–1891), poet and critic, was U.S. minister in London at that time. Emma would write to him in November 1883 when he was appointed rector of Glasgow University:

> [The] pride and rejoicing of your countless friends must enhance, I am sure, the zest of your numerous and gracefully-worn British honors. That much abused book the Talmud has a proverb- "Not the place honors the man, but the man the place." It is in reality far more a subject of congratulations to us at home that you should be called & chosen, than it can possibly be to you to add one more to your laurel. (Lazarus to Lowell, 24 November 1883, Brown University.)

121. The Lillies were close friends of the Gilders'. Lillie had been "in the 'Galaxy' office." Rosamond Gilder, 97.

122. Sir Frederick Leighton (1830–1896) was a British painter with enormous prestige. He was elected president of the Royal Academy in 1878 at which time he was knighted. In 1886 he was made a baronet; in 1896 he became the first British painter to be made a baron. He died one day later.

123. Adelina Patti (1843–1919) was a Spanish-born soprano who was raised in the United States. So brilliant was her voice that she began singing in concert halls in New York at the age of seven. She made her operatic debut in 1859 at the age of sixteen in the title role of Lucia di Lammermoor. From that time she sang successfully until her death. Contralto Sophia Scalchi sang duets with Patti at Covent Garden.

124. Sir Nathaniel (Natty) Mayer Rothschild (1840–1915) succeeded his father, Lionel Nathan (1812–1870), as head of the British branch of the banking house of Rothschild. He became the lay head of the Anglo-Jewish community; he was president of United Synagogues and held other offices. He was made the first Jewish peer in England in 1885, sworn in on a Hebrew Bible. Rothschild was a governor of the Bank of England and the only Jewish member of the Royal Commission on Aliens. In that capacity he resisted strongly attempts to limit immigration. His wife Charlotte, the daughter of Baron Karl von Rothschild of Naples, was in fact his cousin. *Encyclopaedia Judaica* 14: 342.

125. Sir Moses Montefiore (1784–1885) was the most illustrious philanthropist in nineteenth-century England. Born in Italy, he emigrated to England and became a successful stockbroker. He went on to manage the huge Rothschild assets. Retiring at the age of forty in 1824, he devoted the remaining sixty years of his life to Jewish emancipation and to philanthropy. Montefiore was knighted in 1837 while serving as Sheriff of London. He was made a baronet in 1846. He traveled frequently to Palestine, making his last visit in 1875 at the age of ninety-one. *Encyclopaedia Judaica* 12: 270–71.

126. Musicologist Edwin Story.

127. This is probably William Dean Howells.

Letter 29

128. The Peacock Room, the dining room in the home of shipping magnate Frederick R. Leyland, had golden peacocks painted on the walls by James McNeill Whistler in 1876, "against intensities of blue on old Spanish leather." Edel, *A Life*, 316.

129. *The Earthly Paradise*, a collection of poems written by William Morris and illustrated by Edward Burne-Jones, was published in four parts from 1869 to 1871. Interestingly, the poems were written at that painful period of his life when his wife, Jane, "unilaterally undid her marriage," to quote one Pre-Raphaelite scholar, and established at the very least an emotional relationship with Dante Gabriel Rossetti. Jan Marsh, *The Pre-Raphaelite Sisterhood* (New York: St. Martin's Press, 1985), 241.

130. The very striking-looking Jane Morris was the model for many of Dante Gabriel Rossetti's paintings.

131. Merton Abbey was a remodeled abbey where William Morris manufactured textiles for his decorative art shop in London. The factory exemplified all of Morris' ideals. Emma wrote about him and his social and political thought in "A Day in Surrey," her *Century* essay.

132. British philanthropist Frederick David Mocatta (1828–1905) was a member of the distinguished banking firm of Mocatta and Goldsmid. He retired in 1874 to devote himself to a life of public and private philanthropy. Mocatta supported almost every hospital in London, promoted education, especially of the Jewish poor, and better housing for the working classes. A historian himself, he supported Jewish literature and research.

133. The beautiful Mirah Cohen was George Eliot's Jewish heroine in her last novel, *Daniel Deronda*.

134. According to Ralph L. Rusk, Lady Stanley of Alderly was Maude Althea Stanley (1833–1915), the daughter of the second Lord Stanley of Alderly. In 1880, she opened "what has been called the first club for working girls" and wrote on "social problems." See Rusk, ed., *Letters to Lazarus*, 66.

Richard Monckton Milnes (1809–1885) was the first Baron Houghton. An intimate of Tennyson, Hallam, and Thackeray, he sat for a time in Parliament, but this "bird of paradox," as he was called, was too literary for politics. He wrote songs and poems as well as works on politics. He is best known for his *Life of Keats*. Sir Paul Harvey, ed., *The Oxford Companion to English Literature*, 4th ed. (Oxford: Oxford University Press, 1980), 544; Edel, *A Life*, 209–10.

135. We suppose that Emma mentioned Hardy in reference to Helena's new stone studio at Marion; Richard had helped build it.

136. Sir Lawrence Alma-Tadema (1836–1912) painted popular historical idylls. He designed sets for Henry Irving's stage productions.

Letter 30

137. Philippe de Champagne (1602–1674) was a Belgian painter of the French Baroque school. His work is characterized by grave reality depicted in harmonious, somber tones and severe design. Was Emma's comment meant to be sarcastic?

Letter 32

138. This probably refers to Helena's translation of Sensier's *Life of Millet*, which appeared in *Scribner's*, serially, from September to December 1880.

139. The Season in London usually began in April and lasted through August, the period when Parliament was usually in session. The West End was the location for balls and other festivities held in the large and expensive homes. But the Season was also a time for state balls, exhibitions at the Royal Academy, and the Opera. Wolf Von Eckardt et al., *Oscar Wilde's London* (Garden City, N.Y.: Doubleday, Anchor, 1987), 116.

140. The Athanasian Creed states that "the Son is of the same substance as the Father"; the concurrent Arian Creed states that as the Son had not been present since the Creation, he was a separate entity from the Father. We do not know why Emma was so fascinated with this, but it is interesting that she would feel comfortable enough with her Christian friend Helena to speak so disrespectfully.

Letter 33

141. By 1883, Ellen Terry had been married and divorced twice and had given birth to two children out of wedlock. She was married unsuccessfully to English painter and sculptor George Frederic Watts when she was almost seventeen, and to the actor Charles Kelley (Charles Wardell). She lived with the architect Edward Godwin, with whom she had two children. See Nina Auerbach, *Ellen Terry: Player in Her Time* (New York: W. W. Norton, 1987).

142. The acclaimed stage actress Helena Modjeska was a close friend of the Gilders'.

Letter 34

143. Emma's father was terminally ill at that time.

144. Dr. Leopold Damrosch, conductor for the New York Symphony Society, died on 15

February 1885. His funeral was held in the Metropolitan Opera House; it was standing room only. The Reverend Henry Ward Beecher and Felix Adler, founder of the New York Society for Ethical Culture, gave the eulogies. *NYT*, 17 February 1885, 2; 19 February 1885, 5. Damrosch had been brought to New York as music director of the New York Philharmonic but was replaced by Theodore Thomas. It was at that time that his friends, men of wealth and influence, helped him launch the Symphony Society. Charles Edward Russell, *The American Orchestra and Theodore Thomas* (New York: Doubleday, Page, 1927), 137.

Letter 36

145. The clipping, included in the letter, appeared in the *Critic,* 2 August 1884. The poem was read at the opening of the Concord School of Philosophy that summer.

Letter 38

146. Helena was pregnant with her son George Coleman at that time.

147. Henry James' sister Alice James was chronically ill.

148. Emma is referring to Annie Benson Procter, whom she met during her 1883 trip to London.

149. The so-called Home Rule issue in Ireland had caused the crisis. William Gladstone had been turned out of office for the second time with the election of the Marquis of Salisbury.

150. We may assume that the reference is to the Matthew Arnolds. See Letter 41HdeKG, note 160.

Letter 39

151. Emma is probably referring to Helena's pregnancy.

152. Dulwich is a college village five miles south of London. The Dulwich College Picture Gallery was opened in 1814 and houses a "brilliant" collection of Dutch masters, Raphaels, Velásquezes, and Murillos, among others, as well as much British portraiture of the seventeenth and eighteenth centuries.

153. This refers, of course, to St. Patrick's Cathedral, which took twenty-one years, from 1858 to 1879, to be completed. Boyer, *Manhattan Manners,* 131.

Letter 40

154. Joseph Mallord William Turner (1775–1851), the British romantic landscape painter, was a pioneer in the study of light, color, and atmosphere.

155. Mrs. Schuyler Van Rensselaer, born Miriam Griswold, was a close friend of the Gilders' and a historian of New York City. It was at her house that Richard Gilder died in 1909. Rosamond Gilder, conversation with the author, July, 1980.

156. Tolstoy's *Anna Karenina* had been just recently published. Apparently, the English version had not yet reached the Continent.

157. Frédéric Mistral (1830–1914) was a Provençal poet. He was leader of the group of poets in Avignon who called themselves the Félibriges. Mistral won the Nobel Prize for Literature in 1904.

Letter 41

158. John Ruskin and American expatriate artist William Wetmore Story had written these widely read books.

159. Charles Waldstein was an American-born archeologist who taught at Cambridge. In a volume that was published anonymously he refuted the claim that Jews were a race and propounded an ecumenical "neo-Mosaic church." He had been a speaker for the Nineteenth Century Club in New York in 1884. Invitation to Nineteenth Century Club meeting, 8 January 1884, Emma Lazarus Notebook, American Jewish Historical Society Archives.

160. Emma's friend Matthew Arnold, whom she had probably met in New York when he toured the United States several years earlier. See Letter 13RHL and note 21.

Letter 42

161. The Hague, the seat of government in the Netherlands, grew up around a castle built in 1248, which was the first of a group of buildings called the Binnenhof or "inner court."

162. The Mauritshuis was built from 1633 to 1644 for the then governor of Brazil. It became the Royal Museum of Painting of The Hague.

163. The Gevanspaport or so-called Prisoner's Gate was built in 1400.

164. Scheveningen is the Netherlands' principal herring port.

165. Emma is almost certainly referring to Eugène Fromentin's masterpiece *Les Maîtres d'Autrefois: Belgique-Hollande,* which he wrote in 1875. Maxime deCamp's *En Hollande* and Amicis' *Olande* were popular guidebooks at that time.

166. See Letter 7HJ.

167. Olive Chancellor is one of the central characters in Henry James' novel *The Bostonians,* which appeared first, in serial form, in the *Century.* Emma certainly would not be the only person to see the similarities between Olive Chancellor and Alice James' intimate friend, Katherine Loring. See Edel, *A Life,* 312–14.

Letter 43

168. George Coleman, the Gilders' second son.

169. Aleck Oakey was Maria Oakey Dewing's brother. At the time of Mrs. Oakey's remarriage in 1890, the *New York Times* reported that in September 1885, Oakey had disappeared from his New York home. Nearly a year later he was found living under an assumed name in Newark, New Jersey. His wife then divorced him. He was said at the time of her remarriage to be living abroad. *NYT,* 26 February 1890, p. 6.

170. Francisque Sarcey (1828–1899) was a theater critic who was held in high esteem. *NYT,* 16 May 1899, p. 7.

171. Virginie Avegno (1859–1915), wife of wealthy banker and shipowner Pierre Gautreau, sat for John Singer Sargent in Paris in February 1883. Seen as a beauty, she had, in fact, irregular features, and she insisted on powdering her bare arms, shoulders, and face, making the final portrait a "curiosity." The portrait was shown at the Paris Salon in May 1884. Most critics were not so generous as Emma. They found the painting an atrocious curiosity. For a lengthy discussion, see Olson, 104.

Letter 44

172. Gilder's book of poems, *Lyrics,* was published in English in the United States and England in December 1885. As was usually the case, Emma would be sent a copy, early.

Letter 45

173. Claude Lorraine, who died in 1682, was the father of a landscape genre of painting. A Claude Lorraine glass was a piece of tinted framed glass, with a handle. The landscape thus viewed was "transformed into a provincial work of art, framed and suffused by a golden tone like that of the master's paintings." Leo Marx, *The Machine in the Garden: Technology and the Pastoral Ideal in America* (New York: Oxford University Press, 1967), 88–89.

174. That note from Henry James seems to have been lost.

175. Marian Hooper Adams (Mrs. Henry Adams), despondent over the death of her father, committed suicide in December 1885.

Letter 46

176. Bellosguardo is a small mountain in the vicinity of Florence. According to Leon Edel, at least three famous American writers lived there: Nathaniel Hawthorne, James Fenimore Cooper, and Henry James. *The Middle Years,* 201.

177. Luca della Robbia (1399–1482) was the head of a talented Italian family of sculptors renowned for their enameled terra cotta. Luca, however, worked mainly with marble.

Letter 47

178. The noted sculptor William Wetmore Story (1819–1895) lived with his family as an expatriate in the magnificent Palazzo Barberini in Rome. An intimate of the Brownings, he was also a favored friend of Henry James'.

179. Ellen Shaw Barlow was the wife of Civil War hero and attorney Francis Channing Barlow. Mrs. Barlow was the sister of Robert Shaw, who commanded the first Negro regiment from a free state and lost his life in the Civil War. Interestingly, Barlow, a widower, was a good deal older than his wife. Henry James' sister, Alice, wrote to a friend that the news of the engagement "gives one a shiver, does it not?" She went on to say that she had a "prejudice against him," a "sweet young girl like Nelly" should not be marrying a "widower." Jean Strouse, *Alice James: A Biography* (Boston: Houghton Mifflin, 1980), 95.

180. *John Rodman's Testimony* was written by Mary Hallock Foote. We may assume that she named her central character after her dear friend Helena Gilder's son, Rodman.

Letter 48

181. Bessie Ward married Baron Ernest de Schonberg-Roth Schonberg in August 1874. See Gertrude A. Barber, comp., *Marriages Taken from the New York Evening Post from July 16, 1874 to September 11, 1879*, vol. 21, 1938.

182. Emma could be referring to the Causeries du Lundi, organized by Mrs. John Jacob Astor III, a "select group of matrons who met to hear the reading of very intellectual papers." Lloyd Morris, *Incredible New York: High Life and Low Life of the Last Hundred Years* (New York: Random House, 1951), 145.

183. Edith Story Peruzzi was the daughter of the William Wetmore Storys and was noted for her beauty.

184. Robert Underwood Johnson was at that time the associate editor of the *Century*. He would go on to distinguish himself as ambassador to Italy in 1920. He was known as the unofficial poet laureate of the United States because of his prolific output.

185. As stated earlier, Katherine deKay Bronson and Robert Browning were intimate friends. Mrs. Bronson's husband, from whom she had been estranged for many years, died on 2 March 1885. See Meredith, *More Than Friend*, p. 65.

186. Miss Constance Fletcher, whose pseudonym was George Fleming, was the author of several novels and plays and was a good friend of Henry James' and his friend, the brilliant Constance Fenimore Woolson. Edel, *The Middle Years*, 357.

Letter 49

187. Violet Paget was an English author whose pen name was Vernon Lee. A friend of Henry James', she was described by him as a "most astounding young female." Paget, "[t]all, angular, with slightly protruding teeth and peering near-sightedly through her glasses," became a "too ardent admirer" of James. Edel, *A Life*, 303–4.

188. Mary A. F. Robinson, another friend of Henry James', was a poet, essayist, and biographer. She married French orientalist James Darmesteter and, after his death, French scientist Pierre Emile Duclaux. Henry James, *Letters*, 3:51 n6.

Letter 50

189. The government in England had changed parties and therefore prime ministers three times in that year.

190. Emma's sister Agnes was married to British Jew Montague Marks, editor of the popular *Art Amateur,* which was published in London and New York. Marks' father, Rabbi David Marks, was the first Reform Jewish rabbi in England. He was rabbi at the West London Synagogue of British Jews, where Agnes and Montague Marks were married on 17 June 1886. Copy of Marriage Certificate 8277G, General Register Office, London.

Letter 51

191. Although Lisa, Effie, and Bella Stillman were the stepdaughters of Maria Sparlati Stillman, Lisa and Effie were said to be as beautiful as Maria. Emma had known Lisa in New York in the early 1880s when she was studying at the Art Students League. Lisa Stillman to Helena deKay Gilder, n.d., private collection.

192. Anton Rubinstein (1829–1894) was one of the great pianists of the nineteenth century. Said to look remarkably like Beethoven, he brought his own interpretations to those pieces he played, often striking the wrong notes. Rubinstein saw himself as a composer. He is said to have been the model for Klesmer, the musician, in George Eliot's *Daniel Deronda*. Gordon S. Haight, *George Eliot: A Biography* (New York: Oxford University Press, 1968). Rubinstein made his American debut in 1882, giving 215 concerts in 239 days across the country. Harold C. Schonberg, *The Virtuosi: Classical Music's Great Performers from Paganini to Pavarotti* (New York: Vintage Books, 1988), 259.

193. Emma is referring to James Russell Lowell and Oliver Wendell Holmes.

194. Her lengthy essay on William Morris was written in 1884 and published in the *Century* in July 1886. See Letter 13RHL, for first mention of the essay.

Letter 52

195. Emma met and became friendly with Robert Browning during her first trip to London in May and June 1883. See Letters 28, 29HdeKG.

196. Richard Gilder read his poem "Mors Triumphalis" to the graduating class of Smith College in Northampton, Massachusetts, then. Rosamond Gilder, 152.

Letter 53

197. Emma is referring to Frank H. Scott and Robert Underwood Johnson, both staff members of the *Century*. Scott was secretary of the Century Company. See John, 119.

198. For a picture of this celebrated portrait, see "Portrait by Wyatt Eaton," *Art World* 3 (December 1917): 207.

199. Jeannette Gilder was Richard's sister and one of Emma's editors at the *Critic*.

Letter 54

200. The Editor's Cabinet was the *Century*'s informal editorial board that made publication decisions.

Letter 56

201. We do not know if Emma's sister Mary was married by then to Leopold Lindau. Ellen was the family's Irish maid who stayed with Emma and Annie until the end of their stay in Europe.

Letter 57

202. According to biographer Donald Thomas, Browning's "Inn Album," published in 1875, was based on "the conduct of the notorious Lord de Ros, as recorded in the memoirs of Charles Greville. . . . [T]he poem describes the attempt of an elderly roué to prostitute his seduced and discarded mistress to his young companion in exchange for the cancellation of a gambling debt." The poem had "moral objections." Thomas, *Robert Browning: A Life within a Life* (New York: Viking Press, 1983), 248.

203. Frans Hals (1580–1666), the Dutch painter said to have been surpassed only by Rembrandt and Vermeer.

Letter 58

204. Possibly a reference to Les Causeries du Lundi, the group founded by Mrs. John Jacob Astor III. Morris, 145. See Letter 48, n.182.

Letter 59

205. S.L. is Sarah Lazarus, one of Emma's older sisters. Said to have been very beautiful, she spent the last years of her life confined to her room, mentally and physically ill. Letters to Helena deKay Gilder from both Sarah and Josephine Lazarus (1896–1909) describe Sarah's condition. The correspondence is privately held.

206. Joseph Joachim, said to be the greatest classical violinist of the nineteenth century, was born in 1831 in Hungary and first played publicly at the age of eight. Schonberg, 154–56.

207. This probably is Raimundo de Madrazo y Garreta (1852–1917), a member of the family of outstanding Spanish painters. He lived in Paris at that time.

Letter 62

208. "Frankie" Cleveland. See note 211.

209. Amélie Rives (1863–1945) was a noted American author whose first novel, *The Quick or the Dead?* (1888), would establish her as a popular novelist. It is uncertain how Emma knew her.

Letter 65

210. Frances (Frankie) Cleveland was the young bride of President Grover Cleveland. The Clevelands and the Gilders had become and would continue to be close friends. In fact, the Gilders' daughter Francesca was named after the First Lady. Rosamond Gilder, conversation with the author, July 1980. When Emma died on 19 November, Helena wrote

a letter to her friend "Frank" Cleveland in which she told her how much Emma appreciated the flowers. A few leaves would be put away to be kept for the children of the family. Helena deKay Gilder to Frances Cleveland, 19 November 1887, Library of Congress.

10. Thomas Wren Ward

1. Obituary, *NYT,* 9 July 1940, p. 1.

2. Schappes, ed., *Letters,* nos. 19A, 19B, 38A. For a description of the Samuel Gray Ward home in Lenox, Massachusetts, see "American Country Dwellings, II," *Century* 32 (June 1886): 206–20.

3. Gay Wilson Allen, *Waldo Emerson* (New York: Viking Press, 1981), 338–39, 351–55.

4. Margaret Snyder, "The Other Side of the River, Thomas Wren Ward, 1844–1944," *New England Quarterly* 14 (September 1941): 433.

5. Letters from Josephine Lazarus to Thomas and Sophie Ward are located in the Autograph File at the Houghton Library Archives, Harvard University.

Letter 1

6. François Coppée (1842–1908) was a poet of the so-called Parnassian school. He came to be known as a "poète des humbles."

Letter 2

7. *Joseph and His Brethren* was a newly published "dramatic poem" by Charles Wells, with an introduction by Algernon Swinburne. It was published in London by Chatto and Windus in 1876.

Letter 3

8. See Chapter 2, note 1.

Letter 4

9. Emma made her first visit to the Emersons the week of 25 August 1876. For a good description of the effect of the visit on her hosts, see Gregg, 2: 223–25.

10. William Ellery Channing the Younger, named for his famous uncle, had been a close friend of Tom's father, Samuel Gray Ward. In fact, Ward had been so impressed with Channing's poetry, he became his patron. See Frederick T. McGill, Jr., *W. E. Channing of Concord: A Life of William Ellery Channing II* (New Brunswick, N.J.: Rutgers University Press, 1967).

11. Monadnock is a favorite mountain in New Hampshire, one the Concord crowd loved to climb.

12. Emma is referring to Edward Emerson, Ralph Waldo Emerson's son. He roomed with Tom Ward at Harvard.

Letter 5

13. French philosopher and orientalist Ernest Renan (1823–1892) would become a favorite of Emma Lazarus. Her essay "Renan and the Jews," which, according to Lazarus scholar Max Baym, was a paraphrase of two speeches by Renan, would be entered in an essay contest given by the Young Men's Hebrew Association in New York in 1884. The first Renan speech, "Le judaïsme comme race et religion," argues that the prophets' emphasizing social justice made Judaism a universal religion. Isaiah, in fact, was seen as the founder of the Christian church. Renan denied any racial aspect to Jewishness. The second essay, "Identite originelle et séparation graduelle du judaïsme et du christianité," points out the fact that both Christianity and Islam are really Judaism adapted to the Indo-European and Arabic geographical environments. Max Baym, "Emma Lazarus' Approach to Renan in Her Essay 'Renan and the Jews,'" *Publications of the American Jewish Historical Society* 37 (1947): 17–29. Lazarus' essay, written in 1884, diverges from her earlier concepts of Jews and Judaism.

The *Revue des Deux Mondes* was a French-language literary journal popular in the United States at that time. From her correspondence with Ward, we can see that Emma read the magazine regularly.

Letter 7

14. Emma published a book of translations of Heine's poetry in 1881. The article she refers to could be the introductory essay in that collection. See pp. 41–42.

15. Emma's first and only short story, "The Eleventh Hour," appeared in *Scribner's* in June 1878. For further discussion, see pp. 34–35.

16. Ivan Turgenev's *Virgin Soil (Nov')* was published in 1876 to mixed reviews. For a discussion of the work, see Letter 2HdeKG and note 18. Emma and the renowned author corresponded through the services of H. H. Boyesen. See Rusk, ed., *Letters to Lazarus,* 17–19; and *AH,* 9 December 1887.

17. As mentioned, Rudolph Lindau's brother Leopold would marry Emma's sister Mary. The Lindaus' brother Paul was a noted playwright and journalist in Germany. See *NYT,* 2 February 1919, p. 15. Leopold Lindau was a friend of Henry George's. See Rusk, ed., *Letters to Lazarus,* 34. Little more is known of Leopold and Mary Lindau. From the will of Moses Lazarus and the probate document concerning the estate of Emma Lazarus, we can assume that Mary married Leopold some time after her father's death in 1885. We know that in 1892, when Emma's estate was probated, Mary lived in Berlin. See last will and testament of Moses Lazarus, originally admitted to probate, March 18, 1885.

18. The railroad strikes began in mid-July 1877. They occupied the pages of the *New York Times* for several weeks. On 25 July, for example, no less than thirty-nine articles appeared. Seen as a "greater menace to the established order than anything since the Civil War," the

strikes were referred to by the *New York Tribune* as an "insurrection." Other papers called them a Communist Conspiracy or "the awful presence of Socialism." The *Nation* (26 July and 2, 9, and 16 August) published scathing articles against these nationwide strikes that paralyzed the country. It is significant that Emma seems to have sided against the immigrant strikers in what were legitimate grievances about drastic cuts in pay. See Sidney Lens, *Radicalism in America: Great Rebels and the Causes for Which They Fought from 1620 to the Present*, new updated ed. (New York: Thomas Y. Crowell, 1969), 144; Richard Boyer and Herbert M. Morais, *Labor's Untold Story*, 3d ed. (New York: United Electrical Radio and Machine Workers of America, 1971), 59; John A. Garraty, *The New Commonwealth: 1877–1890*, The New American Nation Series (New York: Harper Torchbooks, 1968), 158–60.

19. Jean Richepin (1849–1926), French author of poetry, drama, comedy, and other works including opera, heroic dramas, and several psychological novels. In 1876, he became infamous for his book of inflammatory verse "in defense of the forgotten poor, the tramps, and the homeless, called *La Chanson des Gueux*." In 1883, Richepin and Sarah Bernhardt became lovers. Arthur Gold and Robert Fizdale, *The Divine Sarah: A Life of Sarah Bernhardt* (New York: Alfred A. Knopf, 1991), 204–7.

Letter 8

20. Edward Fitzgerald was best known for his translation of the "Rubaiyat" of Omar Khayyam. His translation of the *Agamemnon* of Aeschylus met with skepticism: rather than giving a literal rendering, he put the Greek into his own words. *Nation*, 24 May 1877, pp. 310–11.

Letter 9

21. We may assume this is the date because Emma mentioned the possibility of being in Ocean City on July 15 for a week. See Emma Lazarus to Charles deKay, 30 June 1879, Emma Lazarus Collection, Clifton Waller Barrett Library, Manuscript division and Special Collections, Alderman Library, University of Virginia. This is the only correspondence thus far discovered of these two friends.

22. Saratoga was a favorite watering place for the wealthy, noted not only for its mineral springs but for gambling and horse racing.

23. The Central Park, as it was called, was purchased by the City of New York in 1856 for $5,500,000 and developed by Frederick Law Olmstead and Calvert Vaux. It extends from 59th to 110th streets and between Fifth and Eighth avenues.

Letter 10

24. *NYT*, 19 July 1940.

25. One of Emma's Jewish poems, "The Guardian of the Red Disk," appeared in the September 1880 number of *Scribner's*. This is significant to the issue of Emma's supposed sudden conversion to her Jewishness in 1882.

Letter 11

26. Emma's unsigned essay on Browning appeared in the November 1880 number of *Scribner's*.

Letter 12

27. Bessie Minturn was probably the daughter of prominent New Yorker Robert Minturn.

Letter 14

28. Charles Victor Cherbuliez's *Noirs and Rouges,* a lesser-known work, was published serially in the *Revue des Deux Mondes* from 25 November 1880 to 15 January 1881. The novel was published in English as *Saints and Sinners.* Cherbuliez, who often wrote under the pseudonym G. Valbert, was elected a member of the French Academy in 1881. Among his works translated into English are *Samuel Brohl* and *The Adventures of Ladislas Bolski.*

29. *Daniel Rochat,* a play by Victorien Sardou, was produced at the Union Square Theatre in New York City on 16 October 1880 and ran until 14 December 1880. We may assume that Emma had seen it. *Daniel Rochat* is the story of two star-crossed lovers, French deputy and ardent atheist Daniel Rochat and American and good Christian Lea Henderson. Having been married in a civil ceremony, Daniel discovers to his horror that Lea insists on being married again by clergy. After an arduous encounter, Daniel tries to compromise, saying that he will be married by clergy but this "fact" must be kept secret, lest his constituents find out. Lea will not agree to this and the two are divorced.

30. Soeur Marie and Mère Amélie were two of the central characters in *Noirs et Rouges.* Soeur Marie, the heroine of this melodramatic story, was the saintly and orphaned Mademoiselle Jetta Maulabret who wants to retreat to the convent to nurse the poor but must live with an uncle for at least two years in order to inherit a fortune left to her with this condition by her mother's surgeon brother. Her aunt, Mère Amélie, is cruel indeed. It is she who insists that Jetta obey her uncle. She demands that Jetta then give the money to the hospital. Jetta falls in love with a "cad" whom she promises to marry in the end. In the meantime she is accosted by another suitor whose mother knows her as a good catch. It is interesting that Emma's friend Rose Hawthorne Lathrop would become a nun, nursing the incurably ill in a setting not unlike the one in *Noirs et Rouges.*

Letter 16

31. Joseph and Jeannette Gilder, Richard Gilder's brother and sister, began publishing their new journal, *The Critic,* in January 1881. There is no signed essay by Emma in that number.

Letter 17

32. Emma apparently objected to Jetta's decision to stay with the cad, Albert Valport.

33. Regnault's correspondence with his family and friends was described by Emma in "Regnault as a Writer," 37.

Letter 18

34. See Letter 7TWW, note 17.

35. John Wesley Powell (1834–1902) was an ethnologist and geologist. He started a daring three-year journey down the Colorado River in 1867. Emma was probably referring to his *Exploration of the Colorado River and Its Tributaries* (1875). *Encyclopaedia Britannica* 18: 390.

36. Bayard Taylor (1825–1878) was known as a rather mediocre travel writer, according to one source. Kunitz and Haycraft, 730–31.

11. Rose Hawthorne Lathrop

1. For an excellent biography of Rose Hawthorne Lathrop, see Valenti.

2. Rose Lathrop to Helena deKay Gilder, n.d., deKG Letters, private collection.

Letter 1

3. Helena deKay and Richard Watson Gilder were renowned for their "Friday Evenings" when artistic and literary luminaries met in their Studio. See Chapter 2 and pp. 67–69.

Letter 2

4. Rose Lathrop's only child, Francis Hawthorne (Francie), who was born in 1876, contracted diphtheria and died on 6 February 1881. After that, Rose left her family home, The Wayside in Concord, never to live there again. Valenti, 63–65.

5. After their son's death, Rose and George Lathrop sailed for England to visit Julian Hawthorne, Rose's brother from whom she had been estranged. Valenti, 66. Rose would make plans with Emma for a European trip in 1883. For reasons unknown, she was unable to go and Emma went, instead, with her youngest sister, Annie. See Letter 27HdeKG.

Letter 3

6. Mrs. George Biddle, née Minnie Rodgers, was one of Emma's childhood friends. See Letter 3HdeKG.

Letter 4

7. Charles Godfrey Leland (1824–1903), poet and writer, often used the pseudonym Hans Breitmann. While living in England he became interested in the methods of teaching the industrial arts. He returned to Philadelphia and became the director of the Public Industrial Art School of Philadelphia. Emma's interest in his work dated from her involvement with unschooled East European Jewish immigrants settling in New York. Leland is mentioned in her letter 3, *Epistle to the Hebrews* (20), when she discusses technical training and manual labor.

8. Oscar Wilde began his celebrated visit to the United States in January 1882, having "nothing to declare, except my genius." He had long hair and wore knee breeches. Had Emma heard his lecture on the Pre-Raphaelites, whom he saw as the inspiration for the revival of art for art's sake in England, she probably would have found much with which to agree. Unfortunately, his theatrics overshadowed the substance of his thought. Many prominent Americans, such as Emma's friend Edmund Stedman, shunned him during his visit. Richard Ellmann, *Oscar Wilde* (New York: Vintage Books, 1988), 157–72.

Letter 5

9. By fall 1882, Emma Lazarus had taken an active interest in the East European Jewish immigrants landing in New York. She was on Ward's Island, which she is said to have visited more than once, the day of the memorable riot among disgruntled immigrant "inmates" of that holding station. She worked in the offices of the Hebrew Emigrant Aid Society and is said to have taught immigrant girls English. Her poems and polemic continued to appear in the *American Hebrew* and the *Century*. For a description of the riot, see *NYT*, 15 October 1882, p. 5. For Emma's visits to Ward's Island, see Philip Cowen, "A Budget of Letters," AH 9 December 1887.

10. Annie Lazarus visited Concord in August 1882. See Gregg, vol. 2, 478.

11. Emma had asked her friend Rabbi Gustav Gottheil of Temple Emanu-El in Manhattan to teach her Hebrew. We know that he was unable to do so, but it has never been made clear just who her teachers were. Morris Schappes offers two sources for this information. First, he reports that Philip Cowen wrote that it was Louis Schnabel (1829–1897), superintendent of the Hebrew Orphan Asylum and a journalist and writer of short stories. Second, Rebekah Kohut, wife of Rabbi Alexander Kohut, reported that Emma took lessons with her cousin Sarah Lyons, daughter of Rev. J. J. Lyons of Congregation Shearith Israel, and later with Professor Arnold B. Ehrlich (1848–1919), Polish-born lexicographer and exegete, at that time an instructor at the Emanu-El Preparatory School. See Schappes, ed., *Letters*, no. 37.

Letter 6

12. Stanford White had helped the Gilders remodel a studio for Helena. The old stone building had been an oil refinery and then a plant for converting seawater into salt. It was in Marion on Buzzards Bay. The main house, interestingly, was the setting for Miss Birdseye's house in *The Bostonians*. See Tharp, *Saint-Gaudens*, 204.

13. We have found no information concerning Stedman's "non-Venetian" holiday. In August 1883, however, his brokerage house was suspended from the New York Stock Exchange because of his son Frederick's ruinous speculation with the defunct Cecil, Ward and Company. For information about this and about Stedman's reinstatement in January 1884, see *NYT*, 16 August 1883, p. 1; 4 January 1884, p. 8. Edmund Stedman, a banker and a poet, through his life would juggle both occupations. He enjoyed an impeccable reputation on Wall Street and was the "touchstone of literary taste." Kunitz and Haycraft, 710–11. He was Richard Gilder's closest friend.

14. It is interesting that Emma was rereading George Eliot then because she would quote

her extensively in *An Epistle to the Hebrews,* which would begin a serial run in the *American Hebrew* in November 1882.

Letter 7

15. *Songs of a Semite* was Emma's book of Jewish poetry that included her celebrated drama *The Dance to the Death.* It was published by The American Hebrew Publishing Company in 1882.

16. Emma's memorial essay, "Emerson's Personality," appeared in the June 1882 number of the *Century.*

Letter 8

17. Traditionally, the London Season began in April and ran through August. Nearly everybody who was anybody in the Empire was lured out of country homes to attend balls and other gala events. See Letter 32HdeKG, note 139.

Letter 10

18. In her own "quiet way" Emma saw no fewer than forty prominent Britishers during her stay in London. For fuller descriptions of Emma's experiences, see Letters 27–29HdeKG.

Letter 11

19. Rose spent Christmas 1883 with her brother. Valenti, 71.

Letter 12

20. Matthew Arnold's lecture on Emerson took place 4 January 1884. See Letter 13RHL.

Letter 13

21. Matthew Arnold lectured in New York City on 4 January 1884. Not everyone agreed with Emma's evaluation of the lecture. For example, her friend naturalist John Burroughs thought Arnold's voice was "too thick and foggy" with "none of the charm and grace of his literary style." Clara Barrus, ed., *The Heart of Burroughs' Journals* (Port Washington, N.Y.: Kennikat Press, 1956), 105.

22. German-born Theodore Thomas, conductor for the New York Philharmonic, was instrumental in setting up a series of so-called Workingmen's Concerts. Unfortunately, the wrong "classes" took advantage of these free concerts. As the *New York Times* reported on 31 March 1884, the "assemblage yesterday was singularly well-to-do in appearance—it was almost too 'dressy,' in fact, to be made up of working men and their families." It was suggested that a small admission fee be charged.

23. Emma's lengthy article on William Morris appeared two years later in the July 1886 number of the *Century*.

Letter 14

24. Moses Lazarus died on 9 March 1885.

12. Edwin Robert Anderson Seligman

1. Nancy-Joan Marks to the author, 1986.
2. Obituary, *NYT*, 19 July 1939, p. 19.
3. See pp. 46–47.

Letter 1

4. Probably Professor Isaac Leopold Rice (1850–1915), who lectured with Seligman at Columbia College in the School of Political Science. See *Epistle to the Hebrews*, xiii, xvii.

Daniel De Leon (1852–1914) was born on the island of Curaçao and came to the United States no later than 1874. He received his LL.B. from Columbia College in 1878 and returned there in 1883 to lecture on Latin American diplomacy for the next six years. De Leon actively supported Henry George for mayor in 1886. He joined the Knights of Labor in 1888 and the Socialist Labor party in 1890. That party chose him as gubernatorial candidate for the state of New York in 1891 and 1902. De Leon played a leading role in the party until 1905, when he helped in the formation of the Industrial Workers of the World. In 1908, his supporters formed a splinter party, the Workers' International Industrial Union, which enjoyed minimal success in the years until his death. *Encyclopaedia Judaica* 5: 1471.

Until the discovery of the letters in this volume, no evidence had been found to indicate that De Leon had any ties with the Jewish community. Emma may have met him through Seligman, his colleague at Columbia.

Letter 2

5. The Jewish Problem or the Jewish Question was a euphemistic phrase popular from that time until Hitler's "Final Solution." For Jews, the "problem" was both the failure of emancipation to eradicate anti-Jewish behavior and laws in western Europe, and the continued excesses against East European Jews, notably in Russia. For non-Jews, the phrase had a more ominous meaning. The perceived inability of Jews to assimilate into the political, social, or economic spheres of their host countries was a persistent concern. Jews as a group were seen to be too capitalistic, too socialistic, or too exclusionary in religious practices. They were seen as a threat to the concept of the nation-state that demanded homogeneity in thought just as religious movements had. See Chapter 7.

Letter 3

6. Laurence Oliphant (1829–1888) was one of the more interesting characters in nineteenth-century England. The author of several travel books and one novel, Oliphant held several minor positions with the British consulate and in the 1860s came to the United States to live with utopian Thomas Lake Harris, who had established a small community, the Brotherhood of the New Life, at Brocton on the shores of Lake Erie. Oliphant first visited Palestine in 1879 and subsequently went there to live. It is interesting that Oliphant's "Hebrew" secretary there was Naphtali Herz Imber (1856–1909), the author of the Israeli national anthem, "Hatikvah." *Epistle to the Hebrews*, 82.

Oliphant would later write Emma, suggesting that she urge the Russian government to put pressure on Turkey to allow Jewish immigration from Russia to Turkey. See Laurence Oliphant to Emma Lazarus, 15 April 1883, Rusk, ed., *Letters to Lazarus*, 51.

Letter 4

7. The "Alliance" or Alliance Israélite Universelle ("All Israel are Comrades"), established in Paris in 1860, was the first international Jewish organization. This world organization of "fortunate" Jews who had achieved emancipation and acculturation in their own countries was to help other Jews who suffered discrimination anywhere. *Encyclopaedia Judaica* 2: 647–48.

8. Emma elucidated her concept of "Internal Reform" in her treatise, *An Epistle to the Hebrews*. In short, she felt that Jews living in eastern Europe had to reform their religion and consequently their way of life, doing away with what she saw as an obscurantism and superstition. What was needed, said Emma, was "Education, Enlightenment, Reformation; a sweeping out of the accumulated cobwebs and rubbish of Kabala and Talmud, darkening their very windows against the day, and incrusting their altars and their hearths with the gathered dust of the ages" (74).

9. DeWitt Seligman, named for Dewitt Clinton, was the son of James and Rosa Content Seligman and Edwin's first cousin.

Frederic deSola Mendes (1850–1927) was rabbi at Congregation Shaarey Tefillah in New York City. He was also one of the founders of the *American Hebrew*. *Encyclopaedia Judaica* 11: 1343.

Nathan Bijur (1862–1930) became a distinguished New York State Supreme Court justice. He would continue to take a leading role in the resettlement of East European Jews in the United States, was among the founders of the National Conference of Jewish Charities and the American Jewish Committee, and was a trustee of the Baron de Hirsch Fund and the Hebrew Free Trade School. He served often as a consultant on legal questions involving Jewish immigration. *Encyclopaedia Judaica* 4: 991.

Julius J. Frank (1852–1931) graduated from the Columbia Law School in 1873. He went on to a distinguished career as an attorney and was active in several independent Democratic movements at the turn of the century. He was active in the B'nai B'rith and was one of the founders of the Young Men's Hebrew Association of New York. Like his friend Seligman, he was a member of the New York Society for Ethical Culture, of which he was a trustee. *NYT*, 23 May 1931, p. 17.

Lazarus could be referring to Nathan Ullmann, art editor of the *American Hebrew.* Cowen, 79.

Minnie Louis would become a leader in philanthropic and educational activities on the Lower East Side. She founded the Louis Downtown Sabbath School in 1880. The institution later became the Hebrew Technical School for Girls. *NYT,* 13 March 1922, p. 15.

Letter 5

10. See pp. 67–69.

11. At that time, Emma was planning to go abroad with Rose Hawthorne Lathrop. When that plan failed, Emma went with her youngest sister, Annie. See Letter 27HdeKG and Letter 8RHL.

12. The Lazaruses moved to 18 West Tenth Street on 25 April 1885.

13. This is the Society for the Improvement and Colonization of East European Jews, established by Emma, Seligman, and their committee in 1883.

Letter 6

14. The Podolian Ghetto was the setting for a series of short stories by Karl Emil Franzos, the so-called Barnow stories. Emma objected to reviews that denegrated the stories of East European Hassidic Jewish life. Her objection seems puzzling, as she disapproved of what she saw as obscurantist Orthodox Judaism. See letter 13, "The Jews of Barnow," *An Epistle to the Hebrews,* 68–72.

Letter 7

15. The Lazaruses lived on Fifty-seventh Street, two houses from Madison Avenue. It is ironic that Emma, who has been seen as such a recluse, would insist on riding in the "cars," a rather inelegant and public way of getting around.

Letter 8

16. The Society for Eastern European Jews is presumably a shortened form of reference to the Society for the Improvement and Colonization of East European Jews.

17. Seligman's uncle, Isaac Seligman, was the London head of J. and W. Seligman and Company. It will be remembered that his grandson, Madron Seligman, married Emma's great-niece Nancy-Joan Marks, whose grandmother was Agnes Lazarus Marks. See Letter 50HdeKG and note 190.

Letter 9

18. Kann was general secretary of the Alliance and president of the Russian Relief Committee in Paris. *Jewish Record,* 25 May 1883.

19. Baron Maurice de Hirsch (1831–1896), German financier and philanthropist, was the first Jewish benefactor to plan large-scale resettlement of Jews from eastern Europe. Interestingly, little has been noted of his philanthropy before 1891, when he founded the Jewish Colonization Association to resettle Jewish immigrants in the United States, South America, and Canada. *Encyclopaedia Judaica* 8: 506.

Letter 10

20. In May of the following year, the Tenement House Building Company was incorporated by Seligman, Felix Adler, and others. Its purpose, according to the *New York Times,* was to "purchase and improve real estate for residences, homesteads, and apartment houses to be leased to and occupied by the stockholders of the company." The company would be capitalized at $150,000 to be divided into 6,000 shares of $25 each. *NYT,* 8 May 1885, p. 8.

Letter 11

21. Felix Adler (1851–1933), professor of Hebrew and Oriental literature, founded the New York Society for Ethical Culture in 1876. It is not clear which committee he headed. He founded the first group for child study in 1883, and was involved in a number of social causes. *Encyclopaedia Judaica* 1: 276.

22. The so-called Workingmen's Concerts were conducted by Theodore Thomas in 1884 and 1885. At first, a "singularly well-to-do" group of people took advantage of this amusement, which was free of charge. *NYT,* 31 March 1884, p. 4. See Letter 13RHL.

13. Henry James

1. R. W. B. Lewis, *The Jameses: A Family Narrative* (New York: Farrar, Straus and Giroux, 1991), 341–42.

2. See Rusk, ed., *Letters to Lazarus,* 426–33.

Letter 1

3. James is referring to Annie Benson Procter. See Letter 27HdeKG and note 111.

Letter 2

4. Leonard Montefiore, who died in 1879 at the age of twenty-six while on a visit to the United States, was someone Emma would have liked. A son of Sir Moses Montefiore, he is said to have been embarrassed by his wealth and lived a penurious life. Chaim Bermant, *The Cousinhood* (New York: Macmillan, 1972), 314–15.

5. Sir Francis Goldsmid (1808–1878) had been the first Jew admitted to the English bar in 1833. He was a member of Parliament as well. Joan Comay, *Who's Who in Jewish History after the Period of the Old Testament* (New York: David McKay, 1974), 170.

Letter 4

6. Florence Bayard Lockwood was a great friend of James. He wrote to Sara Butler Wister that he found Lockwood "a remarkable woman" who was "perhaps too tense and too intense, but so singularly lovely that a tete-a-tete with her is a great bliss." He thought of her as "one of the big figures of one's experience." Edel, *A Life,* 174. For Emma's experiences with Florence Lockwood, see Letters 47, 48HdeKG.

Letter 5

7. Alice James had traveled from Boston to Liverpool with Katherine and Louisa Loring. For an interesting discussion of Alice James' relationship with Katherine Loring and her sister, and Henry James' use of this in *The Bostonians,* see Edel, *A Life,* 308–12.

8. *The Bostonians* appeared serially in the *Century.* The *Atlantic* would serialize *The Princess Casamassima.*

9. James is probably referring to Carlyle's *Reminiscences,* published over a period of years by his biographer, James Anthony Froude.

Letter 8

10. Emma was in Italy at that time.
11. The British had just brought Gladstone back to power.

Glossary of Proper Names

Abbey, Henry (1842–1911). American poet and banker.

Admetus. Hero of Greek mythology. The real hero, however, is Alcestis, his wife, who agrees to die in her husband's place. She is rescued by Hercules, who has wrestled with Death at her grave, and has made him give her back.

Alcott, Amos Bronson (1799–1888). New England teacher, reformer, philosopher, he was a member of the transcendentalist community in Concord, Massachusetts. His life is said to have been a deliberate imitation of Christ, whom he did not think divine. Always poor and in debt, he lived on the largesse of others until his daughter, Louisa May Alcott, gained renown as an author.

Arnold, Matthew (1822–1888). British poet and critic whose central work *Culture and Anarchy* was published in 1869. It was on his triumphal tour of the United States in 1883–1884 that he met Emma Lazarus.

Beecher, Henry Ward (1813–1887). Son of Calvinist minister Lyman Beecher, he was the brother of famed abolitionist storyteller, Harriet Beecher Stowe. Henry Ward Beecher was the legendary pastor of Plymouth Congregational Church in Brooklyn, New York. John Hay called him the "greatest preacher the world has seen since St. Paul preached on Mars' Hill."

Belmont, August (1816–1890). German-Jewish banker Belmont was the American representative of the House of Rothschild. From 1853 to 1855, he was the chargé d'affaires for the United States at The Hague and from 1855 to 1858 he was the American minister resident there. During the Civil War, Belmont was responsible for procuring loans from England and France for the Union effort. A lifelong Democrat, he was chairman of the Democratic National Committee from 1860 to 1872.

Botta, Vincenzio (1818–1894). Botta was professor of Italian at New York University. With his wife, Anne Charlotte Lynch Botta, he opened his home to a variety of intellectuals and artists.

Botticelli, Sandro (1444/5–1510). One of the greatest Renaissance painters. Among those paintings commissioned by his patrons, the Medicis, were *Birth of Venus* and *Adoration of the Magi.* Many of his paintings hang in the Uffizi.

Boyesen, Hjalmar H. (1848–1895). Professor of Germanic literature at Cornell and at Columbia, he was born in Norway and came to this country in 1869. Boyesen was a friend of Turgenev's and translated his pieces into English for publication in the *Century.*

Brandes, Georg Morris Cohen (1842–1927). A Danish Jewish critic and scholar, Brandes was influenced by Nietzsche, whom he discovered in the 1880s. His Danish article on the German philosopher, translated and published in Germany in 1890, is said to have been the starting point for Nietzsche's fame. Thereafter Brandes wrote on such heroes as Goethe, Disraeli, Julius Caesar, Voltaire, and Michelangelo. Brandes was a self-hating Jew who, it is said, was never at home anywhere. He hated his own Jewishness and disliked Jewish characteristics in others.

Brontë, Charlotte (1816–1855). The fifth and youngest daughter of Thomas and Maria Branwell Brontë. Charlotte was a novelist and poet whose best-known work, *Jane Eyre,* was published in 1847 under the pseudonym Currer Bell.

Brown, Ford Madox (1821–1893). This British painter's works resembled those of the Pre-Raphaelite Brotherhood, though he was never a member. He worked for a time as a book illustrator with William Morris.

Burroughs, John (1837–1921). U.S. naturalist and author, Burroughs was seen as Thoreau's successor in writing popular essays on nature. He was a good friend of such nature lovers as John Muir and Theodore Roosevelt.

Campagna di Roma. Low country surrounding Rome. It is bounded on the northwest by hills surrounding Lake Bracciano, on the northeast by the Sabine Mountains, on the southeast by the Alban Hills, and on the southwest by the sea.

Campanile. A bell tower most commonly built beside or attached to a church. A famous example of a round campanile is the Leaning Tower of Pisa, built in the eleventh and twelfth centuries.

Campo Santo. An open cloister in Pisa, built between 1278 and 1283, it was made especially sacred by the fifty-three shiploads of earth brought from Calvary. It is famous for its frescoes, done by various Tuscan artists.

Capitoline Museum. Founded by Pope Sixtus IV at Rome for preserving antique marble statuary.

Caracci, Lodovico (1555–1619), Agostino (1557–1602), and Annibale (1560–1609). Members of a Bolognese family of painters.

Carducci, Giosui (1835–1907). An Italian poet, Carducci was one of the most influential literary figures of his age. He won the Nobel Prize in 1906. In 1860 he became a professor of Italian literature at the University of Bologna and remained there for forty years. He is revered by Italians as a national poet.

Coquelin, Benoit Constant (1841–1909). French actor; by the age of 23 he was a full member of the *Théâtre Français*. Although he was well known for his comedic roles, he was equally at home performing drama and romance.

Cowen, Philip (1853–1943). A member of a German-Jewish family, Cowen founded the *American Hebrew* in 1878 and was editor and publisher for twenty-seven years. In 1903, he went to Russia on a special mission to report on the causes of immigration from eastern Europe with an emphasis on Jewish problems. Then, from 1905 to 1907, he served as an official of the U.S. Immigration Service at Ellis Island.

Cox, Samuel Sullivan (1824–1889). A congressman for two states, Cox represented Ohio from 1857 to 1865 and New York from 1869 to 1895, with an absence in 1885–1886, when he was U.S. minister to Turkey.

Daubigny, Charles François (1817–1878). French landscape painter and engraver who influenced the Impressionists.

Dawes, Anna Laurens (1851–1938). Daughter of Massachusetts Senator Henry L. Dawes, she served as his secretary for many of the thirty-six years of his service as representative and senator. Anna knew Lincoln as a child; her father was an honorary pallbearer at his funeral. Among other published works, Dawes wrote *The Modern Jew: His Present and His Future* (1886).

DeCamps, Alexandre Gabriel (1803–1860). One of the first nineteenth-century

French painters to turn from neoclassicism to romanticism. DeCamps was probably the first of the European painters to represent scenes from scriptural history in their natural and local background.

Delaunay, (Jules) Elie (1828–1891). A French painter whose commissions include *Apollo, Orpheus,* and *Amphion,* at the Paris Opera House. During the last years of his life, he gained great popularity as a portrait painter.

Dodge, Mary Mapes (?–1905). An author, Dodge edited the home department of the magazine *Hearth and Home* and was the editor of *St. Nicholas* magazine. She wrote stories and poems.

Donatello (1386–1466). An important Italian sculptor, he is said to have been one of the founders of Renaissance art.

Drummond, Sir William (1854–1907). Irish-born Canadian poet who wrote sentimentally about the French Canadian peasant.

du Maurier, George Louis Palmella Busson (1834–1896). British illustrator and caricaturist, du Maurier was the author of *Trilby.* His society pictures in *Punch* were acute commentaries on the Victorian scene.

Durance. The Durance River is one of the principal rivers draining the French slope of the Alps into the Mediterranean.

Egan, Maurice Francis (1852–1924). A prolific writer, Egan was professor of English at Catholic University for twelve years. He was appointed by President Theodore Roosevelt to the position of minister at Copenhagen, where he remained through three administrations until June 1918. His friend Robert Underwood Johnson, an editor of the *Century* and ambassador to Italy, said of Egan that he "had not a drop of provincialism in his veins, but lived with the masters of literature of all nations."

Eggleston, Edward (1837–1902). U.S. author best known for *The Hoosier Schoolmaster.* He was editor of both the *Independent* and *Hearth and Home.*

Evarts, William Maxwell (1818–1901). Secretary of state under President Rutherford B. Hayes and later senator from New York.

Fogazzaro, Antonio (1842–1911). An Italian novelist who became popular after Emma's death in 1895 with the publication of *Piccolo mondo antico.* His works were both idealistic and romantic and at the same time presented minute analyses of psychological problems.

Foote, Mary Hallock (1847–1938). An author and artist, Foote was a frequent contributor to the *Century*, among other magazines. She married engineer Arthur De Wint Foote and lived for many years in California, Idaho, and Colorado, where she wrote a number of novels.

Gautier, Théophile (1811–1872). French poet and novelist, Gautier gained renown as a journalist.

Gilder, Rodman (1878–1953). An author and an editor whose best-known literary work was *The Battery*, which is said to have held up a mirror to a great part of the old city of New York. He wrote a small volume on the Statue of Liberty as well.

Gilder, Rosamond (1891–1986). The second daughter of Richard and Helena Gilder was a founder and president of the International Theater Institute, a worldwide organization with sixty-five national centers. She was a vice-president of the American National Theater Academy and editor in chief and drama critic of *Theater Arts* magazine. In 1948, she was awarded a Tony from the American Theater Wing and in 1964 was admitted to the French Order of Arts and Letters.

Godkin, Edwin Lawrence (1831–1902). Born in Ireland, he came to the United States in 1856. He was founding editor of the *Nation* in 1865. In 1881 he sold the journal to the *New York Evening Post*; at the paper he became editor in chief.

Got, François Jules Edmond (1822–1901). French comedic actor, he first appeared in the *Théâtre Français* in 1844 and became a *sociétaire* in 1850.

Gottheil, Gustav (1827–1903). Reform rabbi, liturgist, and U.S. Zionist leader, Rabbi Gottheil was born in Posen, Germany, and emigrated to the United States in 1873 to become rabbi, in New York, at Temple Emanu-El. He was the most prominent American rabbi to publicly support Zionism during the first Zionist Congress at Basle (1897). Furthermore, he was a founder of the Federation of American Zionists.

Guido da Siena (fl. 1250–1275). An Italian painter, he was the earliest representative of neo-Byzantine art that flourished in Siena in the thirteenth century.

HaLevi, Jehudah, also known as Judah Halevi (before 1075–1141). Spanish Jewish poet and philosopher who wrote of God, Zion, and love. His poems were well known and read in both Arabic and Hebrew in his lifetime, outside of Spain. His philosophy is developed in his single volume, *The Book of Argument and*

Proof in Defense of the Despised Faith, most commonly known as the *Book of the Kuzari.*

Harrison, Constance Cary (1843–1920). Born in Virginia, she married Burton Harrison, secretary to Jefferson Davis during the Civil War. They resided in New York City, where she participated in a variety of community endeavors and wrote novels about New York and the South.

Hathaway, Anne (1556–1623). Anne Hathaway married William Shakespeare at the age of twenty-six; he was said to have been only eighteen. Her cottage in the hamlet of Shottery was likely inherited from her father.

Hay, John (1838–1905). U.S. statesman and author. He was assistant private secretary to Lincoln from 1861 to 1864. Thereafter he was secretary of the U.S. legation at Paris, Vienna, and Madrid. Hay was an editorial assistant at the *New York Tribune* from 1879 to 1881 and was then first assistant secretary of state under William Evarts.

Hoffman, James H. A Jewish communal leader who was president of the Hebrew Technical Institute at the time of Emma Lazarus' death.

Holbein, Hans, the Younger (1497–1543). German painter and designer for printers and craftsmen, he is best known for his portraits and historical scenes.

Holmes, Oliver Wendell (1809–1894). Poet, essayist, and novelist who helped found the *Atlantic Monthly.* Born in Cambridge, Massachusetts, he was friends with Emerson and the Concord crowd and was a member with them of the Saturday Club. Although he trained to be a physician, his practice was limited. On his triumphant visit to England in 1886, he received honorary degrees from Oxford, Cambridge, and Edinburgh. Holmes' son, Oliver Wendell, Jr., would distinguish himself as a U.S. Supreme Court justice.

Holt, Henry (1840–1926). Author and publisher. President of his publishing house, Henry Holt and Company, from 1873 to his death.

Homer, Winslow (1836–1910). A self-taught U.S. painter, he has been regarded as one of the greatest American artists. Prout's Neck on the Maine seacoast, where he was a longtime resident, was the subject of many of his naturalistic seascapes.

Kean, Edmund (1787–1833). One of England's theatrical greats, he was a consummate Shakespearean actor. He appeared in New York for the first time in 1820 during a most successful American tour.

Kelmscott Manor. Located in the Upper Thames Valley, it was the holiday home of William Morris, held in joint tenancy for a time with Dante Gabriel Rossetti.

Kohut, Rabbi Alexander (1842–1894). Rabbi Kohut came to the United States in 1885 to serve as rabbi of Congregation Ahabath Chesed in New York and played a major role in the establishment of the Jewish Theological Society of America, where he taught midrash and talmudic methodology. His great work, the eight-volume *Aruka ha-Shalom*, was a lexicon of talmudic terms called the "greatest and finest specimen of Hebrew learning ever produced by a Jew on this conti-nent."
Rebekah (1864–1951), Kohut's second wife, was an expert in vocational educa-tion and a community leader. She married Rabbi Kohut in 1885 and raised his eight children.

Landor, Walter Savage (1775–1864). British author.

Lathrop, George Parsons (1851–1898). Husband of Rose Hawthorne, Lathrop was associate editor of the *Atlantic Monthly*. He edited the collected works of his father-in-law, Nathaniel Hawthorne.

Liptzin, Solomon (1901–?). A literary scholar and educator who edited the *Jewish Book Annual from 1952 to 1956*. He served as visiting professor at Yeshiva Univer-sity, Tel Aviv University, Haifa Technion, and the American College in Jerusalem.

Lohengrin. The so-called knight of the swan, he is the hero of the German version of this medieval legend. He agrees to marry Elsa, a young princess, but makes her promise never to ask his name or background. Some time later, however, she asks the forbidden question. He returns to the castle Grail, from whence he came.

Lowell, James Russell (1819–1891). U.S. poet, critic, and diplomat who was ambas-sador to England from 1880 to 1885. Prior to that, he served as editor of *Atlantic Monthly* and minister to Spain.

Luini, Bernardino (1475–1532). A Lombardi painter who was known for his reli-gious frescoes.

Maimonides, Moses (1135–1204). Rabbinic authority, codifier, philosopher, royal physician known as the Rambam (acronym from Rabbi Moses Ben Maimon). Born in Spain, he was expelled from that country and settled in Fez. His best-known works are the *Mishnah Torah* and *A Guide of the Perplexed*. He is seen as the most illustrious figure in Judaism in the post-talmudic era and one of the greatest men of all time.

Martineau, Harriet (1802–1876). British social and historical writer who was a propagandist for religious liberalism and the abolition of slavery.

Martineau, James (1805–1900). British Unitarian theologian and philosopher, he emphasized the importance of the individual conscience in determining correct moral and religious action. In addition to his work on Spinoza, Martineau wrote *Types of Ethical Theory, A Study of Religion,* and *The Seat of Authority in Religion.*

Mendelssohn-Bartholdy, Jakob Ludwig Felix (1809–1847). German composer Mendelssohn was the grandson of the great German-Jewish thinker Moses Mendelssohn. A child prodigy, he composed *A Midsummer Night's Dream* at the age of seventeen and one half.

Metcalf, Lorettus Sutton (1837–?). Editor of a variety of weeklies, Metcalf was managing editor of the *North American Review* from 1876 to 1885. He founded and edited the *Forum* from 1886 to 1891.

Mino da Fiesole (1429–1484). Popularly esteemed sculptor, known for his works of the Virgin and Child.

Mitchell, Silas Weir (1829–1914). U.S. physician and author who wrote excellent historical romances and other novels that were psychological character studies.

Modjeska, Helena (1840–1909). Polish-born actress who gave her first performance in English in San Francisco in 1877. She played leading Shakespearean roles.

Moroni, Giambattista (Giovanni Battista) (1525–1578). Italian portrait painter.

Mounet-Sully, Jean (1841–1916). French actor and member of the Comédie Française. Henry James described him as an Adonis of the first magnitude.

National Gallery. First among the permanent art collections in London. It is located in Trafalgar Square. The collection originated in 1824.

O'Reilly, John Boyle (1844–1890). Irish-American politician and journalist who came to the United States in 1869.

Orpheus. Son of Apollo, Orpheus is distraught when his wife, Eurydice, is bitten by a serpent and dies. Orpheus descends into Hades to rescue her and is allowed to return with her as long as she walks behind him and he does not look back. He breaks this condition and Eurydice becomes a ghost once more.

Pexiotto, Benjamin F. (1834–?). A cousin of Emma Lazarus, he was appointed consul to Romania by President Ulysses S. Grant. Due to Pexiotto's efforts, three International Jewish Conferences were organized and the Jewish Question was on the agenda at the Congress of Berlin.

Pinturicchio, Bernardino di Betto di Biagio (1454–1513). Italian painter who decorated the Apartmento Borgi, a suite of six rooms in the Vatican, between 1492 and 1494.

Pitti Palace. A residence of the Medici in Florence, it is the site of one of the city's principal art galleries.

Reynolds, Sir Joshua (1723–1792). English painter, perhaps the dominant figure in British art.

Richards, Bernard Gerson (1877–1971). U.S. journalist, widely active in Jewish affairs, he helped found and was executive director of the American Jewish Congress. At the end of World War I, Richards was a member of the American Jewish delegation to the Versailles Peace Conference and a member of the Zionist Organization of America.

Robert II, King of France (970–1031). Son of Hugh Capet, Robert took for his second wife his cousin, Bertha, in 996. From there, the story differs markedly from Emma's version. Robert, known, ironically, as "The Pious," was excommunicated by the Pope because of this marriage, and was made to endure a seven-year penance. After five years, he renounced Bertha, and married, illegally, yet another time. Nevertheless, his rule over France was without event.

Rossetti, Christina Georgina (1830–1894). Sister of Dante and William Rossetti, she was a well-thought-of poet. In addition, she sat as a model for many of the Pre-Raphaelite artists.

Rossetti, Dante Gabriel (1828–1882). English poet and painter, this Pre-Raphaelite was a pupil of Ford Madox Brown and Holman Hunt. For a brief time, he lived with William Morris at Morris' home, Kelmscott Manor.

Rossetti, William Michael (1829–1919). English author and critic who was a founder of the Pre-Raphaelite Brotherhood and edited its paper, the *Germ*. He was known for his writings on Shelley, Whitman, and Blake.

Rossi, Ernesto (1827–1896). Born in Livorno, Italy, Rossi was admired as a Shakespearean actor. He made his first visit to the United States in 1883.

Ruskin, John (1819–1900). British writer, critic, and artist, acknowledged as the chief arbiter of taste in Victorian England.

Sainte-Beuve, Charles Augustin (1804–1869). Eminent literary critic, he was elected to the French Academy in 1844.

Sand, George (1804–1876). The pseudonym of Amandine Lucile Aurore Dupin, Baronne Dudevant. Sand was a nineteenth-century French author who dressed like a man and led an unorthodox life. She had liaisons with such greats as Alfred de Musset and Frédéric Chopin and was a confidante of the great writers of the age.

Sargent, John Singer (1856–1925). British-American painter, Sargent was a good friend of Henry James and many of Emma Lazarus' friends. His portrait of Mrs. John Stewart (Mrs. Jack) Gardner is among his many works that earned him great esteem.

Schiff, Jacob Henry (1847–1920). German-born U.S. financier and philanthropist, he was a descendant of a distinguished rabbinic family and came to this country at the age of eighteen. Eventually, he became head of Kuhn, Loeb, one of the most powerful investment banking houses in the United States. In that capacity, he was influential in the development of a railroad system in the western states. Although he was a Reform Jew, Schiff supported with generosity virtually every significant Jewish institution, Reform, Conservative, or Orthodox. He made an exception in the case of Zionist organizations, which he strongly opposed.

Signorelli, Luca (1441–1523). A painter of the Umbrian school, Italian artist Signorelli, like the Florentines, concentrated on the human form and painted large scriptural and religious frescoes.

Spencer, Herbert (1820–1903). Eminent British thinker who counted as his friends George Eliot, Thomas Huxley, and John Stuart Mill. It was he who coined the term "survival of the fittest" and published his idea of evolution of biological species before the views of Charles Darwin or Alfred Russel Wallace were made known.

Stedman, Edmund Clarence (1833–1908). A stockbroker most of his life, he was one of the most influential and respected poets and critics in the United States. He was president of the American Copyright League and the National Institute of Arts and Letters.

Stendhal (1783–1842). Pseudonym of Marie Henri Beyle. He was one of the most original and distinguished French essayists and novelists. Among his best-known works is *Le Rouge et le Noir*.

Stewart, Alexander Turney (1803–1876). Department store magnate Stewart came to the United States in 1818 and went on to establish a dry-goods empire, with stores and agencies in this country and Europe. His Manhattan home was said to be the most palatial on this continent. At the time of his death, his estate was estimated at forty to fifty million dollars.

Swinburne, Algernon Charles (1837–1909). Known as much for his magnetic personality as for his poetry, the British poet and critic is said to have revolutionized the entire scheme of English prosody.

Szold, Henrietta (1860–1945). Founder of Hadassah, the world's largest Zionist group, in 1912, Szold pioneered in Americanization work after 1882, helped found The Jewish Publication Society of America in 1888, and served as its general editor, translator of Jewish classics, and writer. She became director of Youth Aliyah in 1933, a worldwide movement that rescued young victims of the Holocaust and rehabilitated them in Palestine.

Tasso, Torquato (1544–1595). Greatest Italian poet of the late Renaissance, he was the author of the epic *Gerusalemme liberata*.

Thompson, Maurice (1844–1901). Although he was a poet, he had a variety of occupations from literary editor of the *Independent* to Indiana's state geologist. In 1867, Thompson explored Lake Okeechobee in Florida, recording the birds, animals, and plants there. He also conducted various ornithological explorations in the wilds of northern Michigan and the hill country of Alabama, Mississippi, and Georgia.

Thornycroft, Sir (William) Hamo (1850–1925). A British sculptor whose style was affected by J. F. Millet's peasant realism and later by August Rodin. He was elected to the Royal Academy in 1880 and was knighted in 1917.

Tintern Abbey. One of the most famous ruins in England, located on the River Wye, the abbey was founded in 1131.

Tintoretto (Jacopo Robusti) (1518–1594). An Italian painter, he is considered one of the greatest Mannerists of Venice and one of the giants of the late Renaissance. He was self-taught, studying Michelangelo and Titiano. A Venetian dyer by occupation, he was known as "Tintoretto," or little dyer.

Uffizi Palace. Located in Florence, it is noted for its art gallery built in 1581 on the top floor of the palace in the promenade galleria style.

Van Dyck, Sir Anthony (1599–1641). After Rubens, Van Dyck is said to have been the most prominent Flemish painter of the seventeenth century. He was a prolific painter of portraits, of which about 500 are extant.

Velásquez, Diego Rodríguez de Silvay (1599–1660). Seen as Spain's most important artist, he was court painter to King Philip IV and produced numerous portraits of the various members of the royal family. He was influenced by, among others, Titian and Caravaggio.

Warner, Charles Dudley (1829–1900). U.S. essayist and novelist who collaborated with Mark Twain in writing *The Gilded Age* (1873).

Watts, George Frederic (1817–1904). British painter and sculptor who was married for a short time to actress Ellen Terry. Watts was elected to the Royal Academy in 1867. He was a sculptor and a painter.

Wells, Charles Jeremiah (1798?–1879). Under the pseudonym H. L. Howard, Wells published his play *Joseph and His Brothers,* which was forgotten until Dante Gabriel Rossetti rediscovered it. Rossetti and others saw it as a "rite of initiation into the true poetic culture." Swinburne wrote a review of the poem in 1875, which led to the drama's reprint in 1876.

Whittier, John Greenleaf (1807–1892). U.S. poet and abolitionist.

Wilson, James Grant (1832–1914). Born in Edinburgh, Scotland, Wilson founded and was editor of the *Chicago Record,* a journal of literature and the arts. He served in the Civil War in the Fourth U.S. Colored Cavalry. He headed various organizations, among them the American Authors' Guild and the American Ethnological Society, and was vice-president of the American Society for the Prevention of Cruelty to Animals. He published the works of American poet Fitz-Greene Halleck and wrote a variety of literary and political biographies.

Woodberry, George Edward (1855–1930). Born in Beverly, Massachusetts, he was a prolific author of literary biography and history. He edited multivolume works of Shelley, Bacon, and others. Woodberry was a Fellow of the American Academy of Arts and Sciences and the American Academy of Arts and Letters, and was an Honorary Fellow of the Royal Society of Literature.

Bibliography

Adams, Henry. *The Education of Henry Adams.* Cambridge, Mass.: Riverside Press, 1961.

Adams, Steven. *The Art of the Pre-Raphaelites.* A Quintet Book. Secaucus, N.J.: Chartwell Books, 1988.

Allen, Gay Wilson. *Waldo Emerson.* New York: Viking Press, 1981.

Altick, Richard D. *Lives and Letters: A History of Literary Biography in England and America.* New York: Alfred A. Knopf, 1965.

Amicis, Edmondo de. *Holland.* 2 vols. Philadelphia: Porter and Coates, 1894.

Angoff, Charles. *Emma Lazarus: Poet, Jewish Activist, Pioneer Zionist.* Publications of the Jewish Historical Society of New York, no. 3. New York, 1979.

Aris, Stephen. *But There Are No Jews in England.* New York: Stein and Day, 1971.

Aslin, Elizabeth. *The Aesthetic Movement: Prelude to Art Nouveau.* New York: Excalibur Books, 1981.

Auerbach, Nina. *Ellen Terry: Player in Her Time.* New York: W. W. Norton, 1987.

Baker, Paul R. *Stanny: The Gilded Life of Stanford White.* New York: Macmillan, 1989.

Baldwin, Charles C. *Stanford White.* New York: Da Capo Press, 1976.

Banning, Evelyn. *Helen Hunt Jackson.* New York: Vanguard Press, 1973.

Banta, Martha. *Imaging American Women: Ideas and Ideals in Cultural History.* New York: Columbia University Press, 1987.

Barber, Gertrude A., comp. *Marriages Taken from the New York Evening Post from July 16, 1874 to September 11, 1879.* Vol. 21.

Barrus, Clara. *The Life and Letters of John Burroughs.* Port Washington, N.Y.: Kennikat Press, 1956.

———, ed. *The Heart of Burroughs' Journals.* Port Washington, N.Y.: Kennikat Press, 1956.

Baum, Charlotte, Paula Hyman, and Sonya Michel. *The Jewish Woman in America.* New York: Dial Press, 1976.

Baym, Max I. "Emma Lazarus and Emerson." *Publications of the American Jewish Historical Society* 38 (1949): 261–87.

———. "Emma Lazarus' Approach to Renan in Her Essay 'Renan and the Jews.'" *Publications of the American Jewish Historical Society* 37 (1947): 17–29.

Bell, James B., and Richard L. Adams. *In Search of Liberty: The Story of the Statue of Liberty and Ellis Island.* Garden City, N.Y.: Doubleday, 1984.

Bell, Millicent. *Edith Wharton and Henry James: The Story of Their Friendship.* New York: George Braziller, 1965.

Bender, Thomas. *New York Intellect: A History of Intellectual Life in New York City, from 1750 to the Beginnings of Our Own Time.* New York: Alfred A. Knopf, 1987.

Benét, William Rose, ed. *The Reader's Encyclopaedia: An Encyclopaedia of World Literature and the Arts.* New York: Thomas Y. Crowell, 1948.

Bergmann, Frank. *Robert Grant.* Boston: Twayne, 1982.

Bermant, Chaim. *The Cousinhood.* New York: Macmillan, 1972.

Bernstein, Iver. *The New York Draft Riots: Their Significance for American Society and Politics in the Age of the Civil War.* New York: Oxford University Press, 1990.

Bingham, Madeline. *Henry Irving: The Great Victorian Actor.* New York: Stein and Day, 1978.

Birmingham, Stephen. *The Grandees: America's Sephardic Elite.* New York: Harper and Row, 1971.

———. *"Our Crowd": The Great Jewish Families of New York.* New York: Harper and Row, 1967.

Black, Mary. *Old New York in Early Photographs, 1853–1901.* 2d rev. ed. New York: Dover Publications, 1973.

Blanchard, Paula. *Margaret Fuller: From Transcendentalism to Revolution.* Radcliffe Biography Series. A Merloyd Lawrence Book. New York: Delacorte Press, Seymour Lawrence, 1978.

Blum, Stella, ed. *Victorian Fashions and Costumes from Harper's Bazaar, 1867–1898.* New York: Dover Publications, 1974.

Bowen, Catherine Drinker. *Adventures of a Biographer.* An Atlantic Monthly Press Book. Boston: Little, Brown, 1959.

———. *"Free Artist": The Story of Anton and Nicholas Rubinstein.* New York: Random House, 1939.

Boyer, M. Christine. *Manhattan Manners: Architecture and Style, 1850–1900.* New York: Rizzoli, 1985.

Boyer, Richard, and Herbert M. Morais. *Labor's Untold Story.* 3d ed. New York: United Electrical Radio and Machine Workers of America, 1971.

Bradford, Nancy Margetto. *Costume in Detail: Women's Dress, 1730–1930.* 1st American ed., Boston: Plays, 1968.

Bradley, Ian. *William Morris and His World.* New York: Charles Scribner's Sons, 1978.

Brandes, Georg. *Beaconsfield: A Study*. New York: Charles Scribner's Sons, 1880.

Brooks, Van Wyck. *New England Indian Summer, 1865–1915*. New York: E. P. Dutton, 1940.

———. *The Times of Melville and Whitman*. New York: E. P. Dutton, 1947.

Brown, Arthur W. *Margaret Fuller*. New York: Twayne, 1964.

Brown, Henry Collins. *Brownstone Fronts and Saratoga Trunks*. New York: E. P. Dutton, 1935.

———, ed. *Valentine's Manual of Old New York: New York in the Elegant Eighties*. Hastings-on-Hudson: 1922.

Browning, Robert. *The Poems and Plays of Robert Browning*. New York: Modern Library, 1934.

———. *Robert Browning's Complete Works*. 1898. Vol. 10. New York: Fred DeFau, 1910.

Burke, Doreen Bolger, et al. *In Pursuit of Beauty: Americans and the Aesthetic Movement*. New York: Metropolitan Museum of Art and Rizzoli, 1987.

Burt, Nathaniel. *The Perennial Philadelphians: The Anatomy of an American Aristocracy*. Boston: Little, Brown, 1963.

Burton, Katherine. *Sorrow Built a Bridge: A Daughter of Hawthorne*. London: Longmans, Green, 1939.

Callow, Philip. *From Noon to Starry Night: A Life of Walt Whitman*. Chicago: Ivan R. Dee, 1992.

Cameron, Kenneth Walter. *Transcendental Log: Fresh Discoveries in Newspapers Concerning Emerson, Thoreau, Alcott and Others of the American Literary Renaissance Arranged Annually for a Half Century from 1832*. Hartford: Transcendental Books, 1973.

Campbell, Ian. *Thomas Carlyle*. New York: Charles Scribner's Sons, 1974.

Carter, Morris. *Isabella Stewart Gardner and Fenway Court*. Boston: Houghton Mifflin, Riverside Press, 1925.

Caskey, Willie Malvin. *Secession and Restoration of Louisiana*. Baton Rouge: Louisiana State University Press, 1938.

Century Book Committee. *The Century, 1847–1946*. New York: Century Association, 1947.

Charteris, The Hon. Evan, K.C. *John Sargent*. 1927. Reprint. Detroit: Tower Books, 1971.

Cheskin, Arnold. "Robert Browning's Climactic Hebraic Connection with Emma Lazarus and Emily Harris." *Studies in Browning and His Circle* 10:2 (Fall 1982): 9–22.

Chifferfield, Faith. *In Quest of Love: The Life and Death of Margaret Fuller*. New York: Coward-McCann, 1957.

Christman, Henry M., ed. *One Hundred Years of "The Nation": A Centennial Anthology*. New York: Macmillan, 1965.

Churchill, Allen. *The Splendor Seekers*. New York: Grosset and Dunlap, 1974.

Clark, Harry H., ed. *Transitions in American Literature*. Durham, N.C.: Duke University Press, 1953.

Clemens, Clara. *My Father, Mark Twain*. New York: Harper and Brothers, 1931.

Cochran, Thomas, and William Miller, eds. *The Age of Enterprise: A Social History of Industrial America*. Rev. ed. New York: Harper Torchbooks, 1961.

Cockshut, A. O. J. *Truth to Life: The Art of Biography in the Nineteenth Century*. New York: Harcourt Brace Jovanovich, 1974.

Cohen, Mary M. "Emma Lazarus: Woman; Poet; Patriot." *Poet Lore* 6, 7 (1893): 320–331.

Cohen, Naomi W. *Encounter with Emancipation: The German Jews in the United States, 1830–1914*. Philadelphia: Jewish Publication Society of America, 1984.

Coleman, Marian Moore. *Fair Rosalind: The American Career of Helena Modjeska*. Cheshire, Conn.: Cherry Hill Books, 1969.

Collins, J. A. *Women Artists in America: 18th Century to the Present*. Chattanooga: University of Tennessee, 1973.

Comay, Joan. *Who's Who in Jewish History after the Period of the Old Testament*. New York: David McKay, 1974.

Cowen, Philip. *Memories of an American Jew*. New York: International Press, 1932.

Daly, Gay. *Pre-Raphaelites in Love*. Boston: Ticknor and Fields, 1989.

Damrosch, Walter Johannes. *My Musical Life*. New York: Charles Scribner's Sons, 1924.

Day, Martin S. *History of American Literature*. vol. 1, *From the Beginning to 1910*. Doubleday College Course Guide. Garden City, Doubleday, 1970.

Deiss, Joseph Jay. *The Roman Years of Margaret Fuller: A Biography*. New York: Thomas Y. Crowell, 1969.

deKay, Charles. *Hesperus and Other Poems*. New York: Charles Scribner's Sons, 1880.

———. "Sybil Judaica," *American Hebrew*. 8 February, 1889: 4–5.

deSola Pool, David and Tamar deSola Pool. *An Old Faith in a New World: Portrait of Shearith Israel, 1654–1954*. New York: Columbia University Press, 1955.

Dickason, David Howard. *The Daring Young Men: The Story of the American Pre-Raphaelites*. Bloomington: Indiana University Press, 1953.

Doughty, Oswald. *Dante Gabriel Rossetti: A Victorian Romantic*. New Haven: Yale University Press, 1949.

Dowden, Edward. *The Life of Percy Bysshe Shelley*. New York: Barnes and Noble, 1966.

Draper, John William, M.D., L.L.D. *History of the Conflict Between Religion and Science*. New York: D. Appleton, 1902.

Eby, Cecil D. "America as 'Asylum': A Dual Image." *American Quarterly*. 14 (1962): 483.

Edel, Leon. *Henry James: A Life*. New York: Harper and Row, 1985.

———. *Henry James: The Conquest of London, 1870–1881*. Philadelphia, J. B. Lippincott, 1962.

————. *Henry James: The Middle Years, 1882–1895.* Philadelphia: J. B. Lippincott, 1962.

Edminston, Susan, and Linda D. Corino. *Literary New York.* Boston: Houghton Mifflin, 1976.

Edwards, J. R. *British History: 1815–1939.* New York: Humanities Press, 1970.

Egan, Maurice Francis. *Recollections of a Happy Life.* New York: George H. Doran, 1924.

Elbogen, Ismar. *A Century of Jewish Life.* Translated by Moses Hadas. Philadelphia: Jewish Publication Society of America, 1966.

Eliot, George. *Daniel Deronda.* Edited by Barbara Hardy. New York: Penguin Books, 1983.

————. *Felix Holt, the Radical.* Middlesex, England: Penguin English Library, 1980.

————. *The Works of George Eliot: Adam Bede, Theophrastus Such, Essays.* New York: Thomas Y. Crowell, n.d.

Elliot, Maud Howe. *This Was My Newport.* Cambridge, Mass.: Mythology Co.; A. Marshall Jones, 1944.

Ellmann, Richard. *Oscar Wilde.* New York: Vintage Books, 1988.

Ellsworth, William Webster. *A Golden Age of Authors: A Publisher's Recollection.* Boston: Houghton Mifflin, Riverside Press, 1919.

Emerson, Edward Waldo. *The Early Years of the Saturday Club, 1855–1870.* Boston: Houghton Mifflin, 1918.

Emerson, Ralph Waldo. "Ralph Waldo Emerson's Impressions of Carlyle in 1848." *Scribner's* 22 (May 1881): 89–92.

Ervine, St. John. *Bernard Shaw: His Life, Work and Friends.* New York: William Morrow, 1956.

Feinstein, Marnin. *American Zionism: 1884–1904.* New York: Herzl Press, 1965.

Fido, Martin. *Oscar Wilde.* Leicester, England: Gallery Press, 1988.

Fleming, Gordon. *James Abbott McNeill Whistler: A Life.* New York: St. Martin's Press, 1991.

Foner, Eric. *Reconstruction: America's Unfinished Revolution, 1863–1877.* Perennial Library. New York: Harper and Row, 1989.

Foner, Philip S. *Business and Slavery: The New York Merchants and the Irrepressible Conflict.* New York: Russell and Russell, 1968.

Forbes, S. Russell. *Rambles in Rome.* London: Nelson and Sons, 1882.

Ford, Worthington Chauncey, ed. *Letters of Henry Adams, 1858–1891.* Boston: Mifflin, 1930.

Frances, Whiting Halsey, ed. *Women Authors in Their Homes.* New York: James Pott, 1903.

Frank, Murray. "Emma Lazarus: 100 Years Later." *Jewish Advocate,* 22 September 1949, pp. 8A–9.

Franklin, John Hope. *A Southern Odyssey: Travels in the Antebellum North.* Baton Rouge: Louisiana State University Press, 1976.

Friedenthal, Richard. *Goethe: His Life and Times.* Cleveland: World, 1963.

Friedman, Murray, ed. *Jewish Life in Philadelphia: 1830–1840.* Philadelphia: Institute for the Study of Human Issues, 1983.

Fromentin, Eugene. *The Masters of Past Time: Dutch and Flemish Art from Van Eyck to Rembrandt.* Edited by H. Gerson. A Phaidon Book. Ithaca, N.Y.: Cornell University Press, 1981.

Furnas, J. C. *Fanny Kemble: Leading Lady of the Nineteenth-Century Stage.* New York: Dial Press, 1982.

Gardner, Ralph D. *Horatio Alger or the American Hero Era.* New York: Arco, 1978.

Garraty, John A. *The New Commonwealth: 1877–1890.* The New American Nation Series. New York: Harper Torchbooks, 1968.

Gay, Peter. *The Bourgeois Experience: Victoria to Freud.* Vol. 2, *The Tender Passion.* New York: Oxford University Press, 1986.

Geismar, Maxwell. *Henry James and the Jacobites.* Boston: Houghton Mifflin, Riverside Press, 1963.

George, Henry, Jr. *Henry George.* American Men and Women of Letters Series. General Editor, Daniel Aaron. New York: Chelsea House, 1981.

Gilchrist, Herbert, ed. *Anne Gilchrist: The Life and Writings.* London: T. Fisher Unwin, 1887.

Gilder, Rodman. *Statue of Liberty Enlightening the World.* New York: New York Trust Co., 1943.

Gilder, Rosamond, ed. *Letters of Richard Watson Gilder.* Boston: Houghton Mifflin, Riverside Press, 1916.

Ginger, Ray. *The Age of Excess: The United States from 1877 to 1914.* 2d ed. New York: Macmillan, 1975.

Glasrud, Clarence A. *Hjalmar Hjorth Boyesen.* Authors Series, vol. 1. Northfield, Minn.: Norwegian-American Historical Association, 1963.

Gohdes, Clarence, and Paulli Franklin Baum, eds. *Letters of William Michael Rossetti Concerning Whitman, Blake and Shelley to Anne Gilchrist and Her Son Herbert Gilchrist.* New York: AMS Press, 1968.

Gold, Arthur, and Robert Fizdale. *The Divine Sarah: A Life of Sarah Bernhardt.* New York: Alfred A. Knopf, 1991.

Gottheil, Richard. *The Life of Gustav Gottheil: Memoirs of a Priest in Israel.* Williamsport, Pa.: Bayard Press, 1936.

Grafton, John. *New York in the Nineteenth Century: 321 Engravings from "Harper's Weekly" and Other Contemporary Sources.* New York: Dover Publications, 1977.

Grant, Robert. *The Confessions of a Frivolous Girl: A Story of a Fashionable Life.* Boston: A. Williams, 1880.

Gregg, Edith E. W., ed. *The Letters of Ellen Tucker Emerson.* 2 vols. Kent, Ohio: Kent State University Press, 1982.

Grinstein, Hyman B. *The Rise of the Jewish Community of New York: 1654–1860.* Philadelphia: Jewish Publication Society of America, 1945.

Haight, Gordon S. *George Eliot: A Biography.* New York: Oxford University Press, 1968.

Halleck, Reuben Post. *History of American Literature.* New York: American Books, 1911.

Handlin, Oscar, et al. *The Statue of Liberty.* New York: Newsweek, 1971.

Harap, Louis. *The Image of the Jew in American Literature: From Early Republic to Mass Immigration.* Philadelphia: Jewish Publication Society of America, 1974.

Harrison, Constance Cary. *The Merry Maid of Arcady, His Lordship and Other Stories.* Boston: Lamson, Wolfe, 1897.

———. *Recollections Grave and Gay.* New York: Charles Scribner's Sons, 1911.

Hart, James D. *The Popular Book: A History of America's Literary Taste.* Berkeley and Los Angeles: University of California Press, 1961.

Hartmann, Sadakichi. *A History of American Art.* 2 vols. London: Hutchinson, 1903.

Heine, Heinrich. *Poems and Ballads of Heinrich Heine.* Translated with an introduction by Emma Lazarus. New York: Hurst, 1881.

Hellerstein, Erna Olafson, Leslie Parker Hume, and Karen M. Offen, eds. *Victorian Women: A Documentary Account of Women's Lives in Nineteenth-Century England, France, and the United States.* Stanford: Stanford University Press, 1981.

Hemstreet, Charles. *Literary New York: Its Landmarks and Associations.* New York: G. P. Putnam's Sons; Knickerbocker Press, 1903.

Henderson, Mary C. *The City and The Theatre: New York Playhouses from Bowling Green to Times Square.* Clifton, N.J.: James T. White, 1973.

Hershkowitz, Leo. *Tweed's New York: Another Look.* Garden City, N.Y.: Doubleday Anchor, 1977.

Higginson, Mary Thackery, ed. *Letters and Journals of Thomas Wentworth Higginson.* New York: DeLapo Press, 1969.

Higham, John. *Send These to Me: Jews and Other Immigrants in Urban America.* New York: Atheneum, 1975.

Hilton, Timothy. *The Pre-Raphaelites.* New York: Harry N. Abrams, 1970.

Himmelfarb, Gertrude. *Victorian Minds.* New York: Alfred A. Knopf, 1968.

Hobbs, Susan. "Thomas Wilmer Dewing: The Early Years, 1851–1885." *American Art Journal* 13 (Spring 1981): 5–35.

———. "Thomas Dewing in Cornish, 1885–1905." *American Art Journal.* (Spring 1985): 3–32.

Honan, Park. *Matthew Arnold: A Life.* New York: McGraw-Hill, 1981.

Howe, Winifred E. *A History of the Metropolitan Museum of Art.* New York: Arno Press, 1974.

Howells, William Dean. *A Hazard of New Fortunes.* New York: E. P. Dutton, 1952.

———. *Literary Friends and Acquaintances: A Personal Retrospective of American Authorship.* New York: Harper and Brothers, 1902.

Hunt, John Dixon. *The Wider Sea: A Life of John Ruskin.* New York: Viking Press, 1982.

Hyde, H. Montgomery. *Oscar Wilde: A Biography*. New York: Farrar, Straus and Giroux, 1975.

Inauguration of the Statue of Liberty Enlightening the World by the President of the United States, October 28, 1886. Issued under the authority of the committee. New York: D. Appleton, 1887.

Irving, William, and Park Honan. *The Book, the Ring and the Poet*. New York: McGraw-Hill, 1974.

Jacob, Heinrich E. *The World of Emma Lazarus*. New York: Schocken Books, 1949.

James, Edward T., Editor. Notable American Women, 1607–1950. 3v. Cambridge, Massachusetts: The Belknap Press, Harvard University Press, 1971.

James, Henry. *The Letters of Henry James*. Vol. 1, *1843–1878*. Edited by Leon Edel. Cambridge, Mass.: Belknap Press, 1974.

———. *The Letters of Henry James*. Vol. 3, *1883–1895*. Cambridge, Mass.: Belknap Press, 1980.

———. *Literary Reviews and Essays on American, English and French Literature*. Edited by Albert Mordell. New York: Grove Press, 1975. 1st Black Cat ed., 1979.

———. *The Scenic Art: Notes on Acting and the Drama, 1872–1901*. Edited by Allan Wade. New Brunswick, N.J.: Rutgers University Press, 1948.

James, Robert Rhodes. *The British Revolution: 1880–1939*. New York: Alfred A. Knopf, 1977.

John, Arthur. *The Best Years of the Century: Richard Watson Gilder, Scribner's Monthly and Century Magazine, 1870–1909*. Urbana: University of Illinois Press, 1981.

Johnson, Lee Ann. *Mary Hallock Foote*. Boston: Twayne, 1980.

Jones, Howard Mumford. *The Age of Energy: Varieties of American Experience, 1865–1915*. New York: Viking Press, 1971.

———. *History and the Contemporary: Essays in Nineteenth-Century Literature*. Madison: University of Wisconsin Press, 1964.

Kane, Harnett T. *Deep Delta Country*. Edited by Erskine Caldwell. New York: Duell, Sloan and Pearce, 1944.

Kaplan, Fred. *Thomas Carlyle: A Biography*. Ithaca, N.Y.: Cornell University Press, 1983.

Kaplan, Justin. *Walt Whitman: A Life*. New York: Simon and Schuster, 1980.

Karp, Abraham. *From Haven to Home: A History of the Jews in America*. New York: Schocken Books, 1984.

Karp, Deborah. *Heroes of American Jewish History*. New York: KTAV and Anti-Defamation League of B'nai B'rith, 1972.

Kasson, John F. *Rudeness and Civility: Manners in Nineteenth Century America*. New York: Hill and Wang, 1990.

Kavaler, Lucy. *The Astors: A Family Chronicle of Pomp and Power*. New York: Dodd, Mead, 1966.

Kelley, Elizabeth Burroughs. *John Burroughs: The Story of His Work and Family, by His Granddaughter*. New York: Exposition Press, 1959.

Kessner, Carole S. "From Parnassus to Mount Zion: The Journey of Emma Lazarus, on the Centenary of Her Death." *Jewish Book Annual* 7 (1987): 141–162.

Kobler, Dora. *Leo Pinsker and Emma Lazarus*. London: WIZO World Youth Center, 1943.

Korn, Bertram. *American Jewry and the Civil War*. New York: Schocken Books, 1949.

Kouwenhoven, John A. *The Columbia Historical Portrait of New York: An Essay in Graphic History*. 2d ed. New York: Harper and Row, 1972.

Kramer, Aaron. "The Link Between Heinrich Heine and Emma Lazarus." *Publications of the American Jewish Historical Society* 155 (1957): 248–57.

Kunitz, Stanley J., and Howard Haycraft, eds. *American Authors, 1600–1900: A Biographical Dictionary of American Literature*. New York: H. W. Wilson, 1938.

LaFarge, John. *The Manner is Ordinary*. New York: Harcourt, Brace, 1954.

Landgren, Marchel E. *Years of Art: The Story of the Art Students League of New York*. New York: Robert M. McBride, 1940.

Lazarus, Emma. *Admetus and Other Poems*. 1871. Reprint. Upper Saddle River, N.Y.: Literature House, Gregg Press, 1970.

———. *Alide: An Episode of Goethe's Life*. Philadelphia: J. B. Lippincott, 1874.

———. "American Literature." *Critic* 1 (June 1881): 164.

———. "Browning's 'Dramatic Idyls.' " (Second Series). *Scribner's* 20 (November 1880): 158–159.

———. "By the Waters of Babylon: Little Poems in Prose." *Century* 33 (March 1887): 801–3.

———. "A Day in Surrey with William Morris." *Century* 34 (July 1886): 388–97.

———. "The Death of Rashi." *Independent*, 8 April 1880, p. 27.

———. "Don Pedrillo." *Jewish Messenger*, 18 February 1876, p. 1.

———. "The Eleventh Hour." *Scribner's* 16 (June 1878): 252–56.

———. "Emerson's Personality." *Century* 24 (February 1883): 454–455.

———. *An Epistle to the Hebrews*. Edited by Morris U. Schappes. New York: Jewish Historical Society of New York, 1987. First published in 1900 by the Federation of American Zionists.

———. "Eugene Fromentin." *Critic* 1 (December 1881): 364–65.

———. "Fra Pedro." *Jewish Messenger*, 18 February 1876, p. 1.

———. "The Jewish Problem." *Century* 25 (February 1883): 602–11.

———. *Poems and Translations, Written Between the Ages of Fourteen and Sixteen*. Boston: Printed for Private Circulation, 1866.

———. *The Poems of Emma Lazarus*. 2 vols. Boston: Houghton Mifflin, 1889.

———. "The Poet Heine." *Century* 29 (December 1884): 210–17.

———. "Rashi in Prague." *Independent*, 25 March 1880, pp. 27–28.

———. "Regnault as a Writer." *Critic* 1 (February 1881): 37.

———. "Russian Christianity versus Modern Judaism." *Century* 24 (May 1882): 48–56.

————. "Salvini's King Lear." *Century* 26 (May 1883): 89–91.

————. "The Schiff Refuge." *American Hebrew.* 20 October 1882, p. 114.

————. "Sic Semper Liberatoribus: May 13, 1881." *Scribner's* 22 (June, 1882): 178.

————. *Songs of a Semite: The Dance to the Death and Other Poems.* New York: The American Hebrew, 1882.

————. "Tommaso Salvini." *Century* 23 (November 1881): 110–17.

————. "To R.W.E." *Critic* 5 (2 August 1884): 5–6.

————. "Was the Earl of Beaconsfield a Representative Jew?" *Century* 23 (April 1882): 939–42.

[Lazarus, Josephine.] "Emma Lazarus." *Century* 36 (October 1888): 875–84. Reprinted in *The Poems of Emma Lazarus.* Boston: Houghton Mifflin, 1889.

Lears, T. Jackson. *No Place of Grace: Anti-Modernism and the Transformation of American Culture, 1880–1920.* New York: Pantheon Books, 1981.

Lebeson, Anita Libman. *Recall to Life: Jewish Women in American History.* New York: Thomas Yoseloff, 1970.

Lee, Samuel J. *Moses of the New World: The Work of Baron de Hirsch.* New York: Thomas Yoseloff, 1970.

Lens, Sidney. *Radicalism in America: Great Rebels and the Causes for Which They Fought from 1620 to the Present.* New updated ed. New York: Thomas Y. Crowell, 1969.

Lesser, Allen. "Emma Lazarus, Poet and Zionist Pioneer." *Menorah Journal* 26 (April–June 1938): 212–26.

Lewis, R. W. B. *Edith Wharton.* New York: Harper and Row, 1975.

————. *The Jameses: A Family Narrative.* New York: Farrar, Straus and Giroux, 1991.

Lightfoot, Frederick S., ed. *Nineteenth Century New York in Rare Photographic Views.* New York: Dover Publications, 1981.

Liptzin, Solomon. *Generation of Decision: Jewish Rejuvenation in America.* New York: Bloch, 1958.

————. *The Jew in American Literature.* New York: Bloch, 1966.

Lockwood, Charles. *Manhattan Moves Uptown: An Illustrated History.* Boston: Houghton Mifflin, 1976.

Lyons, Joseph. "In Two Divided Streams." *Midstream* (Autumn 1961): 78–85.

McAllen, John. *Ralph Waldo Emerson: Days of Encounter.* Boston: Little, Brown, 1984.

McCrary, Peyton. *Abraham Lincoln and Reconstruction: The Louisiana Experiment.* Princeton, N.J.: Princeton University Press, 1978.

McGill, Frederick T., Jr. *W. E. Channing of Concord: A Life of William Ellery Channing II.* New Brunswick, N.J.: Rutgers University Press, 1967.

McHenry, Robert, Ed. *Liberty's Women.* Springfield, Massachusetts: Merriam, 1980.

McKay, Ernest A. *The Civil War and New York City.* Syracuse, N.Y.: Syracuse University Press, 1990.

'Mann-a-hatin': The Story of New York. New York: Manhattan Co., 1929.

Manners, Ande. Poor Cousins. Greenwich, Conn.: Fawcett Crest, 1972.

Manvell, Roger. Ellen Terry. New York: G. P. Putnam's Sons, 1968.

Marcus, Jacob. The American Jewish Woman: A Documentary History. New York: KTAV; Cincinnati: American Jewish Archives, 1981.

———. The American Jewish Woman: 1654–1980. New York: KTAV; Cincinnati: American Jewish Archives, 1981.

Markens, Isaac. The Hebrews in America: A Series of Historical and Biographical Sketches. New York: Published by the Author, 1888. Reprint. New York: Arno Press, 1975.

Marsh, Jan. The Pre-Raphaelite Sisterhood. New York: St. Martin's Press, 1985.

———. Pre-Raphaelite Women: Images of Femininity. New York: Harmony Books, 1987.

Martin, George. The Damrosch Dynasty, America's First Family of Music. Boston: Houghton Mifflin, 1983.

Marx, Leo. The Machine in the Garden: Technology and the Pastoral Ideal in America. New York: Oxford University Press, 1967.

Mellquist, Jerome. The Emergence of an American Art. New York: Charles Scribner's Sons, 1942.

Mendes, H. Pereira. "Miss Lazarus and the Restoration of the Jews." Jewish Messenger, 9 February 1883, p. 5.

Meredith, Michael, ed. More Than Friend: The Letters of Robert Browning to Katherine deKay Bronson. Houston: Armstrong Baylor Library, Baylor University; Winfield, Kansas: Wedgewood Press, 1985.

Merriam, Eve. Emma Lazarus: Woman with a Torch. New York: Citadel Press, 1956.

———. The Voice of Liberty: The Story of Emma Lazarus. Philadelphia: Jewish Publication Society of America, 1962.

Meyer, Isidore S., ed. Early History of Zionism in America. New York: American Jewish Historical Society and Theodor Herzl Foundation, 1958.

"Miss Lazarus' Life and Literary Work." Critic 11 (10 December 1887): 293–95.

Modder, Montagu Frank. The Jew in the Literature of England. Philadelphia: Jewish Publication Society of America, 1960.

Montefiore, Claude. "Is Judaism a Tribal Religion?" Contemporary Review 62 (September 1882): 361–82.

Moody, V. Alton. "Slavery on Louisiana Sugar Plantations." Ph.D. diss., University of Michigan. Reprinted from Louisiana Historical Quarterly (April 1924).

Moore, Rayburn S. Constance Fenimore Woolson. New York: Twayne, 1963.

———, ed. Selected Letters of Henry James to Edmund Gosse, 1882–1915: A Literary Friendship. Baton Rouge: Louisiana State University Press, 1988.

Morais, Henry Samuel. Eminent Israelites of the Nineteenth Century: A Series of Biographical Sketches. Philadelphia: Edward Stern, 1880.

———. The Jews of Philadelphia: Their History from the Earliest Settlements to the Present Time. Philadelphia: Levy Type Co., 1894.

Mordell, Albert. "The 100th Birthday of Emma Lazarus: July 22, 1849–November 19, 1887." *Jewish Book Annual* 7 (1949): 79–88.

———. "Some Final Words on Emma Lazarus." *Publications of the American Jewish Historical Society* 39 (1950): 321–27.

———. "Some Neglected Phases of Emma Lazarus' Genius." *Jewish Forum* 32 (October 1949): 181–82, 187.

Morley, Sheridan. *Oscar Wilde*. New York: Holt, Rinehart and Winston, 1976.

Morris, Lloyd. *Incredible New York: High Life and Low Life of the Last Hundred Years*. New York: Random House, 1951.

Mott, Frank Luther. *A History of American Magazines*. Vol. 8, *1865–1885*. Cambridge: Harvard University Press, 1938.

Mushkat, Jerome. *Tammany: The Evolution of a Political Machine*. A New York State Study. Syracuse, N.Y.: Syracuse University Press, 1971.

Nadal, E. S. *A Virginian Village and Other Papers Together with Some Autobiographical Notes*. New York: Macmillan, 1917.

Nevins, Allan. *Grover Cleveland: A Study in Courage*. New York: Dodd, Mead, 1966.

O'Connor, Harvey. *The Astors*. New York: Alfred A. Knopf, 1941.

Oliphant, Laurence. Communication. *American Hebrew,* 16 March 1883, pp. 50–51.

———. "The Jews and the Eastern Question." *Nineteenth Century* 12 (August 1882): 242–55.

Olson, Stanley. *John Singer Sargent: His Portrait*. New York: St. Martin's Press, 1986.

O'Neill, Edward Hayes. *A History of American Biography: 1800–1955*. A Perpetua Book. New York: A. S. Barnes, 1961.

Ostrander, Gilman M. *American Civilization in the First Machine Age: A Cultural History of America's First Age of Technological Revolution and "Rule" by the Young*. New York: Harper and Row, 1970.

O'Toole, Patricia. *The Five of Hearts: An Intimate Portrait of Henry Adams and His Friends, 1880–1918*. New York: Clarkson Potter, 1990.

"The Outrages in Russia." *Century* 23 (April 1882): 949.

Packer, Lona Mosk. *Christina Rossetti*. Berkeley and Los Angeles: University of California Press, 1963.

Parker, Gail, ed. *The Oven Birds: American Women on Womanhood, 1820–1920*. Garden City, N.Y.: Doubleday Anchor, 1972.

Parrington, Vernon Louis. *Main Currents in American Thought: An Interpretation of American Literature from the Beginnings to 1820*. New York: Harcourt, Brace and World, 1958.

Parry, Albert. *Garrets and Pretenders: A History of Bohemianism in America*. Rev. ed. New York: Dover Publications, 1964.

Patterson, Henry E. *The City of New York: A History Illustrated from the Collection of the Museum of the City of New York*. New York: Harry N. Abrams, 1978.

Pauli, Herti, and E. B. Ashton. *I Lift My Lamp: The Way of a Symbol*. New York: Appleton-Century-Crofts, 1948.

Payne, Darwin. *Owen Wister: Chronicler of the West, Gentleman of the East*. Dallas: Southern Methodist University Press, 1985.

Pessin, Deborah. *History of the Jews in America*. New York: United Synagogue Commission on Jewish Education, 1957.

"A Problematic Champion." *Jewish Messenger*, 26 January 1883, p. 4.

Ragozin, Zenaide. "Russian Jews and Gentiles, From a Russian Point of View." *Century* 23 (April 1882): 905–20.

Redinger, Ruby V. *George Eliot: The Emergent Self*. New York: Alfred A. Knopf, 1975.

Review of *Poems and Ballads of Heinrich Heine*. *Century* 23 (March 1882): 785–786.

"Riding an Oliphant." *Jewish Messenger*, 9 February 1883, p. 4.

Rischin, Moses. *The Promised City*. Cambridge: Harvard University Press, 1962.

Roland, Charles P. *Louisiana Sugar Plantations During the Civil War*. Leiden, Netherlands: E. J. Brill, 1957.

Ruchames, Louis. "New Light on the Religious Development of Emma Lazarus." *Publications of the American Jewish Historical Society* 42 (1952): 83–88.

Rugoff, Milton. *The Beechers: An American Family in the Nineteenth Century*. New York: Harper and Row, 1981.

Rusk, Ralph L. *The Life of Ralph Waldo Emerson*. New York: Charles Scribner's Sons, 1949.

———, ed. *The Letters of Ralph Waldo Emerson*. 6 vols. New York: Columbia University Press, 1939.

———. *Letters to Emma Lazarus in the Columbia University Library*. New York: Columbia University Press, 1939.

Russell, Charles Edward. *The American Orchestra and Theodore Thomas*. New York: Doubleday, Page, 1927.

Sachar, Howard Morley. *The Course of Modern Jewish History*. A Delta Book. New York: Dell, 1958.

Saint-Gaudens, Augustus, ed. *The Reminiscences of Augustus St.-Gaudens*. 2 vols. London: Andrew Melrose, 1913.

Samuels, Ernest. *Henry Adams: The Middle Years*. Cambridge, Mass.: Belknap Press, 1958.

Saxton, Martha. *Louisa May: A Modern Biography of Louisa May Alcott*. Boston: Houghton Mifflin, 1977.

Schapiro, Leonard. *Turgenev: His Life and Times*. New York: Random House, 1978.

Schappes, Morris U. Review of *The World of Emma Lazarus*, by Heinrich Jacob. *American Literature* 21 (1950): 506–8.

———, ed. *Emma Lazarus: Selections from Her Poetry and Prose*. IWO Jewish American Section, 1944; New York: Emma Lazarus Federation of Jewish Women's Clubs, 1978.

————. *The Letters of Emma Lazarus, 1868–1885*. New York: New York Public Library, 1949.

Scharnhorst, Gary, with Jace Bales. *The Lost Life of Horatio Alger, Jr*. Bloomington: Indiana University Press, 1985.

Scheyer, Ernst. *The Circle of Henry Adams: Art and Artist*. Detroit: Wayne State University Press, 1970.

Schlesinger, Arthur M. *Learning How to Behave: A Historical Study of American Etiquette Books*. New York: Macmillan, 1947.

————. *The Rise of the City: 1879–1898*. New York: Macmillan, 1933.

Scholnick, Robert J. *Edmund Clarence Stedman*. Boston: Twayne, 1977.

Schonberg, Harold C. *The Virtuosi: Classical Music's Great Performers from Paganini to Pavarotti*. New York: Vintage Books, 1988.

Schuster, M. Lincoln, ed. *A Treasury of the World's Great Letters, from Alexander the Great to Thomas Mann*. New York: Simon and Schuster, 1968.

Simon, Kate. *Fifth Avenue: A Very Social History*. New York: Harcourt Brace Jovanovich, 1978.

Simonhoff, Harry. *Jewish Notables in America, 1776–1865, Links of an Endless Chain*. New York: Greenberg, 1956.

————. *Saga of American Jewry, 1865–1914, Links of an Endless Chain*. New York: Arco, 1959.

Sitterson, J. Carlyle. *Sugar Cane: The Cane Sugar Industry in the South, 1753–1950*. Lexington: University Press of Kentucky, 1953.

Slater, Joseph, ed. *The Correspondence of Emerson and Carlyle*. New York: Columbia University Press, 1964.

Slonimsky, Nicolas. *Baker's Big Dictionary of Musicians*. 7th ed. New York: Macmillan, Schirmer's Books, 1984.

Smith, Bernard. *Forces in American Criticism: A Study in the History of American Literary Thought*. New York: Harcourt, Brace, 1939.

Smith, Goldwin. *A History of England*. 4th ed. New York: Charles Scribner's Sons, 1974.

Smith, Henry Nash, ed. *Popular Culture and Industrialism: 1865–1890*. New York: New York University Press, 1967.

Smith, Herbert F. *Richard Watson Gilder*. New York: Twayne, 1970.

Smith, Page. *Trial by Fire: A People's History of the Civil War and Reconstruction*. Vol. 5. New York: McGraw-Hill, 1982.

————. *The Rise of Industrial America: A People's History of the Post-Reconstruction Era*. Vol. 6. New York: McGraw-Hill, 1984.

Snyder, Margaret. "The Other Side of the River: Thomas Wren Ward, 1844–1940." *New England Quarterly* 14 (September 1941): 426–33.

Sokolow, Nahum. *History of Zionism: 1600–1918*. 2 vols. London: Longmans, Green, 1919.

Spiller, Robert E., et al. *Literary History of the United States*. 3d ed., rev. New York: Macmillan, 1963.

Stauffer, Donald Barlow. *A Short History of American Poetry*. New York: E. P. Dutton, 1974.

Stedman, Edmund Clarence. *Genius and Other Essays*. Port Washington, N.Y.: Kennikat Press, 1966.

———. "Poetry in America." *Scribner's* 22 (August, September, 1881): 540; 817.

———, ed. *An American Anthology, 1887–1900*. Boston: Houghton Mifflin; Cambridge, Mass.: Riverside Press, 1900.

———. *Poets of America*. Boston: Houghton Mifflin; Cambridge, Mass.: Riverside Press, 1885.

Stegner, Wallace. *Angle of Repose*. Greenwich, Conn.: Fawcett Crest, 1971.

Stern, Malcolm. *Americans of Jewish Descent*. Cincinnati: Hebrew Union College Press, 1960.

Still, Bayard. *Mirror for Gotham: New York as Seen by Contemporaries from Dutch Days to the Present*. New York: New York University Press, 1956.

Strouse, Jean. *Alice James: A Biography*. Boston: Houghton Mifflin, 1980.

Sulzberger, Mayer. "Miss Lazarus' Poems." *Jewish Messenger,* 10 November 1882, p. 4.

Swanberg, W. A. *Pulitzer*. New York: Charles Scribner's Sons, 1967.

Tassin, Algernon. *The Magazine in America*. New York: Dodd, Mead, 1916.

Taylor, Ina. *Victorian Sisters: The Remarkable Macdonald Women and the Great Men They Inspired*. Bethesda, Md.: Adler and Adler, 1987.

Taylor, Joshua C. *The Fine Arts in America*. The Chicago History of American Civilization. Edited by Daniel J. Boorstin. Chicago: University of Chicago Press, 1979.

Tharp, Louise Hall. *Mrs. Jack: A Biography of Isabella Stewart Gardner*. Boston: Little, Brown, 1965.

———. *Saint-Gaudens and the Gilded Age*. Boston: Little, Brown, 1969.

Thomas, Donald. *Robert Browning: A Life within a Life*. New York: Viking Press, 1983.

Thomas, Rose Fay. *Memories of Theodore Thomas*. New York: Moffat, Yard, 1911.

Thompson, E. P. *William Morris: Romantic to Revolutionary*. New York: Pantheon Books, 1977.

Thoron, Ward, ed. *The Letters of Mrs. Henry Adams*. Boston: Little, Brown, 1936.

Tomsich, John. *A Genteel Endeavor: American Culture and Politics in the Gilded Age*. Stanford: Stanford University Press, 1971.

Trachtenberg, Alan. *The Incorporation of America; Culture and Society in the Gilded Age*. American Century Series. Consulting Editor, Eric Foner. New York: Hill and Wang, 1982.

Traubel, Horace. *With Walt Whitman in Camden (March 28–July 14, 1888)*. Boston: Small, Maynard, 1906.

Turgenieff, Ivan. *Virgin Soil*. Translated by Isabel Hapgood. New York: Charles Scribner's Sons, 1907.

Valenti, Patricia Dunlavy. *To Myself a Stranger: A Biography of Rose Hawthorne Lathrop.* Baton Rouge: Louisiana State University Press, 1991.

Vogel, Dan. *Emma Lazarus.* Boston: Twayne, 1980.

Von Eckhardt, Wolf, et al. *Oscar Wilde's London.* Garden City: Doubleday, Anchor Press, 1987.

Wagenknecht, Edward. *Daughters of the Covenant: Portraits of Six Jewish Women.* Amherst: University of Massachusetts Press, 1983.

Waters, Clara Erskine Clement, and Laurence Hutton. *Artists of the Nineteenth Century and Their Work.* 1896. Reprint. New York: Arno Press, 1969.

Wecter, Dixon. *The Saga of American Society: A Record of Social Aspiration, 1607–1937.* New York: Charles Scribner's Sons, 1937.

Weintraub, Stanley. *Four Rossettis: A Victorian Biography.* New York: Weybright and Talley, 1977.

Weitkampf, Frank. *Manhattan Kaleidoscope.* New York: Charles Scribner's Sons, 1947.

Wells, Charles. *Joseph and His Brethren: A Dramatic Poem with an Introduction by Algernon Swinburne.* London: Chatto and Windus, 1876.

"Who Are Representative Jews?" *Jewish Messenger,* 31 March 1882, p. 4.

Wiebe, Robert H. *The Search for Order, 1877–1920: The Making of America.* American Century Series. General Editor, David Donald. New York: Hill and Wang, 1967.

Wilkinson, Burke. *Uncommon Clay: The Life and Works of Augustus St.-Gaudens.* Photographs by David Finn. A Helen and Kurt Wolff Book. San Diego: Harcourt Brace Jovanovich, 1985.

Willard, Emma. *Women of the Century.* New York: Mast, Crowell and Kirkpatrick, 1877; reprinted as *American Women,* 2 vols. Detroit: Gale, 1973.

Wilson, Rufus Rockwell, and Otilie Erickson Wilson. *New York in Literature: The Story Told in the Landmarks of Town and Country.* Elmira, N.Y.: Primavera Press, 1947.

Winter, William. *Other Days: Being Chronicles and Memories of the Stage.* New York: Moffat, Yard, 1908.

Wolf, Edwin, II, and Maxwell Whiteman. *The History of the Jews of Philadelphia from Colonial Times to the Age of Jackson.* Philadelphia: Jewish Publication Society of America, 1957.

Wolfe, Theodore F. *Literary Haunts and Homes.* Philadelphia: J.B. Lippincott, 1898.

Wright, Austin, ed. *Victorian Literature: Modern Essays in Criticism.* A Galaxy Book. New York: Oxford University Press, 1961.

Zeiger, Arthur. "Emma Lazarus: A Critical Study." Ph.D. diss., New York University, 1951.

Index

Abbey, Henry, 225n.32
Academy of Design, 223n.15
Academy of Music, 22, 226n.2
Adams, Henry, 108, 242n.118; as member, "Five of Hearts," 242n.119
Adams, Mrs. Henry (Marion "Clover" Hooper), 242n.119; death of, 138, 247n.175
Adler, Felix, 7, 209, 244–45n.144, 261n.21
Aesthetic Movement, 50
Age of ideality, 50
Alcott, Bronson, and Concord School of Philosophy, 73, 232–233n.25
Alcott, Louisa May, views on Concord School of Philosophy, 232–33n.25
Alexander II, Czar, 8, 28, 95, 238n.86
Alliance Israélite Universelle (All Israel Are Comrades), 204, 208, 259n.7, 261n.19
Alma-Tadema, Lawrence, 112, 244n.136
Alma-Tadema, Clara Epps, 240n.110
American Art Association, 223n.15
American Hebrew, and Emma, 9, 57, 60, 224n.21, 230n.4, 256n.9; and memorial issue, 10–11, 221n.1
Amici's *Olande*, 133, 246n.165
Anti-Semitism, Medieval, 36–42; German, 41–42; East European, 56–62; in United States, 46–47
Arnold, Matthew, 21; and Emma, 125, 245n.150; and Emerson Lecture, 198, 199, 257n.20, 257n.21; and "Falkland," 130; and "Mixed Essays," 130, 246n.160
Art Loan Fund Exhibition, in Aid of Bartholdi Pedestal Fund for Statue of Liberty, 3, 221n.1
Art Students League, 68, 233n.28; and Lisa Stillman, 249n.191
Astor, Mrs. John Jacob, III, 248n.182
Authors' Club, 8, 223n.15
Azoff, Sergius, 34–35

Baldwin, Mrs. Alfred (Louise MacDonald), 241n.115
Beck, C.L., and "A Vindication of the Jews," 61
Banks, Major General Nathaniel, 49
Barlow, Ellen Shaw (Nellie), 145, 147, 247n.179
Bastille Day, 113–14
Beecher, Reverend Henry Ward, 37, 47, 244–45n.144
Beeches, The (Lazarus' summer home), 7, 223n.5, 232n.15
Beethoven, 80, 249n.192; and Leonora Overture, 23, 86
Berlin, Irving, 4; and "Miss Liberty," 222n.7
Berlioz, Hector, and "Damnation of Faust," 23, 74, 94, 233n.29, 236n.58; concert, 205
Biddle, Minnie (Mrs. George), 72, 101–2, 188–89, 255n.6
Bijur, Nathan, 204, 208, 259n.9
Booth, William, and Salvation Army, 240n.109
Boyesen, Hjamar H., 223n.8, 223n.15, 225n.32, 252n.16
Bradford, George, 73, 233n.26
Bradish, William Martin, 48
Brafmann, Jacob, and "The Kahal," 57
Bright, John, 107, 241n.115
Broadway Group, and Alma Strettel, 242n.117
Bronson, Edith, 76, 234n.38
Bronson, Katherine deKay, 75, 150, 191, 234n.32; and Robert Browning, 145, 163, 234n.38, 248n.185
Brooklyn Philharmonic, 94, 237n.72; rehearsal of, 238n.82
Brown, Ford Madox, 234n.39
Brown, Oliver Madox, 234n.39; and "Birth Song," 77, 78–79; death of, 238n.63
Browning, Elizabeth Barrett, Emma compared to, 19
Browning, Robert, and "Agamemnon", 176; at

Agnes Lazarus' wedding, 152; and "Balaustion's Adventure," 7; and Emma, 10; and Emma, in London, 107, 108, 110; and Henry James, 211; and "Inn Album", 160, 250n.202; and Katherine deKay Bronson, 145, 163, 234n.38, 248n.185; and "Prince Hohenstein-Schwangau, the Savior of Society," 77, 235n.41

Bryce, James, 241n.115; and Emma, 107; and tickets for Parliament, 153

Burne-Jones, Edward Coley, 241n.115, and Emma, 107, 108, 110–111; illustrates "Earthly Paradise," 243n.129; work of, compared with Thomas Wilmer Dewing's, 114

Burne-Jones, Mrs. Edward (Georgina MacDonald), 241n.115

Burroughs, John, and Emma 8, 10, 12, 19, 225n.32; and Matthew Arnold, 257n.21

Byron, 190; and "Hebrew Melody," 92–93

Carlyle, Thomas, and Emma, 95, 96; Henry James' impressions of, 214; and R.W. Emerson, 93, 237n.70, 238n.81

Carter, Susan, 88; and Cooper Union School of Art, 237n.67

"Causeries" (Causeries du Lundi), 143, 161–62, 248n.182

Central Park, 178, 253n.23; and Cleopatra's Needle, 237n.72; and Metropolitan Museum, 224n.16

Century Magazine, on cultural ideals, 50, 68–69; and Emma, 8, 9, 53, 57, 61, 224n.21, 230n.4, 243n.131, 257n.16, 258n.23; popularity of, in London, 119

Channing, William Ellery, the Younger, 173, 251n.10

Cherbuliez, Charles Victor (G. Vallbert), 181, 182, 254n.28; and The Adventures of Ladislas Bolski, 254n.28; and Noires et Rouges (Saints and Sinners), 181, 182, 254n.28; and Samuel Brohl, 254n.28

Chestnut Hill, Pennsylvania, 101–2, 103

Chickering Hall, 224n.19, 233n.29

Cleopatra's Needle (Egyptian Obelisk), 23–24, 237n.72; and Obelisk Entertainment, 23–24, 90, 92

Cleveland, President Grover, 4, 68

Cleveland, Mrs. Grover (Frances), 167, 169, 250n.208, 250–51n.210

Cohen, Mary M., 11, 225n.32

Commandments (mitzvot), 58

Communism, Emma's views on, 35, 176

Comyn-Carrs, Joseph, and Mrs. Alice (Strettel), 107, 242n.115

Concerts, Free, for Workingmen, 10, 209, 224–25n.28, 257n.22, 261n.22

Concord, 5, 133; and Ellen Emerson's birthday

ball, 91, 238n.77; and Emma's visits, 72–73, 187, 191, 192, 194

Concord School of Philosophy, 73, 232–33n.25, 245n.145

Coppée, François, "Poète des humbles," 88, 172, 175, 176, 251n.6; and "Olivier," 171

Coxon, Miss Ethel, 119

Critic, and Emma, 8, 249n.199, 254n.31

Crosby, Reverend Howard, 224n.19, 233n.30, 237n.72

Crosby, Margaret, and Review Club, 23, 224n.29, 233n.30

Cunliffe, Sir Robert, and Lady Eleanor Leigh, 108, 242n.118

Damrosch, Dr. Leopold, 120, 224n.16, 233n.29, 244–45n.144

Dana, Charles Henry, 10, 19, 225n.32

Darwin, Charles, and Henry Spencer, 60, 61

Dawes, Anna Laurens, 10, 225n.32

DeCamp, Maxime, and En Hollande, 133, 246n.165

Decorative Art Association, 119

deKay, Charles, and Authors' Club, 223n.15; as a Bohemian, 73; and correspondence with Emma, 253n.21; as Emma's "friend," 8, 23, 24, 92, 96, 99, 123, 223n.14; and "Hesperus," 76, 77, 234n.37; in London, 150; and marriage, 27; and Mary Hallock Foote, 44–45; and "Sybil Judaica," 45–46; "The Vision of Nimrod," reviewed by Emma and The New York Times, 85, 236n.60

deKay, Commodore George C., 67

deKay, Janet, 67, 82, 123

deKay, Julia, 122, 123, 129

deKay, Ormonde, 223n.14

deKay Mrs. Sidney, 90, 237n.74

de Leon, Daniel, 21, 202–3, 204, 258n.4

Dengremont, Maurice, 23, 87, 237n.64

Destiny, and nature, Emma's views on, 33–35

Dewing, Maria Oakey, 23; and Aleck Oakey, 246n.169; engagement and marriage of, 80, 81–82, 85, 89, 96–97, 99–100, 235n.47, 235n.48; in England with Emma, 112; and Helena deKay Gilder, 74, 78, 79; and Olivia Ward, 86, 235n.44

Dewing, Thomas Wilmer, 80, 114

Disraeli, Benjamin (Lord Beaconsfield), 13, 28, 53–55, 58

Donnelly, Ignatius, 221n.1

Drake, Joseph Rodman, 67

Draper, Ruth (Mrs. William Henry), 136, 239n.99

duMaurier, George Louis, 9, 107, 108; and Emma's visit to his studio, 111, 241n.115

Eaton, Wyatt, 92, 87, 142; and portrait of Helena deKay Gilder, 155, 238n.78; and Samuel Gray Ward, 97

Editor's Cabinet, 156, 249n.200

Egan, Maurice Frances, 69

Ehrlich, Prof. Arnold, as Emma's Hebrew teacher, 256n.11

Eliot, George (Marianne Evans) and *Daniel Deronda*, 243n.133, 249n.192; Emma reads, 121, 193, 256–57n.14; and "Felix Holt, the Radical," 176; and "George Eliot's" writings, 87; on Jews as a race, 55–56; as quoted by Emma, 55–56, 58, 61, 62, 92

Emerson, Dr. Edward, 173, 252n.12; and Richard Watson Gilder, 104; and Thomas Wren Ward, 170

Emerson, Ellen, and birthday ball, 91, 238n.77; on Concord School of Philosophy, 232–33n.25; and Emma, 44; and Emma's essay on R.W. Emerson, 194

Emerson, Ralph Waldo, and *Century*, 89, 93, 94; and Emma, 6–7, 12, 13, 19, 24, 50, 223n.4, 232n.24; and Emma's visits, 23, 72, 173, 251n.9; and *Parnassus*, 17, 20, 24; and Richard Watson Gilder, 94, 104, 232n.24; as "Sage of Concord," 93, 238n.80; and Samuel Gray Ward, 21; and T. Carlyle, 93, 237n.70, 238n.81

Emersons, The R.W., 173, 194

Emma Lazarus Federation of Women's Clubs, 4–5, 222n.9

Emma Lazarus Foundation, 5

Emma Lazarus Statue of Liberty Dinner, 5

Evarts, William, 224n.19

Exiles, and Emma, 62–63; Heinrich (Harry) Heine as, 41; Jewish, 36

Farragut, Admiral David Glasgow, 239n.n93

Farragut Statue, 24, 99, 239n.93

Fitzgerald, Edward, 176–77, 253n.20; and "Agamemnon of Aeschylus," 253n.20; and "Rubiyat," 253n.20

Fletcher, Constance (George Fleming), author of "Kismet," 145, 248n.186

Fogazzara, and "Daniel Cortis," 146–47

Foote, Mary Hallock (Molly), 100, 118, 223n.14, 239n.94, 239.n98; and "John Rodman's Testimony," 142, 147, 248n.180; and "The Spagnaletto," 25

Frank, J.J., 204, 259n.9

Franzos, Karl, and Barnow Stories, 260n.14; and Podolian Ghetto, 206

Free Religious Association, 31

Free will, 33, 184

Fromentin, Eugene, 28, 82, 133, 235n.49; and "Dominique," 83, 86, 88, 236n.55; and *Le*

Maîtres d'Autrefois: Belgique-Hollande, 246n.165

Froude, James Anthony, and *Thomas Carlyle's Reminiscences*, 238n.85, 262n.9

Garfield, President James A., 28

Gathereau, Mme. (Virginia Avegno, Mme. X), 135, 247n.171

George, Henry, 8, 11, 12; and Daniel DeLeon, 258n.4; and Leopold Lindau, 252n.17; and *Progress and Poverty*, 50, 222n.9, 230n.23

Gilchrist, Alexander, 234n.36

Gilchrist, Anne, 75, 92; and death of daughter, 103; and Emerson, 234n.36

Gilchrist, Herbert, 103, 240n.102

Gilder, Francesca, naming of, 250–51n.210

Gilder, Helena deKay, characteristics of, 67–69; and Emma, 8, 23, 44–45, 67, 187, 188; and Henry James, 210; and letters from Emma, 20–21, 67–169; and Maria Oakey Dewing, 233n.28; and Mary Hallock Foote, 223n.14; and Millet-Rousseau paper, 161–162; and new stone studio, 244n.135, 256n.12; and Olivia Ward, 235n.44; and Rose Hawthorne Lathrop, 186

Gilder, Jeanette, 8, 155, 199, 236n.54, 249n.199, 254n.26

Gilder, Joseph P., 8, 43, 225n.32, 236n.54

Gilder, Richard Watson, 8, 20; and *Century*, 236n.62; characteristics of, 67–69; and Emma, 24, 88, 89, 97–98, 105, 106, 135, 137, 150, 160; and Farragut Statue, 239n.93; and Hymn to Obelisk, 90, 91–92; as member of "genteel aristocracy," 29; and "Mors Triumphalis," 249n.196; and "A New Day," 240n.107; and R.W. Emerson, 89, 93, 94; and *Scribner's*, 68–69; and Statue of Liberty plaque, 221n.2

Gilder, Richard Watson and Helena deKay, as arbiters of culture, 68–69; and Authors' Club, 8, 223n.15; and Emma, 8, 189; and Friday Evening Salons, 23, 67, 187, 189, 205, 210, 255n.3; and J.F. Millet, 235n.45, 244n.138; and Society of American Artists, 8, 223n.15; and "Studio", 67, 76, 87, 238n.89

Goethe, 7, 28, 33–34, 86; and "Faust," 190

Goldsmid, Sir Francis, and Lady, 107, 111, 211, 261n.5

Goldsmid Family, 241n.115

Gosse, Edmund, and Emma, 107, 108, 150, 154, 156; and Henry James, 240n.110

Gosse, Mrs. Edmund (Nellie Epps), 108, 112, 156, 240n.110

Gosses, The E., 110, 112

Gottheil, Gustav, 9–10, 32–33

Grand Union Hotel, 46, 201

Grant, Robert, and *Confessions of a Frivolous Girl*, 83, 236n.53
Great Union Meeting, 227n.3

HaLevi, Judah, and "Longing for Jerusalem" 39
Harrison, Constance Cary, 7, 221n.1, 225n.32
Hart, Jacob, 44
Hay, John, 6, 10, 100, 108, 225n.32, 242n.119
Hebrew Emigrant Aid Society, and Emma Lazarus, 256n.9
Hebrew-English Prayer Book (*The Form of Daily Prayer*), 44
Hebrew Technical Institute, 9, 224n.20
"Hebrews," 45–46
Heine, Heinrich, 7, 9, 28, 36–37, 41; and "Donna Clara," 36–37; and essay by Emma, 20, 41–42; as exile, 41–42; and "The Poet Heine," 41–42; and "Rabbi of Bacharach," 42
Henschel, George, 86, 108, 236n.58, 236
Higginson, Thomas W., 12, 71; as abolitionist, 50, 232n.17; and *Army Life in a Black Regiment*, 232n.17; describes Emma, 44; and First Regiment of South Carolina Volunteers, 232n.17; as member of Town and Country Club, 7; reads Emma's work, 24
Hilton, Judge Henry, 46–47
Hoffman, James H., 225n.32
Holland, Annie, 85, 102, 103, 236n.61
Holland, Josiah G., 23, 90, 103; and "Bonnie Castle," 240n.103; death of, 236n.62, 237n.73
Holmes, Dr. Oliver Wendell, 150, 249n.193
Houghton, Lord, 111
Howe, Julia Ward, and Town and Country Club, 7
Howells, William Dean, 109, 186, 243n.127

Imber, Napthali, and "Hatikvah," 259n.6
Independent, Emma published in, 37
Irving, Henry, 106, 241n.114

James, Alice, and illness, 124, 127, 138, 214–15, 245n.147; and Nelly Barlow, 247n.179; relationship with Katherine Loring, 262n.7
James, Henry, 24; and Alma Strettel, 242n.117; and Annie Benson Procter, 240n.111; and *The Bostonians*, 246n.167, 262n.7; and *Century*, 210, 214, 262n.8; and Constance Fletcher, 248n.186; and Edmund Gosse, 240n.110; and Emma, 108, 133, 134, 148, 152; as member, "Five of Hearts," 242n.119; and J. Comyn-Carrs, 242n.115; and Kathryn Bronson, 234n.32, 248n.185; and letters to Emma, 21, 210–17; and Miss Birdseye, 256n.12; and Olive Chancellor, 113, 246n.167;

and *The Princess Cassamassima*, 262n.8; and sister's illness, *see* Alice James; and Turgenev article, 212; and William Wetmore Story, 247n.178
James, William, 12, 19, and Emma, 210; and Thomas Wren Ward, 170
Jewish Colonization, 202
Jewish Messenger, and Emma's work, 36, 39, 223n.11
Jewish M.P., 106
Jewish Nationalism, 30, 35, 51, 58–59
Jewish Problem/Jewish Question, defined, 43, 258n.5; and Emma, 21, 61–62, 192, 202–203
Jews, British, 9; "Court", "Exception," 45; East European, 35, 57, 62–63; and Emma, 106, 111; German, Prophetic, Reform, 58–59; immigrant, 8, 9, 255n.7, 256n.9; Internal Reform for, 204, 259n.8; in Northausen, Germany, 234n.34; Orthodox, Traditional, 58; in Paris, 112; Progressive, 222n.9; and R. Browning, 110; Representative English, 205; Sephardic, 63; Spanish, expulsion of, 62
Joachim, and Annie Lazarus, 163, 250n.206
Johnson, Bradish, 48–49; owns distillery, 48–49; as slaveholder, 49, 229n.15, 230n.16
Johnson, Bradish, Jr., 49
Johnson, Robert Underwood, as associate editor of *Century*, 248n.184, 249n.197; and Emma in Europe, 143, 148; Emma's letter to, on anti-Semitism, 61; Emma's opinion of, 154, 166
Johnston, John Humphreys, 222n.1
Joseffy, Raphael, 23, 28, 74, 94, 233n.29

Kann, Mr., 207, 208, 261n.19
Keats, John, 140, 142
King, Clarence, 143, 242n.119
Kipling, Alice MacDonald (Mrs. John Lockwood), 241n.115
Kipling, John Lockwood, 241n.115
Kirk, John Foster, 103, 239n.101
Knickerbocker Club, 6, 24, 44
Kohut, Rabbi Alexander, and Rebekah, 256n.11

LaFarge, John, and Emma, 12; and Helena deKay Gilder, 68; and Maria Oakey, 233n.28; and Olivia Ward, 85; and R.W. Gilders, 236n.59; and Town and Country Club, 7
Lathrop, George, 186, 193
Lathrop, Rose Hawthorne, 237n.69; conversion of, 170, 186; and Emma, 8; letters from Emma, 20–21, 186–200; and Rosary Hill Home, 186; and son, Francis, 186, 255n.4; and trip to England, 240n.108
Lazarus, Agnes, and Montague Marks, 148; wedding of, 152, 248n.190

Lazarus, Annie, 14, 237n.75; at Concord, 191, 192–93, 194, 240n.106, 256n.10; and E.C. Burne-Jones, 127; and Edward Emerson, 104; and Ellen Emerson, 194, and Emma's illness, 161–166; in Europe, 105–20, 122–69, 249n.201, 260n.11; and Helena deKay Gilder, 91; and Matthew Arnold, 125; and National Gallery, 125; and Rubenstein concerts, 148; and Stillmans, 149, 152

Lazarus, Emma, *American Hebrew* and, 10–11; ancestors of, 6–7; 43–44; and Jewish immigrants, 9, 256n.9; and Jewish recolonization, *see* Seligman letters; Jewish works of, 52–55; as others saw her, 44–46; and R.W. Emerson, *see* Ralph Waldo Emerson; and the South, 50; work of, 7, 28–35

Lazarus, Emma, European trips of, 105–20, 122–69, 196–97; to British Parliament, 153; to Cambridge, 129–31; to Dulwich Picture Gallery, 126, 245n.152; to Fitzwilliam Museum, 130; to Florence, 136–39, 141, 146–48; to the Hague, 131–33; at King's Procession, 132, 158–59, 440n.161; to London, 105–12, 117–20, 124–27, 142–55, 158; to Merton Abbey, 119, 243n.131; to Paris, 112–114, 133–36, 159–67; to Peacock Room, 109, 243n.128; to Pisa, 137; to Richmond-York, 127–28; to Rome, 140–45; to St. Peter's Basilica, 140; to Sistine Chapel, 140–41, 144–45; to Stratford-on-Avon, 115, 116

Lazarus, Emma, works of, *Admetus and Other Poems*, 7; *Alide: An Episode of Goethe's Life*, 7, 17, 33–34; "American Literature," 29; "Among the Thousand Islands," 227n.92; "Assurance," 18; "The Banner of the Jew," 52–53; "Bertha," 30; Browning essay, unsigned, in *Scribner's*, 179; 254n.26; "By the Waters of Babylon, Little Poems in Prose," 62; "The Crowing of the Red Cock," 52; "The Dance to the Death," 26–27, 39–40, 234n.34, 257n.15; "A Day in Surrey with William Morris," 222n.9, 243n.131; "The Death of Rashi," 37; "Don Pedrillo," 36–37; "Echoes," 28–29; "The Eleventh Hour," 20, 34–35, 252n.15; "Emerson's Personality," 257n.16; "An Epistle," 32; "An Epistle to the Hebrews," 57–61, 224n.31, 256–57n.14; "Eugene Fromentin," 235n.49; "Exodus, August 3, 1492," 62; "Fra Pedro," 37; "The Guardian of the Red Disk," 75, 234n.35, 253n.25; *Poems and Ballads of Heinrich Heine*, 41–42; "In the Jewish Synagogue at Newport," 36; "The Jewish Problem," 61–62, 224n.21; "The New Colossus," 3–4, 15; "Outside the Church," 31; *Poems and Ballads of Heinrich Heine*, 239n.96, 252n.14; *Poems and Translations Written Between the Ages of Fourteen and Seventeen*, 6–7 223n.4; *The Poems of Emma*

Lazarus, Volume I, 50; "The Poet Heine," 41–42; "Progress and Poverty," 222n.9; "Rashi in Prague," 37–39; "To R.W.E.," 122; "Regnault as a Writer," 236n.51; "Renan and the Jews," 252n.13; "Russian Christianity versus Modern Judaism," 56–57, 224n.21; "Salvini's King Lear," 26–27, 237n.65; "Sic Semper Liberatoribus, March 13, 1881," 238n.86; *Songs of a Semite*, 40, 52, 257n.15; "The South," 50–51; "The Spagnaletto," 25–27; "Tannhauser," 30–31; "Tomasso Salvini," 237n.65; "Was the Earl of Beaconsfield a Representative Jew?" 53–55, 224n.21

Lazarus, Esther Nathan, 6, 43

Lazarus, Frank, 49, 73

Lazarus, Jacob Hart, 6

Lazarus, Josephine, 96, 101, 232n20; and Charles deKay, 45; and Emma's illness, 225n.29; in England, 152; and essay on Emma, 13–24; and Georgina Schuyler, 221n.2; and Heine, 41; and Helena deKay Gilder, 69, 78, 87, 111–12; and Thomas Wren Ward, 228n.16

Lazarus, Mary (Lindau), 50, 168, 230n.23, 249n.201, 252n.17

Lazarus, Moses, 6–7; and business, 48–50, 229n.15; and daughters, 24–27; illness and death of, 102–3; 215; 244n.143, 252n.17, 258n.24

Lazarus, Samuel, 44

Lazarus, Sarah, 250n.205; in Europe, 162–63, 166, 168; and Helena deKay Gilder, 83

Lazarus sisters, 27, 222n.1

Leighton, Sir Frederick, 111, 242n.122

Leland, Charles Godfrey (Hans Breitmann), 189–90, 255n.7

Lenox, Massachusetts, and Emma's visit, 191, 192; and Samuel Gray Ward, 170, 175, 178, 251n.2

"Liberty Enlightening the World," 4

Lindau, Leopold, 176, 183, 222n.1; and Mary Lazarus, 230n.23, 249n.201, 252n.17

Lindau, Paul, and "Der Scher," 175–76, 252n.17; and "Nord und Sud"

Lindau, Rudolph, 175, 252n.17

Lippincott's Magazine, and Emma's works, 7, 223n.11

Liszt, Franz, 103, 141, 150

Lockwood, Florence, and Emma, 134–35, 138, 141, 143; and Henry James, 213, 214, 217, 262n.6; and Review Club, 75

London "Season," 195, 196, 244n.139, 257n.17

Longfellow, Henry Wadsworth, 28; and "In the Cemetery at Newport," 36

Loring, Katherine, 127, 151; and Olive Chancellor, 133, 246n.167

Loring, Louise, 262n.7

Lorraine, Claude, Glass 137, 159, 247n.173

Louis, Minnie (Mrs. Alfred), 204, 208, 260n.9;
and Louis Downtown Sabbath School (Hebrew Technical School for Girls), 260n.9
Lowell, James Russell, 3, 19, 108, 150, 242n.120,
249n.193
Lyons, Reverend J. J., 44, 256n.11
Lyons, Sarah, 256n.11

MacDonald sisters, 241n.115
Macy's, R.H., 22, 226n.2
Madison Square, 24, 99, 238n.87, 239n.93
Manhattan Beach at Coney Island, and Jews, 47
Marion, Massachusetts, on Buzzard's Bay (Gild-
ers' summer home), 68, 193, 244n.135, 256n.12
Marks, Rabbi David, 248n.190
Marks, Montague, 222n.1, 248n.190
Marr, Whilhelm, 52
McKim, Annie Bigelow, 100, 239n.95
Mendes, Dr. Frederick deSola, 204, 259n.9
Metropolitan Museum of Art, 8, 22, 224n.16,
226n.2
Metropolitan Opera, 8, 224n.16, 226n.2, 245n.144
Middlemore, Mrs. (Nina Sturgis), 114, 152–53, 157
Millet, Jean François, and Helena deKay Gilder's
manuscript on, 78; and Nation article on, 94;
and R.W. Gilders, 235n.45, 244n.138; and "The
Sower," 104, 240n.107
Milton, Massachusetts, 23, 239n.92
Minturn, Bessie, 180, 254n.27
Mistral Frédéric, leader of "Félibriges," 129, 136,
246n.157
Mocatta, Frederick, 111, 129, 243n.132
Modjeska, Helena, 119, 244n.142
Monadnoc, Mt., 173, 175, 252n.11
Montalbas, The, 107, 241n.115
Montefiore, Claude Joseph Goldsmid, 106, 111,
225n.32, 241n.112
Montefiore, Leonard, 211, 261n.4
Montefiore, Sir Moses, 108–9, 241n.112, 243n.125,
261n.4
Morley, John, and Emma, 107, 158, 196, 241n.115
Morris, William, and "The Earthly Paradise,"
111, 243n.129; and Emma, 107–8, 110–12, 196;
workshop of, 199, 243n.131, 249n.194
Morris, Mrs. William (Jane), 111, 243n.129,
243n.130
Moscheles, Felix, 106–8, 241n.113
Moscheles, Mrs. Felix, and Emma, 149
"Mother of Exiles," 4
Mullaly, John, and "Death in a Jug," 48, 230n17

Nadal, Ehrman Syme, 75, 84, 106, 108, 234n.33
Nathans, and Henderickses, and "Hebrews," 46
Nathan, Benjamin, 6, 18, 44
Nathan, Grace, 6

Nathan, Simon, 6, 44
Nathan, Washington, 18
Nation, and Century, 68; and E.S. Nadal, 84; and
J.F. Millet, 94; and railroad strikes, 176, 253n.18
National Academy of Design, 68, 233n.28
Newport, 5, 7, 71, 172, 175–76; and Lazarus sum-
mer home, 7,
223n.5, 232n.15
New York City, as center of culture, 8, 22; as des-
tination for Jewish immigrants, 8
New York Philharmonic, 10, 224n.16; concerts
of, 189, 209; and Leopold Damrosch, 244n.144;
and Obelisk Entertainment, 237n.72; rehears-
als of, 94, 104; and Theodore Thomas, 257n.22
New York Symphony Society Orchestra, 224n.16,
244–45n.144
New York Times, and anti-Semitism, 46–47; and
Emma 7, 15, 16, 223n.11; and railroad strikes,
253n.18
New York Tribune, and Emma, 15; and railroad
strikes, 253n.18
Nineteenth Century Club, Emma member of, 9,
224n.27

Oakey, Aleck, and Mrs. 78, 157, 235n.42, 246n.169
Oakey, Maria, see Dewing, Maria Oakey
Oliphant, Laurence, 259n.6; and Blackwoods,
203; and The Land of Gilead, 203; and Nine-
teenth Century, 192, 203
Osgood, James, 89, 237n.71

Paget, Violet (Vernon Lee), 147, 248n.187
Palestine, recolonization of, 9; in Emma's essays,
58, 59, 62; and E.R.A. Seligman, 202–4; and L.
Oliphant, 259n.6
Pall Mall Gazette, 161
Paris Salon, 135, 151, 247n.171
Patti, Adelaide, 108, 242n.123
Peruzzi, Mme. Edith Story, 143, 147, 248n.183
Pre-Raphaelite Brotherhood, 235n.40; Wilde's
lecture on, 256n.8
Procter, Annie Benson, 124, 127, and Emma, 106,
107, 112, 150, 245n.148; and Henry James, 210,
211, 240–41n.111, 261n.3
Pursell's Confectionery and Restaurant, 23, 99,
239n.93
Pursell's Ladies Restaurant, 22, 226n.2

Ragozin, Zenaide, and "Russian Jews and Gentiles, from a Russian Point of View", 13, 53,
56–57
Railroad Strikes, 35, 176, 252–53n.18
Rashi (Rabbi Shlomo ben Issac), 28, 37–39, 228–
29n.7

Regnault, Henry, 28, 83, 86, 236n.51; letters of, 82, 183; death of, 236–37n.63

Reinhard, Richard, and "Der Tanz Zum Tode", 234n.34

Renan, Ernest, "Souvenirs d'enfance et de Jeunesse, 174

Review Club, see Crosby, Margaret, 23, 75, 83, 87

Revue des Deux Mondes, 181, 252n.13; and Cherbuliez, 254n.28 and Dominique, 236n.55

Rice, Prof. Isaac Leopold, 202–3, 204, 207, 208, 258n.4

Richipin, Jean, 176, 253n.19

Rossetti, Dante Gabriel, 111; and Anne Gilchrist, 234n.36; and Jane Morris, 243n.129, 243n.130; and Maria Stillman, 235n.40

Rossetti, Olivia Madre, 77

Rossetti, William, and Anne Glichrist, 234n.36, 234n.39

Rousseau, Henri, 113, 235n.50

Rothschild, House of, 243n.124; and Moses Montefiore, 243n.125

Rothschild, Lady Nathaniel, 108, 111, 243n.124

Rubenstein, Anton, 23, 74, 149–50, 154, 249n.192

Ruskin, John, 130, 246n.158; and Maria Stillman, 235n.n40

Saint Gaudens, Augustus, 223n.15, 239n.93

Salvation Army, 106; and William Booth, 240n.109

Salvini, Tomasso, 8, 23, 28, 94; and Emma, 237n.65, 238n.84; Emma's essay on, 94; as King Lear, 26; as Macbeth, 23, 89

Sand, George, correspondence, 192; essay on, 182–83; and Robert Browning, 110, 131

Saratoga Springs, anti-Semitism, 46–47; and Emma's father, 178

Sarcey, Francisque, 134, 246n.170

Sardou, Victorien, and "Daniel Rochat", 181, 254n.29

Sargent, John Singer, 151, and Mme. "X", 135, 247n.171; and Alma Strettel, 242n.117

Schiff, Jacob Henry, 10, 225n.32

Schlachi, Sophia, 108, 242n.123

Schnabel, Louis, 256n.11

Schubert, "Ganymeed," 86

Schuman Concerto, 94

Schuyler, Georgina, 3, 221n.2

Scott, Frank H., 249n.197

Scribner's, and Emma, 75, 75, 179, 223n.11, 238n.86, 254n.26; and Richard Watson Gilder, 67–68, 85; and R.W. Emerson, 89, 93, 94

Seixas, Isaac Mendes, 6, 44

Seixas, Zipporah Levy, 6

Seligman, Edwin Robert Anderson, and "Cooperative" projects, 208, 261n.20; as Dean of

Economics Profession, 201; and Emma, 23, 44, 47, 224n.26; Emma's letters to, 20–21, 201–9

Seligman-Hilton Affair, 46–47, 201, 229n.10; "Hebrew Controversy," 46

Seligman, Isaac, and Emma, 260n.17

Seligman, James, and Rose Content, 259n.9

"Seligman Jews", 46–47

Seligman, Joseph, 46–47, 201

Seligman, J.& W., & Company, 47, 201, 260n.17

Seligman, Madron, 201, 260n.17

Seligman, Nancy-Joan Marks, 201, 241n.115, 260n.17

Shakespeare, William, and "Hamlet," 33–34; and "King Lear," 26–27; and "Macbeth," 23; and "Ophelia," 33–34; and "Othello," 190

Shearith Israel Synagogue, 15, 43–44

Shelley, Percy Bysshe, 77–78, 140, 190

Smalley, Mrs. G.W., 107; and Henry James, 211, 242n.116

Society for the Improvement and Colonization of East European Jews, 9, 21, 202–5, 207–8, 224n.26, 260n.16

Society of American Artists, 8, 68, 223n.15, 233n.28

Solis-Cohen, Solomon, 225n.31

Spencer, Herbert, 59–60, 61

Stanley, Lady Maude of Alderly, 111, 243n.134

Statue of Liberty, and Lazarus plaque, 3, 16, 20; as American icon, 4, 221–22n.5, 222n.6, 222n.8

Stedman, Edmund Clarence, 7, 225n.32; and Authors' Club, 223n.15; and brokerage house, 193, 256n.13; and "genteel aristocracy," 29; and Heine essay, 100, 239n.97; and Oscar Wilde, 256n.8

Stedman, Mrs. Edmund Clarence, 188

Stegner, Wallace, Angle of Repose, 223n.14

Stickney, Bessie, 45, 153, 155, 240n.105

Stillman, Bella, and Effie, 149, 152, 249n.191

Stillman, Lisa, 149, 152, 249n.191

Stillman, Maria Sparlati, 77, 79, 109, 235n.40, 249n.191; and Emma, in London, 141, 149, 152

Stillman, William, 235n.40

Story, Edwin, 109, 243n.126

Story, William Wetmore, 130, 140, 246n.158, 247n.178

Story, Mr. and Mrs. W.W., and Emma, 143

Strettel, Miss Alma, 107, 118, 242n.117; L.A. (Pete) Harrison, 242n.117

Sturgis, Julian, and "John or Dreams," 75, 233n.31

Sully-Prudhomme (Réne François Armand Prudhomme), 83, 86, 88, 236n.56

Szold, Henrietta, 15, 225n.32

Terry, Ellen, n114, 241; and Alice Comyn-Carr, 242n.115; as Beatrice, 106; and Clarence King, 143; and marriages, 244n.141

Thackeray, Anne, and Emma Lazarus, 108
Thomas, Maestro Theodore, 10, 199, 209, 224n.16, 245n.144, 257n.22, 261n.22
Thompson, Mrs. Yates, 161, 164, 166
Tolstoy (Tolstoi), Leo, 128–29, 154–55; "Anna Karenina," 128, 134, 245n.156; "Children and Youth," 157; "Guerre et Paix," 154, 154–55; "Sebastopol Sketches," 157
Town and Country Club, 7
Turgenev, Ivan (Tourgenieff), and Emma, 7, 12, 24, 128–29, 223n.8; and Nedzhanoff, 232n.19; and *Virgin Soil* (Nov'), 29, 71, 252n.16
Twain, Mark, 68, 183; and Clara Clements, 68

Ullmann, Nathan, 204, 208, 260n.9
Union Club, 6, 24, 44
United States Sanitary Commission Fair, 22, 227n.3

Van Rensselaer, Mrs. Schuyler (Marianne Griswold), 128, 245n.155
Von Schoenberg, Bessie (Ward), 142–43, 248n.181

Wagner, Richard, 94, 103, 242n.117
Waldstein, Charles, 130, 246n.159

Ward, Olivia, 235n.44; and Emma, 78, 81–82, 86, 99–101; and Farragut Statue, 24; and John La-Farge, 85; and Mary Hallock Foote, 44–45
Ward, Samuel Gray, 7, 21, 23, 75, 95, 96; and Moses Lazarus, 44; and R.W. Emerson, 170; and William Ellery Channing, 251n.10
Ward, Mrs. Samuel Gray (Anna Barker), 85, 170
Ward, Thomas Wren, 33, 35, 63, 88, 170; and Emma, 23, 24; and Emma's letters to, 20–21, 170–85; and Henry James, 210; and Josephine Lazarus, 228n.16
Ward, Mrs. Thomas (Sophie), 78, 96, 168, 170, 235n.43
Ward's Island, and Emma Lazarus, 224n.20, 256n.9
Watts, George Frederic, 9, 119; and Ellen Terry, 244n.141
West End Synagogue, 248n.190
Whistler, James McNeil, and Peacock Room, 109, 243n.128
White, Stanford, 8, 97, 238n.87, 256n.12
Whitman, Walt, and Anne Gilchrist, 234n.36
Wilde, Oscar, 21, 189, 256n.8; and "Ave Imperiatrix", 189
Wister, Owen, 239n.101
Wister, Sara Butler, 103, 239n.101, 262n.6
Woodberry, George, 29
Woolson, Constance Fenimore, 248n.186